Pocket Dictiona

Pocket Dictionary of
BUSINESS GERMAN

GISELA SHAW

Series editor: C. G. Geoghegan

Hodder & Stoughton

A MEMBER OF THE HODDER HEADLINE GROUP

British Library Cataloguing in Publication Data

A catalogue for this title is available from the British Library

ISBN 0 340 59572 8

First published 1995

Impression number	10 9 8 7 6 5 4 3 2 1
Year	1999 1998 1997 1996 1995

Typeset by Wearset, Boldon, Tyne and Wear.
Printed in Great Britain for Hodder & Stoughton Educational, a division of Hodder Headline Plc, 338 Euston Road, London NW1 3BH by Cox & Wyman Ltd, Reading.

INTRODUCTION

This Pocket Dictionary series is designed for the non-language specialist who needs to find the meaning of a common word used in a business context. The series helps the user read a report or business article in the foreign language and is a useful tool in the preparation of brief reports, faxes, telexes or letters. Selected with general business activities in mind, the words have been chosen for their frequency of use in everyday business dealings rather than for their popularity in theoretical or academic business studies. The list of words has been compiled by analysis of the business press and of business documents. Special attention has also been given to terms in marketing, sales, import and export, finance and accounting, personnel management, transport and distribution.

The German to English section gives the translation, or explanation, of words or expressions commonly found in business and general communication in Germany. This section is designed to help the user understand foreign language communications.

The English to German section provides a general purpose business translation for English words used in business activities. The aim of the section is to help the user communicate effectively in German using the most widely acceptable translation for their needs. The translations are selected for their value to the non-specialist user and are sometimes more general than those in the German to English section.

HOW TO USE THIS BOOK

Where a word has more than one common meaning these are indicated by the numbers **1**, **2**, **3** and so on. To help make these different meanings clear the common area of use is often indicated in brackets. For example:

> **occupy** *vb*, **1** (house), bewohnen. **2** (seat), belegen. **3** (require time, space, energy), beanspruchen. **4** (person, oneself), beschäftigen. **5** (post), innehaben

When you are looking for a possible translation of a word you need to check the part of speech. Be wary of *fixed phrases* or standard business phrases, as you might not be able to understand these by translating the individual words. You will generally find standard or fixed phrases listed under one of the key words they contain. For example:

> **Datenaustausch**, *nm*, **elektronischer Datenaustausch** EDI, Electronic Data Interchange

It is advisable not to use a translation out of the context indicated, as a word may have a number of special meanings. This is a general business dictionary and for very specialist terms you might need a specialist dictionary, such as a dictionary of accounting terminology and practice, or a dictionary of public relations terminology.

A word can have many different meanings according to the context, part of speech and gender (in the case of nouns). Grammatical and contextual information about the word, or expression, is given in the entry.

Abbreviations and symbols

Here are some of the abbreviations used to indicate the area of use of a word:

acct accounts
admin administration

agric	agriculture
comm	commerce
comp	computer
corr	correspondence
cv	curriculum vitae
electr	electronics
eng	engineering
fig	figurative
fin	finance
gen	general
geog	geography
imp/exp	import/export
ins	insurance
maths	mathematics
med	medicine
mktg, sales	marketing, sales
naut	nautical
offce	office
pers	personnel
techn	technical
telec	telecommunications
transp	transport (includes distribution)

Grammatical abbreviations

acc	accusative
adj	adjective
adv	adverb
conj	conjunction
dat	dative
n	noun
nf	noun, feminine
nfpl	noun, feminine, plural
nm	noun, masculine
nmpl	noun, masculine, plural
nn	noun, neuter
nnpl	noun, neuter, plural
pl	plural
prep	preposition

suff	suffix
vb	verb

Occasionally it is not possible to find an exact translation or equivalent for a word or phrase in another language. Similarly it can be difficult to find an exact equivalent for certain official organisations or institutions. In all of these cases the symbol ≈ is used to indicate *roughly equivalent to, roughly the same as.*

GERMAN — ENGLISH

ab|ändern *vb*, amend

Abbau *nm*, **1** (of coal), mining. **2** (of factory, scaffolding), dismantling. **3** (pers), reduction. **4** (of prices), cut, reduction. **5** (of stall), taking down

ab|bauen *vb*, **1** (coal), mine. **2** (factory, scaffolding), dismantle. **3** (pers), reduce. **4** (prices), cut. **5** (stall), take down

ab|bestellen *vb* (order), cancel

Abbestellung *nf* (of order), cancellation

ab|biegen *vb* (vehicle), turn (off); **biegen Sie am Bahnhof links ab**, turn left at the station

Abbildung *nf* (in text), **1** (picture), illustration. **2** diagram

ab|blasen *vb* (event, strike), call off

ab|brechen *vb* (building), demolish

Abbruch *nm* (of building), demolition

ab|buchen *vb*, **1** (payment), debit. **2** pay by standing order

Abbuchung *nf*, **1** (payment), debit. **2** standing order

ab dem (date), as from . . .

Abdruck *nm*, reprint

Abend *nm*, evening; **Abendkleidung** *nf*, evening dress; **Abendkurs** *nm*, evening course

abends *adv*, in the evening

aber *conj*, but

Aber *nn*, **die Sache hat ein Aber**, there's just one snag

ab|fahren *vb*, leave, depart

Abfahrt *nf*, **1** departure. **2** motorway exit

Abfall *nm*, **1** (gen), waste. **2** domestic refuse, rubbish. **3** (in public places), litter; **Abfallbeseitigung** *nf*, waste/refuse disposal; **Abfallprodukt** *nn*, **1** waste product. **2** (research), by-product; **Abfallverwertung** *nf*, waste utilisation

ab|fassen *vb*, write, draft

ab|fertigen *vb*, **1** (goods), prepare for dispatch. **2** (customers), deal with. **3** (customs), clear

Abfertigungsschalter *nm*, **1** (at airport), check-in desk. **2** customs clearance

Abfindung *nf*, compensation

Abflug *nm* (of plane), departure, take-off

abgabenpflichtig *adj*, dutiable

Abgas *nn*, exhaust (pipe), exhaust fumes

abgasarm *adj* (car), low-pollution

abgasfrei *adj* (car), exhaust-free

ab|geben *vb* (luggage), leave, deposit

abgemacht! *interjection*, it's a deal!

abgepackt *adj*, prepacked, prepackaged

abgesehen von (+ dat), apart from

ab|haken *vb* (list), tick

abhanden kommen *vb*, get lost

Abhandenkommen *nn*, loss

ab|hängen von (+ dat) *vb*, depend on; **das hängt ganz vom Preis ab**, that depends entirely on the price

abhängig von (+ dat) *adj*, dependent on

ab|heben *vb* (money), withdraw

ab|heften *vb* (offce), file away

Abhilfe schaffen *vb*, take remedial action

ab|holen *vb*, **1** (load), call for, collect. **2** (person, gen), meet, pick up

Abholmarkt *nm*, cash-and-carry

Abholung *nf*, collection; **zur Abholung bereit**, ready for collection

Abitur *nn*, ≈ A-levels

Abkommen *nn*, agreement

ab|kürzen *vb*, **1** (word), abbreviate. **2** (procedure), shorten. **3** take a short cut

ab|laden *vb*, unload

Ablader *nm* (overseas transport), shipper

Ablage *nf*, **Ablagekorb** *nm* (offce), filing tray

Ablaufdatum *nn*, expiry date

Ablaufplanung *nf*, scheduling

ab|legen *vb*, **1** (ship) sail. **2** (offce), file (away)

ab|lehnen *vb* (offer, proposal, applicant), reject

Ablehnung *nf* (of offer, proposal, applicant), rejection

ab|lösen *vb* (pers), take over from; **Herr Schmidt hat Frau Meier abgelöst**, Herr Schmidt has taken over from Frau Meier

Abmahnungsschreiben *nn* (law), formal letter of caution

ab|melden *vb* (gen), cancel

sich ab|melden *vb*, **1** (of hotel), check out. **2** notify the police that one is moving away

ab|nehmen *vb*, **1** decrease; **die Zahl der Aufträge hat abgenommen**, the number of orders has decreased. **2** (comm), buy. **3** (telec), answer the telephone

Abnehmer(in) *nm/f* (comm), buyer, purchaser; **keine Abnehmer finden**, sell badly

ab|rechnen *vb*, **1** (at end of day), cash up. **2** (with person), settle up with

Abrechnung *nf*, **1** (at end of day) cashing up. **2** (bill), invoice; **Abrechnungen machen**, do the accounts

Abrechnungs-; **Abrechnungstermin** *nm*, accounting date; **Abrechnungsverfahren** *nn*, clearing procedure; **Abrechnungszeitraum** *nm*, accounting period

Abriß *nm* (of text), outline, summary

ab|runden *vb*, round down

Abs., **1 Absatz** *nm*, para., paragraph. **2 Abschnitt** *nm*, sect., section

ab|sagen *vb*, cancel; **ich muß den Termin leider absagen**, unfortunately, I have to cancel the appointment

Absatz *nm*, **1** (in text), paragraph. **2** sales (volume); **erwarteter Absatz**, expected sales; **reißenden Absatz finden**, sell like hot cakes; **Absatzanalyse** *nf*, sales analysis

absatzfähig *adj*, marketable, saleable

Absatz-; **Absatzflaute** *nf*, slump in sales; **Absatzgenossenschaft** *nf*, marketing cooperative; **Absatzkrise** *nf*, sales crisis; **Absatzmarkt** *nm*, outlet (market); **wachsender Absatzmarkt**, growth market; **Absatzpolitik** *nf*, marketing policy; **Absatzprognose** *nf*, sales forecast; **Absatzschwierigkeiten** *nfpl*, sales problems; **Absatzsteigerung** *nf*, increase in sales; **Absatzstrategie** *nf*, sales strategy; **Absatzvolumen** *nn*, sales volume; **Absatzvorsprung** *nm*, sales lead

ab|schalten *vb* (electr, comp), switch off

ab|schicken *vb*, post, send (off); **ist der Brief schon abgeschickt?**, has the letter been posted/sent off yet?

Abschlagszahlung *nf*, part payment

ab|schleppen *vb* (car), tow

ab|schließen *vb*, **1** (door etc), lock. **2** (meeting, business deal), conclude. **3** (books), balance. **4** (stock taking), complete. **5** (agreement), finalise

Abschluß *nm*, bargain, transaction; **zum Abschluß bringen**, finish, finalise

ab|schreiben *vb*, **1** (comm), deduct. **2** (money), write off. **3** (assets), depreciate. **4** (ins), write off

Abschreibung *nf*, depreciation

Abschrift *nf*, copy; **beglaubigte Abschrift**, authenticated copy

ab|senden, *vb*, post, send (off)

Absender *nm*, **1** (corr), sender. **2** (of goods), consignor, shipper; **Absenderadresse** *nf* (corr), return address

ab|setzen *vb*, **1** (goods), sell. **2** (tax), deduct; **das kann man absetzen**, that is tax-deductible

Absicht *nf*, **1** (gen), intention. **2** (law), intent

Absichtserklärung *nf*, letter of intent

Abstand *nm*, **1** (compensation), indemnity. **2** (space), distance, detachment. **3** (time), interval

ab|stimmen *vb*, vote; **wir sollten darüber abstimmen**, we should vote on it

Abstimmung *nf*, vote; **zur Abstimmung kommen**, come to the vote; **Abstimmung durch Handheben**, show of hands

ab|stoßen *vb* (surplus), sell off

ab|streichen *vb* (comm), knock off, deduct

Absturz *nm* (comp), crash

ab|stürzen *vb* (comp), crash

Abteilung *nf*, department

Abteilungsleiter(in) *nm/f*, head of department

Abweichung *nf*, variation, discrepancy; **saisonbedingte Abweichungen**, seasonal variations; **statistische Abweichung**, statistical discrepancy

ab|werben *vb* (pers), poach

ab|werfen *vb* (profit), yield

ab|werten *vb*, devalue

abwesend *adj*, absent

Abwesenheit *nf*, absence; **in Abwesenheit von** (+ dat), in the absence of . . .

ab|zahlen *vb*, pay off

Abzahlung *nf* repayment; **auf Abzahlung kaufen**, buy on hire purchase

ab|zeichnen *vb* initial

abzgl., abzüglich *prep* (comm), minus

ab|ziehen *vb* (fin), deduct

ab|zielen auf (+ acc) *vb* (mktg), target

Abzug *nm* (fin), deduction; **ohne Abzug**, net terms only

abzüglich *prep* (comm), minus

Achtung *nf*, **1 Achtung bitte!**, your attention please! **2 Achtung vor** (+ dat), respect for

ad acta legen *vb*, consider finished

addieren *vb*, add up

Adressat *nm*, **1** (gen), addressee. **2** (of goods), consignee

Adresse *nf*, address

Adressenaufkleber *nm* (offce), address label

adressieren an (+ dat) *vb* (corr), address to

AG *nf*, **Aktiengesellschaft** *nf*, public limited company, plc, joint-stock company

Agendapunkt *nm*, agenda item

Agentur *nf*, agency

Agrar-, agricultural; **Agrarerzeugnisse** *nnpl*, agricultural produce

ähnlich *adj*, similar

Akademiker(in) *nm/f*, graduate

Akkord *nm* (wage), piece rate; **im Akkord arbeiten**, do piecework

Akkreditiv *nn* (fin), letter of credit; **unwiderrufliches Akkreditiv**, irrevocable letter of credit

akkurat *adj*, precise

Akronym *nn*, acronym

Akte *nf*, document, file

Akten-; **Aktenmappe** *nf*, **1** (bag), briefcase. **2** (cover), folder; **Aktenordner** *nm*, file; **kastenförmiger Aktenordner**, box file; **Aktenschrank** *nm*, filing cabinet; **Aktenvermerk** *nm*, memo(randum); **Aktenzeichen** *nn*, reference (number)

Aktie *nf*, share; **notierte Aktie**, quoted share

Aktien-; **Aktienbank** *nf*, joint-stock bank; **Aktienbesitz** *nm*, holding; **Aktienbörse** *nf*, stock exchange; **Aktiengesellschaft** *nf*, **AG** *nf*, public limited company, plc, joint-stock company; **Aktienkurs** *nm*, share price; **Aktienmarkt** *nm*, stock market; **Aktienzertifikat** *nn*, share certificate

Aktionär *nm*, shareholder

Aktionärsversammlung *nf*, shareholders meeting

aktiv *adj*, active

Aktiv-; **Aktivposten** *nm*, asset; **Aktivsaldo** *nm*, credit balance; **Aktivvermögen** *nn*, realisable assets; **Aktivzinsen** *nmpl*, interest receivable

aktualisieren *vb* (data), update

aktuell *adj*, **1** (news), topical; (TV, radio), **eine aktuelle Sendung**, a current-affairs programme. **2** (fin), actual

Akzept *nn* (comm), acceptance; **Dokumente gegen Akzept**, D/A, documents against acceptance

Akzeptanz *nf* (comm), acceptance

akzeptieren *vb*, accept

alkoholfrei *adj*, non-alcoholic; **alkoholfreies Getränk** *nn*, soft drink

Alkoholkonsum *nm*, alcohol consumption

Allein-; **Alleineigentümer(in)** *nm/f*, sole owner; **Alleinvertreter** *nm*, sole agent; **Alleinvertrieb** *nm*, sole distributor; **Alleinvertriebsrechte** *nnpl*, exclusive distribution rights

alljährlich *adj*, *adv*, annual; annually

Allzweck- *in compounds*, multi-purpose

altbewährt *adj*, well-tried

Alter *nn*, **1** (gen), age. **2** old age

Alternative *nf*, alternative

Alters-; **Altersrente** *nf*, (retirement) pension; **Altersversorgung** *nf*, pension scheme; **betriebliche Altersversorgung**, company pension scheme

Alu-Folie *nf*, aluminium foil

amortisieren *vb* (econ), pay for itself

Amt *nn*, **1** (official body), authority; **zum zuständigen Amt gehen**, go to the relevant authority; **Amt für Verbraucherschutz**, ≈ Office of Fair Trading (UK). **2** (post held), office; **kraft seines Amtes**, by virtue of his office; **von Amts wegen**, officially

amtl., **amtlich** *adj*, *adv*, official; officially

Amtsweg *nm*, **den Amtsweg beschreiten**, go through the official channels

sich amüsieren *vb*, have a good time

Analyse *nf*, analysis

analysieren *vb*, analyse

Analytiker(in) *nm/f*, analyst

Anbau *nm* (agric), cultivation

an|bauen *vb* (agric), cultivate

anbei *adv* (corr), enclosed

Anbetracht *nm*, **in Anbetracht** (+ genitive), in view of

an|bieten *vb*, offer; **jemandem das Du anbieten**, suggest the use of the familiar address 'du' (rather than 'Sie')

Anbieter *nm* (comm), supplier

an Bord *adv*, aboard

andauernd *adj*, *adv*, continuous; continuously

ändern *vb*, change, alter

Änderung *nf*, change, alteration

anderweitig *adv*, elsewhere

an|deuten *vb*, hint, indicate

Andeutung *nf*, hint, indication

an|drohen *vb*, threaten

an|erkennen *vb* (achievement), accept, acknowledge

Anerkennung *nf*, recognition; **in Anerkennung seiner Leistungen**, in recognition of his achievements

Anerkennungsschreiben *nn*, letter of commendation

an|fallen *vb*, **1** (fin, interest), accrue. **2** (costs), incur

Anfang *nm*, start; **zu/am Anfang**, at the start; **von Anfang an**, from the (very) start

an|fangen *vb*, start

anfangs *adv*, initially

Anfangsgehalt *nn*, starting salary

Anfangskurs *nm* (fin), opening price

an|fechten *vb*, **1** (not accept), contest, challenge. **2** (law), appeal against

Anforderung *nf*, **1** request. **2** requirement; **eine Anforderung erfüllen**, satisfy a requirement

Anfrage *nf*, inquiry; **auf Anfrage**, on request

Angabe *nf*, **1** (CV), **nähere Angaben**, particulars; **Angaben zur Person**, name and address. **2** (techn), technical specifications

an|geben *vb*, **1** (price), quote. **2** (name, address), give. **3** (preference), state

Angebot *nn*, **1** (gen, comm), offer; **ein Angebot machen/ablehnen**, make/reject an offer. **2** (purchase), bid, tender. **3 Angebot und Nachfrage**, supply and demand

Angebotspreis *nm*, supply price

Angelegenheit *nf*, matter, business; **eine wichtige Angelegenheit**, an important matter; **in einer dienstlichen Angelegenheit**, on official business

angemessen *adj*, *adv*, appropriate; appropriately

angeschmutzt *adj* (goods), shop-soiled

angesehen *adj*, reputable

angesichts (+ genitive) *prep*, in view of; **angesichts der steigenden Nachfrage**, in view of rising demand

angestellt *adj*, employed

Angestellte(r) *nf(m)*, member of staff; **leitende(r) Angestellte(r)**, senior member of staff

an|gleichen *vb*, align

an|gliedern *vb*, affiliate

an|greifen *vb* (supplies, savings), break into

Angriff *nm*, **in Angriff nehmen**, tackle; **die Aufgabe wird gleich in Angriff genommen**, the task will be tackled immediately

Angstkäufe *nmpl*, panic buying

an|halten *vb*, **1** stop. **2** continue, last; **die Rezession hält an**, the recession continues

Anhänger *nm* (for car), trailer

Ankauf *nm*, purchase; **An- und Verkauf von . . .**, we buy and sell . . .

Anklage *nf* (law), charge

an|klagen *vb* (law), accuse, charge; **er wurde des Betrugs angeklagt**, he was charged with fraud

an|kommen *vb*, arrive; **sie kommen am Nachmittag an**, they are arriving in the afternoon

an|kreuzen *vb* (questionnaire), mark with a cross; **Zutreffendes bitte ankreuzen**, mark as appropriate

an|kündigen *vb*, announce

Ankündigung *nf*, announcement

Ankunft *nf*, arrival

an|kurbeln *vb* (economy), boost, stimulate; **die Konjunktur ankurbeln**, boost the economy

Anl., Anlage *nf* (corr), enclosure, enc, encl

Anlage *nf*, **1** (corr), enclosure, enc, encl; **in der Anlage erhalten Sie . . .**, please find enclosed . . . **2** (capital), investment. **3** plant, factory

Anlagekapital *nn*, fixed capital

Anlagen *nfpl*, assets; **flüssige Anlagen**, liquid assets

Anlagevermögen *nn*, fixed assets

an|legen *vb*, **1** (naut), dock, berth. **2** (fin), invest

Anleihe *nf*, loan; **eine Anleihe auflegen**, float a loan; **eine Anleihe aufnehmen**, take out a loan

an|liefern *vb* (comm), deliver

Anlieferung *nf* (comm), delivery

anliegend *adj* (corr), enclosed

Anmeldeformular *nn*, registration form

Anmeldegebühr *nf*, registration fee

sich an|melden *vb*, **1** (in hotel, in exhibition, on course), register. **2** (with company, doctor), make an appointment

Anmeldeschluß *nm* (for conference etc), closing date for registration

annähernd *adj, adv*, approximate; approximately

Annahme *nf*, **1** acceptance. **2** assumption; **in der Annahme, daß . . .**, on the assumption that . . .

annehmbar *adj*, acceptable

an|nehmen *vb*, **1** accept, take. **2** (presume, suppose), assume

Annehmlichkeiten *nfpl* (in hotel), additional facilities, comforts

Annonce *nf*, advertisement (in the paper), ad

annoncieren *vb*, advertise (in a paper)

annullieren *vb*, annul

sich an|passen *vb*, fit in with; **wir passen uns den Bedürfnissen unserer Kunden gern an**, we readily fit in with our clients' needs

an|rechnen *vb* (fin), **1** charge. **2** allow, offset

Anrecht auf (+ acc) *nn* (law), entitlement to

Anreise *nf* journey; **Anreisetag** *nm* day of arrival

Anreiz *nm*, incentive, inducement

Anruf *nm* (telec), call, phone call; **Anrufbeantworter** *nm*, answerphone

an|rufen *vb* (telec), telephone, ring, call

ansässig *adj* (company), established

Ansatz *nm*, approach; **wir brauchen einen ganz anderen Ansatz**, we need a totally different approach

an|schaffen *vb*, acquire

Anschaffung *nf*, acquisition

Anschaffungs-; **Anschaffungskosten** *npl*, purchasing costs; **Anschaffungspreis** *nm*, purchase price; **Anschaffungswert** *nm*, value at the time of purchase

Anschein *nm*, appearance

Anschlag *nm* (fin), estimate; **in Anschlag bringen**, take into account

Anschluß *nm*, **1** (corr), **im Anschluß an** (+ acc), following . . . **2** (train), connection. **3** (machine), installation. **4** (telec), connection; extension; **einen Anschluß beantragen**, apply for a telephone to be connected; **kein Anschluß unter dieser Nummer**, number unobtainable

an|schreiben *vb*, **1** (corr), write to. **2** (debts), chalk up

Anschrift *nf*, address

Ansehen *nn*, (good) reputation, standing

an|sehen *vb*, **1** (gen), look at. **2** (film), view

an|setzen *vb*, **1** fix. **2** estimate; **wir setzen für dieses Projekt 3 Jahre an**, we estimate that this project will take 3 years to complete

Ansicht *nf*, **1** opinion, view; **meiner Ansicht nach**, in my view; **ich bin Ihrer Ansicht**, I share your view. **2** (goods), **zur Ansicht**, on approval

ansonsten *adv*, otherwise

an|sprechen *vb*, appeal to; **dieses Design spricht besonders Jugendliche an**, this design appeals particularly to the young

ansprechend *adj*, *adv*, attractive; attractively

Anspruch *nm*, claim; **Anspruch haben auf** (+ acc), have a claim/be entitled to; **Anspruch erheben auf** (+ acc), claim

Anspruchsberechtige(r) *nf/m* (law), rightful claimant

anspruchsvoll *adj*, **1** (topic), challenging. **2** (task, person), demanding. **3** (quality), upmarket. **4** (reader), discriminating

anstatt (+ genitive) *prep*, instead of

an|steigen *vb* (demand etc), rise, increase; **sprunghaft ansteigen** (prices), soar

anstelle (+ genitive) *prep*, in lieu of

an|stellen *vb* (pers), **1** (have as employee), employ. **2** (staff) appoint; **fest angestellt**, salaried

sich an|stellen *vb*, join the queue, queue; **bitte stellen Sie sich (hinten) an**, please join the queue

Anstellung *nf*, position, employment; **feste Anstellung**, permanent position/employment

Anstieg *nm* (in demand etc), rise; **plötzlicher Anstieg**, surge

Anstoß *nm*, impetus; **den (ersten) Anstoß zu . . . geben**, give the impetus for . . .

anstrengend *adj*, demanding, exhausting

Anteil *nm* (fin), share

anteilig *adj*, *adv*, proportionate; proportionately

Anteilseigner *nm*, shareholder

Antrag *nm*, application; **Antrag auf** (+ acc), application for; **einen Antrag stellen**, make/put in an application; **einen Antrag ablehnen**, reject

Antragsformular *nn*, application form

Antwort *nf*, answer, reply; **Antwortcoupon** *nm*, reply coupon

antworten *vb*, answer

Anwalt *nm*, **Anwältin** *nf*, counsel, lawyer, solicitor

Anwaltskosten *npl*, legal costs

an|weisen *vb*, instruct

Anweisung *nf*, **1** (gen), instruction. **2** (fin), payment, transfer

an|wenden *vb* (knowledge etc), apply

Anwender *nm*, user

anwenderfreundlich *adj*, user-friendly

an|werben *vb*, recruit

Anwesen *nn*, premises

anwesend *adj*, present; **anwesend sein**, attend, be present; **alle Anwesenden**, all those present

Anwesenheitsliste *nf*, attendance list

Anzahl *nf*, number; **beschlußfähige Anzahl** (meeting), quorum

an|zahlen *vb*, pay a deposit

Anzahlung *nf*, deposit

Anzeige *nf* **1** (in press), ad, advertisement; **eine Anzeige aufgeben**, put an ad in the paper; **sich auf eine Anzeige hin bewerben**, reply to an advertisement. **2** (law), **(eine) Anzeige erstatten**, institute legal proceedings

Anzeigen-; **Anzeigenblatt** *nn*, freesheet; **Anzeigenpreise** *nmpl*, advertising rates; **Anzeigenraum** *nm*, advertising space

Apotheke *nf*, chemist's (shop)

Arbeit *nf*, work, job

Arbeiter(in) *nm/f*, (blue-collar) worker

Arbeit-; **Arbeitgeber** *nm* employer; **Arbeitgeber-Arbeitnehmer-Beziehungen** *nfpl*, industrial relations; **Arbeitgeberverband** *nm*, employers' federation; **Arbeitnehmer(in)** *nm/f*, employee

Arbeits-; **Arbeitsamt** *nn*, job centre, employment office; **Arbeitsbedingungen** *nfpl*, working conditions; **Arbeitsbelastung** *nf*, workload; **Arbeitsbeschaffungsprogramm** *nn*, job creation scheme; **Arbeitserlaubnis** *nf*, work permit; **Arbeitsgesetzgebung** *nf*, labour legislation; **Arbeitskampf** *nm*, industrial dispute; **Arbeitskräfte** *nfpl*, workforce; **Arbeitskräftemangel** *nm*, shortage of labour; **Arbeitsleistung** *nf*, performance; **Lohnzahlung nach Arbeitsleistung**, performance-related pay, PRP

arbeitslos *adj*, unemployed; **sich arbeitslos melden**, sign on for the dole

Arbeitslosengeld *nn*, unemployment benefit

Arbeitslosenzahlen *nfpl*, **Arbeitslosenziffern** *nfpl*, number of unemployed or out of work

Arbeitslosigkeit *nf*, unemployment; **saisonbedingte/strukturelle Arbeitslosigkeit**, seasonal/structural unemployment

Arbeits-; **Arbeitsmarkt** *nm*, labour market; **Arbeitsniederlegung** *nf*, walkout; **Arbeitspensum** *nn*, quota of work

Arbeitsplatz *nm*, **1** (in company), workplace; **am Arbeitsplatz**, at work. **2** (pers), job; **sicherer Arbeitsplatz**, secure job; **Arbeitsplatzabbau** *nm*, job cuts; **Arbeitsplatzgarantie** *nf*, job guarantee; **Arbeitsplatzteilung** *nf*, job sharing; **Arbeitsplatzwechsel** *nm*, change of jobs. **3** (offce), workstation

Arbeits-; **Arbeitsschutz** *nm*,

maintenance of industrial health and safety standards; **Arbeitsstelle** *nf*, place of work; **Arbeitssuche** *nf*, search for a job; **Arbeitstag** *nm*, working day; **Arbeitsteilung** *nf*, division of labour; **Arbeitsunfall** *nm*, industrial accident; **Arbeitsvertrag** *nm*, contract of employment; **Arbeitswoche** *nf*, working week; **Arbeitszeit** *nf*, working hours; **gleitende Arbeitszeit**, flexible working hours

Argument *nn*, argument

argumentieren *vb*, argue (a case)

arm *adj*, poor

Ärmelkanal, der Ärmelkanal *nm*, the (English) Channel

arrangieren *vb*, arrange

Artikel *nm* (print, of goods), article

Arzneimittel *nn*, drug; **Arzneimittelgesetz** *nn*, law governing the manufacture and prescription of drugs; **Arzneimittelhersteller** *nm*, drug manufacturer; **Arzneimittelmißbrauch** *nm*, drug abuse

Arzt *nm*, **Ärztin** *nf* (med), doctor

Assekurant *nm* (fin), underwriter

Assembler *nm* (comp), assembler

Assistent(in) *nm/f*, assistant

Atom-; **Atomanlage** *nf*, atomic/nuclear plant; **Atomenergie** *nf*, atomic/nuclear energy; **Atomforschung** *nf*, atomic/nuclear research

Attrappe *nf*, dummy

Aufbau *nm* (economy), building up

auf|bauen *vb* (economy), build up

auf|bereiten *vb*, process

Aufbereitung *nf*, processing

Aufbereitungsanlage *nf*, processing plant

auf|bewahren *vb*, keep, store; **trocken aufbewahren!**, keep in a dry place!

Aufbewahrung *nf*, storage

Aufenthalt *nm*, (gen), stay

Aufenthalts-; **Aufenthaltsberechtigung** *nf*, residence permit; **Aufenthaltsdauer** *nf*, length of stay; **Aufenthaltserlaubnis** *nf*, **Aufenthaltsgenehmigung** *nf*, residence permit

Auffahrt *nf*, ramp

auf|fordern *vb*, request

Aufforderung *nf*, request

auf|führen *vb* (list), detail

Aufgabe *nf*, task

auf|geben *vb*, **eine Bestellung aufgeben**, place an order

Aufgeld *nn*, surcharge

aufgrund (+ genitive) *prep*, owing to; **aufgrund des schlechten Wetters**, owing to the bad weather

auf|halten *vb*, delay; **es tut mir leid, ich bin aufgehalten worden**, I am sorry I have been delayed; **sich aufhalten in**, spend time in

auf|hören *vb*, cease, finish, stop

Aufkleber *nm*, sticker

Auflage *nf* (press), circulation

auf|lösen *vb* (company), wind up

Aufmerksamkeit *nf*, attention

auf|nehmen *vb* (partner), admit

Aufpreis *nm*, additional charge

auf|räumen *vb*, tidy (up)

auf|rufen *vb* (comp), access

auf|runden *vb*, round up

auf|schieben *vb*, delay, shelve

Aufschluß *nm*, **über etwas Aufschluß geben**, provide information about something, help to explain something

auf|schlüsseln *vb* (figures), break down

Aufschlüsselung *nf* (of figures), breakdown

auf|schreiben *vb*, write down

Aufschub *nm*, delay

Aufschwung *nm* (of economy), upswing, upturn

auf|setzen *vb* (document), draft

Aufsicht *nf*, control, supervision

Aufsichtsrat *nm*, supervisory board

Aufsichtsratsmitglied *nn*, member of a company's supervisory board

auf|steigen *vb* (in career), rise, be promoted

Aufstieg *nm* (in career), rise, promotion

Aufstiegsmöglichkeiten *nfpl*, promotion chances

auf|tanken *vb*, **1** (plane), refuel. **2** (car), fill up

Auftrag *nm*, **1** (gen), instruction, order. **2** (comm), order; **einen Auftrag gewinnen**, secure an order; **wir haben diesen Auftrag leider verloren**, unfortunately we (have) lost this order

Auftragnehmer *nm*, contractor

Auftrags-; **Auftragsabwicklung** *nf*, order processing; **Auftragsbestätigung** *nf*, confirmation of order; **Auftragsbuch** *nn*, order book; **Auftragseingang** *nm*, incoming orders; **Auftragserfüllung** *nf*, order fulfilment; **Auftragsformular** *nn*, order form

auftragsgemäß *adj*, *adv*, in accordance with instructions

Auftragsverlust *nm*, loss of an order

Aufwand *nm*, expenditure

Aufwärtstrend *nm* (fin), upward trend

Aufwendungen *nfpl*, expenditure

auf|werten *vb* (currency), revalue

Aufwertung *nf* (of currency), revaluation

auf|zählen *vb*, list

Aufzählung *nf*, list

aufzutreiben, schwer aufzutreiben sein *vb*, be at a premium

Augenblick *nm*, moment; **einen Augenblick bitte!** just a moment please

augenblicklich *adj*, *adv*, current; currently

augenfällig *adj* obvious, eye-catching

Auktion *nf*, auction

aus|beuten *vb*, exploit

Ausbeutung *nf*, exploitation

aus|bilden *vb*, train

Ausbilder(in) *nm/f*, instructor, instructress, trainer

Ausbildung *nf*, training

Ausbildungsvertrag *nm*, training contract, articles of apprenticeship

Ausdruck *nm* (comp), print-out

aus|drucken *vb* (comp), print out

Ausfall *nm*, **1** (of earnings, etc), loss. **2** (of machine), breakdown

aus|fallen *vb*, **1** (engine), break down. **2** (earnings), be lost

Ausfallzeit *nf* (ins), down time

Ausfertigung *nf*, **in doppelter Ausfertigung**, in duplicate; **in mehrfacher Ausfertigung**, multiple copies

Ausfuhr *nf*, export

aus|führen *vb*, **1** (comm), export. **2** (order), execute

Ausfuhrlizenz *nf*, export licence

Ausgabe *nf* (fin), issue; **Ausgabe mit Bezugsrecht**, rights issue;

Ausgaben, expenditure, expenses

Ausgänge *nmpl* (offce), out-tray

aus|geben *vb*, **1** (shares), issue. **2** (money), spend

ausgebucht *adj* (hotel), full

ausgelastet *adj* (with work), fully stretched

ausgestellt *adj*, on display; **die ausgestellten Waren**, goods on display

aus|gleichen *vb*, **1** (differences), even out. **2** (account), balance. **3** (debts), settle. **4** (loss, mistake), make good, compensate for

aus|halten *vb*, be able to take; **dieses Material kann große Hitze aushalten**, this material can take great heat

aus|helfen *vb* (+ dat), help out

Aushilfskraft *nf*, **1** (gen), temporary worker. **2** (offce), temp

Auskunft *nf*, information; (desk), Information/Enquiries

aus|laden *vb* (transp), unload

Auslage(n) *nf(pl)* (shop-window), display

Ausland *nn*, foreign country; **im Ausland**, abroad

Ausländer(in) *nm/f*, **1** (gen), foreigner. **2** (admin, law), alien

Auslands-; **Auslandsabteilung** *nf*, overseas division; **Auslandsgespräch** *nn*, international phone call; **Auslandsreise** *nf*, trip abroad; **Auslandsvertretung** *nf* (of company), foreign branch

aus|lassen *vb*, omit

Auslassung *nf*, omission

aus|lasten *vb* (machine), use to full capacity

aus|laufen *vb*, **1** (liquid), leak. **2** (model, series), be discontinued; **dieses Modell läuft 1995 aus**, this model is to be discontinued from 1995. **3** (ship), sail. **4** (contract), run out

aus|legen *vb* (money), lend (to settle a particular bill)

aus|liefern *vb*, deliver

Auslieferung *nf*, delivery

Ausmaß *nn*, extent; **in einem solchen Ausmaß**, to such an extent

Ausmaße *nnpl*, dimensions

aus|packen *vb*, unpack

Auspacken *nn*, unpacking

aus|probieren *vb*, try out

aus|rechnen *vb*, work out, calculate

Ausrede *nf*, excuse

ausreichend *adj*, *adv*, sufficient; sufficiently

aus|richten *vb*, give a message; **kann ich Frau Schmitz etwas ausrichten?**, can I give a message to Frau Schmitz?

Ausrüstung *nf*, equipment

Aussage *nf* (gen, law), statement

aus|schließen *vb*, exclude; **wir können die Möglichkeit nicht ausschließen, daß . . .** , we cannot exclude the possibility that . . .

ausschließlich *adj*, *adv*, exclusive; exclusively

Ausschnitt *nm*, **1** (from newspaper), cutting. **2** (from text), extract

aus|schreiben *vb*, **1** (job), advertise. **2** (bill), make out. **3** (share, goods), tender

Ausschreibung *nf*, **1** (of job), advertisement. **2** (of share, goods), tender

Ausschuß *nm*, committee; **einem Ausschuß vorsitzen**, chair a committee; **Ausschußmitglied** *nn*, committee member

Ausschußware *nf* (comm), reject

Außendienst *nm*, **im Außendienst**, in the field

Außenhandel *nm*, foreign trade

Außenhandels-; **Außenhandelsbeziehungen** *nfpl*, foreign trade relations; **Außenhandelsbilanz** *nf*, balance of trade; **Außenhandelspolitik** *nf*, foreign trade policy

außer (+ dat), *prep* except (for)

außerdem *adv*, besides

außerfahrplanmäßig *adj*, non-scheduled

außergewöhnlich *adj*, *adv*, unusual, extraordinary; unusually; extraordinarily

sich äußern *vb*, **sich zu . . . äußern**, comment on . . . ; **dazu möchte ich mich nicht äußern**, I would prefer not to comment on that

Aussicht *nf*, future outlook, prospects

Ausstand *nm* (pers), strike, industrial action; **in den Ausstand treten**, take industrial action

aus|statten *vb*, equip

Ausstattung *nf*, equipment

aus|stehen *vb* (debts), be owing; **die Zahlung steht noch aus**, we are still awaiting payment

ausstehend *adj* (payment), outstanding

aus|stellen *vb*, **1** (goods), exhibit. **2** (cheque), make out. **3** raise (an invoice); **dem Kunden eine Rechnung ausstellen**, invoice the customer

Aussteller *nm* (of goods), exhibitor

Ausstellung *nf*, exhibition, show

Ausstellungs-; **Ausstellungsfläche** *nf*, exhibition area; **Ausstellungsgelände** *nn*, exhibition site; **Ausstellungshalle** *nf*, exhibition hall; **Ausstellungskatalog** *nm*, exhibition catalogue; **Ausstellungsraum** *nm*, showroom; **Ausstellungsstand** *nm*, exhibition stand; **Ausstellungsstück** *nn*, exhibit; **Ausstellungszentrum** *nn*, exhibition centre

Ausstoß *nm* (of industry), production

aus|streichen *vb* (on list), cross/strike off

Austausch *nm*, exchange

aus|tauschen *vb*, exchange

aus|üben *vb*, **1** (occupation), practise. **2** (influence), exert

Ausverkauf *nm*, clearance sale

ausverkauft *adj*, sold out

Auswahl *nf*, selection; **eine Auswahl treffen**, make a selection

aus|wählen *vb*, select

Auswahlverfahren *nn*, selection procedure

Ausweg *nm*, way out

aus|weichen *vb*, avoid

Ausweis *nm* (pers), identity card; **Ausweispapiere** *nnpl*, identity papers

aus|weiten *vb*, broaden (out), expand

Ausweitung *nf*, broadening (out), expansion

aus|werten *vb* (results), analyse, evaluate

Auswertung *nf* (of results), analysis, evaluation

aus|wickeln *vb*, unwrap

sich aus|wirken auf (+ acc) *vb*, have an effect on

aus|zahlen *vb*, pay out

Auszahlungsrelation *nf*, pay out ratio

autark *adj*, self-sufficient

Auto *nn*, (motor) car

Autobahn *nf*, motorway;

Autobahnauffahrt *nf*, **Autobahnausfahrt** *nf*, slip road, exit; **Autobahnkreuz** *nn*, motorway intersection; **Autobahnraststätte** *nf*, motorway services

Autobus *nm*, bus

Autofahrer(in) *nm/f*, motorist, driver

Automat *nm*, vending machine

Automatisierung *nf*, automation

Auto-; **Automobil** *nn* (motor) car; **Autonummer** *nf*, (car) registration number; **Autotelefon** *nn*, carphone; **Autoverleih** *nm*, car hire (firm); **Autovermietung** *nf*, car rental (firm); **Autoversicherung** *nf*, car insurance

Avis *nm/nn*, advice note

Azubi *nm*, **Auszubildende(r)** *nf/m*, apprentice, trainee

B

Bahn *nf*, railway; **per Bahn**, by rail; **Bahnfahrt** *nf*, train journey

bahnfrei *adj* (comm), carriage free to station of destination

Bahnhof *nm*, station

Bahnhofsvorplatz *nm*, station forecourt

Baisse *nf*, slump

Baissier *nm* (stock exchange), bear

bald *adv*, soon

baldig *adj*, early; **eine baldige Antwort**, an early response

baldmöglichst *adv*, as soon as possible

Balkendiagramm *nn*, bar chart

Ballen *nm*, bale

Ballungsgebiet *nn*, **Ballungsraum** *nm*, conurbation (area)

Bank *nf*, bank; **Bankangestellte(r)** *nf/m*, bank employee; **Bankanweisung** *nf*, banker's order; **Bankeinlage** *nf*, bank deposit; **Bankfiliale** *nf*, bank branch; **Bankgebühr** *nf*, bank charges; **Bankguthaben** *nn*, bank balance; **Bankhaus** *nn*, **Bankhaus Goldbaum & Co**, Goldbaum & Co., Bankers; **Bankkauffrau** *nf*, **Bankkaufmann** *nm*, (qualified) bank clerk; **Bankkonto** *nn*, bank account; **Bankleitzahl** *nf*, sorting code; **Banknote** *nf*, (bank) note; **Banknotenumlauf** *nm*, notes in circulation

bankrott *adj*, bankrupt; **bankrott machen**, go bankrupt

Bank-; **Banktratte** *nf*, bank draft; **Banküberweisung** *nf*, bank transfer; **Bankverbindung** *nf*, **geben Sie bitte Ihre Bankverbindung an**, please give your account details; **Bankwechsel** *nm*, banker's draft; **Bankwesen** *nn*, banking

bar *adj*, cash; **bares Geld** *nn*, cash; **bar (be)zahlen**, pay cash

Bar-Code *nm*, bar code

Bar-; **Bargeld** *nn*, cash; **Barkauf** *nm*, cash purchase; **Bartransaktion** *nf*, cash transaction; **Barverkauf** *nm*, cash sale; **Barvorschuß** *nm*, cash advance; **Barzahlung** *nf*, cash payment; **Barzahlungsrabatt** *nm*, cash discount

Batterie *nf*, battery

Bau *nm*, building, construction; **im Bau**, under construction; **Baujahr** *nn*, year of construction; **Bauleiter** *nm*, site engineer; **Baumaschinen** *nfpl*, building machinery; **Baumaterial** *nn*, building material

Baumwolle *nf*, cotton

Bauplatz *nm*, building site

bausparen *vb*, save with a building society

Bau-; **Bausparvertrag** *nm*, building society savings agreement; **Baustelle** *nf*, building site; **Baustellenverkehr** *nm*, heavy plant crossing; **Bauunternehmen** *nn*, building contractor; **Bauunternehmer** *nm*, building contractor, builder; **Bauwesen** *nn*, **Bauwirtschaft** *nf*, building/construction industry

beabsichtigen *vb*, intend

beachten *vb*, take into account; **nicht beachten**, ignore

beanspruchen *vb*, claim

beanstanden *vb*, query

Beanstandung *nf*, query

beantragen *vb* (e.g. a visa), apply for

beantworten *vb*, answer (a question); **Sie haben meine Frage noch nicht beantwortet**, you have not yet answered my question

Beantwortung *nf*, answer; **in Beantwortung Ihrer Frage teilen wir Ihnen mit, daß . . .**, in answer to your question, we would like to inform you that . . .

bearbeiten *vb* (offce), deal with

Bearbeitungsfehler *nm*, clerical error

Bearbeitungsgebühr *nf*, handling charge

beaufsichtigen *vb*, supervise

beauftragen *vb*, **1** (company), commission. **2** (committee), appoint. **3** (pers), instruct

sich bedanken *vb*, thank; **ich möchte mich bei Ihnen bedanken für . . .**, I would like to thank you for . . .

bedauerlicherweise *adv*, regrettably

bedauern *vb*, regret

Bedenken *nnpl*, doubts

bedenken *vb*, consider; **bitte bedenken Sie, daß . . .**, please consider that . . .

bedeutend *adj*, significant, important

Bedeutung *nf*, significance, importance

bedienen *vb*, **1** (in restaurant, shop), serve. **2** (machine), operate

Bedienung *nf*, **1** (in restaurant), service. **2** (of machine), operation

Bedingung *nf*, **1** (gen), condition; **unter diesen Bedingungen**, under these conditions. **2** (pers, law), requirement; **der erfolgreiche Bewerber sollte drei Bedingungen erfüllen**, the successful applicant should satisfy three requirements

Bedrohung *nf*, threat

bedürfen *vb*, need

Bedürfnis *nn*, need

beeindrucken *vb*, impress

beeinflussen *vb*, influence

beenden *vb*, finish

befähigen *vb*, enable

Befähigung *nf*, qualification(s)

sich befassen mit (+ dat) *vb* (a problem), deal with, look into; **er wird sich mit der Sache befassen**, he will look into the matter

sich befinden *vb*, be, be situated; **das Hotel befindet sich . . .**, the hotel is (situated) . . .

befolgen *vb* (instructions), follow

befördern *vb*, **1** (goods), transport. **2** (career), promote

Beförderung *nf*, **1** (of goods), transport. **2** (in career), promotion

befrachten *vb*, load

befragen *vb* (survey), canvass

befriedigen *vb* (demand), satisfy

befristen *vb* (project), limit, restrict (in time)

Befugnis *nf*, authorisation

befugt *adj*, authorised

befürworten *vb*, advocate, support

Begebenheit *nf*, occurrence, event

Beginn *nm*, beginning, start

beginnen *vb*, begin; **beginnend am . . .** (date), as from . . .

beglaubigen *vb*, (law), certify, authenticate; **beglanbigte Abschrift**, certified as a true copy

begleiten *vb*, accompany

Begleitung *nf*, **in Begleitung von** (+ dat), accompanied by . . .

begreiflicherweise *adv*, understandably

begrenzen *vb*, impose a limit on; **die Geschwindigkeit begrenzen**, impose a speed limit

begutachten *vb* (damage, market), size up, survey

behalten *vb*, keep

Behälter *nm*, container

behaupten *vb*, state, claim

Behauptung *nf*, statement, claim

beherrschen *vb*, dominate; **den Markt beherrschen**, dominate/control the market

Beherrschung *nf*, domination, control

Behinderte(r) *nf/m*, disabled/handicapped person

Behörde *nf*, authority

bei (+ dat) (corr), c/o, care of

Beifall *nm*, applause

bei|fügen *vb*, enclose

Beilage *nf* (printed), **1** insert. **2** supplement. **3** (corr), enclosure

bei|legen *vb* (corr), enclose

beiliegend *adj* (corr), enclosed

beinahe *adv*, almost

bei|pflichten *vb*, agree with

Beispiel *nn*, example

Beistand *nm*, help, support; **darf ich Sie um Ihren Beistand bitten?**, may I ask you for your support?

Beitrag *nm*, contribution; **einen Beitrag leisten zu** (+ dat), make a contribution to

bei|tragen zu (+ dat) *vb*, contribute to

Bekannte(r) *nf/m*, friend

bekannt|geben *vb*, announce

sich beklagen über (+ acc) *vb*, complain about

Bekleidungsindustrie *nf*, clothing industry

beladen *vb*, load

belangen *vb*, **gerichtlich belangen** (law), sue

belasten *vb*, **ein Konto belasten** (fin), debit an account

Beleg *nm* (fin), receipt; **Belege bitte beilegen!**, please attach any receipts

Belegschaft *nf*, workforce; **das Unternehmen hat eine Belegschaft von 3.500**, the company has a workforce of 3,500

Belegschaftsvertretung *nf*, workers' representatives

belegt *adj*, fully booked; **„belegt"**, "no vacancies"

Beleuchtung *nf*, lighting

beliebig *adj*, **in jeder beliebigen Farbe**, in any colour (you like)

beliebt *adj*, popular

beliefern *vb*, supply

belohnen *vb*, reward

Belohnung *nf*, reward

bemängeln *vb*, find fault with

sich bemühen *vb*, try, make an effort

benachrichtigen *vb*, inform, notify

Benachrichtigung *nf*, **1** (gen), notification. **2** (comm), advice note

benutzen *vb*, use

Benutzer(in) *nm/f*, user

benutzerfreundlich *adj*, user-friendly

Benutzungsgebühr *nf* (road), toll

Benzin *nn*, petrol

beobachten *vb*, observe

beraten *vb*, advise

Berater(in) *nm/f*, consultant

Beratung *nf*, consultation, consultancy

Beratungsunternehmen *nn*, firm of consultants

berechnen *vb*, **1** (figures), calculate. **2** (money), charge; **wir berechnen . . . für** (+ acc), we charge . . . for . . .

Berechnung *nf*, **1** calculation. **2** charge, charging

berechtigen *vb*, entitle, authorise

Bereich *nm*, area

bereinigen *vb* (fin), adjust

Bereinigung *nf* (fin), adjustment

bereit *adj*, ready; **die Waren sind abholbereit**, the goods are ready for collection

Bergegeld *nn*, salvage money

Bericht *nm*, report

berichten *vb*, report

Berichterstatter(in) *nm/f*, reporter

berichtigen *vb*, **1** (gen), correct. **2** (law), rectify

Beruf *nm*, occupation, profession, trade, job; **was sind Sie von Beruf?**, what is your occupation, etc?

beruflich *adj*, occupational, professional; **was tun Sie beruflich?**, what's your job?

Berufs-; **Berufsausbildung** *nf*, vocational training; **Berufsberatung** *nf*, career advice; **Berufsbezeichnung** *nf*, job title; **Berufserfahrung** *nf*, work experience; **Berufsrisiko** *nn*, occupational hazard; **Berufsschaden** *nm*, industrial injury; **Berufsschule** *nf*, commercial/technical college

berufstätig *adj*, working

Berufs-; **Berufsvergehen** *nn*, malpractice; **Berufsziel** *nn* (CV), career objective

Berufung *nf* (law), appeal; **Berufung einlegen gegen** (+ acc), appeal against

beruhen auf (+ dat) *vb*, be based on

Besatzung *nf* (of aeroplane), crew

beschädigt *adj* (goods), damaged

beschaffen *vb*, **1** (law), procure. **2** (informal), get (hold of)

beschäftigen *vb* (company), employ

sich beschäftigen mit (+ dat) *vb*, deal with

beschäftigt *adj*, busy

Beschäftigung *nf*, employment

Bescheid *nm* information; **jemandem Bescheid geben**, let someone know; **bitte geben Sie uns Bescheid, wenn die Waren abgeholt werden können**, please let us know when the goods can be collected

bescheinigt *adj*, certified

Bescheinigung *nf*, certificate, certification

beschlagnahmen *vb* (imp/exp), impound, seize

beschleunigen *vb*, accelerate

beschließen *vb*, decide

Beschluß *nm*, decision; resolution; **der Beschluß wurde einstimmig gefaßt**, the resolution was passed unanimously

beschlußfähig sein *vb*, be quorate

Beschränkung *nf*, restriction; **Beschränkungen auferlegen**, impose restrictions

beschreiben *vb*, describe

Beschreibung *nf*, description

beschriften *vb*, label

beschuldigen *vb*, accuse

Beschwerde *nf*, complaint; **Beschwerde einlegen gegen** (+ acc), put in a complaint against

sich beschweren über (+ dat) *vb*, complain about

besetzt *adj* (WC, telephone), engaged; **die Leitung ist leider besetzt**, sorry, the line is engaged

Besetztzeichen *nn* (telec), engaged tone

besonders *adv*, particularly

besprechen *vb*, discuss

Besprechung *nf*, meeting; **er ist bei einer Besprechung**, he's at a meeting

Besserung *nf*, improvement

Bestand *nm*, stock

beständig *adj*, *adv*, constant; constantly

Bestandsaufnahme *nf*, inventory

Bestandteil *nn*, component

bestätigen *vb*, **1** (gen), confirm. **2** (comm), acknowledge receipt of. **3** certify; **hiermit bestätige ich, daß . . .**, I hereby certify that . . .

Bestätigung *nf*, **1** (gen), confirmation. **2** (law), certification

bestechen *vb*, bribe

bestehen aus (+ dat) *vb* consist of, comprise

bestellen *vb*, **1** (goods), order. **2** (room, stand), book

Bestellung *nf*, **1** (of goods), order; **eine Bestellung aufgeben**, place an order. **2** (of room, stand), booking

Bestellungseingang *nm*, incoming orders

besteuern *vb*, tax

Besteuerung *nf*, taxation

bestimmen *vb*, determine

Bestimmungsort *nm*, destination

bestrebt sein *vb*, endeavour

Besuch *nm*, visit, visitor

besuchen *vb*, visit

Besucher(in) *nm/f*, visitor

beteiligt sein *vb* (fin), have a share in

Beteiligung *nf* (fin), share, holding

betonen *vb*, emphasise, stress

Betonung *nf*, emphasis

Betracht *nm*, **in Betracht ziehen**, take into account

beträchtlich *adj*, *adv*, considerable; considerably

Betrag *nm*, amount; **Betrag dankend erhalten**, payment received with thanks

betragen *vb* (fin), amount to; **die Rechnung beträgt . . .**, the bill amounts to . . .

Betreff *nm* (corr), re(-ference); **Betreff: Ihr Schreiben vom 7.8.1993**, re: your letter of 7.8.1993

betreffen *vb*, **1** (gen), concern; **der Brief betrifft Sie**, the letter concerns you. **2** (comm), regard; **was diese Bestellung betrifft, . . .**, as regards this order . . .

betreffend *adj*, appropriate; **das betreffende Wort**, the appropriate word

betreiben *vb*, **1** (comm), run. **2** (techn), operate

betreten *vb*, enter; **Betreten verboten**! keep off/out!

Betrieb *nm*, **1** (firm), business. **2** factory. **3** place of work. **4 in Betrieb nehmen**, put into operation

betrieblich *adj*, **betriebliche Ausbildung**, on-the-job training

Betriebs-; **Betriebseinkommen** *nn*, operating income; **Betriebsforschung** *nf*, operational research; **Betriebskapital** *nn*, operating/working capital; **Betriebskosten** *npl*, operating costs, overheads; **Betriebsleiter** *nm*, works manager; **Betriebsspesen** *npl*, operating costs, overheads; **Betriebssystem** *nn* (comp), operating system; **Betriebsunfall** *nm*, industrial accident; **Betriebswirtschaftsplan** *nm*, operating budget

betrifft: (corr), re:

beurteilen *vb* (pers), appraise

Beurteilung *nf* (pers), appraisal

Beutel *nm*, carrier bag

bevollmächtigen *vb*, authorise

Bevollmächtigte(r) *nf/m*, appointed agent

bevor *conj*, before

bevorstehend *adj*, forthcoming

bewährt *adj*, proven, tried and tested

bewegen *vb*, move

Beweis für (+ acc), *nm* evidence/proof of

beweisen *vb*, prove

sich bewerben um (+ acc) *vb*, apply for; **er hat sich um die Stelle beworben**, he has applied for the job

Bewerber(in) *nm/f*, applicant; **Bewerberliste** *nf*, list of applicants

Bewerbung um (+ acc), *nf* application for . . .

Bewerbungsformular *nn*, application form

Bewerbungsschreiben *nn*, letter of application

bewerten *vb*, assess

Bewertung *nf*, assessment, evaluation

Bewertungsdurchschnitt *nm*, weighted average

Bewertungsindex *nm*, weighted index

bewilligen *vb*, **1** (credit etc.), grant. **2** (money), award. **3** (plan), approve

Bewohner(in) *nm/f*, **1** (of town, country), inhabitant. **2** (of house), resident, occupant, occupier

bewußt *adj*, aware, conscious; **wir sind uns des Problems bewußt**, we are aware of the problem

bezahlen *vb*, pay

bezahlt *adj*, paid

bezeichnend für (+ acc) *adj*, characteristic of

bezeugen *vb* (law), testify

beziehen *vb* (goods), obtain

Beziehung *nf*, connection, link(s)

Bezirk *nm* (sales), territory

Bezogener *nm* (fin), drawee

Bezug *nm*, **1** (corr), reference; **mit Bezug auf** (+ acc), with reference to. **2** (of goods), purchase

bezüglich (+ genitive) *prep*, with reference to, regarding

Bezugsrecht *nn* (fin), (to subscription), right

Bezugsrechtsausgabe *nf* (fin), rights issue

bieten *vb*, offer

Bilanz *nf* (fin), balance (sheet)

Bilanzierungsperiode *nf*, accounting period

Bilanzwert *nm*, book value

Bild *nn*, picture

Bildmaterial *nn* (mktg, sales), artwork

Bildschirm *nm* (TV, comp), screen; **Bildschirmgerät** *nn*, visual display unit, VDU

Bildung *nf* education

Bildungsweg *nm* (CV), education and training undergone

billig *adj*, *adv*, cheap; cheaply

billigen *vb*, approve

Billigung *nf*, approval

Binnen-; **Binnenhafen** *nm*, inland port; **Binnenhandel** *nm*, domestic trade; **Binnenmarkt** *nm*, home market; **der Europäische Binnenmarkt**, the Internal European Market; **Binnenverkehr** *nm*, inland traffic; **Binnenwährung** *nf*, internal currency; **Binnenwirtschaft** *nf*, domestic economy

Bio- *adj*, organic; **Bioprodukte** *nnpl*, organic products

bis zu (+ dat) *prep*, up to; **der Absatz war um bis zu 20% gesunken**, sales had dropped by up to 20%,

bisher *adv*, **bislang** *adv*, so far

bitten *vb*, ask, request

Bittschrift *nf*, petition

Blanko- *adj*, (fin), open-ended; **Blankoscheck** *nm*, blank cheque

blau|machen *vb*, skip work

Blei *nn*, lead

bleiben *vb*, stay, remain

Bleistift *nm*, pencil; **Bleistiftspitzer** *nm*, pencil sharpener

blicken *vb*, look

Block *nm* (paper), pad

blockieren *vb*, block, obstruct

Blockschrift *nf*, block capitals; **bitte in Blockschrift ausfüllen**, please print in block capitals

bloß *adv*, only

blühend *adj* (economy), booming, flourishing

Bonität *nf* (fin), creditworthiness

Bord *nn*, **an Bord**, on board; **an Bord nehmen**, ship; **frei an Bord** (comm), free on board, fob

borgen *vb*, **1** borrow. **2** lend

Börse *nf*, **1** (for women), purse; (for men), wallet. **2** (fin), stock market, stock exchange

börsenfähig *adj* (fin), negotiable on the stock exchange

Börsen-; **Börsenhändler** *nm*, (stock) jobber; **Börsenkrach** *nm*, stock market crash; **Börsenmakler** *nm*, (stock)broker; **Börsennotierung** *nf*, stock exchange listing; **Börsenspekulant** *nm*, punter

Bote *nm*, messenger

Botschaft *nf*, message

Boykott *nm*, boycott

Brainstorming *nn*, brainstorming

Branche *nf*, line of business, trade

Branchenkenntnis *nf*, knowledge of the trade/industry

Branchenverzeichnis *nn*, ≈ Yellow Pages

Brand *nm*, fire

brauchbar *adj*, **1** (object), useful. **2** (plan), viable

brauchen *vb*, **1** (gen), need; (comm), require. **2** (time), take; **ich habe 2 Stunden gebraucht**, it has taken me 2 hours

breit *adj*, *adv*, wide, extensive, widely, extensively

Breite *nf*, width

Bremse *nf*, brake

bremsen *vb*, brake

Brennstoff *nm*, fuel

Brief *nm*, letter; **Briefbogen** *nm*, (sheet of) stationery; **Brieffach** *nn*, pigeon-hole; **Briefkasten** *nm*, letter box; **Briefmarke** *nf*, (postage) stamp; **Briefpapier** *nn*, notepaper, stationery; **Briefträger(in)** *nm/f*, postman/-woman; **Briefumschlag** *nm*, envelope; **Briefwerbung** *nf*, direct-mail advertising

bringen *vb*, bring, take

Broschüre *nf*, booklet, brochure

brutto *adj*, gross; **brutto verdienen**, gross

Brutto-; **Bruttoeinkommen** *nn*, **Bruttoeinnahmen** *nfpl*, gross earnings; **Bruttogehalt** *nn*, gross salary; **Bruttogewicht** *nn*, gross weight; **Bruttogewinn** *nm*, gross profit; **Bruttoinlandsprodukt** *nn*, gross domestic product, GDP; **Bruttolohn** *nm*, gross wages; **Bruttosozialprodukt** *nn*, gross national product, GNP; **Bruttoverdienst** *nm*, gross income

Btx *nm*, **Bildschirmtext** *nm*, viewdata

Bücher *nnpl*, books; **die Bücher führen**, keep the accounts

Buch- (fin); **Buchhalter** *nm*, accounting clerk; **Buchhaltung** *nf*, accounts department; **die Buchhaltung machen**, keep the accounts; **Buchstabe** *nm*, letter; **ein Wort mit drei Buchstaben**, a three-letter word

buchstabieren *vb*, spell

Buchung *nf*, booking, reservation

Budget *nn*, budget; **Budgetkontrolle** *nf*, budgetary control

Bummelstreik *nm* (pers), go-slow

Bundes- *adj*, federal; **Bundesbahn** *nf*, Federal Railways; **Bundesbehörde** *nf*, Federal authority; **Bundespost** *nf*, Federal Post Office; **Bundestag** *nm*, Federal Parliament; **Bundestagsabgeordnete(r)** *nf/m*, Member of German Parliament; **Bundestagswahl** *nf*, general election

bundesweit *adj*, *adv*, nationwide

Bürge *nm*, **Bürgin** *nf* (law), guarantor

bürgen für (+ acc) *vb* (law), vouch for

Büro *nn*, office

Büro-; **Bürobedarf** *nm*, office supplies; **Büroklammer** *nf*, paper clip; **Büroleiter(in)** *nm/f*, office manager(ess); **Büromaterial** *nn*, office stationery; **Bürosessel** *nm*, office armchair

Busbahnhof *nm*, coach station

bzw., **beziehungsweise** *adv*, respectively, or

C

CAD *nn* (comp), CAD, computer assisted design

CAD/CAM *nn* (comp), CAD/CAM, computer assisted design and manufacture

Cashflow *nm* (fin), cash-flow

CD *nf*, **Compact Disk** *nf*, compact disk

Charter-; **Charterflug** *nm*, charter flight; **Charterflugzeug** *nn*, charter plane; **Chartergesellschaft** *nf*, **1** charter company. **2** (on trip), charter party

chartern *vb*, charter

Chef(in) *nm/f*, (informal), boss; (formal), head, superior

Chefsekretär(in) *nm/f*, director's secretary, personal assistant, P.A.

Chemikalien *nfpl*, chemicals

Chemiker(in) *nm/f*, chemist

cif, **Kosten**, **Versicherung**, **Fracht**, cif, cost, insurance, freight

Codekodierung *nf*, bar code

Container *nm*, container; **versiegelter Container**, sealed container; **auf Container umstellen**, containerise; **Containerladung** *nf*, container load; **Containerlastwagen** *nm*, container lorry; **Containerzug** *nm*, freightliner

Coupon *nm*, coupon; **den ausgefüllten Coupon bitte an obige Adresse schicken**, completed coupon to be returned to above address

D

Dachgesellschaft *nf*, holding company

Dachorganisation *nf*, parent organisation

Dampfschiff *nn*, steamship

Dank *nm*, **haben Sie herzlichen Dank für** (+ acc), thank you very much for

dank (+ genitive or dat) *prep*, thanks to

dankbar *adj*, grateful; **wir wären Ihnen dankbar**, **wenn Sie . . .**, we would be grateful if you . . .

Dankbarkeit *nf*, gratitude

danken *vb*, thank; **danke!**, thanks!; **„dankend erhalten"**, "received with thanks"

Danksagungsadresse *nf*, vote of thanks

dar|bieten *vb*, present

dar|legen *vb*, set out

Darlehen *nn*, credit, loan; **gesichertes Darlehen**, secured loan; **kurzfristiges Darlehen**, short-term loan; **zinsloses Darlehen**, interest-free loan

Darlehensnehmer *nm*, borrower

dar|stellen *vb* **als**, (re)present as

Darstellung *nf*, representation; **falsche Darstellung**, misrepresentation

darüber *adv*, **1** (space), above. **2** about that; **was denken Sie darüber?**, what do you think about that?

da|sein *vb*, be there

Datei *nf* (comp), file

Daten, *npl*, data, information; **Daten eingeben** (comp), key in data; **Daten zugänglich machen**, share information

Daten-; **Datenabruf** *nm*, data retrieval; **Datenaustausch** *nm*, **elektronischer Datenaustausch**, EDI, Electronic Data Interchange; **Datenbank** *nf*, data bank; **Datenerfassung** *nf*, data capture; **Datenfernverarbeitung** *nf*, teleprocessing; **Datenschutz** *nm*, data protection; **Datenübertragung** *nf*, data transmission; **Datenverarbeitung** *nf*, data processing; **auf Datenverarbeitung umstellen**, computerise; **Datenverarbeitungsmanager** *nm*, DP manager, data processing manager

datieren *vb*, date

Datum *nn*, date

Datumsstempel *nm* (offce), date stamp

Dauer *nf*, duration; **auf die Dauer**, in the long term

Dauer-; **Dauerarbeitslose(r)** *nm/f*, long-term unemployed person; **Dauerauftrag** *nm* (fin), standing order; **Dauerbeschäftigung** *nf*, permanent position

dauern *vb* **1** (gen), last. **2** (time), take

Dauerstellung *nf*, permanent position

Debatte *nf*, debate

debattieren *vb*, debate

Debet *nn* (fin), debit

Deck *nn* deck

Decke *nf* (maximum), ceiling

Deckel *nm*, lid

decken gegen (+ acc) *vb* (ins), cover against

Deckladung *nf* (imp/exp), deck cargo

Deckung *nf* (fin), cover, collateral

Defekt *nm*, defect

Defizit *nn*, deficit; **ein Defizit ausgleichen**, make good a deficit

defizitär *adj*, *adv*, adverse; adversely

Dekoration *nf*, (window) decoration

Dekorationsmaterial *nf*, display material

delegieren *vb*, delegate

Delegierte(r) *nf(m)*, delegate

dementsprechend *adj*, *adv*, corresponding; accordingly

denken *vb*, think

Depot *nn*, deposit

Deputat *nn* (agric), payment in kind

derzeitig *adj*, *adv*, current; currently; present; presently

Design *nn*, design

Design-Abteilung *nf*, design department

designiert *adj*, designate

detailliert *adj*, *adv*, detailed, in detail

deutlich *adj*, *adv*, clear; clearly

deutsch *adj*, German

Deutsche Bundesbahn *nf*, **DBB** *nf*, German Federal Railways

Deutsche Bundespost *nf*, **DBP** *nf*, German Federal Post Office

Deutscher Gewerkschaftsbund *nm*, **DGB** *nm*, Federation of German Trade Unions, ≈ TUC

Devisen *nfpl*, foreign currency; **Devisenankauf** *nm*, foreign currency purchase; **Devisenhandel** *nm*, foreign exchange dealing; **Devisenkonto** *nn*, foreign currency account; **Devisenkontrolle** *nf*, exchange control; **Devisenkurs** *nm*, rate of exchange; **Devisenmakler** *nm*, foreign exchange broker/dealer;

Devisentransfer *nm*, foreign exchange transfer; **Devisenverkauf** *nm*, foreign currency sale

dezentralisieren *vb*, decentralise

Dezimalstelle *nf*, decimal point

d.h., das heißt, that is, i.e.

d.i., das ist, that is, i.e.

Dia *nn*, slide, transparency

Diagramm *nn*, diagram; **Diagramm der Unternehmensstruktur**, organisation chart

Diaprojektor *nm*, slide projector

-dicht *adj suffix*, -proof; -tight; **wasserdicht**, water-tight

Diebstahl *nm*, theft

Diebstahlversicherung *nf*, insurance against theft

dienen *vb*, serve

Dienst *nm*, service; **öffentlicher Dienst**, public service

Dienstalter *nn*, years of service; **höheres Dienstalter**, seniority

dienstälter *adj*, senior

Dienstgeheimnis *nn*, official secret

Dienstleistung *nf*, service

Dienstleistungsbranche *nf*, service industry

dienstlich *adj*, *adv*, **1** business. **2** on business; **mein Chef ist leider dienstlich unterwegs**, I am sorry but my boss is away on business

Dienst-; **Dienstreise** *nf*, business trip; **Dienststunden** *nfpl*, office hours; **Dienstweg** *nm*, official channel; **den Dienstweg beschreiten**, go through the official channels

Dieselmotor *nm*, diesel engine

Dieselöl *nn*, diesel oil

Differenz *nf*, difference

digital *adj*, **Digital-** *adj*, digital

digitalisieren *vb* (comp), digitise

Digitaluhr *nf*, digital watch

Diktaphon *nn*, dictaphone

diktieren *vb*, dictate

Diktiergerät *nn*, dictaphone

DIN, Deutsche Industrie-Norm *nf*, German Industrial Standard; **DIN A4, DIN A4-Format** *nn*, German standard paper size (A4)

Dipl.-Ing. *nm*, **Diplomingenieur** *nm*, engineer (university graduate)

Diplom *nn*, diploma

direkt *adj*, *adv*, direct; directly

Direkt-; **Direktabbuchung** *nf*, direct debit; **Direktmarketing** *nn*, direct marketing; **Direktverbindung** *nf*, **1** (train), through train. **2** (flight), direct flight; **Direktverkauf** *nm*, direct sales; **Direktversand** *nm*, direct mail(ing)

Direktion *nf*, management

Direktor(in) *nm/f*, director

Diskette *nf* (comp), (floppy) disk

Diskont *nm*, discount, rebate; **Diskontsatz** *nm*, bank rate, discount rate; **Diskontwert** *nm*, discount value

Diskrepanz *nf*, discrepancy

diskret *adj*, **1** (person), discreet. **2** (matter, talk), confidential

Diskussion *nf*, discussion

Diskussionsbeitrag *nm*, contribution to the discussion

disponibel *adj*, available

Disziplin *nf*, discipline

Disziplinarverfahren *nn*, disciplinary procedure

diversifizieren *vb*, diversify

Dividende *nf*, dividend; **eine Dividende ausschütten**, pay a dividend; **die Dividende erhöhen**, raise the dividend

Dividendenertrag *nm*, dividend yield

d.J., dieses Jahres (corr), of this year

d.M., dieses Monats (corr), inst., instant; **unser Brief vom 3. d.M.**, our letter of the 3rd instant

DM *nf*, **Deutsche Mark** *nf*, DM, deutschmark, German mark

Dock *nn*, dock; **Dockgebühren** *nfpl*, dock dues

Dokument *nn*, document

dokumentarisch *adj*, *adv*, documentary, in documentary form

Dokumentation *nf*, documentation

Dollar *nm*, dollar

dolmetschen *vb*, interpret

Dolmetscher(in) *nm/f*, interpreter

Doppel- *adj*, double; **Doppelbelegung** *nf*, double booking; **Doppelbesteuerungsnachlaß** *nm*, double taxation relief; **Doppelbrief** *nm*, letter weighing over 20 g; **Doppelhaushälfte** *nf*, semi-detached house, semi; **Doppelstecker** *nm*, two-way adaptor; **Doppelsteuerabkommen** *nn*, reciprocal taxation agreement

doppelt *adj*, *adv*, double; twice

Doppelverdiener *nm*, person/family with two incomes

Dose *nf*, can, tin

Dosenerbsen *nfpl*, canned/tinned peas

dotieren *vb*, remunerate

Dr., Doktor *nm*: **Dr. rer. nat, Dr. rer. pol., Dr. phil.**, PhD; **Dr. theol.**, DD; **Dr. iur.**, LLD; **Dr. med.**, MD

Draht *nm*, wire

drahtlos *adj*, **drahtloses Telefon** *nn*, mobile telephone

dreifach *adj*, triple; **in dreifacher Ausfertigung**, in triplicate

dringend *adj*, *adv*, **dringlich** *adj*, *adv*, urgent; urgently

Drittel *nn*, third

Dritte Welt *nf*, Third World

drohen *vb*, threaten

Drohung *nf*, threat

Druck *nm*, pressure

Druckbuchstaben *nfpl*, printed letters; **in Druckbuchstaben schreiben**, print

drucken *vb*, print

drücken *vb*, press, push

Drucker *nm* (comp), printer

Druckmesser *nm*, pressure gauge

Drucksache *nf*, printed matter

Druckschrift *nf*, printing; **bitte in Druckschrift schreiben**, please print

Drucktaste *nf* (comp), key

Dumping *nn*, dumping

dünn *adj*, *adv*, thin, thinly; fine, finely

Duplikat *nn*, duplicate

durch (+ acc) *prep*, through, by

durchaus *adv*, definitely, quite, perfectly

Durchbruch *nm*, breakthrough

durchdringen *vb* (market), penetrate

Durchdringung *nf* (of market), penetration

durchführbar *adj* (plan), feasible, viable

Durchführbarkeit *nf*, feasibility, viability

Durchführbarkeitsstudie *nf*, feasibility study

durch|führen *vb*, **1** (order), carry out; (plan), implement. **2** (survey), conduct

durchgehend *adj*, *adv*, **1** (opening times), round-the-clock.

2 (connection), direct. **3** (train), non-stop, through, direct, directly. **4** (goods), in transit

durch|halten *vb*, hold out, persevere

durchlässig *adj*, permeable, porous

Durchlauf *nm* (comp), run

durch|lesen *vb*, read through

durch|machen *vb*, experience

durchschauen *vb*, see through

durchschlagend *adj*, **1** (success), sweeping. **2** (measure), decisive. **3** (proof), conclusive

Durchschlagpapier *nn*, carbon paper

Durchschnitt *nm*, average; **im Durchschnitt**, on average; **den Durchschnitt berechnen**, calculate the average

durchschnittlich *adj*, *adv*, average, on average

durch|setzen *vb*, enforce

durchsichtig *adj*, transparent

durch|streichen *vb*, cross out

Durchwahl *nf* (telec), direct dialling

durch|wählen *vb*, dial direct; **Sie können von hier aus durchwählen**, you can dial direct from here

Durchwahlnummer *nf*, dialling code

Durchzug *nm* (of air), draft

Dusche *nf*, shower; **Zimmer mit Dusche**, room with shower

Dutzend *nn*, **Dtzd.** *nn*, dozen

dutzendweise *adv*, by the dozen

duzen *vb*, address someone as 'du' (rather than 'Sie')

DV *nf*, **Datenverarbeitung** *nf*, data processing

dynamisch *adj*, dynamic, vigorous

D-Zug *nm*, fast train (stops only in major cities); **D-Zug-Zuschlag** *nm*, travel supplement on fast trains

E

Ebene *nf*, level; **auf höchster Ebene**, at the highest level

echt *adj*, *adv*, genuine; genuinely; **echtes Leder**, genuine leather

Echtzeit *nf*, real time

Eckwert *nm*, benchmark

Eckzins *nm* (fin), base rate

EDV *nf*, **elektronische Datenverarbeitung** *nf*, electronic data processing; **EDV-Abteilung** *nf*, computer department

Effekt *nm*, effect

Effekten *nmpl* (fin), securities; **Effektenemission** *nf*, capital issue; **Effektenhändler** *nm*, securities trader; **Effektenmarkt** *nm* (fin), securities market

effektiv *adj*, *adv*, effective; effectively

effizient *adj*, *adv*, efficient; efficiently

Effizienz *nf*, efficiency

EG *nf*, **Europäische Gemeinschaft** *nf*, European Union, EU

egal *adj*, **das ist egal**, that doesn't matter, that doesn't make any difference; **das ist mir egal**, it's all the same to me

ehemalig *adj*, former

eher *adv*, earlier, sooner; **je eher desto besser**, the sooner the better

Ehre *nf*, honour

ehrenamtlich *adj*, *adv* (work), unpaid

Ehrgeiz *nm*, ambition

ehrlich *adj*, *adv*, honest; honestly

eichen *vb* (scales), calibrate

Eichung *nf*, calibration

eifrig *adj, adv*, keen; keenly

Eigen-; **Eigenbedarf** *nm*, **1** (of person), personal use. **2** (of state), domestic requirements; **Eigenfinanzierung** *nf*, self-financing; **Eigenkapital** *nn*, equity capital; **Eigenname** *nm*, proper name

eigentlich *adj, adv*, real, actual; really, actually

Eigentum *nn*, property

Eigentümer(in) *nm/f*, proprietor, proprietress

Eigentumsübertragung *nf* (law), conveyancing

Eigentumswohnung *nf*, privately owned flat

eigenverantwortlich *adv*, autonomously

Eignung *nf*, aptitude

Eil-; express; **Eilauftrag** *nm*, rushed job; **Eilbote** *nm*, courier; **Eilbrief** *nm*, express letter

Eile *nf*, hurry; **in Eile**, in a hurry

eilen *vb*, hurry

eilig *adj, adv*, urgent; urgently

Eilzug *nm*, fast stopping train

Eilzustellung *nf*, express delivery

sich ein|arbeiten *vb*, get used to one's work

Einbahnstraße *nf*, one-way street

Einbauten *nmpl*, fittings

einbegriffen *adj*, included

ein|berufen *vb*, convene

ein|büßen *vb*, lose, forfeit

ein|brechen *vb*, **1** (thief), burgle. **2** (economy), collapse

Einbruch *nm*, **1** (crime), burglary. **2** (of economy), collapse

ein|checken *vb* (at airport), check in

Eindruck *nm*, impression

einfach *adj, adv*, simple; simply

Einfachflug *nm*, single flight

Einfluß *nm*, influence; **Einfluß nehmen**, lobby; **Einflußbereich** *nm*, sphere of influence

ein|frieren *vb* (food, prices), freeze

ein|fügen *vb*, insert

Einfuhr *nf*, import

ein|führen *vb*, **1** (product), launch. **2** (comm), import

Einfuhr-; **Einfuhrgenehmigung** *nf*, import permit; **Einfuhrkontingent** *nn*, import quota; **Einfuhrstopp** *nm*, ban on imports

Einführungspreis *nm*, introductory price

Einfuhrverbot *nn*, ban on imports

Einfuhrzoll *nm*, import duty

Eingabe *nf*, **1** (to authority), petition. **2** (comp), input

Eingang *nm*, **1** (of building), entrance. **2** (of goods), delivery, receipt

Eingänge *nmpl* (offce), in-tray

Eingangs-; **Eingangsbestätigung** *nf* (comm), acknowledgement of receipt; **Eingangsdatum** *nn* (comm), date of receipt; **Eingangsvermerk** *nm* (comm), notice of receipt

eingehend *adj, adv*, detailed, thorough; thoroughly

eingeschränkt *adj*, restricted

eingeschriebener Brief *nm*, registered letter

eingespannt *adj*, busy, stressed

Eingeständnis *nn*, admission, confession

ein|gestehen *vb*, admit (to); **wir gestehen unseren Fehler ein**, we admit (to) our mistake

eingetragen *adj*, registered

ein|gliedern *vb*, incorporate

ein|greifen *vb*, intervene

Eingriff *nm*, intervention

ein|halten *vb*, **1** (promise), keep. **2** (rules), follow. **3** (obligations), carry out. **4** (deadline), meet.

ein|hängen *vb* (telec), hang up

einheimisch *adj* (product), homegrown

Einheit *nf* (of goods), unit

einheitlich *adj*, *adv*, uniform; uniformly

Einheitskosten *npl*, unit costs

ein|holen *vb*, catch up with

einig *adj*, **sich einig sein mit** (+ dat), agree with . . .; **wir sind uns einig, daß . . .**, we agree that . . .; **sie können sich nicht einig werden**, they are unable to agree

sich einigen über (+ acc) *vb*, agree on

Einigkeit *nf*, unanimity

Einigung *nf*, agreement; **Einigung erzielen**, reach an agreement

Einkauf *nm*, **1** (gen), shopping. **2** (comm), purchasing

ein|kaufen *vb*, **1** (gen), buy, shop; **einkaufen gehen**, go shopping. **2** (comm), buy, do the buying

Einkaufen *nn*, shopping; **preisbewußtes Einkaufen**, shopping around

Einkäufer(in) *nm/f* (comm), buyer

Einkaufs-; **Einkaufsabteilung** *nf*, buying department; **Einkaufsgenossenschaft** *nf*, consumers' cooperative society; **Einkaufsleiter** *nm*, purchasing manager; **Einkaufsmarkt** *nm*, superstore; **Einkaufspassage** *nf*, shopping arcade; **Einkaufsstraße** *nf*, shopping street; **Einkaufswagen** *nm*, (shopping) trolley; **Einkaufszentrum** *nn*, shopping centre; **Einkaufszettel** *nm*, shopping list

Einklang *nm*, **in Einklang stehen mit** (+ dat), comply with

Einkommen *nn*, income; **festes Einkommen**, fixed income; **geregeltes Einkommen**, regular income; **persönliches Einkommen**, personal income; **verfügbares Einkommen**, disposable income

Einkommensausfall *nm*, loss of income

Einkommensgrenze *nf*, income limit

einkommensschwach *adj*, low-income

einkommensstark *adj*, high-income

Einkommenssteuer *nf*, income tax; **Einkommenssteuererklärung** *nf*, income tax return; **Einkommenssteuerformular** *nn*, income tax form

Einkünfte *npl*, earnings; **unsichtbare Einkünfte**, invisible earnings

ein|laden *vb*, invite

Einladung *nf*, invitation

ein|leiten *vb* (procedure), initiate

Einlieferungsschein *nm*, certificate of posting

ein|lösen *vb* (cheque), cash

einmal *adv*, once

einmalig *adj*, **1** one-off. **2** (unequalled), unique; **eine einmalige Leistung**, a unique achievement

Einmannbetrieb *nm*, one-man business

Einmischung *nf*, interference

einmütig *adj*, *adv*, unanimous; unanimously; **einmütig beschließen**, agree unanimously

Einnahmen *nfpl*, earnings, revenue, takings

Einnahmequelle *nf*, source of income

Einnahmereserven *nfpl*, revenue reserves

ein|nehmen *vb* (money), earn, take

ein|ordnen *vb* (files), file

ein|räumen *vb* (credit, extra time), grant

ein|reichen *vb*, submit; **seine Kündigung einreichen**, tender one's resignation

Einrichtung *nf* (in laboratory, shop), equipment

ein|schalten *vb* (machine), switch on

Einschaltquote *nf* (TV, radio), ratings

einschließlich (+ genitive) *prep*, inclusive

ein|schränken *vb*, limit, restrict

Einschreibebrief *nm*, (letter sent by) recorded delivery

Einschreiben *nn*, registered letter; **per Einschreiben**, by registered post

Einschub *nm* (in text), insertion

ein|sehen *vb* (document), look at, see

ein|senden *vb* (to competition), send in

Einsendeschluß *nm*, last date for entries, closing date

ein|sparen *vb*, save

ein|springen für (+ acc) *vb*, stand in for

Einspruch *nm*, objection; **Einspruch erheben** object

Einstandspreis *nm* (comm), introductory price

ein|stellen *vb*, **1** (production), cease. **2** (for post), recruit, appoint. **3** (machine), adjust

sich ein|stellen auf (+ acc) *vb*, adapt to; **sich auf Kundenwünsche einstellen**, tailor one's service to clients' needs

Einstellung *nf*, **1** (pers), appointment. **2** attitude. **3** (of machine), adjustment

Einstellungsgespräch *nn*, job interview

Einstellungstermin *nm*, starting date

einstimmig *adj*, *adv*, unanimous; unanimously

ein|stufen *vb*, classify

einstweilig *adj*, *adv*, temporary; temporarily

ein|tragen *vb* (on list), enter one's name, register

Eintragung *nf* (on list), entry, registration

Eintragungsnummer *nf*, registration number

ein|treten für (+ acc) *vb*, advocate (a point of view)

Eintritt *nm*, admission, entry charge; **Eintritt frei**, admission free

Eintrittsgebühr *nf*, admission charge

Eintrittskarte *nf*, admission ticket

Einvernehmen *nn*, agreement; **in beiderseitigem Einvernehmen**, by mutual agreement

einverstanden *adj*, agreed; **ich bin völlig einverstanden mit Ihrem Vorschlag**, I am perfectly in agreement with your proposal; **er ist damit einverstanden, daß . . .**, he is in agreement that . . .

Einwand *nm*, objection; **einen Einwand erheben gegen** (+ acc), raise an objection to

Einwanderer *nm*, immigrant

einwandfrei *adj* (goods), perfect

ein|wenden *vb*, object

Einweg-, non-returnable; **Einwegflasche** *nf*, non-returnable bottle

ein|wickeln *vb*, wrap (up)

ein|zahlen *vb*, deposit

Einzelfahrschein *nm*, single ticket

Einzelhandel *nm*, retail trade; **im Einzelhandel verkaufen**, retail

Einzelhandels-; **Einzelhandelsbank** *nf*, retail bank; **Einzelhandelsgeschäft** *nn*, retail shop; **Einzelhandelspreis** *nm*, retail price

Einzelhändler *nm*, retailer

Einzelheit *nf*, detail; **in allen Einzelheiten**, in all detail

Einzelzimmer *nn*, single room

einzigartig *adj*, *adv*, unique; uniquely

Eisen *nn*, iron; **Eisenbahn** *nf*, railway (train); **Eisenbahnfahrkarte** *nf*, rail(way) ticket

Eisenhütte *nf*, iron works, iron foundry

Eisenwaren *nfpl*, hardware; **Eisenwarenhändler** *nm*, ironmonger

Eisfach *nn*, freezer compartment

Eisgetränk *nn*, iced drink

Eisschrank *nm*, refrigerator, fridge

elektrisch *adj* electric(al); **elektrisches Gerät** *nn*, electrical appliance; **elektrischer Strom** *nm*, electricity

Elektrizität *nf*, electricity

Elektrizitätsversorgung *nf*, electricity supply

Elektronik *nf*, electronics

elektronische Post *nf*, **E-Mail** *nf*, electronic mail, E-mail

Elektrowaren *nfpl*, electrical supplies

Embargo *nn*, embargo; **ein Embargo verhängen über** (+ acc), place an embargo on

Emission *nf* (of shares), issue

emittieren *vb* (shares), issue

Empfang *nm*, **1** (in hotel), reception. **2** (corr), receipt; **wir bestätigen den Empfang Ihres Schreibens vom 3. Mai**, we acknowledge receipt of your letter of 3rd of May

empfangen *vb*, receive

Empfänger *nm*, addressee; **Empfänger unbekannt**, not known at this address

Empfangs-; **Empfangsbereich** *nm* (in hotel), reception area; **Empfangsbescheinigung** *nf*, advice of receipt, AR; **Empfangsbestätigung** *nf*, advice of receipt; **Empfangsdame** *nf*, (lady) receptionist

empfehlen *vb*, recommend

Empfehlung *nf*, **1** (gen), recommendation, advice; **auf Empfehlung von Herrn Schmidt**, on the recommendation of Herr Schmidt. **2** (pers), testimonial, reference. **3** (corr), **mit freundlichen Empfehlungen**, with best regards

empfindlich *adj*, sensitive

Endbetrag *nm* (fin), grand total

enden *vb*, finish; **die Ausstellung endet am 9. August**, the exhibition finishes on August 9

End-; **Endergebnis** *nn*, final result; **Endlospapier** *nn* (comp), continuous paper; **Endprodukt** *nn*, end product; **Endstation** *nf*, terminus; **Endverbraucher** *nm*, end user

Energie *nf*, energy

energiesparend *adj*, energy-saving

Energieverbrauch *nm*, energy consumption

energisch *adj*, *adv*, energetic; vigorous; energetically; vigorously

eng *adj*, *adv*, tight; tightly; **auf engem Raum**, in a small space; **im engeren Sinne**, in the narrow sense; **in die engere Wahl kommen**, be short-listed

Engpass *nm*, bottleneck

entdecken *vb*, discover

Entdeckung *nf*, discovery

entfernt *adj*, distant

Entfernung *nf*, distance

entflechten *vb* (cartel), break up

Entflechtung *nf* (of cartel), breaking up

entfrosten *vb*, defrost

entgegen (+ dat) *prep*, contrary to; **entgegen meinen Erwartungen**, contrary to my expectations

entgegen|gehen *vb*, **1** (move towards), approach. **2** go to meet

entgegen|kommen (+ dat) *vb*, oblige

Entgegenkommen *nn*, concession

entgegen|sehen *vb* (corr), look forward to; **ich sehe Ihrer baldigen Antwort entgegen**, I look forward to your early reply

entgegen|wirken (+ dat) *vb*, counteract

entgegnen *vb*, reply

enthalten *vb*, contain

entladen *vb*, unload

entlassen *vb*, **1** (pers), dismiss. **2** (from hospital), discharge

Entlassung *nf* (pers), dismissal; **unrechtmäßige Entlassung**, wrongful dismissal

entlasten *vb*, relieve

entlohnen *vb*, remunerate

entmutigen *vb*, discourage

Entnahme *nf* (of money), withdrawal

entnehmen *vb*, gather; **wir entnehmen Ihrem Brief, daß Sie . . .**, we gather from your letter that you . . .

entschädigen *vb*, compensate

Entschädigung *nf*, compensation, indemnity

entscheiden *vb*, decide, make up one's mind; **wir haben entschieden, daß . . .**, we have decided that . . . ; **haben Sie sich schon entschieden?**, have you made up your mind yet?

entscheidend *adj*, decisive, crucial

Entscheidung *nf*, decision; **eine Entscheidung fällen/treffen**, take a decision

Entscheidungsträger *nm*, decision maker

sich entschließen *vb*, **sich entschließen, etwas zu tun**, decide to do something

Entschluß *nm*, decision; **einen Entschluß fassen**, take a decision

entschuldigen *vb*, excuse, forgive; **bitte entschuldigen Sie mein Zuspätkommen**, please forgive my being late; **sich entschuldigen**, apologise; **Sie brauchen sich bei mir nicht zu entschuldigen**, you need not apologise to me

Entschuldigung *nf*, **1** excuse. **2** apology; **um Entschuldigung bitten**, apologise

entsprechen (+ dat) *vb*, **1** (figures), correspond to. **2** (expectations), meet

entsprechend *adj*, *adv*, corresponding; correspondingly; accordingly; **er benahm sich entsprechend**, he behaved accordingly

enttäuschen *vb*, disappoint

Enttäuschung *nf*, disappointment

entwerfen *vb*, **1** (document), draft. **2** (fashion), design

entwickeln *vb*, develop

Entwicklung *nf*, development; **wirtschaftliche Entwicklung**, economic development

Entwicklungsland *nn*, developing country

Entwurf *nm* (of document), draft; **der Vertrag existiert bisher nur im Entwurf**, so far the contract only exists in draft form

entziehen (+ dat) *vb*, withdraw from

entziffern *vb*, decipher

erbauen *vb*, build

erbitten *vb*, request

Erbschaftssteuer *nf*, estate duty

Ereignis *nn*, event

erfahren *vb*, hear, learn; **wir haben aus Manchester erfahren, daß . . .**, we have heard from Manchester that . . .

erfahren *adj*, experienced; **wir suchen einen erfahrenen Praktiker** (pers), we are looking for an experienced practitioner

Erfahrung *nf*, experience; **nach unserer Erfahrung**, in our experience; **Erfahrung sammeln**, gain experience

erfinden *vb*, discover

Erfindung *nf*, discovery

Erfolg *nm*, success, achievement

erfolgreich *adj*, *adv*, successful; successfully

Erfolgs-; **Erfolgskonto** *nn* (fin), trading account; **Erfolgskurs** *nm*, **auf Erfolgskurs**, on the road to success; **Erfolgs- und Leistungsnachweis** *nm*, track record

Erfrischung *nf*, refreshment

Erfrischungszelt *nn*, hospitality tent

erfüllen *vb* (conditions), satisfy

ergänzen *vb* (comments), add; **darf ich Frau Holzers Ausführungen noch etwas ergänzen?**, may I add a few comments to Frau Holzer's presentation?

Ergebnis *nn*, result; **Ergebnisse**, findings

ergebnislos *adj*, *adv*, unsuccessful; unsuccessfully

ergreifen *vb*, seize; **die Gelegenheit ergreifen**, seize the opportunity

Erhalt *nm* (of goods etc), receipt

erhalten *vb* (get), receive

sich erholen *vb*, get better, recover

Erholung *nf*, recovery

erinnern an (+ acc) *vb*, remind; **sich erinnern an** (+ acc), remember

Erinnerung *nf*, **1** memory; **zur Erinnerung an Ihren Aufenthalt in München**, in memory of your stay in Munich. **2** (jogging someone's memory), reminder

erkennen *vb*, recognise

Erkenntnis *nf*, realisation

erklären *vb*, **1** (gen), explain. **2** declare, state

Erklärung *nf*, **1** explanation. **2** declaration, statement

erkranken *vb*, be taken ill

Erkrankung *nf*, illness

Erkrankungsfall *nm*, **im Erkrankungsfall**, in case of illness

sich erkundigen *vb*, inquire

Erkundigung *nf*, inquiry

erlangen *vb*, achieve, gain

erlauben *vb*, allow, permit

Erlaubnis *nf*, permission

erläutern *vb*, explain

erledigen *vb*, deal with, handle, finish

erledigt *adj*, dealt with

erleichtern *vb*, **1** (make easier), facilitate. **2** (reduce worry, pressure), relieve

Erleichterung *nf*, relief; **zu meiner großen Erleichterung**, to my great relief

Erlös *nm*, proceeds

ermangeln *vb*, lack

ermäßigen *vb* (price), reduce

Ermäßigung *nf* (of price), reduction

ermessen *vb*, estimate, gauge

Ermessen *nn*, **1** judgment, estimation; **nach meinem Ermessen**, in my estimation. **2** discretion; **nach eigenem Ermessen handeln**, act at one's discretion; **wir stellen es in Ihr Ermessen, ob Sie . . .**, we leave it to your discretion whether you . . .

Ermessensspielraum *nm*, discretionary powers

ermitteln *vb*, investigate

ermöglichen *vb*, make possible, facilitate

ermutigen *vb*, encourage

ernennen *vb*, appoint

Ernennung *nf*, appointment

Ernennungsschreiben *nn*, letter of appointment

Ernennungsurkunde *nf*, certificate of appointment

erneuern *vb*, renew

ernsthaft *adj*, *adv*, serious; seriously

eröffnen *vb* (business), open (up)

errechnen *vb*, work out, calculate

erreichen *vb*, **1** (gen), reach. **2** (train etc), catch. **3** (contact), get in touch with; **wann kann ich Sie morgen am besten erreichen?**, when is the best time tomorrow to get in touch with you? **4** (succeed), achieve; **haben Sie etwas erreicht?**, have you achieved anything?

Ersatz *nm*, replacement, substitute; **Ersatzreifen** *nm*, spare tyre; **Ersatzteil** *nn*, spare part

erscheinen *vb*, **1** (gen), appear. **2** (on the market), come out

erschöpfen *vb*, exhaust

erschweren *vb*, make more difficult, aggravate

erschwinglich *adj* (price), reasonable

ersetzen *vb*, **1** (objects, people), replace. **2** (cost), reimburse

ersparen *vb*, save

Ersparnis *nf*, savings

erstatten *vb* (expenses), refund

Erstattung *nf*, reimbursement

erstaunen *vb*, astonish, amaze

Erstbestellung *nf* (comm), initial order

erstklassig *adj*, **1** (gen), first-class. **2** (shares), blue-chip

ersuchen *vb*, request

Ertrag *nm*, (fin), yield

ertragen *vb*, bear, put up with

ertragreich *adj*, profitable

Ertragsfähigkeit *nf*, earning potential

erwachsen *adj*, adult

erwachsen *vb* (costs), result

erwägen *vb*, consider

erwähnen *vb*, mention; **wie oben erwähnt**, as mentioned above

erwarten *vb*, await, expect; **das war zu erwarten**, that was to be expected

erweitern *vb*, expand

Erweiterung *nf* expansion; **Erweiterung des Produktangebots**, product diversification

Erwerb *nm*, acquisition

erwerben *vb*, acquire

erwerbslos *adj*, unemployed; **die Erwerbslosen**, the unwaged

Erwerbstätigkeit *nf*, gainful employment

erwerbsunfähig *adj*, unable to work

erwidern *vb*, reply

erwirtschaften *vb* (profit), make

erwünscht *adj*, desired

Erz *nn*, ore

erzählen *vb*, tell

erzeugen *vb*, produce

Erzeugnis *nn*, **1** (of industry), product. **2** (of agriculture), produce

Erzfrachter *nm*, ore carrier

Erziehung *nf*, education

erzielen *vb* (result), achieve, obtain

eskalieren *vb*, snowball

eßbar *adj*, edible; **nicht (mehr) eßbar**, inedible

Essensmarke *nf*, luncheon voucher, LV

Etage *nf*, floor; **in der 1. Etage**, on the first floor

Etat *nm*, budget; **in den Etat einplanen**, budget for

Etatkontrolle *nf*, budgetary control

Etikett *nn*, label

etikettieren *vb*, label

etwa *adv*, about, roughly

europäisch *adj*, European

Europäisch; **Europäische Gemeinschaft** *nf*, **EG** *nf*, European Community, EC; **Europäischer Gerichtshof** *nm*, European Court of Justice; **Europäische Union** *nf*, EU *nf*, European Union; **Europäische Währungseinheit** *nf*, European currency unit, ECU; **Europäische Wirtschaftsgemeinschaft** *nf*, **EWG** *nf*, European Economic Union

Euroscheck *nm*, Eurocheque

exakt *adj*, *adv*, exact; exactly

Examen *nn*, exam, examination

Exemplar *nn*, **1** (of goods) specimen. **2** (of book, journal) copy

expandieren *vb*, expand

experimentieren *vb*, experiment

Export *nm*, export; **sichtbare Exporte**, visible exports; **Exportanreiz** *nm*, export incentive; **Exportausführung** *nf*, export model

Exporteur *nm*, exporter

Exportgenehmigung *nf*, export permit

exportieren *vb*, export

Export-; **Exportleiter** *nm*, export manager; **Exportlizenz** *nf*, export licence; **Exportquote** *nf*, export ration; **Exportzoll** *nm*, export duty

Expreß *nm*, express; **per Expreß**, express

Extrabezüge *nmpl*, fringe benefits

Extras *nnpl*, optional extras

Extravergütung *nf*, fringe benefits

E-Zug *nm*, **Eilzug** *nm*, fast stopping train

F

F, **nach Schema F**, in the usual way

Fa., **Firma** *nf* (corr), firm, company

Fabrik *nf*, factory; **Fabrikananlage** *nf*, plant; **Fabrikarbeiter(in)** *nm/f*, blue-collar worker, factory worker

Fabrikat *nn*, make

Fabrikation *nf*, manufacture, production

Fabrikationsnummer *nf*, serial number

Fabrikhalle *nf*, factory floor

fabrikmäßig *adj*, **fabrikmäßige Herstellung** *nf*, mass production

Fabrikpreis *nm*, factory (gate) price, price ex factory

-fach *adj suffix*, -fold; **zwanzigfach**, twentyfold

Fach *nn*, **1** (of knowledge), subject, field; **vom Fach (sein)**, (be) an expert; **ich bin nicht vom Fach**, I am not an expert in this. **2** trade

Fach-; **Facharbeiter(in)** *nm/f*, skilled worker; **Fachausdruck** *nm*, technical term; **Fachfrau** *nf*, (female) expert; **Fachhändler** *nm*, stockist; **Fachkollege** *nm*, professional colleague; **Fachkreisen** *nfpl*, **in Fachkreisen**, among experts; **Fachleute** *npl*, experts; **Fachmann** *nm*, (male) expert; **Fachsprache** *nf*, technical terminology; **Fachterminus** *nm*, technical term; **Fachzeitschrift** *nf*, specialist journal

fähig *adj*, capable, competent

Fähre *nf*, ferry

fahren *vb*, **1** (car), drive; **ich fahre mit dem Auto nach München**, I am driving to Munich. **2** (public transport), use, go by; **wir fahren mit dem Bus nach Bonn**, we're going to Bonn by bus

Fahrer *nm*, driver

Fahrkarte *nf*, ticket; **einfache Fahrkarte**, one-way ticket, single ticket; **eine Fahrkarte nach Bonn lösen**, buy a ticket to Bonn

Fahrkartenschalter *nm*, booking office, ticket office

Fahrlässigkeit *nf*, negligence

Fahrplan *nm*, (train/coach/flight) timetable

Fahrpreis *nm*, fare; **einfacher/halber/voller Fahrpreis**, single/half/full fare

Fahrt *nf*, **1** (in car), drive, ride. **2** journey, trip; **gute Fahrt!**, safe journey!

Fahrzeug *nn*, vehicle

Faktor *nm*, factor

Fall *nm* (instance), case

fallen *vb*, fall; **plötzlich fallen**, slump

fallen|lassen *vb*, drop

fällig *adj*, due; **fälliger Betrag** *nm*, amount due; **fällig werden** (bills), mature

Fälligkeit *nf*, maturity

Fälligkeitstag *nm*, expiry date

falsch *adj*, false, wrong; **falsch berechnen**, miscalculate; **falsch darstellen**, misrepresent

fälschen *vb*, **1** (gen), forge. **2** (comm, books, facts) falsify

falten *vb*, fold

Familienname *nm*, family name

Familienunternehmen *nn*, family business

Farbe *nf*, colour

Farbfernsehen *nn*, colour TV

Farbkopierer *nm*, colour copier

Farbton *nm*, shade

Faß *nn*, barrel, bbl

fassen *vb*, **1** (volume), take. **2** (mind), grasp, comprehend

Fassung *nf* (draft), version

Fassungsvermögen *nn*, **1** (of volume), capacity. **2** (of mind), comprehension

fast *adv*, almost

faulen *vb*, rot

faxen *vb*, fax

Fehl-; **Fehlbetrag** *nm*, deficit, shortfall; **Fehldeutung** *nf*, misinterpretation; **Fehleinschätzung** *nf*, false estimation, misreading

fehlen *vb*, be lacking or missing; **hier fehlt etwas**, something is missing here; **es fehlt mir an** (+ dat), I lack . . .

Fehlentscheidung *nf*, wrong decision

Fehler *nm*, **1** error, mistake. **2** fault, defect

Fehleranalyse *nf*, error analysis

fehlerfrei *adj*, **1** (goods), perfect. **2** (work), faultless, flawless

fehlerhaft *adj*, **1** (goods), imperfect. **2** (work). faulty, flawed

Fehler-; **Fehlerquelle** *nf*, source of error; **Fehlerquote** *nf*, error rate; **Fehlerspielraum** *nm*, margin of error

Fehlkalkulation *nf*, miscalculation

Fehlschlag *nm*, failure

fehl|schlagen *vb*, fall through, fail

Fehlzeiten *nfpl*, working hours lost through absenteeism

feiern *vb*, **1** (gen), celebrate. **2** stay off work

Feiertag *nm*, public holiday

feilschen *vb*, haggle

Feinarbeit *nf*, precision work

Felduntersuchung *nf*, field work

Feld-, **Wald- und Wiesen-** *adj*, common-or-garden, run-of-the-mill

Feldzug *nm*, campaign

Fensterumschlag *nm* (offce), window envelope

Ferien *npl*, holidays

Ferngespräch *nn* (telec), long-distance call

fern|laden *vb* (comp), download

Fernmeldewesen *nn*, telecommunications system

Fernschreiben *nn*, **Fernschreiber** *nm*, telex; **per Fernschreiber**, by telex

Fernsehapparat *nm*, TV (set)

Fernsehen *nn*, television, TV; **im Fernsehen**, on TV

Fernseher *nm*, TV (set)

Fernseh-; **Fernsehgebühr** *nf*, television licence fee; **Fernsehgerät** *nn*, TV (set); **Fernsehkanal** *nm*, TV channel; **Fernsehzeitschrift** *nf*, TV guide

Fernspediteur *nm*, road haulier

Fernsprecher *nm*, telephone; **öffentlicher Fernsprecher**, public telephone

Fernsprechteilnehmer(in) *nm/f*, telephone subscriber

Fernsteuerung *nf*, remote control

Fernverkehr *nm*, long-distance traffic

fertig *adj*, **1** finished; **die Arbeit ist fertig**, the job is finished; **sind Sie mit dem Brief fertig?**, have you finished the letter? **2** ready-made; **etwas fertig kaufen**, buy something ready-made. **3** ready; **alle sind fertig zur Abfahrt**, everyone is ready to go; **fertig zur Auslieferung**, ready for dispatch

Fertig-; **Fertiggericht** *nn*, convenience food, **Fertigkeiten**

nfpl, skills; **Fertigstellung** *nf*, completion

Fertigung *nf*, manufacturing, production

Fertigungsstraße *nf*, assembly or production line

Fertigwaren *nfpl*, finished goods

fest *adj*, **1** firm; **wir haben einen festen Plan**, we have a definite plan. **2** fixed; **fester Satz** *nm*, fixed rate

festigen *vb*, strengthen

Festigkeit *nf* (of material), strength

Festkosten *npl*, running costs

Festland *nn*, mainland

fest|legen *vb*, **1** (date etc), determine, fix. **2** (resources), tie up

Festplatte *nf* (comp), hard disk

Festpreis *nm*, fixed price

fest|stellen *vb*, ascertain

festverzinslich *adj* (fin), fixed-rate

feucht *adj*, **1** (material), damp; **in feuchtem Zustand**, in a damp condition. **2** (air), humid

Feuchtigkeit *nf*, **1** (of material), dampness. **2** (of air), humidity. **3** (in walls), damp; **vor Feuchtigkeit schützen!**, keep dry!

feuchtigkeitsbeständig *adj*, damp-proof

Feuer *nn*, fire

feuerfest *adj*, **1** (gen), fireproof. **2** (dishes), heat-resistant

feuergefährlich *adj*, (in)flammable

Feuerlöscher *nm*, fire extinguisher

feuern *vb* (from job), fire, sack

Fiasko *nn*, fiasco

Filiale *nf* (of bank etc), branch.

Filialleiter(in) *nm/f*, branch manager(ess)

Finanz *nf*, financial world; **Finanzberater** *nm*, financial adviser; **Finanzbericht** *nm*, financial report; **Finanzfrage** *nf*, question of finance; **Finanzgebaren** *nn*, management of public finances; **Finanzhilfe** *nf*, financial assistance

finanziell *adj*, *adv*, financial; financially; **finanziell unabhängig**, self-supporting, self-funding

finanzieren *vb*, finance

Finanzierung *nf*, financing, funding

Finanz-; **Finanzjahr** *nn*, financial year; **Finanzlage** *nf*, financial status; **Finanzminister** *nm*, minister of finance; **Finanzplanung** *nf*, financial planning, budgeting; **Finanzprüfung** *nf*, financial review; **Finanzvereinbarungen** *nfpl*, financial arrangements; **Finanzverwaltung** *nf*, Inland Revenue

finden *vb*, find

Firma *nf* (pl: **Firmen**), firm, company; **angesehene Firma**, company of good standing; **eine Firma gründen**, set up a company; **eine Firma leiten**, run a firm

Firmen-; **Firmenansehen** *nn*, goodwill; **Firmenbogen** *nm*, headed paper; **Firmen(mitbe)gründer** *nm*, company promoter; **Firmengründung** *nf*, formation of a company; **Firmenimage** *nn*, corporate image; **Firmenkopf** *nm*, company letterhead; **Firmenwagen** *nm*, company car; **Firmenzeichen** *nn*, logo; **Firmenzentrale** *nf*, headquarters

fiskalisch *adj*, fiscal

flau *adj* (economy), slack, sluggish

Flaute *nf*, (economic) downturn

fliegen *vb*, fly

Fließband *nn*, conveyor belt

fließend *adj, adv*, fluent; fluently; **leider spreche ich noch nicht fließend Deutsch**, I am afraid I am not yet fluent in German

Flip-Chart *nf*, flip chart

florierend *adj*, flourishing

Flug *nm*, flight; **Flugabfertigung** *nf*, check-in; **Flughafen** *nm*, airport; **Flughafengebühr** *nf*, airport tax; **Fluglotse** *nm*, air traffic controller; **Flugsicherheit** *nf*, airport security; **Flugsteig** *nm*, gate; **Flugtauglichkeit** *nf*, airworthiness; **Flugzeug** *nn*, aircraft, plane

Fluktuation *nf*, fluctuation

fluktuieren *vb*, fluctuate

Flußdiagramm *nn*, flow chart

flüssig *adj*, liquid

flüssig|machen *vb* (resources), free

Folge *nf*, consequence, result; **mit der Folge, daß . . .** , with the result that . . .; **zur Folge haben**, result in

folgen (+ dat) *vb*, follow; **im folgenden**, hereafter

folgendermaßen *adv*, as follows

folgerichtig *adj, adv*, consistent; consistently

Folgeschreiben *nn*, follow-up letter

folglich *adv*, consequently

Folie *nf*, **1** (cling)film. **2** (metal), (aluminium) foil. **3** (OHP), transparency

Fonds *nm*, **1** (gen), fund. **2** (fin), government bond

fordern *vb*, demand

fördern *vb*, **1** (gen), promote. **2** (fin), sponsor. **3** (coal), mine, produce

Forderung *nf*, claim, demand

Förderung *nf*, **1** (gen), promotion. **2** (fin), sponsorship. **3** (mining), production

Formalität *nf*, formality; **eine bloße Formalität**, a mere formality

Format *nn*, **1** (of paper), format, size. **2 hervorragendes Format haben**, be of excellent quality

formatieren *vb* (comp), format

formell *adj, adv*, formal; formally

Formsache *nf*, formality

Formular *nn*, form; **ein Formular ausfüllen**, fill in/complete a form

formulieren *vb*, (agreement etc), word, phrase

Formulierung *nf*, wording

forschen *vb*, (do) research

Forscher(in) *nm/f*, researcher

Forschung *nf*, research; **Forschung und Entwicklung**, research and development, R&D

Forschungs-; **Forschungsgelder** *nnpl*, research funds; **Forschungsgruppe** *nf*, research unit; **Forschungsinstitut** *nn*, research institute

fortgeschritten *adj*, advanced

Fortschritt *nm*, advance, progress

Fortschrittsbericht *nm*, progress report

fort|setzen *vb*, continue

Fortsetzung *nf*, continuation; **Fortsetzung folgt**, to be continued

Fotoapparat *nm*, camera

Fotokopie *nf*, photocopy

fotokopieren *vb*, photocopy

Fotokopierer *nm*, photocopier

Fracht *nf*, cargo, freight; **Fracht aufladen**, take on freight; **Frachtbrief** *nm*, consignment note, shipping note, waybill; **Frachter** *nm*, freighter

frachtfrei *adj, adv*, carriage-free

Fracht-; **Frachtgebühren** *nfpl*, cargo rates; **Frachtkosten** *npl*, freight costs, freightage; **Frachtnachnahme** *nf*, carriage forward, freight forward; **Frachtschiff** *nn*, cargo ship

Frage *nf*, question; **noch eine Frage**, one more question; **eine Frage stellen**, ask a question; **in Frage stellen**, query

Fragebogen *nm*, questionnaire; **einen Fragebogen ausfüllen**, complete or fill in a questionnaire; **Fragebögen ausgeben**, issue questionnaires

fragen *vb*, ask

fraglich *adj*, uncertain, doubtful

fragwürdig *adj*, questionable, shady

Franchise *nf*, franchise; **Franchisebasis** *nf*, **auf Franchisebasis vergeben**, franchise; **Franchisegeber** *nm*, franchisor; **Franchisenehmer** *nm*, franchisee

frankieren *vb*, **1** (by hand), stamp. **2** (machine), frank

Frankiermaschine *nf*, franking machine

frankierter Rückumschlag *nm*, stamped addressed envelope, SAE

franko *adj* (comm), carriage paid

Frau *nf*, **1** (gen), woman. **2** wife. **3** (address), Mrs; **Frau Vorsitzende**, Madam Chairman

Frauenzeitschrift *nf*, women's magazine

Fräulein *nn*, Miss (no longer used as form of address)

frei *adj*, **1** free; **„Zimmer frei"**, "vacancies"; **ist dieser Platz noch frei?**, is anyone sitting here? **2** (imp/exp), **frei ab Grenze**, DAF, delivered at frontier; **frei ab Kai**, free alongside quay; **frei Schiff**, free alongside ship; **frei an Bord**, free on board; **frei Bahn**, free on rail; **frei Haus**, free delivery; **frei Lkw ab Lager**, free on truck

freiberuflich *adj*, *adv*, **freiberuflich tätig sein**, work freelance, be self-employed

Frei-; **Freihafen** *nm*, free port; **Freihandel** *nm*, free trade; **Freihandelszone** *nf*, free trade area; **Freikarte** *nf*, complimentary ticket

freilich *adv*, admittedly

frei|machen *vb*, **1** (by hand), stamp. **2** (machine), frank

Freiplatz *nm*, complimentary seat

freischaffend *adj*, freelance

freiwillig *adj*, *adv*, voluntary; voluntarily

Freizeichen *nn* (telec), dialling tone

Freizeit *nf*, leisure time, spare time

Freizeitbeschäftigung *nf*, hobby

Freizeitkleidung *nf*, leisure wear

Fremdenverkehr *nm*, tourism

Fremdenverkehrsbüro *nn*, tourist information office

Fremdkapital *nn* (fin), borrowings; **Fremdkapitalaufnahme** *nf*, **festverzinsliche Fremdkapitalaufnahme**, gearing

Fremdsprache *nf*, foreign language

Fremdwährung *nf*, foreign currency

Frequenzmodulation *nf*, frequency modulation, FM

freuen *vb* **1**, **es freut mich, daß . . .**, I I'm glad that . . . **2 sich freuen auf** (+ acc), look forward to; **wir freuen uns auf Ihren Besuch**, we're looking forward to your visit. **3 sich freuen über** (+ acc) *vb*, be pleased with, be happy about

freundlich *adj*, kind; **mit freundlichen Grüßen** (corr), **1** (addressed by name), Yours sincerely. **2** (no name), Yours faithfully

Freundlichkeit *nf*, kindness

Friedensrichter *nm*, magistrate

frisch *adj, adv*, fresh; freshly

Frische-Datum *nn*, sell-by date

Frischhaltebeutel *nm*, air-tight bag

Frist *nf*, period (with a deadline); **eine Frist einhalten**, meet a deadline; **eine Frist verlängern**, extend a deadline; **eine Frist versäumen**, miss a deadline

fristgerecht *adj, adv*, within the period stipulated

fristlos *adj, adv*, **fristlos entlassen**, dismiss without notice

Fristverlängerung *nf*, extension

frostbeständig *adj*, frost-resistant

Frostschutzmittel *nn* (in car), antifreeze

früh *adj, adv*, early; **er kam zu früh**, he came early

früher *adj, adv*, **1** earlier. **2** former; formerly

frühestmöglich *adj, adv*, earliest possible; as soon as possible

Frühling *nm*, spring; **im Frühling**, in the spring

Frühpensionierung *nf*, early retirement

Frührente *nf*, early retirement

Frühschicht *nf*, early shift

Frühstück *nn*, breakfast; **Frühstück bestellen**, order breakfast

Frühstückspause *nf*, coffee break

Fühlungnahme *nf*, contact

führen *vb*, **1** lead. **2** (goods), carry, stock

führend *adj*, leading

Führerschein *nm*, driving licence

Führung *nf*, **1** (gen), guidance, direction. **2** (comm), management

Führungs-; **Führungskraft** *nf*, (member of the) executive; **nach Führungskräften suchen**, headhunt; **Führungsnachwuchs** *nm*, management trainee(s), young people with leadership potential; **Führungsspitze** *nf*, top management

Funk *nm*, radio; **per Funk**, by radio; **Funkausstellung** *nf*, radio and television exhibition

funkelnagelneu *adj*, brand-new

Funk-; **Funkkontakt** *nm*, radio contact; **Funkrufempfänger** *nm*, pager; **Funksprechgerät** *nn*, radiotelephone; **Funktelefon** *nn* cordless telephone

Funktion *nf*, function

funktionieren *vb*, function, work (properly)

Fürsorge *nf*, welfare

Fusion *nf*, merger

fusionieren *vb*, merge

Fusionierung *nf*, merger

Fußboden *nm*, floor

Fußgänger *nm*, pedestrian; **Fußgängerzone** *nf*, pedestrian precinct, shopping precinct

Futures-Markt *nm* (fin), futures market

G

g, **Gramm** *nn*, gram(me)

Gabelstapler *nm*, forklift

Gang *nm*, **1** corridor. **2** (at exhibition), walkway. **3** (in aircraft), aisle. **4** (techn), gear; **im dritten Gang**, in third gear. **5 in Gang**, going; **in Gang bringen** initiate; **in Gang kommen**, get off the ground; **in Gang setzen**, get going

ganz *adj*, *adv*, whole, entire; wholly, entirely, quite

ganzjährig *adv*, all the year round

gänzlich *adv*, completely

ganztägig *adj*, *adv*, all-day

Ganztags-, full-time; **Ganztagsarbeit** *nf*, full-time job

Ganzzahl *nf*, integer

Garant *nm*, guarantor

Garantie *nf*, guarantee, warranty

garantieren *vb*, guarantee

Garantieschein *nm*, (certificate of) guarantee

Garantieverletzung *nf*, breach of warranty

Gartenlokal *nn*, beer garden

Gast *nm*, **1** (gen), guest. **2** (at exhibition), visitor

gastfreundlich *adj*, hospitable

Gast-; **Gastfreundschaft** *nf*, hospitality; **Gastgeber(in)** *nm/f*, host(ess); **Gastland** *nn*, host country; **Gaststätte** *nf*, restaurant; **Gaststättengewerbe** *nn*, catering (trade); **Gastwirtschaft** *nf*, restaurant

Gebäude *nn*, building; **Gebäudereinigung** *nf*, cleaning contractors, commercial cleaning

Gebiet *nn*, area, district

gebildet *adj*, educated

geboren *adj*, born; **geboren am 9. Marz 1972**, born on March 9th 1972

Gebr., **Gebrüder** *nmpl* (comm), Brothers; **Gebrüder Meier**, Meier Brothers

Gebrauch *nm*, use

gebrauchen *vb*, use

Gebrauchsanweisung *nf*, directions for use

Gebrauchsgüter *nnpl*, consumables; **langlebige Gebrauchsgüter**, consumer durables

gebrauchsfertig *adj*, ready for use

gebraucht *adj*, used, second-hand

Gebrauchtwaren *npl*, second-hand goods; **Gebrauchtwarenhändler** *nm*, second-hand dealer

Gebühr *nf*, **1** (gen), charge; **über Gebühr**, excessively. **2** (for professional services), fee. **3** postage; **Gebühr bezahlt**, postage paid; **Gebühr bezahlt Empfänger**, freepost

gebührend *adj*, *adv*, appropriate; appropriately

Gebühreneinheit *nf* (telec), unit

Gebührenordnung *nf*, **Gebührentabelle** *nf*, scale of charges

Geburtenrate *nf*, birth rate

Geburtsdatum *nn*, date of birth

Geburtstag *nm*, birthday; **ich gratuliere Ihnen zum Geburtstag!**, happy birthday!

Geburtsurkunde *nf*, birth certificate

Gedächtnis *nn*, memory; **ein gutes/schlechtes Gedächtnis**, a good/poor memory

gedr., gedruckt *adj*, printed

Gedränge *nn*, crowd, crush

gedrängt (voll) *adj* (with people), packed (full)

Gedrucktes *nn*, print

Geduld *nf*, patience

sich gedulden *vb*, be patient

geeignet *adj*, *adv*, suitable; suitably; **jemand Geeignetes**, a suitable person

Gefahr *nf*, danger, risk; **auf die Gefahr hin**, at the risk of; **es besteht die Gefahr, daß . . .**, there is the danger that . . .; **in Gefahr bringen**, jeopardise

gefährden *vb*, endanger

gefahrene Kilometer *nmpl*, mileage

Gefahrenzulage *nf*, danger money

gefährlich *adj*, *adv*, dangerous; dangerously

gefallen (+ dat) *vb*, like, please; **das gefällt mir**, I like that

Gefälligkeit *nf*, favour; **aus Gefälligkeit**, as a favour

gefälscht *adj*, counterfeit, forged

gefärbt *adj*, **1** (gen), dyed. **2** (foodstuffs), coloured

Geflügel *nn*, poultry; **Geflügelzucht** *nf*, poultry farming

Gefrier-; **Gefrierfach** *nn*, freezer compartment; **Gefrierkost** *nf*, frozen food; **Gefrierschrank** *nm*, **Gefriertruhe** *nf*, freezer

gegebenenfalls *adv*, should the situation arise

gegen (+ acc) *prep*, against, counter to; **gegen . . . sein**, be against . . ., object to . . .; **gegen bar**, for cash; **gegen Bezahlung/Quittung**, against payment/receipt

Gegenangebot *nn*, counteroffer

Gegenforderung *nf*, counterclaim

Gegend *nf*, area, neighbourhood

gegenseitig *adj*, *adv*, reciprocal; reciprocally

Gegenstand *nm*, **1** (gen), object. **2** (on list), item

Gegenteil *nn*, contrary; **im Gegenteil**, on the contrary

Gegenwart *nf*, presence

gegenwärtig *adj*, *adv*, current, present; currently; at present

gegenzeichnen *vb*, countersign

Gehalt *nn*, salary; **ansprechendes Gehalt**, attractive salary

Gehalts-; **Gehaltsabrechnung** *nf*, payslip; **Gehaltsanspruch** *nm*, salary claim; **Gehaltsaufbesserung** *nf*, salary increase; **Gehaltserhöhung** *nf*, salary rise; **Gehaltsklasse** *nf*, salary bracket; **Gehaltskürzung** *nf*, salary cut; **Gehaltsvorstellung** *nf*, salary expectations; **Gehaltszahlung** *nf*, salary payment

geheim *adj*, *adv*, secret; secretly

Geheimhaltung *nf*, secrecy

Geheimhaltungspflicht *nf*, obligation to maintain secrecy

Gehilfe *nm*, **Gehilfin** *nf*, **1** (gen), assistant. **2** (comm), trainee

gehören (+ dat) *vb*, belong to

Gehtnichtmehr *nn*, **sich bis zum Gehtnichtmehr verschulden** (informal), get up to one's ears in debt

Geistesgegenwart *nf*, presence of mind

geizig *adj*, mean, stingy

Gelände *nn*, premises, grounds

gelangen *vb*, reach

geläufig *adj*, common, familiar

Gelbe Seiten *nfpl*, Yellow Pages

Geld *nn*, money; **Geld anzahlen**, pay a deposit; **Geld einbüßen**, lose money; **Geld verdienen**, make money; **Geld verlieren**, lose money; **Geldabwertung** *nf*, currency devaluation; **Geldanlage** *nf*, financial investment; **Geldausgabe** *nf*, (financial) expenditure; **Geldautomat** *nm*, cash dispenser, automatic teller machine, ATM; **Geldentwertung** *nf*, currency depreciation; **Geldgeber** *nm*, financial backer; **Geldgeschäft** *nn*, financial transaction

geldlich *adj*, *adv*, financial; financially

Geld-; **Geldmangel** *nm*, lack of money; **Geldmärkte** *nmpl*, money markets; **Geldmittel** *nnpl*, funds; **Geldstrafe** *nf*, fine; **Geldstück** *nn*, coin; **Geldwäsche** *nf*, money laundering; **Geldwechsler** *nm*, change machine; **Geldwert** *nm*, cash value

gelegen sein *vb*, be situated

Gelegenheit *nf*, opportunity

Gelegenheitsarbeit *nf*, casual work

Gelegenheitskauf *nm*, bargain

gelegentlich *adj*, *adv*, occasional; occasionally

gelingen (+ dat) *vb*, succeed; **es gelang uns, den Umsatz zu erhöhen**, we succeeded in raising the turnover

gelten *vb*, **1** (gen), be valid; **gelten lassen**, accept. **2** (law), be in force. **3** (coin), be legal tender

Geltung *nf*, validity

Gemeinde *nf*, (admin), municipality; **Gemeindeabgaben** *nfpl*, rates; **Gemeindeamt** *nn*, local authority; **Gemeindeverwaltung** *nf*, local government

gemeinsam *adj*, *adv*, joint, collective, together; jointly, collectively

Gemeinwohl *nn*, public welfare

Gemüse *nn*, vegetables

genau *adj*, *adv*, exact; exactly

genaugenommen *adv*, strictly speaking

genehmigen *vb*, **1** (gen), approve, give permission. **2** (official, e.g. visa), authorise

genehmigt *adj*, **1** (gen), approved. **2** (official), authorised

Generaldirektor *nm*, managing director

genießbar *adj*, **1** edible; **2** drinkable

Genossenschaft *nf*, cooperative society

Gepäck *nn*, luggage; **Gepäckaufbewahrung** *nf*, left-luggage (office)

gepflegt *adj* (food, wines), excellent

Gerät *nn*, **1** piece of equipment; device. **2** electrical appliance. **3** (kitchen) utensil

Geratewohl *nn*, **aufs Geratewohl**, at random

geräumig *adj*, spacious

Geräusch *nn*, noise

gerecht *adj*, just

Gerechtigkeit *nf*, justice

Gericht *nn*, (law) court; **vor Gericht erscheinen**, appear in court

gerichtlich vor|gehen *vb*, take legal action

Gerichts-; **Gerichtstermin** *nm*, date of trial; **Gerichtsverfahren** *nn*, legal proceedings; **Gerichtsverhandlung** *nf*, trial

gering *adj*, low, marginal, minor; **es gab nur geringen Schaden**, there was only minor damage

geringfügig *adj*, marginal, negligible; **ein geringfügiger Fehler**, a marginal error

Gesamt- *adj*, total; **Gesamtplan** *nm*, overall plan; **Gesamtsumme** *nf*, sum total; **Gesamttonnage** *nf*, deadweight tonnage

Geschäft *nn*, **1** (gen), business. **2** shop

geschäftlich *adv*, business, on business; **geschäftlich in London zu tun haben**, be in London on business

Geschäfts-; **Geschäftsadresse** *nf*, business address; **Geschäftsbericht** *nm*, annual report; **Geschäftsbriefe** *nmpl*, business correspondence; **Geschäftsführer** *nm*, managing director; **Geschäftsjahr** *nn*, financial year, trading year; **Geschäftsleitung** *nf*, directorate; **Geschäftsräume** *nmpl*, business premises; **Geschäftsreise** *nf*, business trip; **Geschäftsschluß** *nm*, closing time; **Geschäftsstelle** *nf*, branch office; **Geschäftsverbindung** *nf*, business contact; **Geschäftszeit** *nf*, business hours

Geschenk *nn*, gift

Geschenkgutschein *nm*, gift token

Geschenkpapier *nn*, gift wrapping

geschlossen *adj*, closed; **montags geschlossen**, closed on Mondays

Geschmack *nm*, **1** (gen), taste. **2** (aroma), flavour

Geschwindigkeit *nf*, speed

Geschwindigkeitsgrenze *nf*, speed limit

Gesellschaft *nf*, **1** society. **2** (firm), company; **Gesellschaft mit beschränkter Haftung, GmbH**, public limited company, plc; **nahestehende Gesellschaft**, associate company

gesellschaftlich *adj*, social

Gesellschaftskleidung *nf*, formal dress

Gesetz *nn*, act, law, statute; **gegen das Gesetz verstoßen**, break the law

Gesetzesvorlage *nf*, (in parliament), bill

gesetzlich *adj*, *adv*, legal; legally; **gesetzlich geschützt**, patented; **gesetzlich vorgeschrieben**, statutory

gesetzwidrig *adj* (action), unlawful

Gespräch *nn*, **1** (gen), chat, conversation. **2** (formal), interview. **3** telephone call; **ein Gespräch annehmen**, take a call

gestohlen *adj*, stolen

Gesundheit *nf*, health

Gesundheits-; **Gesundheitsamt** *nn*, public health department; **Gesundheitsschaden** *nm*, health defect; **Gesundheitszeugnis** *nn*, health certificate

Getränk *nn*, drink; **alkoholfreies Getränk**, soft drink

getrennt *adj*, **mit getrennter Post**, under separate cover

Getriebe *nn* (techn), gears

Gewähr *nf* (gen), guarantee; **„ohne Gewähr"** (on price list), "subject to change"

gewähren *vb*, give, grant; **wir gewähren 5% Rabatt**, we give a 5% discount

gewährleisten *vb*, ensure, guarantee

Gewebe *nn* (textile), fabric

Gewerbe *nn*, trade; **ein Gewerbe ausüben**, carry on/practise a trade; **Gewerbeaufsicht** *nf*, factory safety and health control; **Gewerbeaufsichtsamt** *nn*, factory inspectorate; **Gewerbebetrieb** *nm*, commercial enterprise; **Gewerbegebiet** *nn*, trading estate; **Gewerbesteuer** *nf*, trade tax

gewerblich *adj*, *adv*, commercial; commercially; **gewerblich nutzen**, use for commercial purposes

Gewerkschaft *nf*, trade(s) union

Gewerkschaftsfunktionär *nm*, union official

Gewerkschaftsmitglied *nn*, union member

Gewicht *nn*, weight

Gewinn *nm*, profit; **Gewinn vor Steuern**, pre-tax profit; **Gewinnbeteiligung** *nf*, profit sharing

gewinnen *vb*, **1** win. **2** (acquire), gain; **an Wert gewinnen**, gain in value; **Erfahrung gewinnen**, gain experience

Gewinn-; **Gewinnmarge** *nf*, profit margin; **Gewinnrückgang** *nm*, fall in profits; **Gewinnspanne** *nf*, profit margin; **Gewinnsteuer** *nf*, tax on profits; **Gewinnstreben** *nn*, profiteering; **Gewinn- und Verlustrechnung** *nf*, profit and loss account

Gewohnheit *nf*, **1** (personal), habit. **2** (collective), custom. **3** (business), practice

gewöhnlich *adj*, *adv*, usual; usually

Gezeiten *nfpl*, tide

Girokonto *nn*, giro account

Giroscheck *nm*, giro cheque

glauben *vb*, believe

Glauben *nm*, belief; **in gutem Glauben**, bona fide

Gläubiger *nm*, creditor

gleich *adj*, equal; **gleiche Rechte**, equal rights

gleich *adv*, in a moment; **er kommt gleich**, he is on his way, he'll be here in a moment

Gleichstrom *nm*, direct current, DC

gleitend *adj*, sliding; **gleitende Arbeitszeit** *nf*, flexible working hours, flexitime; **gleitende Skala** *nf*, sliding scale

Gleitzeit *nf*, flexible working hours, flexitime; **Gleitzeitleser** *nm*, flexitime reader; **Gleitzeitregelung** *nf*, flexitime ruling

Glück haben *vb*, be fortunate/lucky

Glückwunsch *nm*, congratulation; **herzlichen Glückwunsch!**, congratulations!

gratis *adv*, free (of charge); **gratis bekommen**, get as a freebie

Gratisprobe *nf*, free sample

gratulieren *vb*, congratulate; **gratulieren zu** (+ dat), congratulate on . . .

Gremium *nn*, committee

Grenze *nf*, **1** (national), border, frontier; **an der deutschen Grenze**, on the German border/frontier. **2** (of property), boundary. **3 wir haben die Grenzen unserer Geduld erreicht**, our patience has reached its limits/is running out

Grenzübergangsstelle *nf*, customs entry point

grenzüberschreitend *adj*, transnational

Grenzwert *nm*, marginal value

Großabnehmer *nm*, bulk purchaser

Großbuchstaben *nmpl*, capital letters, block capitals

Größe *nf*, size; **von mittlerer Größe**, medium-sized

Groß-; **Großeinkauf** *nm*, bulk purchase; **Großhandel** *nm*, wholesale (trade); **Großhandelspreis** *nm*, trade price; **Großhändler** *nm*, wholesale dealer; **Großindustrie** *nf*, big business; **Großraumbüro** *nn*, open-plan office; **Großrechner** *nm* (comp), mainframe computer

großzügig *adj*, *adv*, generous; generously

grün *adj*, green; **grünes Licht geben**, give the go-ahead/thumbs up

Grund *nm*, **1** (cause), reason. **2** (physical), ground; **Grund und Boden** land(ed property); **Grundbesitz** *nm*, land, property; **Grundbesitzer** *nm*, landowner; **Grundbuch** *nn*, land register;

Grundbuchamt *nn*, land registry; **Grundeigentumsurkunde** *nf*, title deed

gründen *vb*, found

Grund-; **Grundfläche** *nf* (building, room), floor space; **Grundgebühr** *nf*, flat rate; **Grundlage** *nf*, basis

grundlegend *adj*, *adv*, fundamental; fundamentally

gründlich *adj*, *adv*, thorough; thoroughly

Grund-; **Grundmaterial** *nn*, commodity, raw material; **Grundsatz** *nm*, principle; **Grundschuld** *nf*, mortgage; **Grundstein** *nm*, foundation stone; **Grundsteuer** *nf*, local property tax; **Grundstoff** *nm*, basic material; **Grundstoffindustrie** *nf*, basic/primary industry

Grundstück *nn*, **1** (piece of land), plot. **2** (developed), property

Grundstücks-; **Grundstücksmakler** *nm*, estate agent; **Grundstücksspekulant** *nm*, property speculator; **Grundstückswartung** *nf*, site maintenance

Gruppe *nf*, group

Gruppierung *nf*, grouping

Gruß *nm* (in letter), greeting; **viele Grüße**, best wishes; **mit freundlichem Gruß**, Yours sincerely, (if addressee's name used); Yours faithfully, (with no name); **viele Grüße an Ihre Kollegen**, (give my) regards to your colleagues

grüßen *vb*, **1** (gen), greet. **2** (informal), say hello. **3** (formal), give/send regards; **ich soll Sie von Frau Schmitz grüßen**, Frau Schmitz sends her regards; **mein Chef läßt Sie (herzlich) grüßen**, my boss sends his regards

Grußformel *nf*, **1** (gen), form of greeting. **2** (at start of letter), salutation. **3** (at close of letter), complementary close, ending

gültig *adj*, valid; **gültig vom . . . bis zum . . .**, valid from . . . until . . .

Gültigkeit *nf*, validity

Gummi *nm/nn*, rubber; **Gummiband** *nn*, rubber band

günstig *adj*, **1** (time), convenient. **2** (disposition, weather, assessment), favourable; **günstig abschneiden**, do well; **günstig kaufen/verkaufen**, buy/sell at a good price

Gußeisen *nn*, cast iron

gut *adj*, *adv*, good; well; **er spricht gut Deutsch**, he speaks good German; **das ist gut gegen/für** (+ acc), it's good for . . .; **das ist ja alles gut und schön, aber . . .**, that's all very well but . . .; **gute Besserung!**, get well soon; **auf gutes Gelingen!**, here's to success!; **lassen wir es damit gut sein**, let's stop at this point, that'll do; **schon gut!**, it's OK; **nun gut!**, fair enough; **seien Sie so gut, und schreiben Sie mir das auf**, would you mind writing that down for me?

Gutachten *nn*, expert opinion

Gutachter *nm*, **1** (gen), consultant, expert. **2** (law), expert witness

gutbezahlt *adj*, highly-paid

Güter *nnpl*, goods, freight; **Güter zollamtlich abfertigen**, clear goods through the customs; **Güterabfertigung** *nf*, **1** dispatch of freight/goods. **2** freight/goods office; **Güterbahnhof** *nm*, freight/goods depot; **Güterdepot** *nn* goods depot; **Güterfernverkehr** *nm*, long-distance haulage; **Güterkraftverkehr** *nm*, road haulage; **Güternahverkehr** *nm*, short-distance haulage; **Güterschuppen** *nm*, freight depot, goods shed; **Güterumschlag** *nm*, cargo handling; **Güterwagen** *nm*, goods truck; **Güterzug** *nm*, freight/goods train

Guthaben *nn* (fin), credit; **auf Ihrem Konto ist ein Guthaben von DM 3.500**, your account is DM 3,500 in credit

Gutschein *nm*, coupon, voucher

gut|schreiben *vb*, credit with; **bitte schreiben Sie die Summe meinem Konto gut**, please credit my account with that sum

Gutschrift *nf*, **1** (process), crediting. **2** (note), credit note. **3** (amount), credit (item)

gutverdienend *adj*, high-income

Haben *nn*, credit; **im Haben stehen**, be on the credit side

Hafen *nm*, port, harbour; **Hafenanlagen** *nfpl*, docks, harbour/port installations; **Hafenbehörde** *nf*, harbour/port authorities; **Hafengebühr** *nf*, harbour/port dues; **Hafenstadt** *nf*, port

haften für (+ acc) *vb* (law), be legally responsible for, accept liability for

haftpflichtversichert sein *vb* (driver), have third-party insurance

Haftpflichtversicherung *nf*, third-party insurance

Haftung *nf* (law), liability; **Haftung übernehmen für** (+ acc), accept liability for

halb *adj*, half; **eine halbe Stelle haben**, have a half-day job; **zu halbem Preis**, half-price

halbe-halbe machen *vb*, go fifty-fifty

halbieren *vb*, halve; **die Kosten halbieren**, halve the costs

Halbjahresbericht *nm*, half-yearly report

halbjährlich *adj*, *adv*, half-yearly

Halbpension *nf* (in hotel), half board/bed, breakfast and evening meal

Hälfte *nf*, half; **die Hälfte davon gehört ihm**, half of it is his

haltbar *adj*, **haltbar bis . . .**, best before . . .; **haltbar sein**, keep

Haltbarkeit *nf*, shelf-life

Haltbarkeitsdatum *nn*, best-before

date, eat-by date

sich halten an (+ dat) *vb* (regulations), comply with

Hand *nf*, **zu Händen von . . ., z.H(d).** (corr), for the attention of

Handel *nm*, trade; **Handel treiben mit** (+ dat), trade with

handeln *vb*, **1** (comm), trade (with). **2** (take action), act. **3** (negotiate price), haggle

Handels-; **Handelsabkommen** *nn*, trade agreement; **Handelsartikel** *nm*, commodity; **Handelsbeziehungen** *nfpl*, trade relations; **Handelsbilanz** *nf*, trade balance; **Handelsembargo** *nn*, trade embargo; **ein Handelsembargo verhängen**, impose a trade embargo; **Handelsgesetzbuch** *nn*, Code of Commercial Law; **Handelskammer** *nf*, chamber of commerce; **Handelskette** *nf*, chain of retail shops; **Handelslücke** *nf*, trade gap; **Handelsmarke** *nf*, trademark, tradename; **Handelsmesse** *nf*, trade fair; **Handelspreis** *nm*, trade price; **Handelsregister** *nn*, register of companies; **Handelsschule** *nf*, commercial school/college

handelsüblich *adj*, customary (in the trade)

Handelsvertrag *nm*, trade agreement

handeltreibend *adj*, trading

Händler *nm*, **1** (gen), trader, dealer. **2** shopkeeper

Händlerrabatt *nm*, trade discount

Handwerk *nn*, craft

Handwerker *nm*, **1** (gen), workman. **2** (professional status), craftsman

Handwerkskammer *nf*, Chamber of Crafts

Handzettel *nm*, flier/flyer

häufig *adj*, *adv*, frequent; frequently, often

Häufigkeit *nf*, frequency

Haupt- *adj*, chief, main, principal; **Hauptbahnhof** *nm*, main (railway) station

hauptberuflich *adj*, *adv*, full-time

Haupt-; **Hauptbuch** *nn*, ledger; **Hauptbüro** *nn*, central office; **Haupterzeugnis** *nn*, staple commodity/product; **Hauptgeschäftsstelle** *nf*, head office, headquarters; **Hauptgeschäftsstraße** *nf*, High Street; **Hauptindustriezweig** *nm*, staple industry; **Hauptpost** *nf*, **Hauptpostamt** *nn*, main post office; **Hauptprodukt** *nn*, staple commodity/staple product

hauptsächlich *adj*, *adv*, main; mainly

Haupt-; **Hauptsaison** *nf*, busy season; **Hauptsendezeit** *nf*, prime time; **Hauptsitz** *nm*, headquarters; **Hauptspeicher** *nm* (comp), main memory; **Hauptstadt** *nf*, capital city; **Hauptverdiener** *nm*, main/principal earner; **Hauptverkehrszeit** *nf*, peak period, rush hour; **Hauptversammlung** *nf*, annual general meeting, AGM

Haushalt *nm* (fin), budget, household; **. . . im Haushalt einplanen**, budget for . . .

Haushalts-; **Haushaltsgerät** *nn*, domestic appliance; **elektrische Haushaltsgeräte**, white goods; **Haushaltsjahr** *nn*, financial year; **Haushaltswaren** *nfpl*, hardware; **Haushaltswarengeschäft** *nn*, hardware shop

Haushaltungskosten *npl*, household expenses

hausintern *adj*, *adv*, in-house

Haus-; **Hausmarke** *nf*, own brand; **Hausmüll** *nm*, domestic rubbish; **Hausnachrichten** *nfpl*, house magazine; **Hausnummer** *nf*, house number

Hausse *nf* (stock exchange), boom

Haussier *nm* (stock exchange), bull

Haustelefon *nn*, internal telephone

Haus-zu-Haus *adj*, *adv*, door-to-door

Havarie *nf* (imp/exp), average, av; **besondere Havarie**, particular average; **große Havarie**, general average, GA, ga

Hebel *nm*, lever

Hefter *nm* (offce), stapler

Heftklammer *nf* (offce), staple

Heftzwecke *nf*, drawing-pin

Heim *nn*, home

Heimarbeit *nf* (in industry), homework, outwork

Heimat *nf*, home; **Heimatadresse** *nf*, **Heimatanschrift** *nf*, home address; **Heimathafen** *nm*, port of registry; **Heimatland** *nn*, home country

Heimcomputer *nm* (comp), home computer

heimlich *adj*, *adv*, secret; secretly

heim|reisen *vb*, travel home

Heimwerker *nm*, handyman; **Heimwerkerprodukte** *nnpl*, DIY/Do It Yourself products

heiß *adj*, hot

heißen *vb*, **1** be called; **wie heißt er?**, what is he called? **2** mean. **3** say; **das heißt**, . . ., that is (to say) . . .; **es heißt** . . ., it says . . .; **es heißt in diesem Brief** . . ., it says in this letter . . .

heizen *vb*, heat

Heizkosten *npl*, heating charge

Heizöl *nn*, fuel-oil

Heizung *nf*, heating

helfen (+ dat) *vb*, help, be of help; **damit ist uns wenig geholfen**, that's not much help to us

hemmen *vb*, check, slow down

Hemmnis *nn*, bar, check

herab|setzen *vb* (price), mark down, reduce; **wir haben unsere Preise stark herabgesetzt**, we have reduced our prices considerably

herauf|setzen *vb* (price), put up

heraus|bringen *vb* (product), bring out, launch

heraus|fordern *vb*, challenge

Herausforderung *nf*, challenge

Herausgeber(in) *nm/f*, editor

herbei|führen *vb*, bring about

Herbst *nm*, autumn; **im nächsten Herbst**, next autumn

herein|bitten *vb*, ask (to come) in

Herkunft *nf*, origin

Herkunftszertifikat *nn* (imp/exp), certificate of origin

Hermes Kreditversicherung *nf* (imp/exp), Export Credit Guarantee

hermetisch versiegelt *adj*, *adv*, hermetically sealed

Herr *nm*, **1** gentleman; **drei Herren warten auf Sie**, three gentlemen are waiting for you. **2** Mr; **Herr Müller hat angerufen**, Mr. Müller has rung. **3** (corr), **Herrn Dr. Hans Schneider**, Dr. Hans Schneider

Herren *nmpl*, **1** Messrs; **Herren X, Y and Z**, Messrs X, Y and Z. **2** (WC) **„Herren"**, "Gentlemen"; **Herrenbekleidung** *nf*, menswear

herrschen *vb*, **es herrscht**, there is; **es herrscht kaum Nachfrage nach** (+ dat), there is hardly any demand for . . .; **es herrscht Hochkonjunktur**, there is a boom

her|stellen *vb*, manufacture, produce

Hersteller *nm*, manufacturer, producer; **Herstellerpreis** *nm*, manufacturer's price; **empfohlener Herstellerpreis**, manufacturer's recommended price, MRP

Herstellung *nf*, manufacture, production; **serienmäßige Herstellung**, mass production

Herstellungs-; **Herstellungsfehler** *nm*, manufacturing defect; **Herstellungskosten** *npl*, production costs; **Herstellungspreis** *nm*, prime cost; **Herstellungsverfahren** *nn*, manufacturing/production method

herunter|setzen *vb* (price), mark down, reduce

hervor|heben *vb*, emphasise, stress

heute *adv*, today; **von heute an**, from today; **bis heute**, to date; **heute früh, heute morgen**, this morning

heutig *adj*, of today; **unser heutiges Schreiben** (corr), our letter of today

heutzutage *adv*, nowadays

hier *adv*, here; **von hier aus**, from here; **hier und heute**, here and now

hier|bleiben *vb*, stay (here)

hiermit *adv*, hereby; **hiermit bestätigen wir** . . ., we hereby acknowledge . . .

hiesig *adj*, local; **die hiesige Produktion**, local production

Hi-Fi-Anlage *nf*, hi-fi set, hi-fi system

Hilfe *nf*, assistance, help; **um Hilfe bitten**, ask for help

Hilfs-; **Hilfsarbeiter(in)** *nm/f* (in factory), unskilled worker; **Hilfsmittel** *nn*, aid; **Hilfsprogramm** *nn* (comp), utility programme

hinaus|komplimentieren *vb*, usher out

hinaus|laufen auf (+ acc) *vb*, result in

hinaus|schieben *vb*, postpone, put off

hindern *vb*, **1** (progress), hamper, impede. **2** (person), prevent, stop

Hindernis *nn*, hindrance, obstacle

Hinderungsgrund *nm*, excuse

hinein|gehen *vb*, enter

hinein|passen *vb*, fit in

Hinfahrt *nf*, **1** (gen), journey there. **2** (rail), outward journey

hinfällig *adj* (argument, reason), invalid

Hinflug *nm*, outward flight

hinlänglich *adj*, *adv*, sufficient; sufficiently

hin|nehmen *vb* (something undesirable), take, accept

hinreichend *adj*, *adv*, adequate, sufficient; adequately, sufficiently

hinsichtlich (+ genitive) *prep*, with respect to; **hinsichtlich Ihrer Anfrage vom 3. April**, with respect to your enquiry of 3 April

hinten *adv*, behind

hinter|legen *vb* (money), deposit

Hin- und Rückfahrkarte *nf* (rail etc), return ticket

Hin- und Rückflug *nm*, return flight

Hinweis *nm*, indication; **es gibt Hinweise darauf, daß** . . ., there are indications that . . .

hin|weisen auf (+ acc) *vb*, draw attention to . . .; **wir möchten Sie darauf hinweisen, daß** . . ., we would like to draw your attention to the fact that . . .

hinzu|fügen *vb*, add

hinzu|kommen *vb*, **hinzukommt, daß** . . ., added to which . . .

hitzeabweisend *adj*, heat-repellent

hitzebeständig *adj*, heat-resistant

hitzeempfindlich *adj*, sensitive to heat

hochachtungsvoll *adv* (corr), Yours faithfully

hochbezahlt *adj* (pers), highly paid

Hoch-; **Hochdruck** *nm* (physics), high pressure; **Hochfinanz** *nf*, high finance; **Hochfrequenz** *nf* (electr), high frequency; **Hochgarage** *nf*, multi-storey car park; **Hochgeschwindigkeitszug** *nm*, high-speed train

hochgestellt *adj* (pers), highly placed

Hochkonjunktur *nf* (econ), boom

Hochleistung *nf*, first-class performance

hochprozentig *adj* (drinks), high-proof

hochqualifiziert *adj* (pers), highly qualified

hoch|schnellen *vb* (price), shoot up

hoch|schrauben *vb* (demands), increase (steadily)

Hochschulabsolvent(in) *nm/f*, graduate

Hochschule *nf*, higher education institution, college, university

Hochseeschiffahrt *nf*, deep-sea shipping

Hochspannung *nf* (electr), high voltage

höchst *adj*, highest, largest; **der höchste Betrag**, the largest sum

Hochstapler *nm*, confidence trickster, con man

Höchstbetrag *nm*, maximum amount

höchstens *adv*, not more than, at the most

Höchst-; **Höchstgeschwindigkeit** *nf*, maximum speed; **Höchstgeschwindigkeitsgrenze** *nf*, speed limit; **Höchstgewinn** *nm*, record profit; **Höchstgrenze** *nf*, ceiling, upper limit; **Höchstpreis** *nm*, top/maximum price; **Höchststand** *nm*, highest level, peak

höchstwahrscheinlich *adv*, in all probability

Höchstwert *nm*, maximum value

Hochtouren *nfpl*, **auf Hochtouren arbeiten**, work flat out; **auf Hochtouren laufen** (machines), operate at full throttle

hoch|treiben *vb* (price), force up

Hoch- und Tiefbau *nm*, structural and civil engineering

hochverschuldet *adj*, deep in debt

hochverzinslich *adj*, yielding a high rate of interest

hochwertig *adj*, high-quality

Hof *nm* (factory), yard

hoffen *vb*, hope; **es bleibt nur zu hoffen, daß . . .**, one can only hope that . . .; **wir hoffen darauf, daß . . .**, we are hoping that . . .

Hoffnung *nf*, hope; **in der Hoffnung, bald von Ihnen zu hören**, hoping to hear from you soon; **wir machen uns keine Hoffnung, daß . . .**, we hold out no hopes that . . .

hoffnungslos *adj*, *adv*, hopeless; hopelessly

höflich *adj*, *adv*, polite; politely

Hoheitsgewässer *nnpl*, territorial waters

Höhepunkt *nm* (of development), climax, peak

Holdinggesellschaft *nf*, holding company

Holz *nn*, **1** (gen), wood; **aus Holz**, wooden. **2** (for building), timber

hölzern *adj*, wooden

Honorar *nn*, fee, honorarium; **Honorarvorschuß** *nm*, retainer

hören *vb*, hear; **etwas von sich hören lassen**, get in touch

Hörensagen *nn*, hearsay; **vom Hörensagen**, by/from hearsay

Hörer *nm* (telec), receiver; **Hörer bitte auflegen**, please put down the receiver; **bitte nehmen Sie den Hörer ab**, please pick up the receiver

horten *vb* (goods), stockpile

Hotel *nn*, hotel; **Hotelgewerbe** *nn*, hotel trade; **Hotelhalle** *nf*, lobby; **Hotelkette** *nf*, hotel chain; **Hotel- und Gaststättengewerbe** *nn*, catering industry; **Hotelunterbringung** *nf*, hotel accommodation; **Hotelverzeichnis** *nn*, hotel register

Hubschrauber *nm*, helicopter; **mit dem Hubschrauber**, by helicopter

Huckepack *nn* (rail), piggy-back; **Huckepackverfahren** *nn*, piggy-back system

Hypermarkt *nm*, hyper-market

Hypothek *nf*, mortgage; **eine Hypothek aufnehmen**, take out a mortgage

hypothekarisch belasten *vb*, mortgage

Hypothekenbrief *nm*, mortgage deed/certificate

hypothekenfrei *adj*, unmortgaged

Hypotheken-; **Hypothekengläubiger** *nm*, mortgagee; **Hypothekenschuldner** *nm*, mortgager; **Hypothekentilgung** *nf*, mortgage payments; **Hypothekenzinsen** *nmpl*, mortgage interest

I

i.A., im Auftrag (corr), p.p.

i.allg., im allgemeinen, in general

IC, Intercity(-Zug) *nm*, intercity (train); **IC-Zuschlag** *nm*, intercity supplement

Idee *nf*, idea; **eine gute Idee**, a good idea

Ideenaustausch *nm*, exchange of ideas

identifizieren *vb*, identify

IG, Industriegewerkschaft *nf*, industrial trade(s) union

ignorieren *vb*, ignore

IHK *nf*, **Industrie- und Handelskammer** *nf*, Chamber of Industry and Commerce

illegal *adj*, *adv*, illegal; illegally

immaterielle Werte *nmpl* (fin), intangible assets

immer *adv*, always; **immer mehr**, more and more, increasingly

Immobilien *npl*, real estate; **Immobilienmakler** *nm*, estate agent

Import *nm*, import; **sichtbare/unsichtbare Importe**, visible/invisible imports; **Importabgabe** *nf*, import surcharge; **Importbeschränkungen** *nfpl*, import barriers; **Importgenehmigung** *nf*, import licence/permit; **Importgeschäft** *nn*, import business; **Importhandel** *nm*, import trade

importieren *vb*, import

Import-; **Importkonnossement** *nn*, inward bill; **Importquote** *nf*, import quota; **Importwaren** *nfpl*, imported goods

Index *nm*, index; **Indexanleihe** *nf* (fin), index-linked loan; **Indexbindung** *nf* (fin), indexation

Indexierung *nf* (fin), indexation

Indikator *nm*, indicator

indirekt *adj*, *adv*, indirect; indirectly

individuell *adj*, *adv*, individual; individually

Indossament *nn* (comm), endorsement

indossieren *vb* (comm), endorse

industrialisieren *vb*, industrialise

Industrialisierung *nf*, industrialisation

Industrie *nf*, industry; **verarbeitende Industrie**, manufacturing industry

industriell *adj*, *adv*, industrial; industrially

inflationär *adj*, inflationary

Inflationsrate *nf*, rate of inflation

Informationsaustausch *nm*, exchange of information

Informationstechnologie *nf*, information technology

informieren *vb*, inform; **sich informieren**, find out

Ingenieur *nm*, engineer; **Dipl. Ing.**, title of university graduate in engineering; **Ing. (grad)**, title of polytechnic ('Fachhochschule') graduate in engineering

Inhaber(in) *nm/f*, **1** (of hotel), proprietor, proprietress. **2** (fin), bearer; **Inhaberscheck** *nm* (fin), negotiable cheque; **Inhaberschuldverschreibung** *nf* (fin), bearer bond

Inhalt *nm*, content

Inhaltsverzeichnis *nn*, **1** (in book), contents. **2** (of goods), docket

Inkasso *nn* (fin), encashment, collection **Inkassobüro** *nn* (fin), (debt) collection agency; **Inkassostelle** *nf* (fin), (debt) collection point

Inkaufnahme *nf* (formal), acceptance (of undesirable feature)

inkl., **inklusive**, inclusive

Inklusivpreis *nm*, all-in price

inkompetent *adj*, *adv*, incompetent; incompetently

inkonsequent *adj*, *adv*, inconsistent; inconsistently

inkorrekt *adj*, *adv*, incorrect; incorrectly

Inland *nn* (comm), home; **im Inland hergestellt**, home-produced; **im Inland**, inland; **Inlandbedarf** *nm*, home/domestic requirements; **Inlandflug** *nm*, domestic/internal flight

Inlands-; **Inlandsabsatz** *nm*, home/domestic sales; **Inlandsgespräch** *nn* (telec), inland call; **Inlandsmarkt** *nm*, domestic market; **Inlandsporto** *nn*, inland postage; **Inlandsverbrauch** *nm*, home/domestic consumption

Innen-; **Innenarchitekt(in)** *nm/f*, interior designer; **Innenbeleuchtung** *nf*, interior lighting; **Innendienst** *nm*, office duty; **Innenministerium** *nn*, Home Office; **Innenstadt** *nf*, city centre

innerbetrieblich *adj*, *adv*, in-house, internal; internally

innerhalb (+ genitive) *prep*, within

inoffiziell *adj*, *adv*, unofficial; unofficially

insbesondere *adv*, in particular

Inserat *nn*, ad; **ein Inserat aufgeben**, put an ad in the paper

Inserent *nm*, (in a paper), advertiser

inserieren *vb*, (in a paper), advertise

insgesamt *adv*, altogether, in total

Insidergeschäft *nn*, insider deal

Inspektion *nf*, inspection

Installateur *nm*, **1** (gen), plumber. **2** (electr) electrician. **3** gas-fitter

Installation *nf*, installation

installieren *vb*, install

instand setzen *vb*, repair

Instandsetzung *nf*, repair

Instandsetzungskosten *npl*, upkeep

Instrument *nn*, instrument

Integration *nf*, integration

integrieren *vb*, integrate

Interesse *nn*, concern, interest; **persönliches Interesse**, vested interest

Interessen-; **Interessengemeinschaft** *nf*, interest group; **Interessengruppe** *nf*, interest group, lobby; **Interessenkonflikt** *nm*, conflict of interests

Interessent(in) *nm/f*, potential customer

Interessenverband *nm*, lobby

Interimszahlung *nf*, interim payment

intern *adj*, *adv*, internal; internally

Inventar *nn*, stock (inventory)

inventarisieren *vb*, make an inventory

Inventarverzeichnis *nn*, inventory

Inventur *nf*, stocktaking; **Inventur machen**, stocktake

investieren *vb*, invest

Investition *nf*, investment

Investitions-; **Investitionsausgaben** *nfpl*, capital outlay; **Investitionsgüter** *nnpl*, capital equipment; **Investitionsniveau** *nn*, level of investment; **Investitionszuschuß** *nm*, investment grant

Investmentbank *nf*, merchant bank

Investmentgesellschaft *nf*, unit trust

Investor *nm*, investor

IQ *nm*, **Intelligenzquotient** *nm*, IQ, intelligence quotient

irre|führen *vb*, mislead

sich irren *vb*, be wrong

Irrtum *nm*, error; **Irrtümer vorbehalten**, EE, errors excepted

irrtümlich *adv*, in error; **„Brief irrtümlich geöffnet"**, "letter opened in error"

Ist-Bestand *nm*, **1** (money), cash in hand. **2** (goods), actual stock

Ist-Wert *nm*, actual value

i.V., in Vertretung (corr), on behalf of

J

Jahr *nn*, year

Jahres-; **Jahresabschluß** *nm*, annual accounts; **Jahresbeginn** *nm*, beginning of the year; **Jahresbilanz** *nf*, annual balance sheet; **Jahreseinkommen** *nn*, annual income; **Jahreshälfte** *nf*, half of the year; **Jahreshauptversammlung** *nf*, AGM, annual general meeting; **Jahresrente** *nf*, annuity; **Jahresschlußverkauf** *nm*, annual stock-taking sale; **Jahreszeit** *nf*, season

jahreszeitlich bedingt *adj*, seasonal; **jahreszeitlich bedingte Arbeitslosigkeit**, seasonal unemployment

Jahrgang *nm*, **Jg.**, **1** (of wine), vintage. **2** (pers), year of birth, age group. **3** (of periodical), volume

Jahrhundert *nn*, **Jh.** *nn*, century; **Jahrhundertfeier** *nf*, centenary

jährlich *adj*, *adv*, **1** annual; annually. **2** (payment), per annum

je *adv*, **1** each, every; **für je 5 Stück bieten wir 10% Rabatt**, we offer a 10% discount for every 5 purchased; **die Firmen zahlen je 1.000 DM**, firms pay 1,000 marks each. **2** ever; **haben Sie je einen solchen Preisanstieg erlebt?**, have you ever seen a price increase like this?

jedenfalls *adv*, in any case

jederzeit *adv*, at any time

jedoch *adv*, however

jemand *pron*, somebody

jetzt *adv*, now; **von jetzt an**, from now on

juristisch *adj*, *adv*, legal; legally; **ein juristisches Problem**, a legal problem

Justiz *nf*, judiciary; **Justizministerium** *nn*, Ministry of Justice

K

Kabel *nn*, cable; **Kabelfernsehen** *nn*, cable television, cable TV

Kabine *nf*, **1** (for changing, shower etc), cubicle. **2** (naut), cabin. **3** (telec), booth. **4** (film), projection-room

Kaffeepause *nf*, coffee break

Kai *nm*, quay; **ab Kai** (imp/exp), ex quay, ExQ, Exq

Kalender *nm*, **1** (on wall, desk), calendar. **2** (in pocket), diary; **Kalenderjahr** *nn*, calendar year; **Kalendermonat** *nm*, calendar month

Kalkulation *nf*, calculation, computation

kalkulieren *vb*, **1** (work out figures), calculate, compute. **2** (assume), reckon

kalt *adj*, cold

Kaltlagerung *nf*, cold storage

Kamera *nf*, camera

Kampagne *nf*, campaign; **überregionale Kampagne**, national campaign

Kampf *nm*, struggle; **der Kampf um die Macht**, the struggle for power; **Kampfgeist** *nm*, fighting spirit

Kanal *nm* (waterway, TV), canal

Kandidat(in) *nm/f*, candidate

Kapazität *nf*, **1** (strength), capacity; **ungenutzte Kapazität**, spare capacity. **2** (person), expert; **er ist eine Kapazität in seinem Fach**, he is a leading expert in his field

Kapital *nn*, capital; **arbeitendes Kapital**, productive capital; **totes Kapital**, dead capital; **verfügbares Kapital**, available capital; **Kapital schlagen aus** (+ dat), capitalise on; **Kapitalanlage** *nf*, investment; **Kapitalanleger** *nm*, investor; **Kapitalaufwand** *nm*, capital spending; **Kapitaldecke** *nf*, capital resources; **Kapitaleinkommen** *nn*, unearned income; **Kapitalgesellschaft** *nf*, corporation

kapitalintensiv *adj*, capital intensive

Kapital-; **Kapitalmarkt** *nm*, money market; **Kapitalversicherung** *nf*, capital insurance; **Kapitalzuwachssteuer** *nf*, capital gains tax

kaputt *adj*, broken

kaputt|gehen *vb*, break

Karriere *nf*, career

Karte *nf*, **1** (post)card. **2** (offce), (file) card. **3** (on bus, train etc), ticket. **4** (in restaurant), menu. **5** (introducing oneself), (business) card. **6** (geog), map

Kasse *nf* (in store), cash-desk; **Kasse machen**, cash up

Kassen-; **Kassenabschluß** *nm*, cashing-up; **Kassenarzt** *nm*, National Health general practitioner, GP; **Kassenbeleg** *nm*, sales receipt; **Kassenbon** *nm*, sales slip, receipt; **Kassenschlager** *nm* (comm) (informal), sales hit; **Kassenstand** *nm*, cash in till; **Kassenwart** *nm*, treasurer; **Kassenzettel** *nm*, sales slip

kassieren *vb* (money), collect/take (the) money

Kassierer(in) *nm/f*, cashier

Kasten *nm*, (wooden) box

Katalog *nm*, catalogue; **Katalogpreis** *nm*, list price

Katasteramt *nn*, land registry

Kauf *nm*, purchase; **ein guter/schlechter Kauf**, a

good/bad purchase; **Kauf mit Rückgaberecht**, sale or return; **Kaufanreiz** *nm*, sales appeal

kaufen *vb*, buy, purchase

Käufer(in) *nm/f*, purchaser; **ein ernsthafter Käufer**, a genuine purchaser; **Käufermarkt** *nm*, buyer's market

Kauf-; **Kauffrau** *nf*, business woman; **Kaufhaus** *nn*, department store; **Kaufkraft** *nf*, purchasing power; **Kaufmann** *nm*, businessman; **Kaufpreis** *nm*, purchase/purchasing price; **Kaufvertrag** *nm*, bill of sale

Kaution *nf*, bail; **gegen Kaution freilassen**, release on bail

Kenntnis *nf*, knowledge; **meine Deutschkenntnisse sind noch nicht gut**, my knowledge of German isn't very sound yet; **ohne Kenntnis der Umstände**, without knowing the circumstances; **in Kenntnis setzen**, inform; **zur Kenntnis nehmen**, note

Kenntnisnahme *nf*, **zur Kenntnisnahme an** (+ acc) (offce), for the attention of; **nach Kenntnisnahme bitte an mich zurück**, please return to me after perusal

Kennwort *nn*, **1** (gen), codename. **2** (comm), reference

Kennzeichen *nn*, **1** (gen), particular characteristic, distinguishing feature. **2** (on car), registration number. **3** (sticker), label

kennzeichnen *vb*, **1** (gen), be characteristic of, characterise; **das kennzeichnet dieses Unternehmen**, that is characteristic of this company. **2** (imp/exp), label; **die Kisten müssen noch gekennzeichnet werden**, the crates still need to be labelled

Kernkraft *nf*, nuclear power

Kette *nf* (techn), chain

Kettenantrieb *nm*, chain drive

Kettenladen *nm*, chain store

kg, **Kilogramm** *nn*, kilogramme

KHz, **kHz**, **Kilohertz** *nn*, kilohertz

Kilometer *nm*, **km**, kilometre; **gefahrene Kilometer**, mileage; **Kilometerpauschale** *nf*, mileage allowance (against tax); **Kilometerzähler** *nm*, mileage counter

Kinder *nnpl* (CV), children; **Kinderzulage** *nf*, child benefit

kippen *vb* (e.g. load), tip

Kiste *nf*, crate; **eine Kiste Äpfel**, a crate of apples; **in Kisten verpacken**, pack into crates

Klage *nf*, **1** (gen), complaint; **Grund zur Klage**, reason for complaint. **2** (law), action, legal proceedings; **eine Klage erheben gegen** (+ acc), take legal action against, sue; **zivilrechtliche Klage**, civil action

klagen *vb*, **1** (gen), complain. **2** (law), sue

Klang *nm* (gen), reputation; **der Name hat einen guten Klang**, the name has a good reputation

klar *adj*, *adv*, clear; clearly

Kläranlage *nf*, **1** (gen), sewage plant. **2** (in factory), purification plant

klären *vb*, **1** (air), purify. **2** (sewage), treat. **3** (situation), clarify, clear up. **4** (issue), settle

klar|machen *vb*, make clear

Klarsichtfolie *nf*, clear film

Klarsichtpackung *nf*, see-through pack

Klausel *nf*, clause

kleben *vb*, stick

Klebstoff *nm* (offce), glue

Klebstreifen *nm* (offce), adhesive tape

klein *adj*, small

Klein-; Kleinaktionär *nm*, small shareholder; **Kleinanzeige** *nf*, small ad; **Kleinarbeit** *nf*, detailed work; **Kleinbetrieb** *nm*, small business; **Kleingedrucktes** *nn*, small print

Kleinigkeit *nf*, detail

Klima *nn*, climate; **Klimaanlage** *nf*, air-conditioning system; **mit Klimaanlage**, air-conditioned

klingeln *vb*, ring; **das Telefon klingelt**, the telephone is ringing; **es klingelt**, there is a ring at the door

Klon *nm*, clone

knapp *adj*, *adv*, scarce; scarcely; **meine Zeit ist knapp**, my time is scarce; **das Problem zeigte sich vor knapp 3 Monaten**, the problem emerged scarcely 3 months ago

Knappheit *nf*, scarcity

Kohle *nf*, coal

Kohlenbergbau *nm*, coal-mining

Kohlenbergwerk *nn*, coal-mine, pit

Kohlensäure *nf*, carbonic acid

kohlensäurehaltig *adj* (drink), carbonated

Kohlepapier *nn* (offce), carbon paper

Kollege *nm*, **Kollegin** *nf*, colleague; **„Kollege kommt gleich"** (in restaurant), "somebody will be with you right away"

Kollektion *nf*, **1** (of goods), range. **2** fashion collection

kollidieren *vb*, collide

Kollision *nf*, collision

Kombination *nf*, combination

kombinieren *vb*, combine

Kombiwagen *nm*, estate car

Komitee *nn*, committee

Kommanditgesellschaft *nf*, **KG** *nf*, limited partnership

kommend *adj*, **in der kommenden Woche**, in the coming week

kommissarisch *adj*, *adv*, temporary; temporarily

Kommission *nf*, commission

kommunal *adj*, *adv*, municipal, local; locally

Kommunalabgaben *nfpl*, local rates

Kommunikation *nf*, communication

Kompetenz *nf*, competence

Kompromiß *nm*, compromise; **einen Kompromiß schließen**, reach a compromise

Konferenz *nf*, conference; **Konferenz zur Absatzförderung** sales conference; **Konferenzleitung** *nf*, conference organiser(s); **Konferenzprogramm** *nn*, conference programme; **Konferenzprotokoll** *nn*, conference proceedings; **Konferenzraum** *nm*, conference room; **Konferenzteilnehmer(in)** *nm/f*, conference delegate

konfiszieren *vb*, confiscate

Konflikt *nm*, conflict

Kongreß *nm*, congress; **Kongreßteilnehmer(in)** *nm/f*, congress/conference delegate; **Kongreßzentrum** *nn*, congress/conference centre

Konjunktur *nf*, economic situation, economic trend; **steigende/rückläufige Konjunktur**, upward/downward economic trend; **Konjunkturaufschwung** *nm*, economic upturn; **Konjunktureinbruch** *nm*, slump; **Konjunkturindustrie** *nf*, boom industry; **Konjunkturprognose** *nf*, economic forecast; **Konjunkturrückgang** *nm*, slowdown in the economy; **Konjunkturtief** *nn*, trough

Konkurrent(in) *nm/f*, competitor

Konkurrenz *nf*, competition; **die Konkurrenz verdrängen**, freeze out the competition; **Konkurrenzdruck** *nm*, pressure of competition

konkurrenzfähig *adj*, competitive

Konkurrenzkampf *nm*, **1** (comm), competition. **2** (between people), rivalry

konkurrieren *vb*, compete

Konkurs *nm*, bankruptcy, insolvency; **in Konkurs gehen/Konkurs machen**, go bankrupt, go into receivership; **Konkursmasse** *nf*, bankrupt's estate; **Konkursverwalter** *nm*, receiver

können *vb*, can, be able to; **ich kann kein Englisch**, I can't speak English; **werden sie pünktlich liefern können?**, are they going to be able to deliver on time?

Konnossement *nn* (imp/exp), bill of lading, B/L

Konsens *nm*, consensus

konsequent *adj*, *adv*, consistent; consistently

konsolidierte Bilanz *nf* (fin), consolidated accounts

Konsul(in) *nm/f*, consul

konsularisch *adj*, consular

Konsulat *nn*, consulate

Konsum *nm*, consumption

Konsument *nm*, consumer

Konsumergesellschaft *nf*, consumer society

Konsumgüter *nnpl*, consumer goods

konsumieren *vb*, consume

Kontakt *nm*, contact

kontaktieren *vb*, contact

Konto *nn* (fin), account; **Geld auf ein Konto einzahlen**, pay money into an account; **ein Konto eröffnen**, open an account; **ein Konto schließen**, close an account; **laufendes Konto**, current account; **überzogenes Konto**, overdrawn account; **Kontoauszug** *nm*, statement of account; **Kontoführung** *nf*, handling of account; **Kontokorrent** *nn*, current account; **Kontoüberziehung** *nf*, overdraft

Kontrolle *nf*, **1** (of goods), check. **2** (of passport), control

kontrollieren *vb* (examine), check; **die Warenqualität kontrollieren**, check the quality of the goods

konvertierbare Währung *nf* (fin), convertible currency

Konzentration *nf*, concentration

sich konzentrieren auf (+ acc) *vb*, concentrate on

Konzept *nn*, **1** (document), (rough) draft, rough copy. **2** plan, programme

Konzernbilanz *nf*, consolidated accounts

Konzession *nf* (comm), concession, licence, franchise

Konzessionär *nm* (comm), concessionaire, licensee, franchisee

koordinieren *vb*, coordinate

Kopf *nm*, head; **pro Kopf**, per capita/head; **Kopfjäger** *nm*, head-hunter

Kopie *nf*, copy; **unterschriebene Kopie**, signed copy

kopieren *vb*, copy

Kopiergerät *nn*, copier

körperlich *adj*, **1** (gen), physical. **2** (work), manual; **körperliche Arbeit**, manual work

Körperschaft *nf*, corporation

Körperschaftssteuer *nf*, corporation tax

korrekt *adj*, *adv*, correct; correctly

Korrektur *nf*, correction

Korrespondenz *nf*, correspondence; **in Korrespondenz stehen**, be in correspondence

korrespondieren *vb*, correspond

korrigieren *vb*, correct

korrupt *adj*, corrupt

Korruption *nf*, corruption

Kosten *npl*, costs; **die Kosten decken**, break even; **die Kosten tragen**, bear the costs; **auf Kosten des Steuerzahlers**, at the expense of the tax-payer; **auf seine Kosten kommen**, cover one's expenses; **Kosten spielen keine Rolle**, money is no object; **Kosten und Fracht** (imp/exp), C&F, cost and freight

kosten *vb*, **1** cost; **was kostet das?**, how much does it cost? **2** (food, drink), taste, sample; **wollen Sie mal kosten?**, would you like to taste this?

Kosten-; **Kostenanalyse** *nf*, cost analysis; **Kostenaufwand** *nm*, expenses; **Kostenberechnung** *nf*, costing

kostendeckend *adj*, *adv*, **kostendeckend arbeiten**, break even

Kostendeckungspunkt *nm*, break-even point

Kostenersparnis *nf*, cost savings

kostenlos *adj*, *adv*, free, free of charge; **kostenlos zur Probe**, free trial

Kostenminderung *nf* **durch große Serien**, economy of scale

Kosten-Nutzen-Analyse *nf*, cost-benefit analysis

Kostensenkung *nf*, cost-cutting

kostensparend *adj*, *adv*, economical; economically

Kosten(vor)anschlag *nm*, estimate; **einen Kosten(vor)anschlag machen**, put in an estimate

kostenwirksam *adj*, *adv*, cost-effective; cost effectively

kostspielig *adj*, costly

Kraftfahrzeug *nn*, **Kfz** *nn*, motor vehicle; **Kraftfahrzeugkennzeichen** *nn*, (vehicle) registration; **Kraftfahrzeugsteuer** *nf*, motor vehicle tax, road tax; **Kraftfahrzeugversicherung** *nf*, motor/car insurance

Kran *nm*, crane

krank *adj*, sick; **krank geschrieben sein**, be on sick leave

Kranken-; **Krankenakte** *nf*, medical file; **Krankengeld** *nn*, sick pay, sickness benefit; **Krankenhaus** *nn*, hospital; **Krankenkasse** *nf*, medical insurance scheme; **Krankenschein** *nm*, certificate of illness; **Krankenversicherung** *nf*, health/medical insurance

krank|feiern *vb*, be off sick

Krankfeiern *nn*, absenteeism

Krankheit *nf*, illness, sickness

Krankmeldung *nf*, notification of illness

Kredit *nm*, credit, loan; **auf Kredit**, on credit; **kurzfristiger Kredit**, short-term credit/loan; **langfristiger Kredit** extended credit/loan; **offener Kredit**, open credit; **prolongierter Kredit**, extended credit; **revolvierender Kredit**, revolving credit; **auf Kredit kaufen**, buy on credit; **Kredit gewähren**, give credit; **einen Kredit kündigen**, withdraw a credit/credit facilities; **seinen Kredit überziehen**, exceed one's credit limit; **Kreditaufnahme** *nf*, credit borrowing; **Kreditbank** *nf*, credit bank; **Kreditbedingungen** *nfpl*, credit terms; **Kreditbrief** *nm*, letter of credit

Kredite *nmpl*, **eingefrorene Kredite**, frozen credits

Kredit-; **Kreditfähigkeit** *nf*, borrowing power; **Kredithai** *nm*, loan shark; **Kreditinstitut** *nn*, financial institution; **Kreditkarte** *nf*, credit card; **Kreditkontrolle** *nf*, credit control; **Kreditlimit** *nn*, credit limit; **Kreditmodalitäten** *nfpl*, credit facilities; **Kreditnehmer** *nm*, borrower, debtor; **Kreditrestriktionen** *nfpl*, credit squeeze; **Kreditsaldo** *nm*, credit balance; **Kredittransfer** *nm*, credit transfer

kreditwürdig *adj*, creditworthy

Kreditwürdigkeit *nf*, creditworthiness

Kreis *nm*, circle; **Kreisdiagramm** *nn*, pie chart; **Kreisstadt** *nf*, ~ county town; **Kreisverkehr** *nm* (transp), roundabout

Kreuzung *nf* (transp), crossroads

Krise *nf*, crisis; **eine Krise durchmachen**, go through a crisis

Krisenmanager *nm*, crisis manager

Krisenmaßnahme *nf*, emergency measure

Kritik *nf*, criticism

Kritiker *nm*, critic

kritisieren *vb*, criticise

Kto, **Konto** *nn*, a/c, account

kühl *adj*, *adv*, cool; coolly; **kühl lagern**, store in a cool place

kühlen *vb*, refrigerate

Kühl-; **Kühlhauslagerung** *nf*, cold storage; **Kühlschrank** *nm*, refrigerator, fridge; **Kühltruhe** *nf*, deep freeze

kündbar *adj*, **1** (contract), terminable. **2** (loan), redeemable

Kunde *nm*, customer, client

Kunden-; **Kundenbetreuer** *nm*, account executive; **Kundendaten** *npl*, customer details; **Kundendatenbank** *nf*, client data base; **Kundendienst** *nm*, after-sales service; **Kundenfang** *nm*, **auf Kundenfang sein**, tout for customers; **Kundenkreditkarte** *nf*, charge card; **Kundenkreis** *nm*, clientele; **Kundentreue** *nf*, customer loyalty

kündigen *vb*, **1** (employee), give in one's notice. **2** (employer), dismiss, give notice. **3** (contract, credit), terminate

Kündigung *nf*, **1** (by employee), handing in one's notice. **2** (by employer), dismissal. **3** (of contract, credit), termination

Kündigungs-; **Kündigungsfrist** *nf*, period of notice; **Kündigungsgrund** *nm*, reason for giving notice; **Kündigungsschutz** *nm* (in job), protection against wrongful dismissal

Kundin *nf*, (female) customer or client

Kundschaft *nf*, clientele, customers

künftig *adj*, *adv*, future, in future

Kunst *nf*, art; **Kunstfaser** *nf*, man-made fibre; **Kunstgewerbe** *nn*, arts and crafts; **Kunsthandwerk** *nn*, craft industry

Kupfer *nn*, copper; **Kupferblech** *nn*, sheet copper

Kurve *nf*, **1** (in road), bend. **2** (diagram), curve

Kurs *nm*, **1** (lessons), course; **einen Kurs mitmachen**, do a course. **2** (fin), rate (of exchange); **Kurs-Gewinn-Verhältnis** *nn*, price/earnings ratio, P/E ratio; **Kursmanipulation** *nf*, stock market manipulation; **Kursnotierung** *nf*, **Kursquotierung** *nf* (fin), rate of exchange; **Kurstreiberei** *nf* (fin), rigging the market

kurz *adj*, *adv*, short, brief; briefly; **vor kurzem**, a little while ago

Kurzarbeit *nf*, short time (work)

kurz|arbeiten *vb*, be on short time

Kurzausbildung *nf*, short training course

Kürze *nf*, **in Kürze**, soon

kürzen *vb*, cut (down), reduce

Kurzfassung *nf*, abridged version

kurzfristig *adj*, *adv*, short-term

kürzlich *adj*, *adv*, recent; recently

Kurz-; **Kurzschrift** *nf*, shorthand; **Kurzstreckenflug** *nm*, short-haul flight; **Kurzübersicht** *nf*, profile

Kürzung *nf*, cut(back), reduction

Kurzurlaub *nm*, short holiday

L

Labor *nn*, lab(oratory)

Laborant(in) *nm/f*, lab(oratory) assistant

Ladefaktor *nm* (imp/exp), load factor

Ladeliste *nf* (imp/exp), manifest

Laden *nm* (comm), shop

laden *vb*, **1** (freight), load. **2** (comp), (down)load

Laden-; **Ladenbesitzer(in)** *nm/f*, shopkeeper; **Ladendieb(in)** *nm/f*, shop-lifter; **Ladenhüter** *nm*, non-seller; **Ladenkette** *nf*, chain of shops; **Ladenpreis** *nm*, retail price; **Ladenräume** *nmpl*, shop premises; **Ladenschluß** *nm*, closing time; **Ladenstraße** *nf*, shopping street; **Ladentisch** *nm*, counter

Lade- (imp/exp); **Ladeplatz** *nm*, loading bay; **Laderampe** *nf*, loading ramp; **Laderaum** *nm* (of ship), hold; **Ladeschein** *nm*, bill of lading

Ladung *nf* (imp/exp), **1** (gen), load, shipment; **zwei Lkw-Ladungen Zement**, two lorry-loads of cement. **2** (of ship, aircraft), cargo

Lage *nf*, situation; **die wirtschaftliche Lage**, the economic situation

Lager *nn*, **1** (of shop), stockroom. **2** (for storage only), warehouse; **auf Lager haben**, have in stock; **das Lager auffüllen**, restock, stock up; **frei Lkw ab Lager**, free on truck, FOT; **ab Lager(haus)** (imp/exp), ex warehouse; **Lagerarbeiter** *nm*, warehouseman; **Lagerbestand** *nm*, stock; **Lagerbestandsaufnahme**

nf, inventory; **Lagerfähigkeit** *nf* (of product), shelf-life; **Lagergeld** *nn*, storage; **Lagerhausgarantie** *nf*, warehouse warrant, W/W

Lagerist(in) *nm/f*, storeman, storewoman

Lagerkontrolle *nf*, stock control

Lagerumschlag *nm*, stock turnover

Lagerung *nf*, storage, warehousing

Lagerverwalter(in) *nm/f*, stores supervisor

laminieren *vb*, laminate

Land *nn*, country; **auf dem Land**, in the country

Landehafen *nm*, port of entry, POE

landesweit *adj*, *adv*, nationwide

Landwirt(in) *nm/f*, farmer

Landwirtschaft *nf*, farming; **gemischte Landwirtschaft**, mixed farming

landwirtschaftlich *adj*, *adv*, agricultural; agriculturally

Länge *nf*, length; **sich in die Länge ziehen**, go on and on

langfristig *adj*, *adv*, long-term; **ein langfristiger Vertrag**, a long-term contract; **langfristig betrachten**, take the long-term view

langlebig *adj* (goods), durable; **langlebige Verbrauchsgüter**, durables

langsam *adj*, *adv*, slow; slowly; **langsam fahren!**, slow!

Laptop-Computer *nm*, laptop (computer)

Lasten *nfpl*, **zu Ihren Lasten** (fin), payable by you

Last(kraft)wagen *nm*, **Lkw**, lorry

Lastschrift *nf*, debit

Lastwagenfahrer *nm*, lorry-driver

Lastwagenladung *nf*, lorry-load

Laufbahn *nf*, career

laufend *adj*, current; **laufendes Konto**, current account; **laufende Nummer**, serial number

laufenden, sich auf dem laufenden halten *vb*, keep up-to-date

Laufzeit *nf* (of contract, credit), term, period of validity

Laufzettel *nm* (for files, machines), docket

laut (+ genitive) *prep*, according to; **laut Ihrem Brief vom 6. Juni**, according to your letter of 6 June

lauten *vb*, say, read; **der Text lautet**, the text reads

lebend *adj*, **Transport lebender Tiere**, shipment of live animals

Lebenshaltungskosten *npl*, cost of living; **Lebenshaltungskostenindex** *nm*, cost of living index

Lebenslauf *nm*, curriculum vitae, CV

Lebensmittel *npl*, foodstuffs, groceries; **Lebensmittelchemiker(in)** *nm/f*, food analyst; **Lebensmittellieferant** *nm*, caterer

Lebensstandard *nm*, standard of living

lebhaft *adj*, *adv*, (comm), brisk; briskly

Leder *nn*, leather; **aus Leder**, (made of) leather; **Lederwaren** *nfpl*, leather goods

ledig *adj* (CV), single

leer *adj*, empty

leeren *vb*, empty

Leergut *nn*, empties

leer|stehen *vb*, be vacant

Leertaste *nf* (comp), space-bar

Lehrgang *nm*, course; **einen Lehrgang besuchen**, attend a course

Leibrente *nf*, life annuity

leicht *adj*, **1** (not difficult), easy; **leicht verderblich**, perishable. **2** (not heavy), light

leicht *adv*, easily

Leichtindustrie *nf*, light industry

leiden *vb*, suffer; **leiden an/unter** (+ dat), suffer from

leihen *vb*, **1** (from someone), borrow; **dürfte ich eben Ihren Stift leihen?**, could I just borrow your pen? **2** (to someone), lend. **3** (car), hire

Leihgebühr *nf*, rental charge

Leihwagen *nm*, hire(d) car

leisten *vb*, **1** achieve. **2 wir können uns keine Verluste leisten**, we cannot afford any losses

Leistung *nf*, achievement

Leistungs-; **Leistungsbeurteilung** *nf*, performance assessment; **Leistungsbilanz** *nf*, trade balance

leistungsfähig *adj*, efficient

leiten *vb*, **1** (organisation), manage, be in charge of. **2** (meeting), chair

leitend *adj* (pers), managerial, senior; **eine leitende Stellung**, a senior post; **ein leitender Angestellter**, an executive

Leiter(in) *nm/f* (pers), manager(ess), director; **Leiter der EDV-Abteilung**, computer manager; **Leiter der Verkaufsabteilung**, sales manager

Leiterplatte *nf* (comp), circuit board

Leitung *nf* (pers), **1** (gen), management. **2** (of meeting), chairmanship. **3** (electr), cable, wire

Leitzins *nm* (fin), base rate

lesbar *adj*, **1** (handwriting), legible. **2** (text), readable

Leserschaft *nf*, readership

letzt *adj*, final; **letzter Versuch**, final attempt

Leuchtschrift *nf*, neon writing

Leuchtstift *nm* (offce), marker

leugnen *vb*, deny

Leverage *nn*, leverage

Lieferant *nm*, **1** (provider of goods), supplier. **2** (transporter of goods), deliveryman

Liefer-; **Lieferauftrag** *nm*, delivery order; **Lieferbedingungen** *nfpl*, **1** (provision), terms of supply. **2** (delivery), terms of delivery; **Lieferdatum** *nn*, delivery date; **Lieferfrist** *nf*, delivery period

liefern *vb*, **1** (provide with goods), supply. **2** (transport goods), deliver

Lieferschein *nm*, delivery note

Liefertermin *nm*, delivery date

Lieferung *nf*, delivery; **Lieferung gegen Nachnahme**, cash on delivery, C.O.D.

Liefer-; **Liefervertrag** *nm*, contract of delivery; **Lieferwagen** *nm*, delivery van; **Lieferzeit** *nf*, delivery time, lead time

Liegegeld *nn* (imp/exp), demurrage

liegen *vb* (place), be located/situated; **die Fabrik liegt im Nordwesten der Stadt**, the factory is situated in the northwest of the city

liegen|lassen *vb* (fail to do), leave; **ich lasse dies bis zu meiner Rückkehr liegen**, I shall leave this until my return

Liegeplatz *nm*, **1** (of ship), mooring. **2** (on train, ship), berth

Linie *nf*, **in erster Linie**, above all, mainly

Linien-; **Linienflug** *nm*, scheduled flight; **Linienmanagement** *nn*, line management; **Linienschiff** *nn*, liner; **Linienverkehr** *nm*, regular traffic

linke(r,s) *adj*, left, left-hand; **die linke Seite**, the left(-hand) side; **auf der linken Seite**, on the left(-hand) side

links *adv*, (on the/to the) left; **fahren**

Sie an der Ampel (nach) links, turn left at the traffic lights

Linkssteuerung *nf* (in car), left-hand drive

Liquidation *nf* (fin), liquidation; **freiwillige Liquidation**, voluntary liquidation; **in Liquidation gehen**, go into liquidation

liquidieren *vb* (fin), liquidate

Liquidität *nf* (fin), liquidity

Lizenz *nf*, licence, franchise; **Lizenznehmer** *nm*, licensee, franchisee

Lkw, **Lastkraftwagen** *nm*, lorry

loben *vb* (pers), commend

Loch *nn*, hole

Lockartikel *nm* (mktg, sales), loss leader

lockern *vb*, ease, loosen, relax

Lohn *nm*, **1** (regular pay), wage, pay. **2** (one-off bonus), reward; **zum Lohn**, as a reward; **Lohnabbau** *nm*, reduction of earnings; **Lohnabkommen** *nn*, pay agreement; **Lohnausfall** *nm*, loss of earnings; **Lohnbuchhalter(in)** *nm/f*, wages clerk

sich lohnen *vb*, be worth it; be worthwhile; **es lohnt sich nicht**, it isn't worth it

Lohn-; **Lohnerhöhung** *nf*, wage increase, wage rise; **Lohnfortzahlung** *nf*, continued payment of wages; **Lohngefälle** *nn*, pay differential; **Lohngruppe** *nf*, wage group; **Lohnkosten** *npl*, wage costs; **Lohnkürzung** *nf*, wage cut; **Lohnliste** *nf*, payroll; **Lohnrunde** *nf*, pay round; **Lohnsenkung** *nf*, pay cut; **Lohnsteuer** *nf*, income tax; **Lohnsteuerjahresausgleich** *nm*, annual adjustment of income tax; **Lohnstückkosten** *npl*, unit wage costs; **Lohnsummensteuer** *nf*, payroll tax; **Lohntüte** *nf*, wage packet; **Lohnverhandlungen** *nfpl*, pay talks; **Lohnzettel** *nf*, pay slip

Lokalblatt *nn*, local (news)paper

lösbar *adj* (problem), soluble

löschen *vb*, **1** (ship's load), unload. **2** (comp), delete

Löschung *nf* (of ship's load), unloading

lösen *vb*, **1** (problem), solve. **2** (conflict), resolve. **3** (contract), cancel. **4** (ticket), buy

Lösung *nf*, **1** (of problem), solution. **2** (of conflict), resolution. **3** (of contract), cancellation

los|werden *vb*, get rid of

löten *vb*, solder

Lotse *nm* (naut), pilot

Luft *nf*, air

luftdicht *adj*, *adv*, airtight

lüften *vb*, ventilate

Luftfahrt *nf*, aviation

Luftfracht *nf* (imp/exp), aircargo, airfreight; **per Luftfracht senden**, airfreight; **Luftfrachtbrief** *nm*, consignment note, air waybill; **Luftfrachtnachnahme** *nf*, airfreight collection; **Luftfrachtversandanzeige** *nf*, consignment note

Luftkissenfahrzeug *nn*, hovercraft

Luftpost *nf*, airmail; **per Luftpost**, by air(mail); **Luftpostaufkleber** *nm*, airmail sticker; **Luftpostbrief** *nm*, airmail letter; **Luftpostumschlag** *nm*, airmail envelope

Lüftung *nf*, ventilation

Luftverkehr *nm*, air traffic

Luftverschmutzung *nf*, air pollution

Luftweg *nm*, **auf dem Luftwege**, by air

lügen *vb*, (tell a) lie

Luxus *nm*, luxury; **Luxussteuer** *nf*, levy on luxury items; **Luxuswaren** *nfpl*, luxury goods

Machart *nf*, design, style

Macht *nf*, control, power; **wir werden alles tun, was in unserer Macht steht**, we shall do everything in our power

Machtbefugnis *nf*, authority

Magazin *nn*, **1** (media), magazine. **2** (room), storeroom

mahnen *vb* (debts), send a reminder

Mahnung *nf*, reminder (letter)

Makler *nm*, broker; **Maklergebühr** *nf*, brokerage

Mal *nn*, time; **das erste Mal**, the first time; **dieses Mal**, this time; **ein ums andere Mal**, time after time; **kein einziges Mal**, not once; **mit einem Mal**, all at once; **zu wiederholten Malen**, repeatedly

Management *nn*, management; **mittleres Management**, middle management

managen *vb*, (informal), manage

Manager(in) *nm/f*, manager, manageress; **stellvertretender Manager**, assistant manager; **Managerkurs** *nm*, management course

manchmal *adv*, sometimes

Mangel *nm*, **1** lack, shortage. **2** (in goods), defect, fault

Mängelbericht *nm*, list of faults

mangelfrei/mängelfrei *adj*, free of defects/faults

mangeln *vb*, **es mangelt uns an qualifiziertem Personal**, we lack qualified staff

mangels (+ genitive) *prep*, for lack of

Mangelware *nf*, scarce commodity

Männerberuf *nm*, male occupation/profession

Manteltarifvertrag *nm* (pers), general agreement on conditions of employment

Mappe *nf*, **1** (offce), file. **2** briefcase

Marge *nf* (fin), margin

Marke *nf*, **1** (comm), (of food), brand. **2** (of industrial goods), make

Marken-; **Markenartikel** *nmpl*, **Markenerzeugnisse** *nnpl*, branded goods; **Markenhersteller** *nm*, manufacturer of proprietary goods; **Markenname** *nm*, brand (name); **Markenprofil** *nn*, brand profile; **Markenschutz** *nm*, protection of trademarks; **Markentreue** *nf*, brand loyalty

Marketing-; **Marketing-Abteilung** *nf*, marketing department; **Marketing-Manager** *nm*, marketing manager; **Marketing-Mix** *nm*, marketing mix

markieren *vb*, mark

Markierstift *nm* (offce), highlighter

Markierungszeichen *nn* (comp), marker

Markt *nm*, market; **den Markt beherrschen**, corner/dominate the market; **auf den Markt bringen**, put on the market; **einen Markt erschließen**, open up a market; **auf den Markt werfen**, flood the market; **flauer Markt**, depressed market; **offener Markt**, open market; **potentieller Markt**, potential market; **Marktabsprache** *nf*, marketing agreement; **Marktanalyse** *nf*, market analysis; **Marktanteil** *nm*, market share; **Marktbeherrschung** *nf*, market domination; **Marktbewertung** *nf*, market valuation; **Marktdurchdringung** *nf*, market penetration; **Marktentwicklung**

nf, market trend; **Marktforschung** *nf*, market research; **Marktführer** *nm*, market leader; **Marktkräfte** *nfpl*, market forces; **Marktlücke** *nf*, gap in the market; **Marktnische** *nf*, market niche; **Marktsättigung** *nf*, market saturation; **Marktstudie** *nf*, market survey; **Marktwert** *nm*, market value; **Marktwirtschaft** *nf*, market economy; **freie Marktwirtschaft**, free market economy

Maschine *nf*, **1** (gen), machine. **2** (short for 'Schreibmaschine'), typewriter; **mit der Maschine schreiben**, type

maschinell *adj*, *adv*, mechanical; mechanically, machine; by machine

Maschinen-; **Maschinenantrieb** *nm*, machine drive; **Maschinenbau** *nm*, mechanical engineering; **Maschinenbauer** *nm*, mechanical engineer; **Maschinenindustrie** *nf*, engineering industry; **Maschinenlesbarkeit** *nf*, machine readability; **Maschinenöl** *nn*, lubricating oil; **Maschinenschaden** *nm*, mechanical fault; **Maschinenschlosser** *nm*, machine fitter; **Maschinenschrift** *nf*, **1** (process), typing. **2** (outcome), typescript; **Maschinenwärter** *nm*, machine minder

Maschinist(in) *nm/f*, (machine) operator

Maß *nn*, **1** (unit), measure; **Maße und Gewichte**, weights and measures. **2** extent, degree; **in hohem Maße**, to a great extent/to a high degree

Masse *nf*, bulk, mass

Maßeinheit *nf*, unit of measurement

Massen-; **Massenarbeitslosigkeit** *nf*, mass unemployment; **Massenartikel** *nm*, mass-produced article; **Massenbedarfsgüter** *nnpl*, basic consumer goods; **Massenfertigung** *nf*, mass production; **Massengüter** *nnpl*, bulk goods; **Massengutfrachter** *nm* (transp) bulk carrier; **Massenproduktion** *nf*, mass production; **Massenspeicher** *nm* (comp), bulk storage, mass memory

maßgeblich *adj*, **1** (influence), decisive. **2** (opinion), definitive. **3** (text, expert), authoritative. **4** (personality), leading. **5** (contribution), substantial

mäßig *adj*, *adv*, moderate; moderately

Maßnahme *nf*, measure

Maßstab *nm* (criterion), standard

Material *nn*, material; **Materialförderung** *nf*, materials handling

Maus *nf* (comp), mouse

maximal *adj*, *adv*, maximum, at the most

maximieren *vb*, maximise

Maximum *nn*, maximum

mechanisieren *vb*, mechanise

Mechanismus *nm*, mechanism

Medien, **die Medien** *npl*, the media

Medizin *nf*, medicine

mehr *adv*, more; **mit mehr oder weniger Erfolg**, with more or less success; **wir haben uns lange nicht mehr gesehen**, we haven't seen each other for a long time

Mehr-; **Mehrarbeit** *nf*, overtime; **Mehraufwand** *nm*, additional expenditure; **Mehrbedarf** *nm*, increased demand; **Mehrbetrag** *nm*, additional amount; **Mehreinname** *nf*, additional revenue

mehrfach *adj*, multiple; **bitte senden Sie die Unterlagen in mehrfacher Ausfertigung ein**, please submit the documents in multiple copies

mehrfach *adv*, many times, repeatedly

Mehrheit *nf*, majority; **die Mehrheit (der Stimmen) gewinnen**, gain a majority (of votes cast)

Mehrheitsbeschluß *nm*, majority decision

Mehrheitsbeteiligung *nf*, majority interest

Mehrkosten *npl*, additional costs

Mehrverbrauch *nm*, additional consumption

Mehrweg- *adj*, returnable reusable; **Mehrwegflasche** *nf*, returnable bottle; **Mehrwegverpackung** *nf*, reusable packaging

Mehrwert *nm*, added value; **Mehrwertsteuer** *nf*, value-added tax, VAT

meinetwegen *adv*, as far as I am concerned

Meinung *nf*, opinion, view; **meiner Meinung nach**, in my opinion/view

Meinungs-; **Meinungsaustausch** *nm*, exchange of views; **Meinungsumfrage** *nf*, **1** (gen), opinion poll. **2** (of market), survey; **Meinungsverschiedenheit** *nf*, disagreement

meist *adv*, mostly

Meister *nm*, **1** master craftsman. **2** (in industry), foreman

Meisterwerk *nn*, masterpiece

Meistgebot *nn*, highest bid

meistgefragt *adj*, most popular

meistgekauft *adj*, best-selling

Meldebestätigung *nf* (police), confirmation of registration

melden *vb* (inform), report; **bitte melden Sie das der Behörde**, please report this to the authorities

sich melden *vb*, **1** (telec), answer; **es meldet sich niemand**, no one is answering. **2** get in touch with. **3 sich melden bei** (+ dat), report to, register with; **sich bei der Polizei melden**, register with the police

Meldepflicht *nf* (police), compulsory registration

Meldestelle *nf*, registration office

Menge *nf*, **1** (gen), amount, quantity. **2** (people), crowd; **eine Menge Aussteller kamen zur Messe**, lots of exhibitors came to the exhibition

Mengeneinkauf *nm*, bulk buying

mengenmäßig *adv*, as far as quantity is concerned

Mengenpreis *nm*, bulk price

Mengenrabatt *nm*, bulk discount

menschenmöglich *adj*, humanly possible

Menu *nn*, **Menü** *nn*, **1** (in restaurant), set meal. **2** (comp), menu

Merchandising *nn*, merchandising

merken *vb*, notice

sich merken *vb* (not forget), remember

Merkmal *nn*, characteristic feature

Messe *nf* (comm), fair, exhibition; **Messegast** *nm*, visitor to the fair; **Messegelände** *nn*, exhibition centre; **Messehalle** *nf*, fair pavilion

messen *vb*, measure

Messe-; **Messeneuheit** *nf*, trade fair first; **Messestadt** *nf*, (city with an) exhibition centre; **Messestand** *nm*, exhibition stand

Metall *nn*, metal; **Metallarbeiter** *nm*, metalworker; **Metallermüdung** *nf*, metal fatigue; **Metallverarbeitung** *nf*, metal processing; **Metallwaren** *nfpl*, hardware

Meter *nm/nn*, metre; **in einer Entfernung von 3 Metern**, at a distance of 3 metres

meterlang *adv*, metres long

meterweise *adv*, by the metre

Methode *nf*, method

Miete *nf*, **1** (of flat), rent; **eine symbolische Miete**, a nominal rent. **2** (of objects), rental. **3** (of services), charge

mieten *vb*, hire, rent; **einen Wagen mieten**, hire/rent a car

Mieter(in) *nm/f*, **1** (gen), tenant. **2** (subletting), lodger

Mieterhöhung *nf*, rent increase

Miet-; **Mietpreis** *nm*, rent; **Mietpreisbindung** *nf*, rent control; **Mietvertrag** *nm*, lease; **Mietvorauszahlung** *nf*, key money; **Mietwagen** *nm*, hire(d) car

Mikrofon *nn*, microphone

Mikrowelle *nf*, microwave

Millionengeschäft *nn*, a business (deal) worth millions

Millionenschaden *nm*, damage amounting to millions

Minderheit *nf*, minority

Minderheitsinteresse *nn*, minority interest

minderwertig *adj* (goods), inferior, low-quality

Mindestbetrag *nm*, minimum amount

Mindesteinkommen *nn*, minimum income

mindestens *adv*, at least

Mindest-; **Mindestlohn** *nm*, minimum wage; **Mindestpreis** *nm*, reserve price; **Mindestumtausch** *nm*, minimum obligatory exchange; **Mindestzinssatz** *nm*, minimum lending rate, MLR

Mineralöl *nn*, mineral oil

minimal *adj*, minimal

Minimum *nn*, minimum

Minirechner *nm* (comp), minicomputer

Minister(in) *nm/f*, minister

Ministerium *nn*, ministry

Ministerrat *nm* (EU), Council of Ministers

Mißbrauch *nm*, **1** (of power etc), abuse. **2** (of tool), improper use

Mißerfolg *nm*, failure

mißglücken *vb*, fail

Mißtrauen *nn*, mistrust, suspicion

Mißtrauensantrag *nm*, motion of no confidence

Mitarbeit *nf*, cooperation, collaboration; **unter Mitarbeit von** (+ dat), in collaboration with

mit|arbeiten *vb*, cooperate

Mitarbeiter(in) *nm/f*, **1** (pers), employee; **wir haben hier 750 Mitarbeiter**, we have 750 employees. **2** colleague; **darf ich Ihnen meine Mitarbeiterin, Frau Schmitz, vorstellen?**, I would like you to meet my colleague, Frau Schmitz. **3 freier Mitarbeiter, freie Mitarbeiterin**, freelancer

Mitarbeiterstab *nm*, staff

Mit-; **Mitbegründer** *nm*, co-founder; **Mitbestimmung** *nf*, worker participation; **Miteigentum** *nn*, co-ownership, joint ownership

Mitglied *nn*, member

Mitgliedsausweis *nm*, membership card

Mitgliedsbeitrag *nm*, membership fee

Mitgliedschaft *nf*, membership

Mitgliedsstaat *nm*, member state

Mittagessen *nn*, lunch

mittag|essen *vb*, have lunch

mittags *adv*, at lunchtime; **treffen wir uns mittags in der Kantine!**, let's meet at lunchtime in the canteen

Mittagspause *nf*, lunch-break

mit|teilen *vb*, **1** (a person, informally), let know; **bitte teilen Sie uns mit, was Sie von diesem Plan halten**, please let us know what you think of this plan. **2** (a person, formally), inform; **er hat uns seine Lieferschwierigkeiten nie mitgeteilt**, he never informed us of his delivery problems. **3** (publicly), announce

Mittel *nn*, **1** (gen), way, method; **Mittel und Wege finden**, find ways and means. **2** (transp), means of transport. **3** medicine. **4** (fin), means, resources

mittelbar *adj*, *adv*, indirect; indirectly

mittelfristig *adj*, *adv*, medium-term

mittelgroß *adj*, medium-sized

Mittel-; **Mittelstand** *nm*, middle classes; **Mittelständler** *nm* (comm), medium-sized company; **Mittelweg** *nm*, middle course; **einen Mittelweg einschlagen**, steer a middle course

mittlere Reife *nf*, ≈ O-Levels (now: GCSE)

Mitverantwortung *nf*, share of responsibility

Mitverfasser(in) *nm/f*, co-author

Mitwirkung *nf*, collaboration, cooperation; **wir sind Ihnen für Ihre Mitwirkung sehr dankbar**, we are grateful to you for your cooperation

Möbelwagen *nm*, removal van

Mode *nf*, fashion; **in Mode/aus der Mode kommen**, come into/go out of fashion; **Modejournal** *nn*, fashion magazine

Modell *nn*, model; **das neuste Modell**, the latest model

modern *adj*, **1** (gen), modern. **2** fashionable, "in"

modernisieren *vb*, modernise

modifizieren *vb*, modify

Modul *nn*, module

modular *adj*, modular

mögen *vb*, like; **ich möchte gern . . .**, I would like to . . .; **ich möchte gern Frau Müller sprechen**, I would like to talk to Frau Müller

möglich *adj*, possible; **es ist durchaus möglich, daß . . .**, it is perfectly possible that . . .

möglicherweise *adv*, possibly

Möglichkeit *nf*, chance, possibility

Moment *nm*, moment; **einen Moment, bitte!**, one moment please!; **im letzten Moment**, at the last moment

momentan *adj*, *adv*, current; currently

Monat *nm*, month; **am 5. des laufenden Monats**, on the 5th (of this month); **vorletzten Monat**, the month before last; **was verdienen Sie im Monat?**, how much do you earn a month?

monatelang *adj*, *adv*, for months

monatlich *adj*, *adv*, monthly

Monats-; **Monatsanfang** *nm*, beginning of the month; **Monatsende** *nn*, the end of the month; **Monatsgehalt** *nn*, monthly salary; **Monatsrate** *nf*, monthly instalment

monetär *adj*, monetary

Monopol *nn*, monopoly

Montage *nf* (techn), **1** (setting up), installation. **2** (putting together), assembly; **auf Montage sein**, be away on a job

Monteur *nm*, **1** (techn), fitter. **2** car mechanic. **3** (heating, telec), engineer. **4** (electr), electrician

morgen *adv*, tomorrow

morgens *adv*, in the morning

Motor *nm*, engine

müde *adj*, tired, weary

Mühe *nf*, effort, trouble; **es lohnt die Mühe**, it's worth the effort/trouble; **sich große Mühe geben**, take great trouble; **wir haben uns die Mühe umsonst gemacht**, our efforts have been wasted; **ohne Mühe**, without any trouble;

verlorene Mühe, a waste of effort

Müll *nm*, **1** (domestic), rubbish. **2** (industry), waste; **Müllabfuhr** *nf*, refuse collection; **Müllabladeplatz** *nm*, rubbish tip; **Müllcontainer** *nm*, rubbish skip; **Mülldeponie** *nf*, **Müllhalde** *nf*, rubbish tip; **Müllsortierung** *nf*, sifting of waste; **Müllverbrennung** *nf*, incineration; **Müllverbrennungsanlage** *nf*, incineration plant

mündelsichere Wertpapiere *nnpl* (fin), gilt-edged securities

mündlich *adj*, **eine mündliche Vereinbarung**, a verbal agreement

Münze *nf*, coin

Münzfernsprecher *nm*, payphone

müssen *vb*, have to, must; **er mußte den Brief sofort schreiben**, he had to write the letter immediately; **leider müssen wir Ihnen mitteilen, daß . . .**, unfortunately we have to inform you that . . .

Muster *nn* (comm), sample; **entspricht nicht dem Muster**, not up to sample

Mustervertrag *nm*, standard agreement/contract

Mutter-; **Muttergesellschaft** *nf*, parent company; **Mutterschaftsurlaub** *nm*, maternity leave; **Mutterschutz** *nm*, legal protection of expectant and nursing mothers

Muttersprachler(in) *nm/f*, native speaker

nach (+ dat) *prep*, **1** (place), to; **nach Frankreich**, to France. **2** (time), after; **nach 5 Uhr**, after 5 o'clock

nach|ahmen *vb*, imitate

Nachahmung *nf*, imitation, copy

nach|bestellen *vb*, reorder

Nachbestellung *nf*, repeat order

nach|datieren *vb*, postdate

nach|denken über (+ acc) *vb*, think about; **darüber muß ich erst einmal nachdenken**, I'll have to think about that

Nachdruck *nm*, **„Nachdruck verboten"**, "no part of this publication may be reproduced without prior permission of the publishers"

nach|drucken *vb*, reprint

nachdrücklich *adj*, *adv*, emphatic; emphatically; **nachdrücklich hinweisen auf** (+ acc), point out, highlight; **wir müssen Sie nachdrücklich darauf hinweisen, daß . . .**, we have to point out to you that . . .

Nachfolge *nf* (in office), succession

nach|folgen (+ dat) *vb*, **1** (gen), follow. **2** (in office), succeed

nachfolgend *adj*, following

Nachfolger(in) *nm/f*, successor

nach|forschen *vb*, investigate

Nachfrage *nf* (comm), demand; **es herrscht große Nachfrage nach** (+ dat), there is keen demand for; **die Nachfrage läßt nach**, demand is dropping; **eine**

Nachfrage befriedigen/stillen, satisfy a demand

nach|fragen *vb*, enquire; **bitte fragen Sie am Schalter nach**, please enquire at the counter

nachher *adv*, afterwards

nach|holen *vb* (what was missed), catch up on, make up for

Nachkriegs- *adj*, post-war; **Nachkriegsentwicklungen** *nfpl*, post-war developments

nach|lassen *vb* (trend, demand etc), slacken

nach|liefern *vb* (comm), deliver at a later date

nach|lösen *vb*, **1** (gen), buy a ticket on the train. **2** (for an extension of the journey), pay extra, pay a supplement

nachmittags *adv*, in the afternoon

Nachnahme *nf*, **per Nachnahme schicken**, send cash on delivery; **Nachnahmegebühr** *nf*, COD charge

Nachporto *nn*, excess postage

nach|prüfen *vb*, check, verify

Nach-; **Nachprüfung** *nf*, check, verification; **Nachredner** *nm* **mein Nachredner**, the speaker after me; **Nachricht** *nf*, message, news; **wir geben Ihnen Nachricht, wann . . .**, we'll let you know when . . .; **Nachsaison** *nf* (tourism), off-season

nach|schicken *vb* (mail), forward; **„bitte nachschicken!"**, "please forward"

nach|sehen *vb*, have a look, look up

Nachsicht *nf*, leniency, forebearance

Nacht *nf*, night; **in der Nacht**, during the night

Nachteil *nm*, drawback; **die Sache hat einen Nachteil**, there is a drawback; **im Nachteil sein**, be at a disadvantage

nachteilig *adj*, *adv*, adverse; adversely

Nachtflug *nm*, night flight

Nachtragshaushalt *nm*, mini budget

Nacht-; **Nachtschalter** *nm*, night desk; **Nachtschicht** *nf*, night shift; **Nachtstrom** *nm*, off-peak electricity; **Nachttarif** *nm*, night rate; **Nachttresor** *nm*, night safe; **Nachtwächter** *nm*, night watchman

Nachweis *nm*, proof, evidence; **bitte erbringen Sie einen Nachweis, daß Sie . . .**, please provide some evidence that you . . .

nach|weisen *vb*, prove

Nachwuchs *nm* (pers), **es fehlt bei den Ingenieuren an Nachwuchs**, there are not enough young people wanting to be engineers; **wir brauchen mehr Nachwuchs**, we need new blood

nach|zahlen *vb* (on a train), pay extra

nach|zählen *vb* (money after purchase), check

nahe *adj*, **in naher Zukunft**, in the near future

Nähe *nf* (place), closeness; **in der Nähe**, in the vicinity, close by

nahe|legen *vb*, suggest; **ich möchte Ihnen folgendes nahelegen**, I would like to suggest to you the following

nahe|liegend *adj*, which suggests itself, obvious; **ein naheliegender Gedanke**, an obvious idea

näher *adj*, *adv*, closer, more closely; **wir müssen die Sache näher betrachten**, we have to examine the matter more closely; **der Termin rückt näher**, the deadline is coming closer

näher|kommen *vb*, **1** come closer. **2** be nearer the mark; **das kommt der Sache näher**, that's nearer the mark

näher|liegen *vb*, make more sense;

es liegt eigentlich näher, noch etwas abzuwarten, it makes more sense to wait a little longer

nahezu *adv*, nearly, almost

Nahrung *nf*, food

Nahrungs-; **Nahrungsmittel** *npl*, foodstuffs; **Nahrungsmittelabteilung** *nf* (in store), food department; **Nahrungs- und Genußmittelindustrie** *nf*, food and allied industries

Nahverkehr *nm*, local traffic

Nahverkehrszug *nm*, commuter train

Name *nm*, name; **ich kenne ihn dem Namen nach**, I know him by name; **im Namen meines Chefs**, on behalf of my boss; **mein Name ist Schmitz**, my name is Schmitz; **wie war doch Ihr Name?**, what was the name?

namens *adv*, by the name of

Namens-; **Namensliste** *nf*, **Namensverzeichnis** *nn*, list of names; **Namenszug** *nm*, signature

namhaft *adj*, famous, well-known; **eine namhafte Firma**, a well-known firm

naß *adj*, wet

Nässe *nf*, wetness, dampness, moisture; **„vor Nässe schützen"**, "keep dry"

natürlich *adj*, natural

natürlich *adv*, naturally, of course

neben (+ dat) *prep*, **1** (place), beside, next to. **2** apart from

Neben-; **Nebenabsicht** *nf*, secondary objective; **Nebenanschluß** *nm* (telec), extension; **Nebenausgaben** *nfpl*, incidental expenses; **Nebenberuf** *nm*, second job, sideline

nebeneinander *adv*, side by side

Neben-; **Nebeneingang** *nm*, side entrance; **Nebeneinnahmen** *nfpl*, additional income

nebenher *adv*, in addition, on the side

Neben-; **Nebenkosten** *npl*, incidental expenses; **Nebenleistungen** *nfpl*, fringe benefits; **Nebenprodukt** *nn*, by-product; **Nebensache** *nf*, minor matter; **Nebensaison** *nf*, off-season, quiet season; **Nebenstraße** *nf*, side street; **Nebenwirkung** *nf*, side effect

negativ *adj*, negative

neigen *vb*, **dazu neigen, etwas zu tun**, tend to do something; **zu der Annahme neigen, daß . . .** be inclined to think that . . .

nennenswert *adj*, considerable, significant; **es besteht kein nennenswerter Unterschied**, there is no significant difference

Nenner *nm* (maths), denominator; **gemeinsamer Nenner**, common denominator

Nennwert *nm* (fin), face value

netto *adj* (comm), net; **er verdient DM 3.000 netto im Monat** his monthly net income is DM 3,000

Netto-; **Nettoeinnahmen** *nfpl*, net income; **Nettogehalt** *nn*, net salary; **Nettogewicht** *nn*, net weight; **Nettogewinn** *nm*, net profit; **Nettopreis** *nm*, net price; **Nettoumsatz** *nm*, net sales

Netz *nn* (system), network; **Netzanschluß** *nm*, **mit Netzanschluß**, runs on mains electricity; **Netzwerk** *nn* (comp), network

neu *adj*, new

neuartig *adj*, novel

Neu-; **Neuausgabe** *nf* (of book), new issue; **Neubau** *nm*, new house or building; **Neubaugebiet** *nn*, development area; **Neubeginn** *nm*, (new) departure

neuerdings *adv*, recently; **er duzt mich neuerdings**, he recently started calling me 'du'

Neuerer *nm*, innovator

Neuerung *nf*, innovation

Neu-; **Neuerwerbung** *nf*, new acquisition; **Neugründung** *nf*, start-up; **Neuordnung** *nf*, reorganisation; **Neuzulassung** *nf* (of car), registration of a new vehicle

nicht *adv*, not; **nicht berühren!**, do not touch!

nichtamtlich *adj*, non-official

Nicht-; **Nichtanerkennung** *nf*, non-recognition; **Nichterfüllung** *nf* (law), default; **Nichterscheinen** *nn*, failure to appear

nichtig *adj* (law), invalid, null and void; **der Vertrag wurde für nichtig erklärt**, the contract was declared invalid/null and void

Nichtigkeit *nf* (law), invalidity

Nicht-; **Nichtlieferung** *nf*, non-delivery; **Nichtraucher** *nm*, „**Nichtraucher**" (train), "No smoking"; **ich bin Nichtraucher**, I don't smoke; **Nichtrancherabteil** *nt* **ich möchte einen Platz im Nichtraucherabteil**, I would like a seat in a no-smoking compartment; **Nichtverfügbarkeit** *nf*, unavailability; **Nichtzahlung** *nf*, non-payment; **bei Nichtzahlung**, in case of non-payment

nie *adv*, never; **nie wieder**, never again

Niederlage *nf* (transp), warehouse

sich nieder|lassen *vb*, **1** (gen), settle. **2** (comm), set up in business

Niederlassung *nf* (comm), branch, registered office

nieder|legen *vb*, **die Arbeit niederlegen**, walk out

niedrig *adj*, low; **niedrige Löhne** *nmpl*, low wages

Niedrigpreis *nm*, cut price

Niedrigstpreise *nmpl*, rock-bottom prices

noch *adv*, **1** (until now), still; **er ist noch nicht da**, he still isn't here. **2** (in addition), else; **was haben Sie noch gesehen?**, what else did you see? **3** (comparison) even; **das war noch besser**, that was even better. **4 weder . . . noch**, neither . . . nor; **er hat weder Kraft noch Zeit dafür**, he has neither the energy nor the time for it

nochmal(s) *adv*, once again

nominieren *vb*, nominate

Nominierung *nf*, nomination

Norden *nm*, north; **Hamburg liegt im Norden Deutschlands**, Hamburg is situated in the north of Germany

Norm *nf*, norm

normal *adj*, **1** (gen), normal. **2** (subject to standardisation), standard

normalerweise *adv*, normally

Normalrabatt *nm*, basic discount

Normalverbraucher *nm*, average consumer

Normblatt *nn*, standard specifications sheet

Normung *nf*, standardisation

Notar *nm*, notary, conveyancer

Notausgang *nm*, emergency exit

Notfall *nm*, emergency; **im Notfall**, in an emergency

notieren *vb*, **1** (order), note. **2** (on stock exchange), list, quote

Notiz *nf*, note; **Notizen machen**, take notes; **Notizblock** *nm*, writing pad

nötig *adj*, necessary

Notlage *nf*, plight, difficulty

Notstand *nm*, emergency

notwendig *adj*, necessary

notwendigerweise *adv*, necessarily

Notwendigkeit *nf*, necessity, need; **es besteht keine Notwendigkeit, ihn anzurufen**, there is no need to ring him

Null *nf*, zero, nought; **null Komma drei (0,3)**, nought point three, 0.3; **Nullinflation** *nf*, zero inflation; **Nullpunkt** *nm*, rock-bottom; **zum Nulltarif**, free; **Nullwachstum** *nn*, zero growth

numerieren *vb*, number

Nummer *nf* (of house, car, telephone etc), number

Nummernkonto *nn* (fin), numbered account

Nummernschild *nn* (of car), number plate

nur *adv*, only

nutzen *vb*, make use of, exploit

Nutz-; **Nutzfahrzeug** *nn* (comm), commercial vehicle; **Nutzfläche** *nf*, utilisable floor space; **Nutzlast** *nf* (transp), payload

nutzlos *adj*, *adv*, useless; uselessly

oben *adv*, at the top

Oberfläche *nf*, surface

Oberflächenfinish *nm*, finish

oberflächlich *adj*, *adv*, superficial, superficially; **nach oberflächlicher Schätzung**, at a rough estimate

obgleich *conj*, although

Obligation *nf* (fin), bond

obligatorisch *adj*, compulsory

offen *adj*, **1** (gen), open. **2** (speech), frank; **offene Rechnung** *nf*, outstanding bill; **offene Stelle** *nf*, vacancy; **Tag der offenen Tür**, open day; **offenes Ticket** *nn*, open ticket

offen|bleiben *vb*, remain open; **diese Frage ist offengeblieben**, this question remained open

Offenheit *nf*, frankness, openness

offen|stehen *vb*, **1** (gen), be open. **2** (comm), remain unpaid. **3** be open to; **auch Nichtmitgliedern steht die Teilnahme an der Ausstellung offen**, the exhibition is also open to non-members

öffentlich *adj*, public; **öffentlicher Fernsprecher** *nm*, public telephone; **öffentliche Mittel** *nnpl*, public funds; **der öffentliche Sektor**, the public sector; **der öffentliche Verkehr**, public transport

Öffentlichkeit *nf*, general public; **in/vor aller Öffentlichkeit**, in public

Öffentlichkeitsarbeit *nf*, public relations

öffentlich-rechtlich *adj* (law), (under) public law; **die deutschen Industrie- und Handelskammern sind öffentlich-rechtliche Einrichtungen**, German chambers of industry and commerce have been set up under public law

öffnen *vb*, open; **„hier öffnen"**, "open this end", "open here"

oft *adv*, often, frequently

OHG, **Offene Handelsgesellschaft** *nf*, general partnership

ohne (+ acc) *prep*, without; **ohne Probleme**, without problems

Ökologe *nm*, **Ökologin** *nf*, ecologist

Ökologie *nf*, ecology; **Ökologiebewegung** *nf*, ecological movement

ökologisch *adj*, *adv*, ecological; ecologically

Ökonomie *nf*, **1** economy. **2** (science), economics

ökonomisch *adj*, *adv*, economic; economically; **wir müssen ökonomischer arbeiten**, we have to operate more economically; **ökonomisch ist das Unsinn**, in economic terms this is nonsense

Ökopapier *nn*, recycled paper

Öl *nn*, oil; **Ölexportland** *nn*, oil-exporting country; **Ölgesellschaft** *nf*, **Ölkonzern** *nm*, oil company; **Ölkrise** *nf*, oil crisis

Operation *nf*, operation

operieren *vb*, operate

optimal *adj*, optimal; **optimale Ergebnisse** *nnpl*, optimal results

optimieren *vb*, optimise

Optimist(in) *nm/f*, optimist

Option *nf*, option

Options-; **Optionsanleihe** *nf* (fin), optional bond; **Optionspreis** *nm*, option price; **Optionsrecht** *nn* (fin), option right

ordentlich *adj*, *adv*, tidy, neat; neatly

Organisation *nf*, organisation

organisatorisch *adj*, *adv*, organisational; organisationally

organisch *adj*, *adv*, organic; organically

organisieren *vb*, organise

Organogramm *nn*, organisation chart

orientieren *vb*, inform, provide/contain information; **unser Katalog orientiert über unsere Sonderangebote**, our catalogue contains information about our special offers

Orientierung *nf*, information; **zu Ihrer Orientierung**, for your information

Original *nn*, original; **Originalausstattung** *nf*, original equipment; **Originalverpackung** *nf*, original packaging

originell *adj*, (independent, novel), original, **eine originelle Idee**, an original idea

Ordnung *nf*, **1** (gen), order; **Ordnung schaffen**, put things in order; **in Ordnung sein**, be in order, be OK. **2** (rules), **der Ordnung gemäß**, according to the rules

Ort *nm* (gen), place, spot; **am Ort**, locally, in town; **das beste Hotel am Ort**, the best hotel in town; **vor Ort**, on location, in situ

örtlich *adj*, *adv*, local; locally

ortsansässig *adj*, local, resident; **sind Sie hier ortsansässig?**, are you a resident here?

Ortsgespräch *nn* (telec), local call

Ortszulage *nf*, (local) weighting allowance

Oxid *nn*, **Oxyd** *nn*, oxide

Ozean *nm*, ocean; **Ozeanriese** *nm*, ocean liner

Ozon *nm*, ozone; **Ozonschicht** *nf*, ozone layer

P

Paar *nn*, **ein Paar**, a pair (of)

paar *adj*, **ein paar**, a few; **ein paar Minuten**, a few minutes

Pacht *nf*, lease, rent; **etwas in Pacht geben**, lease something (out); **etwas in Pacht nehmen**, lease something

pachten *vb*, lease, rent

Pächter *nm*, leaseholder, lessee

Pachtgrundstück *nn*, leasehold property

Pachtvertrag *nm*, lease

Päckchen *nn*, **1** (gen), (small) parcel. **2** (post), (small) packet. **3 ein Päckchen Zigaretten**, a packet of cigarettes

packen *vb* (packet, suitcase), pack

Packmaterial *nn*, packing material

Packpapier *nn*, wrapping paper, brown paper

Packung *nf* (mktg, sales), packet, pack; **eine 5-kg-Packung**, a 5 kg pack

Packzettel *nm* (imp/exp), packing list, packing note

Paket *nn* (post), parcel; **Paketannahme** *nf*, **Paketausgabe** *nf*, parcels office; **Paketkarte** *nf*, dispatch form; **Paketschalter** *nm*, parcels counter

Palette *nf*, **1** (of goods), range; **eine reichhaltige Palette**, a wide range. **2** (transp), pallet

palettieren *vb* (transp), palletise

Panne *nf*, **1** (gen), hitch, trouble. **2** (of

car), breakdown. **3** (in tyre), puncture

Pannendienst *nm*, breakdown service

Papier *nn*, paper; **Papier mit Briefkopf** (offce), headed paper; **Papiere**, papers, documents; **Papierfabrik** *nf*, paper mill; **Papierkorb** *nm* (offce), wastepaper basket; **Papierkram** *nm*, bumf; **Papierkrieg** *nm*, red tape; **Papierschneider** *nm* (offce), guillotine; **Papierwaren** *nfpl*, stationery

Pappe *nf*, cardboard

Pappkarton *nm*, **1** (material), cardboard. **2** (object), cardboard box

Paragraph *nm*, **1** (law), section. **2** (part of text), paragraph

Parität *nf*, parity

parken *vb* (car), park

Park-; **Parkplatz** *nm*, car park; **Parkuhr** *nf*, parking meter; **Parkverbot** *nn*, parking ban, no parking; **Parkverbotsschild** *nn*, no-parking sign

Parlament *nn*, parliament

Parlamentswahl(en) *nf(pl)*, parliamentary election(s)

Partei *nf* (politics, law), party

parteiisch *adj*, bias(s)ed, partial

Partner(in) *nm/f*, partner; **Partnerschaft** *nf*, partnership

Paß *nm*, passport

Passagier(in) *nm/f*, passenger

Paßbild *nn*, passport photo(graph)

passen *vb*, **1** (correct size), fit. **2** (be convenient), suit; **leider paßt mir das Datum nicht besonders gut**, unfortunately, the date doesn't suit me very well. **3** (colour, style), **passen zu** (+ dat), match, fit in with; **der Sessel paßt nicht zu Ihrer sonstigen Büroeinrichtung**, the armchair doesn't fit in with the rest of your office furniture

passend *adj*, **1** (acceptable), convenient; **eine passende Zeit**, a convenient time. **2** (colour, style) matching. **3** (right for the occasion), fitting, appropriate

passieren *vb*, **1** happen; **was ist passiert?**, what's happened? **2** pass, cross; **wir haben gerade die Grenze passiert**, we have just crossed the border

Passiva *npl* (comm), liabilities

Passivposten *nm* (comm), debit entry

Paßkontrolle *nf*, passport control

Paßwort *nn* (comp), password

Patent *nn*, patent

patentieren *vb*, patent

pauschal *adj*, *adv*, **1** (gen), estimated. **2** flat rate; **der Strom wird pauschal berechnet**, we'll charge you a flat rate for electricity. **3** (price), inclusive

Pauschalarrangement *nn*, package deal

Pauschalbetrag *nm*, lump sum

Pauschale *nf*, **1** (gen), estimated amount. **2** flat rate

Pauschalreise *nf*, package holiday, package tour

Pauschalversicherung *nf*, comprehensive insurance

Pause *nf*, break

peinlich *adj*, embarrassing

pendeln *vb* (travel to work), commute

Pendelverkehr *nm*, **1** (to work), commuter traffic. **2** (e.g. to airport, station), shuttle service

Pendler(in) *nm/f*, commuter; **Pendlerzug** *nm*, commuter train

sich pensionieren lassen *vb*, retire

Pensionierung *nf*, retirement

periphäre Geräte *nnpl* (comp), peripherals

Personal *nn*, personnel, staff, manpower; **Personalabteilung** *nf*, personnel department; **Personalbeschaffung** *nf*, recruitment; **Personalchef(in)** *nm/f*, personnel manager(ess); **Personalcomputer** *nm*, personal computer, PC; **Personalleitung** *nf*, personnel management; **Personalmangel** *nm*, staff shortage; **Personalplanung** *nf*, manpower planning; **Personalstärke** *nf*, staff(ing) level; **Personalvertretung** *nf*, staff association

Personen-; **Personengesellschaft** *nf*, partnership; **Personenstand** *nm*, legal status; **Personenzug** *nm*, passenger train

persönlich *adj*, *adv*, personal, personalised; personally; **mit persönlicher Note** (mktg), personalised; **persönliches Eigentum** *nn*, personal property; **persönliche Sekretärin** *nf*, personal secretary

Pfand *nn* (on bottle), deposit; **Pfandflasche** *nf*, returnable bottle

Pflicht *nf*, duty; **Pflichtversicherung** *nf*, compulsory insurance

Pfund *nn*, **1** (currency), **Pfund Sterling**, pound sterling. **2** (weight), pound (= 500 g)

pharmazeutisch *adj*, pharmaceutical; **pharmazeutische Industrie** *nf*, pharmaceutical industry; **pharmazeutische Produkte** *nnpl*, pharmaceutical products

Plakat *nn*, poster; **Plakatkampagne** *nf*, poster campaign; **Plakatwand** *nf*, advertisement hoarding

Plan *nm*, **1** (of city, future), plan. **2** (timing), schedule

planen *vb*, plan; **eine Werbekampagne planen**, plan an advertising campaign

Plantafel *nf*, wall chart

Planung *nf*, planning

Planwirtschaft *nf*, planned economy

Plastik *nn*, plastic; **Plastiktüte** *nf*, plastic bag

pleite *adj*, broke; **pleite gehen**, go bust

Pleite *nf*, **1** bankruptcy. **2** flop; **das war eine totale Pleite**, that was a total flop

Plombe *nf* (customs), customs seal

Police *nf* (ins), policy

politisch *adj*, *adv*, political; politically

Polizei *nf*, police

Portfolio *nn*, portfolio

Porto *nn*, postage; **Porto zahlt Empfänger**, postage paid

Portokasse *nf*, petty cash

Post *nf*, **1** (letters etc), mail; **mit gewöhnlicher Post**, by surface mail; **elektronische Post**, electronic mail, E-mail. **2** (institution), post office

Post-; **Postamt** *nn*, post office; **Postbote** *nm*, postman; **Postbotin** *nf*, postwoman; **Postdienst** *nm*, postal service

Posten *nm*, **1** (pers), post, position. **2** (in list), entry, item

Post-; **Postfach** *nn*, (mail) box; **Postgebühren** *nfpl*, postage, postal charges; **Postleitzahl** *nf*, post code; **Poststelle** *nf*, mail room; **Poststempel** *nm*, postmark; **Postversand** *nm*, mail order; **Postwurfsendung** *nf*, mailing piece

PR-Abteilung *nf*, PR department, public relations department

Praktikum *nn*, work placement

praktisch *adj*, **1** practical. **2** (suitable), convenient. **3** (useful), handy

Prämie *nf*, **1** (ins), premium. **2** (reward), bonus

Präsentation *nf*, presentation; **eine Präsentation machen**, make a presentation

Präsentationspackung *nf*, presentation pack

Präsident *nm*, president

Präzedenzfall *nm*, precedent

präzise *adj*, *adv*, precise; precisely

Präzision *nf*, precision

Prazisionsinstrument *nn*, precision instrument

Preis *nm*, **1** (reward), prize; **der erste Preis**, first prize. **2** (cost), price; **der Preis ist angemessen**, the price is fair; **der geforderte Preis**, the asking price; **der vereinbarte Preis**, the agreed price; **die Preise drücken**, force prices down; **einen Preis auf . . . festsetzen**, price at . . . ; **die Preise hochtreiben**, force up prices; **Preis ab Kai**, price ex quay; **Preis ab Lager**, price ex warehouse; **Preis ab Werk**, price ex works, price ex factory; **Preisabsprache** *nf*, price rigging; **Preisaufschlag** *nm*, mark-up; **Preisbildung** *nf*, pricing; **Preisempfehlung** *nf*, recommended price; **unverbindliche Preisempfehlung**, manufacturer's recommended price, MRP, recommended retail price, RRP; **Preiserhöhung** *nf*, price increase; **Preisgefälle** *nn*, price differential; **Preiskrieg** *nm*, price war; **Preislage** *nf*, price range; **Preisliste** *nf*, price list; **Preisnachlaß** *nm*, discount; **Preisnotierung** *nf*, quotation; **Preispolitik** *nf*, pricing policy; **Preisschild** *nn*, price label; **Preissenkung** *nf*, price cut; **Preisstopp** *nm*, price freeze; **Preis/Verdienst-Relation** *nf*, price-earning ratio

Preisverlosung *nf*, prize draw

Premierminister(in) *nm/f*, prime minister

Presse *nf*, press; **Pressebericht** *nm*, press report; **Presseberichte über die Ausstellung**, press coverage of the exhibition; **Pressemitteilung** *nf*, press release; **Pressenotiz** *nf*, press notice; **Pressestelle** *nf*, press office

Prestige *nn*, prestige; **Prestigeverlust** *nm*, loss of status

Prinzip *nn*, principle; **im Prinzip**, in principle

Priorität *nf*, priority

privat *adj*, *adv*, private; privately

privatisieren *vb*, privatise

privatisiert *adj*, privatised

Privatisierung *nf*, privatisation

Probe *nf*, **1** (of goods), sample; **kostenlose Probe**, free sample. **2** (pers), **auf Probe**, on probation; **Probeexemplar** *nn*, specimen (copy)

probe|fahren *vb* (car), test-drive

Probe-; **Probefahrt** *nf* (of car), test drive; **Probelauf** *nm*, test run, trial run; **Probesendung** *nf*, sample pack; **Probezeit** *nf* (pers), probation

probieren *vb* (food, drink), sample, taste

Problem *nn*, problem; **Problemlösung** *nf*, solution

Produkt *nn*, product; **Produktgestaltung** *nf*, product design; **Produkthaftung** *nf*, product liability; **Produktmanager** *nm*, product manager; **Produktnutzen** *nm* (mktg), product benefits

Produktion *nf*, production

Produktions-; **Produktionsanlage** *nf*, plant; **Produktionsausfall** *nm*, loss of production;

Produktionskosten *npl*, production costs; **Produktionskraft** *nf*, production capacity; **Produktionsmittel** *nnpl*, means of production; **Produktionsstand** *nm*, production level; **Produktionsstätte** *nf*, production centre

produktiv *adj, adv*, productive; productively

Produktivität *nf*, productivity

Produktivitätsprämie *nf* (pers), productivity bonus

produzieren *vb*, produce

Profit *nm*, profit

profitabel *adj, adv*, **profitbringend** *adj, adv*, profitable; profitably

profitieren von (+ dat) *vb*, profit from

pro forma *adv*, pro forma

Pro-forma-Rechnung *nf*, pro-forma invoice

Programm *nn* (gen, comp), programme

programmieren *vb* (comp), programme

Programmierer(in) *nm/f* (comp), programmer

Programmiersprache *nf*, programming language

Projekt *nn*, project

projektieren *vb*, plan, project

Projekt-; **Projektleiter(in)** *nm/f*, project manager; **Projektphase** *nf*, project phase; **die letzte Projektphase**, the last phase of the project; **Projektplanung** *nf*, project planning

pro Kopf *adv*, per capita

promovieren *vb*, do a doctorate

prompt *adj, adv*, prompt; promptly

Prospekt *nm* (advertising), brochure, leaflet

Protokoll *nn*, (of a meeting), minutes; **Protokoll führen**, take minutes

Provision *nf* (comm), commission

provisorisch *adj, adv*, provisional; provisionally

Prozent *nn*, per cent; **Prozentbasis** *nf*, **auf Prozentbasis**, on a commission basis; **Prozentsatz** *nm*, percentage

Prozeß *nm* (law), (legal) proceedings

prüfen *vb*, **1** (gen), examine. **2** (company), inspect

Prüfung *nf*, **1** (gen), examination. **2** (of company), inspection

Publikation *nf*, publication

Pufferbestand *nm*, buffer stock

Punkt *nm*, **1** (in debate), point. **2** (on agenda, list), item.

pünktlich *adj, adv*, prompt; promptly; on time; **pünktlich bezahlen**, pay on the nail; **pünktlich sein**, be on schedule/on time

Quadrat *nn*, square

quadratisch *adj*, square

Quadratkilometer *nm*, **qkm**, square kilometre

Quadratmeter *nm*, **qm**, square metre

Qualifikation *nf*, qualification

qualifizieren *vb*, **sich qualifizieren** *vb*, **sich als . . . qualifizieren,** qualify as . . .

Qualität *nf*, quality

Qualitäts-; **Qualitätsarbeit** *nf*, quality work; **Qualitätserzeugnis** *nn*, quality product; **Qualitätskontrolle** *nf*, **Qualitätssicherung** *nf*, quality control; **Qualitätsware** *nf*, quality goods; **Qualitätswein** *nm*, wine of certified origin and quality

Quantität *nf*, quantity

Quartal *nn* (part of year), quarter

Quelle *nf*, source

Quellenbesteuerung *nf*, deduction at source

quer *adv*, crossways, diagonally, at right angle

quittieren *vb*, get/give a receipt for

Quittung *nf*, receipt; **gegen Quittung**, on production of a receipt

Quittungsblock *nm*, receipt book

Quorum *nn*, quorum

Quote *nf*, quota

Quotensystem *nn*, quota system

quotieren *vb* (comm), quote

Quotierung *nf* (comm), quotation

R

Rabatt, *nm*, discount, rebate; **mit 25% Rabatt**, at a 25% discount; **Rabatt gewähren**, discount, grant a discount

Rabattmarke *nf*, (comm), trading stamp

Rad *nn*, wheel

Radiergummi *nm*, (India) rubber

radikal *adj*, radical, drastic, total; **eine radikale Maßnahme**, a radical measure; **wir müssen ganz radikal vorgehen**, we must take drastic steps

Radio-; **Radiogeschäft** *nn*, electrical shop; **Radiosender** *nm*, radio station; **Radiowecker** *nm*, radio alarm

Raffinerie *nf* (for sugar, oil), refinery

raffinieren *vb* (sugar, oil), refine

Rahmen *nm*, framework; **aus dem Rahmen fallen**, be different, not fit in; **Rahmenbedingung** *nf*, general condition; **Rahmengesetz** *nn*, framework legislation; **Rahmenvertrag** *nm* (for industry), general agreement

Rang *nm* (in company), position; **jemandem den Rang streitig machen**, challenge someone's position; **Rangordnung** *nf*, hierarchy; **Rangstufe** *nf*, rank; **Rangunterschied** *nm*, professional/social distinction

Rat *nm*, advice; **darf ich Sie um Rat fragen?**, may I ask your advice?; **wir brauchen Ihren Rat**, we need your advice

Rate *nf*, instalment; **in Raten zahlen**, pay in instalments

raten *vb*, **1** advise. **2** guess

rationalisieren *vb*, rationalise, streamline

Rationalisierung *nf*, rationalisation, streamlining

rauben *vb*, rob

rauchen *vb*, smoke; **„Rauchen verboten"**, "no smoking"

Rauchverbot *nn*, ban on smoking

Raum *nm*, **1** (in building), room. **2** area; **der Raum München**, the Munich area

Raumausstatter(in) *nm/f*, interior decorator

räumen *vb* (building, warehouse etc), clear

Raumfahrt *nf*, space travel/flight; **Raumfahrttechnik** *nf*, space technology

Räumlichkeit(en) *nf(pl)*, rooms, premises

Raumpflegerin *nf*, cleaning lady

Räumungsverkauf *nm*, clearance sale

Raumverschwendung *nf*, waste of space

Raumverteilungsplan *nm*, floor plan

reagieren auf (+ acc) *vb*, react to; **wir haben bisher auf Ihren Brief noch nicht reagiert, weil . . .**, we have not yet answered your letter because . . .

Reaktion *nf*, reaction

Reaktor *nm*, reactor

realisieren *vb*, realise

realistisch *adj*, *adv*, realistic; realistically

Realität *nf*, reality, the facts; **die Realität anerkennen**, face the facts

Rechenanlage *nf*, computer

Rechenmaschine *nf*, adding machine

Rechenschaft *nf*, account; **Rechenschaft ablegen über** (+ acc), account for; **zur Rechenschaft verpflichtet sein**, be accountable

Rechenschaftsbericht *nm*, report

Rechen-; **Rechenschieber** *nm*, **Rechenstab** *nm*, slide-rule; **Rechenzentrum** *nn*, computer centre

rechnen *vb*, **1** (add etc), work out, calculate. **2** (estimate), reckon; **wir rechnen mit 3 Tagen**, we reckon on three days. **3** (expect), **mit etwas rechnen**, reckon with, be prepared for; **wir rechnen mit dem Schlimmsten**, we are prepared for the worst

Rechner *nm*, **1** (gen), computer. **2** pocket calculator

rechnergesteuert *adj*, computer-controlled

Rechnernetz *nn*, **lokales Rechnernetz** (comp), local area network

Rechnung *nf*, account, bill, invoice; **eine Rechnung begleichen**, settle a bill; **eine detaillierte Rechnung**, a detailed account; **laut Rechnung**, as per invoice; **unbezahlte Rechnung**, unpaid invoice; **eine Rechnung vorlegen**, present a bill; **eine Rechnung ausstellen**, invoice; **in Rechnung stellen**, bill

Rechnungs-; **Rechnungsabteilung** *nf*, invoicing department; **Rechnungsausstellung** *nf*, invoicing; **Rechnungsbetrag** *nm*, total invoice value; **Rechnungsbuch** *nn*, account book; **Rechnungseinheit** *nf*, unit of account; **Rechnungsjahr** *nn*, financial year

Rechnungsprüfer *nm*, accountant, auditor; **außerbetrieblicher Rechnungsprüfer**, external auditor; **betriebsinterner Rechnungsprüfer**, internal auditor; **unabhängiger Rechnungsprüfer**, external auditor

Rechnungsprüfung *nf*, audit; **außerbetriebliche Rechnungsprüfung**, external audit; **betriebsinterne Rechnungsprüfung**, internal audit; **unabhängige Rechnungsprüfung**, external audit

Rechnungswesen *nn*, accountancy, accounting

Recht *nn*, **1** (body of rules), law; **bürgerliches Recht**, civil law; **nach englischem Recht**, according to English law. **2** (entitlement), right; **seine Rechte geltend machen**, insist on one's rights

recht *adj*, right, correct; **ganz recht!**, quite right!; **recht behalten**, be proved right; **jemandem recht geben**, agree with someone; **recht gehen in der Annahme, daß . . .**, be correct in assuming that . . . ; **recht haben**, be right

rechte(r, s) *adj*, right, right-hand; **auf der rechten Seite**, on the right; **im rechten Winkel**, at right angle

rechtfertigen *vb*, justify

Rechtfertigung *nf*, justification

rechtlich *adj*, *adv*, legal; legally; **eine rechtliche Frage**, a legal issue; **rechtlich belangen**, take to court

rechtmäßig *adj*, *adv*, lawful, legitimate; lawfully, legitimately

rechts *adv*, on/to the right; **halten Sie sich rechts**, keep to the right

Rechts-; **Rechtsangelegenheit** *nf*, legal matter; **Rechtsanwalt** *nm*, **Rechtsanwältin** *nf*, lawyer, solicitor; **Rechtsauskunft** *nf*, legal advice; **Rechtsberater(in)** *nm/f*, legal adviser

rechtsgültig machen *vb*, validate

rechtskräftig *adj*, **1** (contract), legally

valid. **2** (legislation), in force

Rechts-; **Rechtslage** *nf*, legal situation; **Rechtspflege** *nf*, administration of justice; **Rechtsstaat** *nm*, state under the rule of law; **Rechtsstreit** *nm*, court case, litigation; **Rechtstitel** *nm*, legal title

Rechtsverkehr *nm*, **1** (transp), right-hand traffic. **2** (law), legal transactions

rechtswidrig *adj*, *adv*, illegal; illegally

rechtzeitig *adj*, *adv*, punctual, on time

Redaktion *nf*, **1** (process), editing. **2** (pers), editorial board

Rede *nf* (at conference), speech, address; **eine Rede halten**, give a speech

reden *vb*, **1** (gen), talk, speak; **reden wir morgen darüber!**, let's talk about it tomorrow; **darüber läßt sich reden** (price, conditions etc), we could discuss that. **2** (give a speech), speak

redlich *adj*, *adv*, honest; honestly, **sein Geld redlich verdienen**, make an honest living

Redner(in) *nm/f*, speaker

reduzieren *vb*, reduce

Reederei *nf* (naut), shipping company

Referat *nn*, (admin), department

Referenz *nf*, reference, testimonial; **dürfte ich Sie um eine Referenz bitten?**, might I ask you for a reference?

referieren *vb*, give a report

Refinanzierung *nf*, refinancing

Reform *nf*, reform

reformbedürftig *adj*, in need of reform

Reformkurs *nm*, policy of reform

Regal *nn* (gen, comm), shelves; **Regalauffüller** *nm* (comm), shelf-filler; **Regalfläche** *nf* (gen, comm), shelf space

rege *adj*, **1** (traffic), busy. **2** (trade), brisk

Regel *nf* (norm), rule; **in der Regel**, as a rule; **Regelarbeitszeit** *nf*, core working hours; **Regelfall** *nm*, **im Regelfall**, as a rule

regelmäßig *adj*, *adv*, regular; regularly

Regelmäßigkeit *nf*, regularity

regeln *vb*, **1** (traffic), control. **2** (temperature), regulate. **3** (task), see to. **4** (disagreement), settle

Regelung *nf*, **1** (of traffic), control(ling). **2** (of temperature), regulation. **3** (task), dealing with. **4** (of disagreement), settlement

regieren *vb* (market), control, dominate

Regierung *nf*, government

regional *adj*, *adv*, regional; regionally; **regional verschieden**, with regional variations

Register *nn*, register; **ein Register führen**, keep a register

Registratur *nf*, **1** (department), registry. **2** (storage place), filing cabinet

registrieren *vb*, (enter in record), register

Registrierkasse *nf*, cash register

Regreß *nm* (law), recourse, redress; **Regreßanspruch** *nm*, claim for compensation

regulieren *vb*, **1** (process), control, regulate. **2** (machine), adjust. **3** (bill, claim), settle

Reibung *nf*, friction

reichen *vb*, **1** (distance), extend to, reach. **2** be enough, suffice; **der Konferenzraum reicht nicht für 200 Leute**, the conference room won't be large enough for 200 people

reichlich *adj*, ample, generous

Reichtum *nm*, wealth

Reife *nf* (pers), maturity

Reihe *nf*, **1** (seating, number), row; **man saß in einer Reihe**, people were seated in a row. **2** series; **eine Reihe von Beispielen**, a series of examples. **3** (next), **er ist an der Reihe**, it's his turn

Reihenfertigung *nf*, serial production

Reihenfolge *nf*, order; **in alphabetischer Reihenfolge**, in alphabetical order; **in zahlenmäßiger Reihenfolge**, in numerical order

rein *adj*, **1** pure, plain; **die reine Wahrheit**, the plain truth. **2** (not dirty), clean; **die Hände rein behalten**, keep one's nose clean. **3** (clear, neat), **ins reine schreiben**, write out a fair copy

Reinemachen *nn*, cleaning

Reingewinn *nm*, net profit

reinigen *vb*, clean

Reinigung *nf*, cleaning; **(chemische) Reinigung**, dry cleaning

Reinschrift *nf*, fair copy

reinseiden *adj*, (of) pure silk

Reinvermögen *nn* (fin), net assets

Reise *nf*, journey, trip; **sie ist auf Reisen**, she is away on a trip; **Reiseantritt** *nm*, start of journey; **Reisebüro** *nn*, travel agency; **Reisegenehmigung** *nf*, travel permit; **Reisegepäck** *nn*, luggage; **Reiseleiter(in)** *nm/f*, courier

reisen *vb*, travel

Reisende(r) *nf(m)*, traveller

Reise-; **Reiseroute** *nf*, itinerary; **Reisescheck** *nm*, traveller's cheque; **Reisespesen** *npl*, travelling expenses; **Reiseveranstalter** *nm*, tour operator; **Reiseziel** *nn*, destination

Reißbrett *nn*, drawing board

Reißzwecke *nf*, drawing pin

Reiz *nm*, appeal; **Reiz haben für** (+ acc), appeal to

reizen *vb*, **1** appeal to . . . ; **das reizt mich gar nicht**, that doesn't appeal to me at all. **2** irritate

reizend *adj*, charming

Reklame *nf*, **1** (individual, gen), advertisement, ad. **2** (TV, radio) commercial. **3** (mktg), advertising, publicity; **Reklameartikel** *nm*, free gift; **Reklamebroschüre** *nf*, advertising brochure; **Reklamefeldzug** *nm*, advertising campaign; **Reklameplakat** *nn*, (advertising) poster; **Reklamesendung** *nf*, commercial; **Reklametafel** *nf*, **Reklamewand** *nf*, advertising hoarding

reklamieren *vb*, **1** complain. **2** (bill), query

Rekord *nm*, record; **einen Rekord halten**, hold a record; **Rekordverluste** *nmpl*, record losses

Relevanz *nf*, relevance

Rendite *nf* (fin), yield, return on capital

rentabel *adj*, **1** (fin), profitable; **eine rentable Investition**, a profitable investment. **2** (firm), viable; **das Unternehmen ist nicht rentabel**, the company is not viable

Rentabilität *nf*, **1** (fin), profitability. **2** (of firm), viability

Rente *nf*, **1** (for old age, invalidity), pension. **2** (ins), annuity. **3** (from assets), income. **4** (on stock exchange), fixed-income security

Renten-; **Rentenalter** *nn*, pensionable age; **Rentenanpassung** *nf*, tying of pension to national average wage; **Rentenanspruch** *nm*, right to a pension; **Rentenempfänger(in)** *nm/f*, pensioner; **Rentenfonds** *nm*, pension fund;

Rentenversicherung *nf*, pension scheme

Rentner(in) *nm/f*, pensioner

reorganisieren *vb*, reorganise

Reparatur *nf*, repair

reparaturbedürftig *adj*, in need of repair

Reparaturkosten *npl*, cost of repair

reparieren *vb*, mend, repair

Reportgeschäft *nn* (fin), contango

Repräsentant(in) *nm/f*, representative

Repräsentationswerbung *nf*, prestige advertising

Repräsentativumfrage *nf*, representative survey

repräsentieren *vb*, represent

Reserve *nf*, **1** (gen, fin), reserve; **stille Reserven** (fin), hidden assets, hidden reserves. **2** (money), savings; **Reservefonds** *nm*, reserve fund; **Reservereifen** *nm*, spare tyre; **Reservewährung** *nf*, reserve currency

reservieren *vb* (e.g. seat, room), reserve, book

Reservierung *nf* (of seat, room), reservation

Resonanz *nf* (mktg, sales), response, feedback; **große Resonanz finden**, meet with a good response

Ressort *nn*, department

Rest *nm*, **1** (gen), remainder, rest. **2** (of material), remnant

Restaurierung *nf*, restoration; **„wegen Restaurierung geschlossen"**, "closed for restoration"

Restbetrag *nm* (fin), balance

Restlaufzeit *nf* (fin), remaining term

restlich *adj*, remaining

restlos *adj*, *adv*, complete; completely

Restposten *nm* (comm), remaining stock

Resultat *nn*, result

Retourwaren *npl* (comm), returns

retten *vb*, **1** (gen), rescue, save. **2** (lost goods), recover

Rettung *nf*, **1** (gen), rescue, salvation. **2** (of lost goods), recovery

reüssieren *vb*, succeed

sich revanchieren *vb*, reciprocate

Revision *nf*, **1** (comm), audit. **2** (law), appeal; **Revision einlegen**, appeal (on points of law)

Revisor *nm* (comm), auditor

rezensieren *vb* (a publication), review

Rezept *nn*, **1** (med), prescription. **2** (gen, cooking), recipe

Rezeption *nf*, reception

Rezession *nf*, recession

R-Gespräch *nn* (telec), reverse charge call

richten *vb*, **richten an** (+ acc), address to; **der Brief sollte an den Direktor gerichtet werden**, the letter should be addressed to the Director; **sich richten an** (+ acc), talk/turn to; **bitte richten Sie sich an Frau Schmitz**, please consult Frau Schmitz **sich richten nach** (+ dat); abide by; **sich nach den Vorschriften richten**, abide by/follow the regulations

Richter(in) *nm/f* (law), judge

Richtgeschwindigkeit *nf*, recommended speed

richtig *adj*, *adv*, accurate, correct; accurately, correctly

Richtpreis *nm*, **empfohlener Richtpreis**, recommended price

Richtung *nf*, direction; **die Richtung ändern**, change direction; **in Richtung Bonn fahren**, drive in the direction of Bonn; **eine andere**

Richtung nehmen, turn in a different direction

richtungweisend *adj*, pointing the way (ahead)

Richtwert *nm*, guideline

riesig *adj*, gigantic

Ringordner *nm* (offce), ring-binder

Risiko *nn*, risk; **Risikokapital** *nn*, venture capital; **Risikostreuung** *nf*, diversification

riskant *adj*, risky

riskieren *vb*, risk

Rivale *nm*, **Rivalin** *nf*, rival

Roboter *nm*, robot; **Robotermontage** *nf*, robot assembly

roh *adj*, **1** (uncooked), raw. **2** (unfinished), rough

Roh-; **Rohbau** *nm* (of a building), shell; **Rohbilanz** *nf*, trial balance sheet; **Roheisen** *nn*, pig iron; **Rohentwurf** *nm*, rough draft; **Rohertrag** *nm*, gross proceeds; **Rohfaser** *nf*, raw fibre; **Rohgewicht** *nn*, gross weight; **Rohmaterial** *nn*, raw material; **Rohöl** *nn*, crude oil

Rohr *nn* (techn), pipe

Rohseide *nf*, wild silk

Rohstoff *nm* (primary), commodity, raw material; **Rohstoffindustrie** *nf*, primary industry

Rolle *nf*, role; **das spielt keine Rolle**, it doesn't matter

Rollfeld *nn* (aviat), runway

ROM *nn* (comp), ROM

Rost *nm*, rust

rosten *vb*, rust

rostfrei *adj*, rustproof

Rotation *nf*, rotation

rotieren *vb*, rotate

Route *nf*, route

Routine *nf*, routine; **Routineangelegenheit** *nf*, routine matter

routinemäßig *adj*, *adv*, routine, by way of routine

routiniert *adj*, experienced

rück|erstatten *vb*, refund

Rück-; **Rückerstattung** *nf*, refund; **Rückfahrkarte** *nf*, return ticket; **Rückfahrt** *nf*, return journey; **Rückflug** *nm*, return flight; **Rückforderung** *nf*, clawback; **Rückfrage** *nf*, query; **Rückgabe** *nf*, return; **Rückgang** *nm*, decline, drop

rückgängig machen *vb* (order, contract), cancel

Rückhalt *nm*, support

Rückkauf *nm*, repurchase; **Rückkaufwert** *nm*, surrender value

rückläufig *adj*, **1** (sales), dropping. **2** (trend), downward

Rück-; **Rücknahme** *nf* (goods), taking back; **Rückporto** *nn*, return postage; **Rückschlag** *nm* (in business), setback; **Rückschluß** *nm*, conclusion

Rückseite *nf*, **1** (of book), back. **2** (of building), rear

Rücksendung *nf*, return

Rücksicht *nf*, consideration; **aus Rücksicht auf** (+ acc), out of consideration for

rücksichtslos *adj*, inconsiderate

Rücksprache *nf*, consultation; **nach Rücksprache mit Frau Schultz**, following consultation with Frau Schultz; **Sie sollten Rücksprache mit** (+ dat) **nehmen**, you ought to talk to/consult with

Rückstand *nm*, delay, arrears; **im Rückstand sein**, be behind/in arrears; **mit seinen Zahlungen in Rückstand geraten**, get in arrears

rückständig *adj*, (payment), overdue

Rückstellung *nf*, deferred liability

Rücktransport *nm*, return transport

Rücktritt *nm*, **1** (pers), resignation. **2** (from contract etc), withdrawal

Rücktrittsklausel *nf*, cancellation clause, escape clause

Rückvergütung *nf*, refund

Rückversicherung *nf*, reinsurance

rückwärts *adv*, backwards

Rückweg *nm*, way back

Rückwirkung *nf*, **eine Zahlung mit Rückwirkung vom Mai**, a payment backdated to May

rückzahlbar *adj*, repayable

Rückzahlung *nf*, back payment, payback, rebate, redemption

Rückzahlungsklausel *nf*, payback clause

Rückzahlungswert *nm*, redemption value

Rufnummer *nf* (telec), telephone number

Ruhegehalt *nn*, superannuation

Ruhestand *nm*, retirement; **in den Ruhestand treten**, retire

ruhig *adj*, **1** (still), quiet, **2** (sales), slack

Ruin *nm* (comm), ruin, bankruptcy

ruinieren *vb* (comm), ruin

rund *adv*, roughly; **rund 500 Geschäftsleute**, roughly 500 business people

Rundfahrt *nf*, tour

Rundfunk *nm*, broadcasting, radio; **Rundfunkprogramm** *nn*, radio programme; **Rundfunksender** *nm*, radio station; **Rundfunkübertragung** *nf*, radio broadcast

Rundreise *nf*, tour

Rundschreiben *nn*, circular (letter)

S

S., Seite *nf*, p., page

Sachbearbeiter(in) *nm/f*, clerk (with specified responsibilities)

Sachbeschädigung *nf* (law), damage to property

Sache *nf*, **1** (gen), thing; **eine merkwürdige Sache**, a funny thing. **2** (3-dimensional), object; **die Sachen in diesem Raum**, the objects in this room. **3** (issue, case), matter; **diese Sache muß der Direktor selbst entscheiden**, this is a matter the Director has to decide himself; **nichts zur Sache tun**, be irrelevant

Sachgebiet *nn*, subject area

Sachkenner(in) *nm/f*, expert

Sachkenntnis *nf*, **Sachkunde** *nf*, expertise

sachkundig *adj*, experienced

Sachlage *nf*, situation, state of affairs

sachlich bleiben *vb*, not get carried away, stay objective

Sachmängel *nmpl*, material defects

Sachschaden *nm*, damage to property

Sachverstand *nm*, expertise

Sachverständigenausschuß *nm*, panel of experts

Sachverständigengutachten *nn*, expert's report

Sachwerte *nmpl*, material assets

sagen *vb*, say, tell; **sagen Sie mal, . . .**, tell me . . .; **das kann man wohl sagen!**, you can say that again!

Sagen *nn*, **das Sagen haben**, have the say

Saison *nf*, season; **Saisonarbeiter(in)** *nm/f*, seasonal worker

saisonbedingt *adj*, seasonal; **saisonbedingte Nachfrage** *nf*, seasonal demand; **saisonbedingte Beschäftigung** *nf*, seasonal employment

Saisonbeschäftigung *nf*, seasonal job

Saisongewerbe *nn*, seasonal trade

Saldo *nm* (fin), balance, balance brought down; **per Saldo bezahlen**, pay off the balance in full; **Saldoübertrag** *nm*/**Saldovortrag** *nm* (fin), balance brought/carried forward

Sammelbestellung *nf*, joint/collective order

Sammelladung *nf* (transp), consolidated shipment

sammeln *vb*, collect

Sammelnummer *nf* (telec), private exchange number, switchboard number

Sammelpunkt *nm*, assembly point

sämtliche *adj*, all; **sämtliche Telefonnummern haben gewechselt**, all telephone numbers have changed

sanieren *vb*, **1** (housing), redevelop. **2** (company), put back on its feet, turn round

Sanierungsgebiet *nn*, redevelopment area

Sanierungsmaßnahme *nf*, **1** (of city quarter), redevelopment measure. **2** (of company), rehabilitation measure

sanitär *adj*, sanitary; **sanitäre Anlagen**, sanitary installations

sanktionieren *vb*, sanction

Satellitenfernsehen *nn*, satellite TV

Sattelschlepper *nm* (transp), articulated lorry

sättigen *vb* (market), saturate

Sättigung *nf*, saturation; **Sättigungspunkt** *nm*, saturation point

saturiert *adj*, saturated

Satz *nm*, **1** (complete collection), set. **2** (costs), rate; **der übliche Satz**, the going rate; **der volle Satz**, the full rate

Satzung *nf*, articles of association/incorporation

satzungsgemäß *adj*, constitutional, according to the rules

sauber *adj*, clean

säubern *vb*, clean

sauer *adj*, **1** (milk), sour. **2** (wine, rain), acid. **3** (gherkin, herring), pickled

Sauerstoff *nm*, oxygen

saugen *vb*, suck

Säulendiagramm *nn*, bar chart

Säure *nf*, acid

S-Bahn *nf*, suburban train; **S-Bahn-Netz** *nn*, suburban train network

Scanner *nm* (med, comp), scanner

Schablone *nf*, stencil

schachern um (+ acc) *vb*, haggle over

Schachtel *nf*, box

schade! (interjection), what a pity!

Schaden *nm*, damage, harm; **Schaden aufweisen**, be defective; **Schaden verursachen**, cause damage/harm

schaden *vb*, damage, harm

Schadensbegrenzung *nf*, damage limitation

Schadensersatz *nm*, compensation, damages; **Schadensersatzanspruch** *nm*, claim for compensation

schadensersatzpflichtig *adj*, liable for compensation

Schadensfall *nm*, **im Schadensfall**, in the event of claim

Schadensprüfung *nf*, damage survey

schadhaft *adj*, faulty, defective

schädigen *vb*, damage, harm

schädlich *adj*, damaging, harmful

Schadstoff *nm*, harmful substance

schadstoffarm *adj*, **schadstoffarm sein**, contain a low level of harmful substances

Schadstoff-; **Schadstoffbelastung** *nf*, pollution; **Schadstoffgehalt** *nm*, level of harmful substances; **Schadstoffkonzentration** *nf*, concentration of harmful substances

schaffen *vb* (gen), achieve

Schall *nm*, sound; **Schalldämpfer** *nm* (car), silencer

schalldicht *adj*, soundproof

Schallplatte *nf*, record

Schaltbrett *nn* (techn), switchboard, control panel

Schalter *nm*, **1** (in post office etc), counter. **2** (at station), ticket office. **3** (electr), switch; **Schalterstunden** *nfpl*, hours of business

Schaltkreis *nm* (techn), (switching) circuit

scharf *adj* (competition), fierce, tough

schätzen *vb*, **1** (value), estimate, assess. **2** regard highly, value; **wir schätzen ihn als Kollegen sehr**, we value him highly as a colleague

Schatzkanzler *nm*, Chancellor of the Exchequer

Schätzpreis *nm*, valuation price

Schätzung *nf*, estimate

schätzungsweise *adv*, approximately

Schätzwert *nm*, estimated value

Schaubild *nn*, diagram

Schaufenster *nn*, shop window; **Schaufensterbummel** *nm*, window shopping; **Schaufensterdekoration** *nf*, window display

Schaukasten *nm*, display case, showcase

Schaupackung *nf*, display pack/dummy pack

Scheck *nm*, cheque; **einen Scheck ausstellen**, write out a cheque; **bestätigter Scheck**, certified cheque; **einen Scheck einlösen**, cash a cheque; **einen Scheck sperren**, put a stop on a cheque; **einen Scheck stornieren**, cancel a cheque; **einen Scheck unterschreiben**, sign a cheque; **per Scheck bezahlen**, pay by cheque; **ungedeckter Scheck**, dud cheque; **Scheckfälschung** *nf*, cheque forgery; **Scheckheft** *nn*, cheque book; **Scheckkarte** *nf*, cheque card

Schein *nm*, **1** (money), (bank)note. **2** (formal confirmation), certificate. **3** (travel), ticket. **4** appearance

Scheinfirma *nf*, fictitious firm

scheitern *vb*, **1** (efforts), fail. **2** (negotiations), break down. **3** (plan), fall through

Schema *nn*, pattern

schenken *vb*, make a present, give as a present; **keinen Glauben schenken**, give no credence to; **jemandem sein Vertrauen schenken**, trust someone

Schenkung *nf* (law), gift

Schere *nf* (offce), scissors

scheuen *vb* (avoid), spare; **weder Mühe noch Kosten scheuen**, spare neither trouble nor expense

Schicht *nf*, **1** (gen), layer; (thin layer), film. **2** (of paint), coat. **3** (of population), section. **4** (of work), shift; **Schicht arbeiten**, work shifts; **Schichtarbeit** *nf*, shift-work; **Schichtarbeiter(in)** *nm/f*, shift-worker

schichten *vb* (wood, books), stack

Schicht-; Schichtleiter(in) *nm/f*, shift manager(ess); **Schichtlohn** *nm*, shift rates; **Schichtstoff** *nm*, laminate; **Schichtwechsel** *nm*, change of shifts

schick *adj*, *adv*, elegant, smart; elegantly, smartly

schicken *vb*, **1** (letters), send, mail. **2** (goods), dispatch

Schicksal *nn*, fate, destiny

Schieber *nm*, black marketeer

Schiebung *nf*, fiddle, shady deal

Schiedsgericht *nn*, industrial tribunal

Schiedsrichter *nm*, arbitrator

schief|gehen *vb*, go wrong

Schiene *nf*, rail

Schienenbus *nm*, rail bus

Schienennetz *nn*, rail network

Schiff *nn*, boat, ship; **ab Schiff** (imp exp), ex ship, EXS, Exs

Schiffahrt *nf*, shipping

Schiffahrtsgesellschaft *nf*, shipping company

Schiffahrtslinie *nf*, shipping route

schiffbar *adj*, navigable

Schiffbau *nm*, shipbuilding

schiffbrüchig *adj*, shipwrecked

Schiffs-; Schiffsbesatzung *nf*, ship's company; **Schiffslieferant** *nm*, chandler; **Schiffspapiere** *nnpl*, ship's papers

Schild *nn*, **1** (gen, traffic), sign. **2** (price), ticket. **3** (for firm), plate

schildern *vb*, describe

Schilderung *nf*, description

Schlafwagen *nm* (on train), sleeper; **Schlafwagenabteil** *nn*, sleeping compartment

Schlagbaum *nm* (at customs), barrier

schlagen *vb*, beat; **Profit aus** (+ dat) **schlagen**, make a profit from

schlagend *adj*, **1** (observation, comparison), apt, appropriate. **2** (proof), striking, convincing

Schlagzeile *nf*, headline; **Schlagzeilen machen**, hit the headlines

Schlange *nf* (of people), queue; **Schlange stehen**, queue

schlau *adj*, clever, shrewd

schlecht *adj*, *adv*, **1** (gen), bad; badly; **das können wir uns schlecht leisten**, we can ill afford it. **2** poor; **in schlechtem Zustand**, in a poor condition

schleichen *vb*, creep; **schleichende Inflation**, creeping inflation

Schleichhandel *nm*, illicit trading

schleppen *vb*, **1** (heavy burden), lug. **2** (car, ship), tow

schleppend voran|gehen *vb*, drag on

Schleuderpreis *nm*, give-away price

Schleuse *nf* (for ships), lock

schlicht *adj*, *adv*, plain, simple; simply; **die schlichte Wahrheit**, the plain truth; **das ist schlicht falsch**, that is simply wrong

schlichten *vb* (in industry), arbitrate

Schlichter *nm* (in industry), arbitrator

Schlichtung *nf* (in industry), arbitration

Schlichtungs-; Schlichtungskommission *nf*, arbitration tribunal; **Schlichtungsverhandlungen** *nfpl*, arbitration negotiations; **Schlichtungsversuch** *nm*, attempt at arbitration

schließen *vb*, shut, close; **„montags geschlossen"**, "closed on Mondays"; **schließen aus** (+ dat) conclude from

Schließfach *nn*, **1** (at station), left-luggage locker. **2** (at post office), post-office box, PO box. **3** (in bank), safe-deposit box

schließlich *adv*, finally, eventually

Schließung *nf*, **1** (of company), closure. **2** (of meeting), closing. **3** (of business), closing(-time)

Schließungstag *nm*, closing date

schlimm *adj*, serious, bad; **ist es schlimm?** is it serious/bad?

schlimmstenfalls *adv*, at (the) worst

Schlitz *nm* (in machine), slot

Schloß *nn*, (door) lock

Schluß *nm*, **1** (gen), end. **2** (end of speech), conclusion; **Schlußabrechnung** *nf*, final statement, final account; **Schlußbestand** *nm*, closing stock; **Schlußbilanz** *nf*, final balance (sheet)

Schlüssel *nm*, **1** (gen), key. **2** (for distribution), ratio (of distribution), **Schlüsselindustrie** *nf*, basic industry

schlußfolgern *vb*, conclude; **aus Ihrer Antwort müssen wir schlußfolgern, daß . . .**, from your answer we have to conclude that . . .

Schluß-; **Schlußformel** *nf*, **1** (corr), complimentary close. **2** (in contract), final clause; **Schlußkurs** *nm*, **Schlußnotierung** *nf* (fin), closing price; **Schlußsitzung** *nf*, closing session; **Schlußverkauf** *nm*, end-of-season sale, the sales

schmieren *vb*, **1** (with money), bribe. **2** (car), lubricate

Schmiergeld *nn*, bribe

schmutzig *adj*, dirty

Schmutzkampagne *nf*, smear campaign

Schnäppchen *nn*, bargain; **ein Schnäppchen machen**, get a bargain

Schneeballeffekt *nm*, snowball effect

Schneeballsystem *nn* (comm), pyramid selling

schneiden *vb*, cut

schnell *adj*, *adv*, quick; quickly, fast; **schnell machen**, hurry (up)

Schnellbahn *nf*, **S-Bahn** *nf*, (high-speed) suburban train

Schnelle *nf*, rush; **das kann man nicht auf die Schnelle machen** that can't be done in a rush

Schnellgericht *nn*, convenience food

Schnelligkeit *nf*, speed

Schnellreinigung *nf*, express cleaning service

schnellstens *adv*, as quickly as possible

Schnellzug *nm*, fast train; **Schnellzugzuschlag** *nm*, supplementary charge for travel on fast train

Schock *nm*, shock

schockieren *vb*, shock, scandalise

schon *adv*, already; **waren Sie schon einmal dort?**, have you been there (before)?; **ich bin schon drei Jahre hier in München**, I have been here in Munich for three years (now); **die Sache ist schon längst erledigt**, the matter was dealt with ages ago; **schon die Tatsache, daß . . .**, the very fact that . . .; **was sind schon heute 100 Mark?**, 100 mark goes nowhere these days; **wenn schon!**, so what?; **danke, es geht schon**, thanks, I'll manage

schön *adj*, beautiful, nice; **alles ist in schönster Ordnung**, everything is OK; **haben Sie einen schönen Urlaub gehabt?**, did you have a nice holiday?, **schönes Wochenende!**, have a good weekend!

Schonfrist *nf*, period of grace

Schongang *nm* (in washing machine), gentle action wash

schöpferisch *adj*, creative

schräg *adv*, **1** at an angle; **schräg gegenüber**, diagonally opposite. **2** (print), **schräg gedruckt**, in italics

Schrägstrich *nm*, oblique

Schrank *nm*, **1** (for clothes), wardrobe. **2** (offce), cabinet

Schranke *nf*, **1** (obstacle), barrier. **2** limit

Schraube *nf*, **1** screw. **2** bolt

schrauben *vb*, screw

Schreckensbotschaft *nf*, **Schreckensnachricht** *nf*, terrible (piece of) news

schrecklich *adj*, *adv*, terrible; terribly

Schreib-; **Schreibarbeiten** *nfpl*, clerical work, paperwork; **Schreibbedarf** *nm*, writing materials, stationery; **Schreibdienst** *nm*, **zentraler Schreibdienst**, typing pool

Schreiben *nn* (comm corr), letter; **wir danken Ihnen für Ihr Schreiben vom 5.6.1994**, thank you for your letter of 5.6.1994

schreiben *vb*, **1** write; **bitte schreiben Sie uns nach Ihrer Rückkehr**, please write to us on your return. **2** spell; **wie schreiben Sie Ihren Namen?**, how do you spell your name?

Schreib-; **Schreibfehler** *nm*, clerical error; **Schreibkraft** *nf* (pers), (copy) typist; **Schreibkräfte** *nfpl*, clerical staff; **es fehlt uns an wirklich guten Schreibkräften**, we are short of really qualified clerical staff; **Schreibmaschine** *nf*, typewriter; **mit der Schreibmaschine schreiben**, type; **Schreibmaschinepapier** *nn* typing paper; **Schreibtisch** *nm*, desk; **Schreibtischjob** *nm*, office job; **Schreibwaren** *nfpl*, stationery

Schrift *nf*, (hand-)writing; **Schriftdeutsch** *nn*, written German; **Schriftform** *nf* (law), **dieser Vertrag erfordert die Schriftform**, this contract must be drawn up in writing; **Schriftführer(in)** *nm/f*, secretary, clerk; **Schriftleiter(in)** *nm/f*, editor

schriftlich *adj*, *adv*, written, in writing; **eine schriftliche Prüfung**, a written examination; **bitte legen Sie mir das schriftlich vor**, please submit this to me in writing

Schriftstück *nn*, document

Schriftverkehr *nm*, correspondence; **wir stehen im Schriftverkehr**, we are in correspondence

Schritt *nm*, step; **Schritte ergreifen**, take steps; **Schritt halten mit** (+ dat), keep up with

schrittweise *adj*, *adv*, gradual; gradually; step by step; **schrittweise einführen**, phase in

Schrott *nm*, scrap metal

schrottreif *adj*, ready for the scrap heap

Schrottwert *nm*, scrap value

schrumpfen *vb*, shrink

schrumpfend *adj*, **schrumpfende Erträge** *nmpl*, diminishing returns; **ein schrumpfender Markt**, a dwindling market; **eine schrumpfende Industrie**, a declining industry

Schrumpfpackung *nf*, shrinkwrapping

Schublade *nf*, drawer

schubweise *adv*, in batches

Schuld *nf*, **1** (gen), blame; **die Schuld haben an** (+ dat), be to blame for. **2** (law), guilt. **3** (fin), debt

schuld haben/sein *vb*, be to blame; **wir sind nicht schuld daran, daß . . .**, it's not our fault that . . .

Schulden *nfpl*, debts; **aufgenommene Schulden**, borrowings; **fällige Schulden**, debts due; **kurzfristige Schulden**, short-term debts; **Schulden begleichen**, settle a debt; **Schulden eintreiben**, collect a debt; **Schulden haben**, be in debt; **Schulden machen**, run up debts; **Schulden tilgen**, pay off a debt

schulden *vb*, owe

schuldig *adj*, **1** (gen), to blame. **2** (law), guilty

Schuldner(in) *nm/f*, debtor; **säumiger Schuldner**, defaulter

Schuldschein *nm*, **1** (bank), bond. **2** (personal), IOU, promissory note

Schuldverschreibung *nf* (fin), debenture bond

Schulung *nf*, training

Schulungskurs *nm*, training course

schütteln *vb*, shake; **den Kopf schütteln**, shake one's head

Schutz *nm*, protection, security

schützen *vb*, safeguard, protect

Schutz-; **Schutzmaßnahme** *nf*, precautionary measure; **Schutzschicht** *nf*, protective layer; **Schutzumschlag** *nm*, dust jacket; **Schutzzoll** *nm*, protective tariff

schwach *adj*, *adv*, **1** (gen), weak; weakly. **2** (comm); **schwache Nachfrage**, slack demand. **3 die Ausstellung war nur schwach besucht**, the exhibition was poorly attended

Schwäche *nf*, weakness

schwächen *vb*, weaken

schwanken *vb* (comm), fluctuate, vary; **die Preise begannen zu schwanken**, prices began to fluctuate

schwankend *adj*, fluctuating, unstable, variable

Schwankung *nf* (comm), fluctuation

schwarz *adj*, *adv*, black, illegal; illegally; **der schwarze Markt**, the black market; **schwarz über die Grenze gehen**, cross the border illegally

Schwarzarbeit *nf*, moonlighting

Schwarzes Brett *nn*, noticeboard

Schwarz-; **Schwarzfahrer** *nm*, **1** (on public transp), fare dodger. **2** (in motorcar), driver without a licence; **Schwarzhandel** *nm* (activity), marketeering; **Schwarzmarkt** *nm*, black market; **Schwarzmarktpreis** *nm*, black-market price

schwarz|sehen *vb*, be pessimistic about; **da sehe ich schwarz!**, I am not very optimistic there

schwarzweiß *adj*, black-and-white

schwebend *adj* (comm), **1** (business), pending. **2** (debts), floating

Schwefel *nm*, sulphur; **Schwefeldioxid** *nn*, sulphur dioxide

schweigen *vb*, be silent, not say anything

Schwellenpreis *nm*, threshold price

schwer *adj*, *adv*, **1** heavy; heavily. **2** difficult; with difficulty

Schwer-; **Schwerfahrzeug** *nn*, heavy goods vehicle; **Schwergut** *nn*, deadweight cargo; **Schwerindustrie** *nf*, heavy industry; **Schwermaschinen** *nfpl*, heavy equipment, heavy machinery; **Schwermetall** *nn*, heavy metal; **Schwerpunkt** *nm*, focus; **Schwerpunktindustrie** *nf*, main industry

schwerverständlich *adj*, *adv*, difficult to understand

schwerwiegend *adj*, serious; **ein schwerwiegender Fehler**, a serious mistake

Schwesterfirma *nf*, sister company, associate(d) company

schwierig *adj*, difficult

Schwierigkeiten *nfpl*, difficulties, trouble; **in Schwierigkeiten geraten/kommen**, get into difficulty; **Schwierigkeiten machen**, make trouble

Schwindel *nm*, swindle, fraud; **die Reklame ist reiner Schwindel**, the advertisement is a complete swindle/fraud; **Schwindelfirma** *nf*, bogus firm; **Schwindelgeschäft** *nn*, fraudulent transaction

Schwindler *nm* (fraud), con-man

schwören *vb* (law), swear; **ich hätte schwören können, daß . . .**, I could have sworn that . . .

Schwund *nm*, **1** (of material), shrinkage. **2** (techn), wastage

Schwung *nm*, **in Schwung bringen**, get things going; **in Schwung kommen**, gather momentum

Schwungkraft *nf*, centrifugal force

schwungvoll *adj* (speech), lively

See *nm*, lake

See *nf*, sea; **auf hoher See**, on the high seas; **Seerecht** *nn* (law), maritime law; **Seereise** *nf*, voyage; **See(transport)versicherung** *nf*, marine insurance; **Seeweg** *nm*, **auf dem Seeweg**, by sea (mail)

Segmentierung *nf*, segmentation

sehen *vb*, **1** (gen), see. **2** meet; **wir haben uns zuletzt auf der Leipziger Messe gesehen**, we last met at the Leipzig Fair. **3 sich sehen lassen, die neue Marke läßt sich sehen**, the new brand is something to be proud of. **4 sich sehen lassen bei** (+ dat), come to see; **lassen Sie sich bald wieder hier bei Siemens sehen!**, come to see us again soon here at Siemens

sehenswert *adj*, worth seeing

sehr *adv*, very; **Sehr geehrte(r) . . .** (corr, formal), Dear . . .

seit (+ dat), *prep*, **1** (point in time), since; **seit Montag**, since Monday. **2** (period), for; **seit 3 Monaten**, for three months

Sekretär(in) *nm/f*, secretary

Sekretariat *nn* (of company), office

Sektor *nm*, sector; **staatlicher Sektor**, public sector

sekundär *adj*, secondary

selbständig *adj*, **1** (gen), independent. **2** self-employed

Selbständige(r) *nf/m*, **1** independent businesswoman/businessman. **2** self-employed person

Selbstbedienung *nf*, self-service

selbstfinanzierend *adj*, self-financing

Selbst-; **Selbstkosten** *npl* (fin), prime costs; **Selbstkostenpreis** *nm*, **zum Selbstkostenpreis**, at cost; **Selbstversicherung** *nf* personal insurance; **Selbstversorgung** *nf* (tourism), self-catering; **Selbstverwaltung** *nf*, self-regulation; **Selbstwählferndienst** *nm* (telec), automatic dialling service, subscriber trunk dialling

selten *adv*, seldom

Seltenheitswert *nm*, rarity value

senden *vb*, **1** (mail), send. **2** (comm), dispatch. **3** (TV, radio), transmit

Sender *nm* (telec), transmitter

Sendezeit *nf* (TV, radio), slot

Sendung *nf*, **1** (gen), mail, post. **2** (of goods), consignment, shipment. **3** (on TV, radio), programme

senken *vb* (price), lower, reduce

senkrecht *adj*, *adv*, vertical; vertically

Senkrechtstarter *nm* (pers) high-flyer, whizz kid

Senkung *nf* (in price), reduction

separat *adj*, **1** (gen), separate. **2** (accommodation), self-contained

Serie *nf*, batch, series; **in Serie gehen**, go into production; **in Serie herstellen**, mass-produce

seriell *adj*, *adv*, **serieller Anschluß** *nm* (comp), serial connector; **seriell herstellen**, mass-produce

Serienfabrikation *nf*, **Serienfertigung** *nf*, **Serienherstellung** *nf*, batch production

serienmäßig *adj*, *adv*; **das wird serienmäßig eingebaut**, that's a standard fitting

Seriennummer *nf*, batch number, serial number

Serienproduktion *nf*, batch production

serienreif *adj* (cars), ready to go into production

serienweise herstellen *vb*, mass-produce

seriös *adj*, **1** (firm), reputable. **2** (person), respectable

setzen *vb*, put, set; **setzen Sie das mit auf die Rechnung**, put it on the bill; **das Unternehmen hat sich ein festes Ziel gesetzt**, the company has set itself a firm target

sicher *adj*, **1** (gen), sure, certain. **2** safe, secure; **eine sichere Investition**, a safe/secure investment

Sicherheit *nf*, **1** certainty; **ich kann das mit einiger Sicherheit sagen**, I can say that with some certainty. **2** safety; **die öffentliche Sicherheit**, public safety. **3** (comm, labour market), security, collateral; **Sicherheit des Arbeitsplatzes**, job security

Sicherheitsbestimmungen *nfpl*, safety regulations

sicherheitshalber *adv*, for safety

Sicherheits-; **Sicherheitsmarge** *nf*, safety margin; **Sicherheitsmaßnahme** *nf*, safety precaution; **Sicherheitsnormen** *nfpl*, safety standards

sicherlich *adv*, certainly

sicher|stellen *vb*, **1** make sure; **bitte stellen Sie sicher, daß der Computer ausgeschaltet ist**, please make sure the computer is turned off. **2** (customs), impound

Sicht *nf*, **1** (weather), visibility. **2 auf lange Sicht**, in the long term. **3** (comm), sight; **nach Sicht**, after sight

sichtbar *adj*, *adv*, visible; visibly

Sichttratte *nf*, **Sichtwechsel** *nm*, sight draft

Siegel *nn* (corr), seal

siezen *vb*, address as 'Sie'

Signal *nn*(corr), signal

signalisieren *vb*, signal

sinken *vb* (price), drop, fall; **im letzten Jahr sind die Preise um 8 Prozent gesunken**, last year prices dropped by 8 per cent

Sinn *nm*, **1** mind; **was haben Sie im Sinn?**, what have you in mind? **2** interest; **das ist nicht im Sinne unserer Kunden**, this is not in the interest of our customers. **3** point; **das hat keinen Sinn**, there is no point

Sinnesänderung *nf*, change of mind

sinnlos *adj*, pointless

Sitz *nm* (company), headquarters

sitzen|lassen *vb* (abandon), leave in the lurch

Sitzordnung *nf*, seating plan

Sitzung *nf*, **1** (conference), meeting. **2** (court), session; **eine Sitzung eröffnen**, open a meeting; **eine Sitzung leiten**, chair/conduct a meeting; **die Sitzung ist geschlossen**, the meeting is closed. **3** (of parliament), sitting

Sitzungs-; **Sitzungsbericht** *nm*, minutes; **Sitzungsort** *nm*, venue; **Sitzungsperiode** *nf* (of parliament), session; **Sitzungssaal** *nm*, boardroom; **Sitzungszimmer** *nn*, conference room

Skala *nf*, scale

sobald *conj*, as soon as

soeben *adv*, just (today/this moment); **wir hören soeben, daß . . .**, we have just learnt that . . .

sofort *adv*, immediately, right away

sofortig *adj*, immediate, instant; **wir bitten um eine sofortige Antwort**, we would ask for an instant reply

Sofortliquidität *nf*, spot cash

Software *nf* (comp), software

solange *conj*, as/so long as

solidarisch *adj*, **sich mit** (+ dat) **solidarisch erklären**, declare one's solidarity with

Soll *nn*, **1** (fin), debit, debit side; **Soll und Haben**, debit and credit. **2** (comm), target; **wir haben unser Soll erfüllt**, we have achieved our target; **Sollbuchung** *nf*, debit entry; **Sollsaldo** *nm*, debit balance; **Sollseite** *nf*, debit side; **Sollzinsen** *nmpl*, interest charges

Solvenz *nf* (fin), solvency

somit *adv*, consequently

Sommer *nm*, summer; **(im) nächsten Sommer**, next summer; **Sommerferien** *npl*, summer holidays; **Sommerkleidung** *nf*, summer clothing; **Sommersaison** *nf*, summer season; **Sommerurlaub** *nm*, summer leave; **Sommerzeit** *nf*, Summer Time

Sonder-; **Sonderanfertigung** *nf*, special model; **das ist eine Sonderanfertigung**, this has been made specially; **Sonderangebot** *nn*, special offer; **Sonderangebotsabteilung** *nf*, budget department; **Sonderangebotsstand** *nm*, bargain counter; **Sonderausführung** *nf* (car), custom-built model; **Sonderbedingungen** *nfpl*, special requirements; **Sonderfall** *nm*, special case, exception; **Sondergenehmigung** *nf*, **1** (act), special permission. **2** (paper), special permit; **Sondergewinnsteuer** *nf*, windfall tax; **Sondermarke** *nf* (post), special stamp; **Sondernummer** *nf* (of journal), special issue; **Sonderpreis** *nm*, bargain price; **Sonderschicht** *nf*, special shift; **Sondersitzung** *nf* (of company), special meeting; **Sonderzubehör** *nn*, optional extras

sondieren *vb*, explore, sound out

Sondierungsgespräch *nn*, exploratory discussion

Sonnenkraftwerk *nn*, solar power station

Sonn- und Feiertage *nmpl*, Sundays and public holidays

sonst *adv*, **genau wie sonst**, the same as usual; **ich denke, er ruft mich an; sonst muß ich ihn anrufen**, I think he'll ring me, otherwise I'll have to ring him; **wenn Sie sonst noch Fragen haben, . . .**, any further queries?; **wo waren Sie sonst noch?**, where else did you go?; **war der Absatz sonst auch so schlecht?**, have sales always been so poor?

sonstwie *adv*, in some other way

Sorge *nf*, concern, worry; **wir beobachten diese Entwicklung mit Sorge**, we view these developments with concern; **sich Sorge machen um** (+ acc), be concerned about, worry about; **machen Sie sich deshalb keine Sorgen**, don't worry about it; **Herr Braun wird dafür Sorge tragen, daß . . .**, Herr Braun wil see to it that . . .

Sorgfalt *nf*, care; **mit großer Sorgfalt vorgehen**, proceed with great care

sorgfältig *adj*, *adv*, careful; close; carefully, closely; **die Sache muß sorgfältig geprüft werden**, the matter needs to be studied closely

Sorte *nf*, **1** (goods), variety, type. **2** (quality), grade

sortieren *vb*, **1** (gen), sort, sort out. **2** (comp), sort

Sortiermaschine *nf*, sorting machine, sorter

Sortiment *nn* (of goods), product line, range

Sortimentsbuchhandlung *nf*, retail bookshop

Sortimentserweiterung *nf*, product diversification

soundso *adv*, such and such; **soundso lange**, for such and such a time; **das soundso machen**, do it in such and such a way

soviel/soweit *conj*, as far as

sowieso *adv*, anyway; **ich bleibe sowieso noch eine Nacht**, I am staying on another night anyway

sozial *adj*, *adv*, social; socially

Sozial-; **Sozialhilfe** *nf*, supplementary benefit; income support; welfare; **Sozialleistungen** *nfpl*, employers' contribution; **Sozialstaat** *nm*, welfare state; **Sozialversicherung** *nf*, National Insurance; **Sozialversicherungsbeiträge** *nmpl*, National Insurance contributions

sozusagen *adv*, as it were

Spalte *nf* (of text), column

Spannungsregler *nm* (electr), voltage regulator

Spar- (fin); **Sparbrief** *nm*, savings certificate; **Sparbuch** *nn*, savings book; **Spareinlage** *nf*, savings deposit

sparen *vb* (gen), save

Spar-; **Sparguthaben** *nn*, **Sparkonto** *nn*, savings account; **Sparmaßnahme** *nf*, economy measure; **Sparpackung** *nf*, economy pack/size; **Sparpolitik** *nf*, cost-cutting policy; **Sparpreis** *nm*, economy price

sparsam *adj*, *adv*, economical; economically

Spartarif *nm*, **zum Spartarif einkaufen**, shop at discount prices

Sparte *nf* (comm), line of business

Sparzins *nm*, interest (on savings account)

spät *adj*, *adv*, late; **es tut mir leid, daß ich zu spät komme**, sorry I am late

später *adj*, *adv*, later; **an später denken**, think of the future

spätestens *adv*, at the latest; **bis in spätestens einer Woche**, by next week at the latest

Spätschaden *nm*, long-term damage

Spätschicht *nf*, late shift

Spediteur *nm*, road haulier, haulage contractor, shipper

Spedition *nf*, carrier, haulage firm, shipping company

Speditionskosten *npl*, haulage, haulage costs

Speicher *nm*, **1** (building), storehouse. **2** (comp), memory

Speicherfunktion *nf* (comp), memory function

speichern *vb*, **1** (goods), store. **2** (comp), save

Speicherung *nf*, storage

Speicherverwaltung *nf* (comp), memory management

Spekulant(in) *nm/f* (gen, fin), speculator

Spekulation *nf* (gen, fin), speculation

Spekulations- (fin); **Spekulationsaktie** *nf*, speculative share; **Spekulationsgewinn** *nm*, speculative gains; **Spekulationsobjekt** *nn*, object of speculation

spekulieren *vb* (gen, fin), speculate

Spende *nf*, donation, contribution

Spendenkonto *nn* (fin), donations account

Sperre *nf* (comm), embargo

sperren *vb*, **1** (road, harbour), close. **2** (wage, account), stop. **3** (imp/exp), ban. **4** (electr, telec), cut off

sperrig *adj*, bulky

Sperr-; **Sperrklausel** *nf*, exclusion clause; **Sperrkonto** *nn*, blocked account; **Sperrmüll** *nm*, bulky refuse; **Sperrzoll** *nm*, prohibitive tariff

Spesen *npl* (fin), expenses

spesenfrei *adv*, free of charge

Spesenkonto *nn*, expense account

Spezial- *adj*, special(ist); **Spezialausbildung** *nf*, specialised training; **Spezialausführung** *nf*, special model; **Spezialfall** *nm*, special case; **Spezialgeschäft** *nn*, specialist shop

sich spezialisieren auf (+ acc) *vb*, specialise in

Spezialität *nf*, speciality

Spiegel *nm*, mirror; **im Spiegel der Öffentlichkeit**, as seen by the public

Spielautomat *nm*, fruit machine, one-armed bandit

spielen lassen *vb*, bring to bear; **seine Beziehungen spielen lassen**, bring one's connections to bear

Spirale *nf*, spiral

Spirituosen *npl*, spirits

spitz *adj*, pointed

Spitze *nf*, **1** (thin end), point. **2** (highest level of achievement), peak. **3** (leadership), head, top; **er wurde an die Spitze des Unternehmens gestellt**, he was put at the head of the company

Spitzen-; **Spitzenbedarfszeit** *nf*, time of peak demand; **Spitzenbelastung** *nf*, peak (load); **Spitzenerzeugnis** *nn*, top(-quality) product; **Spitzenklasse** *nf*, top class; **Spitzenleistung** *nf*, top performance; **Spitzenposition** *nf*, leading position, top position; **Spitzenqualität** *nf*, top quality; **Spitzenreiter** *nm*, leader; **Spitzenumsätze** *nmpl*, record sales; **Spitzenverkehrszeit** *nf*, peak period; **Spitzenwert** *nm*, peak

sponsern *vb*, sponsor

Sponsor(in) *nm/f*, sponsor; **als Sponsor finanzieren**, sponsor

Sponsoring *nn*, sponsorship

spontan *adj*, *adv*, spontaneous, on impulse

Spontankäufer(in) *nm/f*, impulse buyer

Sportausrüstung *nf*, sports equipment

Sportzentrum *nn*, sports centre

Spottpreis *nm*, bargain price

Sprache *nf*, language; **etwas zur Sprache bringen**, raise an issue

Sprachkenntnisse *nfpl*, linguistic knowledge

Sprachkurs *nm*, language course

Spray *nm*, spray

sprechen *vb*, speak, chat, have a word, talk; **kann ich Sie kurz sprechen?**, can I have a word with you?; **ich möchte gern Frau Sauer sprechen**, could I speak to Frau Sauer?; **mit jemandem sprechen**, chat/talk to someone;

mit wem spreche ich? (telec), who is speaking please?; **sprechen Sie Englisch?**, do you speak English?; **für Sie bin ich jederzeit zu sprechen**, I am always available/at your disposal (to talk to you)

Sprecher(in) *nm/f*, **1** (gen), speaker. **2** (for company), spokesperson, spokesman, spokeswoman

spritzen *vb*, **1** (with can), spray. **2** (med), inject

spruchreif *adj*, **die Sache ist noch nicht spruchreif**, the matter is not yet decided (and it is therefore too early to say more about it)

Sprünge *nmpl*, **das Unternehmen kann keine großen Sprünge machen**, the firm has to watch its expenditure very carefully

sprunghaft *adj*, *adv* (rise), sharp; sharply; **sprunghaft ansteigen**, rise sharply

spurlos *adv*, without trace

SSV, **Sommerschlußverkauf** *nm*, summer sales

staatlich *adj*, *adv*, state; (by the) state/government; **staatlicher Besitz** *nm*, state/state-owned property; **staatliche Unterstützung** *nf*, state aid, state subsidy; **staatlich anerkannt**, state approved, registered; **staatlich gefördert**, state/government sponsored; **staatlich gelenkt**, government regulated; **staatlich geprüft**, state certified; **staatlich subventioniert**, state subsidised

Staats-; **Staatsabgaben** *nfpl*, taxes; **Staatsangehörige(r)** *nf/m*, national; **Staatsangehörigkeit** *nf*, nationality; **Staatsanleihen** *nfpl*, government bonds; **Staatsanwaltschaft** *nf*, public prosecution service; **Staatsausgaben** *nfpl*, public spending; **Staatsbesitz** *nm*, state property; **Staatsbetrieb** *nm*, state enterprise; **Staatsbürger(in)** *nm/f*, citizen; **Staatsdienst** *nm*, the civil service

staatseigen *adj*, state-owned

Staats-; **Staatsfeiertag** *nm*, national holiday; **Staatsfinanzen** *nfpl*, public finance; **Staatshaushalt** *nm*, the budget; **Staatspapiere** *nnpl*, gilt-edged securities; **Staatsverschuldung** *nf*, national debt; **Staatsvertrag** *nm*, treaty

stabil *adj*, stable

stabilisieren *vb*, stabilise

Stadium *nn*, stage; **in diesem Stadium der Entwicklung**, at this stage of development

Stadt *nf*, town; city; **Stadtbahn** *nf*, **S-Bahn** *nf*, suburban train

städtisch *adj*, **1** (gen), urban. **2** (referring to one particular town), municipal; **die städtische Verwaltung**, the municipal administration

staffeln *vb*, stagger; **gestaffelt**, on a sliding scale

stagnieren *vb*, stagnate

Stagnierung *nf*, stagnation

Stahl *nm*, steel; **Stahlbeton** *nm*, reinforced concrete; **Stahlindustrie** *nf*, steel industry; **Stahlkassette** *nf*, strongbox; **Stahlwerk** *nn*, steel works

Stamm-; **Stammaktie** *nf*, ordinary share; **Stammaktionär** *nm* (fin), ordinary shareholder; **Stammbelegschaft** *nf*, permanent/regular workforce; **Stammdaten** *npl* (comp), master data; **Stammgesellschaft** *nf*, parent company; **Stammhaus** *nn* (comm), parent company; **Stammkapital** *nn* (fin), ordinary share capital; **Stammkundschaft** *nf*, regular clients/customers, regulars

Stand *nm*, **1** (gen), state, situation; **der gegenwärtige Stand**, the current situation. **2** (fin, of exchange rate), level. **3** (at exhibition), stand. **4 auf den neusten Stand bringen**, update; **auf dem neusten Stand sein**, be up-to-date.

standardisieren *vb*, standardise

Standesorganisation *nf*, professional association

ständig *adj*, *adv*, **1** permanent; **ein ständiges Problem**, a permanent problem. **2 ein ständiges Mitglied**, a full member. **3 ein ständiges Einkommen haben**, have a regular income. **4** (without a break), constant; constantly; continually

Standort *nm*, location; **Standort Deutschland**, Germany as industrial location; **seinen Standort haben in** (+ dat), be based in

Standpunkt *nm*, opinion, (point of) view; **er steht auf dem Standpunkt, daß . . .**, he takes the view that . . .; **ich vertrete den Standpunkt, daß . . .**, I take the view that . . .; **von unserem Standpunkt aus**, from our point of view

Stange *nf*, **bei der Stange bleiben**, remain firm, not be deterred; **jemandem die Stange halten**, stick up for someone

Stanniol(papier) *nn*, silver foil

stanzen *vb* (holes), punch

Stapel *nm*, **1** (transp), batch, pile, stack. **2** (comm), store, depot. **3** (naut), stocks; **vom Stapel lassen**, launch; **vom Stapel laufen**, be launched

stapeln *vb*, batch, pile (up), stack (up)

Stapelverarbeitung *nf* (comp), batch processing

stark *adj*, *adv* (gen), strong, powerful; strongly; **ein starker Motor**, a powerful engine; **seine starke Seite**, his strong point, his forte; **stark fallen** (prices), plummet; **stark verschuldet**, deeply in debt

stärken *vb*, strengthen, reinforce

starr *adj*, *adv*, inflexible; inflexibly; **starr an etwas festhalten**, stick rigidly to

Start *nm*, start; **einen schlechten Start haben**, get off to a bad start; **Starthilfe** *nf* (business), pump-priming (money); **Startkapital** *nn*, starting capital

Statistik *nf*, statistics; **eine offizielle Statistik**, an official statistic

statistisch *adj*, *adv*, statistical; statistically; **statistisch erfassen**, record

statt|finden *vb*, take place; **die Eröffnung fand am 6. Dezember statt**, the opening (ceremony) took place on December 6

Statut *nn*, statute

Stau *nm*, traffic jam, tailback

Staub *nm*, dust

Staubsauger *nm*, vacuum cleaner, hoover

Stechkarte *nf*, clocking-in card

Stechuhr *nf*, time-clock

Steckdose *nf* (electr), socket

Stecker *nm* (electr), plug

Stegreif *nm*, **eine Rede aus dem Stegreif halten**, give an impromptu speech

stehen *vb*, **1** (gen, fin), stand; **wie steht die DM heute?**, how does the deutschmark stand today? **2** (formal), **das steht bei Ihnen**, this is up to you. **3** (in newspaper), **das steht in . . .**, it says so in . . .; **4** (views), **wie stehen Sie dazu?**, what are your views on that? **5** (promise), **das Unternehmen steht zu der Vereinbarung**, the company stands by the agreement

Stehvermögen *nn*, stamina

steigen *vb* (price, figure etc), increase, go up; **seit letztem Jahr sind die Preise durchschnittlich um 5 Prozent gestiegen**, prices have gone up by an average of 5 per cent since last year

steigern *vb* (efforts, figures), increase; **die Firma hat ihren Umsatz um 3 Prozent steigern können**, the company has been able to increase its turnover by 3 per cent

Steigerung *nf* (prices), increase

steil *adj*, *adv*, steep, rapid; rapidly; **eine steile Karriere**, a rapid (career) rise; **ein steiler Preisanstieg**, a steep price rise

Stein *nm*, **1** stone. **2** jewel. **3 einen Stein im Brett haben bei** (+ dat), be well in with

Stelle *nf*, **1** (location), place, spot; **hier ist eine gute Stelle zum Parken**, this is a good place for parking; **an seiner Stelle würde ich . . .**, if I were in his place I would . . . **2** (in time), point; **ich möchte an dieser Stelle betonen, daß . . .**, I would like to stress at this point that . . . **3** (employment), job; **er hat jetzt eine gute Stelle bei Krupp**, he has now got a good job with Krupp; **offene Stelle** (pers), vacancy

stellen *vb* (gen), put, set, place; **eine Bedingung stellen**, set a condition; **eine Frage stellen**, ask a question; **jemandem eine Aufgabe stellen**, confront someone with a task

Stellen-; **Stellenangebot** *nn*, job offer; **Stellenanzeige** *nf*, **Stellenausschreibung** *nf*, job advertisement; **Stellenbeschreibung** *nf*, job description; **Stellengesuch** *nn*, job application; **„Stellengesuche"**, "situations wanted"; **Stellenmarkt** *nm*, job market; **Stellenvermittlung** *nf*, **1** (public), employment centre. **2** (private), job agency

Stellung *nf*, **1** (gen), position; **eine untergeordnete Stellung**, a subordinate position. **2** status; **seine gesellschaftliche Stellung**, his social status

Stellungnahme *nf*, statement; **das Unternehmen hat noch keine Stellungnahme abgegeben**, the company has not yet made a statement

Stellungswechsel *nm*, change of job

stellvertretend *adj*, vice-, deputy; **stellvertretender Vorsitzender** *nm*, vice-chairperson

Stellvertreter(in) *nm/f*, **1** deputy. **2** representative

Stempel *nm*, **1** (offce), stamp. **2** (post), postmark. **3** (for gold, silver), hallmark

stempeln *vb*, **1** (offce), stamp. **2** (post), postmark. **3** (stamp), frank. **4 stempeln gehen**, go on the dole

Stempelsteuer *nf*, stamp duty

Steno *nf*, shorthand; **Stenoblock** *nm*, shorthand pad; **Stenografie** *nf*, shorthand

stenografieren *vb*, take down in shorthand/do shorthand; **können Sie stenografieren?**, can you do shorthand?

Stenogramm *nn*, text in shorthand

Stenotypist(in) *nm/f*, shorthand typist

Stereoaufnahme *nf*, stereo recording

Stereogerät *nn*, stereo unit

stetig *adj*, *adv*, **1** (without interruption), continuous; **eine stetige Verbesserung**, continuous improvement. **2** (at the same pace), steady; steadily; **ein stetiges Ansteigen der Preise**, a steady rise in prices

stets *adv*, always

Steuer *nn*, **1** (of car), steering wheel. **2** (of plane), controls

Steuer *nf*, tax; **Steuer zahlen**, pay tax; **der Steuer unterliegen**, be taxable; **Steueraufkommen** *nn*, revenue

steuerbefreit *adj*, tax-exempt

Steuerbefreiung *nf*, tax exemption

steuerbegünstigt *adj*, **1** (investment, mortgage), tax-deductible. **2** (goods), taxed at a lower rate

Steuer-; **Steuerbegünstigung** *nf*, tax concession; **Steuerberater** *nm*, tax consultant; **Steuererklärung** *nf*, tax return; **Steuererlaß** *nm*, tax exemption; **Steuererstattung** *nf*, tax rebate; **Steuerflucht** *nf*, tax evasion

steuerfrei *adj*, *adv*, tax-free

Steuer-; **Steuerfreiheit** *nf*, tax exemption; **Steuerfreiheit genießen**, be exempt from tax; **Steuergelder** *nnpl*, taxes; **Steuerhinterziehung** *nf*, tax evasion; **Steuerklasse** *nf*, tax bracket

steuerpflichtig *adj*, taxable

Steuer-; **Steuerprüfer** *nm*, tax inspector; **Steuerrecht** *nn*, tax law; **Steuerreform** *nf*, tax reform; **Steuerrückzahlung** *nf*, tax repayment; **Steuersatz** *nm*, rate of taxation; **Steuerschulden** *nfpl*, taxes owing; **Steuersenkung** *nf*, tax cut; **Steuersünder** *nm*, tax evader

Steuerungsball *nm* (comp), trackball

Steuer-; **Steuerveranlagung** *nf*, tax assessment; **Steuervorteil** *nm*, tax advantage; **Steuerzahler** *nm* taxpayer

stichhaltig *adj*, **1** (reason), sound. **2** (proof), conclusive

Stichprobe *nf*, **1** (gen), spot check. **2** (mktg), sample survey

Stichprobenbefragung *nf* (mktg), sample opinion

Stichprobenverfahren *nn*, sampling

Stichtag *nm*, deadline

Stichwort *nn*, clue; **in Stichworten**, in note form

stichwortartig *adj*, *adv*, in note form, in outline

Stichwortverzeichnis *nn*, index

Stift *nm* (offce), pencil, pen

stiften *vb* (money), **1** donate. **2** (church, university), endow

still *adj*, **1** (comm), **stiller Teilhaber** *nm*, sleeping partner. **2** (fin), **stille Reserven** *nfpl*, hidden reserves

stillegen (separable **still legen**) *vb*, (company), close, shut down

Stillegung *nf* (of company), closure, shut-down

stillschweigend *adj*, silent, tacit; **stillschweigendes Einverständnis** *nn*, tacit agreement

Stillstand *nm* (in production, negotiations), stoppage; (temporary) interruption; **zum Stillstand bringen**, stop

Stimmabgabe *nf*, voting; **geschlossene Stimmabgabe**, block vote

Stimme *nf*, vote; **seine Stimme abgeben**, cast one's vote; **ausschlaggebende Stimme**, casting vote

stimmen *vb*, **1** (in election), vote. **2** be correct; **das stimmt**, that's right/correct

Stimmenauszählung *nf* (of votes), count

Stimmenmehrheit *nf* (of votes), majority

Stimmenthaltung *nf*, abstention

Stimmzettel *nm*, ballot paper

Stock *nm* (of building), floor; **im ersten Stock**, on the first floor

stocken *vb*, **1** (work, traffic), slow down. **2** (trade etc), slacken, stagnate

Stockung *nf*, **1** (of work) interruption. **2** (of business, trade), slackening. **3** (in traffic), congestion, traffic jam, hold-up

Stoff *nm*, **1** (gen), material. **2** (chemical), substance; **giftige Stoffe**, toxic substances

stolz *adj*, proud; **wir sind stolz auf** (+ acc), we are proud of

Stopp *nm*, **1** (gen), stop, halt. **2** (of wage), freeze

Stoppuhr *nf*, stop-watch

stören *vb*, bother, disturb, mind; **entschuldigen Sie, wenn ich Sie störe**, I am sorry to disturb/bother you; **stört es Sie, wenn ich . . .?**, do you mind if I . . .?; **das stört mich nicht**, it doesn't bother me, I don't mind

störend *adj*, disturbing, bothersome

stornieren *vb* (comm), **1** (order), cancel. **2** (mistake in book-keeping), reverse

Storno *nm/nn* (comm), **1** (of order), cancellation. **2** (mistake in book-keeping), reversal

Störung *nf*, **1** (gen), disturbance. **2** (techn), fault

Störungsstelle *nf* (telec), faults service

stoßdämpfend *adj*, shock-absorbent

stoßfest, **stoßsicher** *adj*, shock-proof

Stoßzeit *nf*, **1** (business), peak period. **2** (traffic), rush-hour

Straf-; **Strafandrohung** *nf* (law), threat of penalty; **Strafantrag** *nm* (law), **Strafantrag stellen**, institute legal proceedings; **Strafanzeige** *nf* (law), **Strafanzeige erstatten gegen** (+ acc), bring a charge against

strafbar *adj* (law), punishable; **eine strafbare Handlung**, a punishable offence; **sich strafbar machen**, commit an offence

Strafe *nf* (law), **1** (gen), penalty. **2** (money), fine; **Strafe zahlen**, pay a fine. **3** prison sentence

Straf-; **Strafgebühr** *nf*, surcharge; **Strafgeld** *nn* (law), fine: **Strafjustiz** *nf* (law), criminal justice; **Strafklausel** *nf* (law), penalty clause; **Strafporto** *nn*, postal surcharge; **Strafprozeß** *nm*, criminal proceedings; **Strafrecht** *nn*, criminal law; **Straftat** *nf*, criminal offence, crime; **Strafverfolgung** *nf*, criminal prosecution; **Strafverteidiger** *nm*, counsel for the defence; **Strafzettel** *nm*, ticket

Strandgut *nn*, flotsam and jetsam

Strapaze *nf*, strain

strapazierfähig *adj* (clothes, shoes), hard-wearing

Straße *nf*, road, street; **der Mann auf der Straße**, the man in the street

Straßen-; **Straßenbahn** *nf*, tram; **Straßenbahnhaltestelle** *nf*, tram stop; **Straßenbau** *nm*, road construction; **Straßenbauarbeiten** *nfpl*, road works; **Straßenbenutzungsgebühr** *nf*, (road) toll; **Straßenhandel** *nm*, street trading; **Straßenhändler** *nm*, street vendor; **Straßenkreuzung** *nf*, crossroads; **Straßennetz** *nn*, road network; **Straßenschild** *nn*, street sign; **Straßenverkauf** *nm*, take-away sales, off-licence sales; **Straßenverkehr** *nm*, (road) traffic; **Straßenzustand** *nm*, road conditions

Strategie *nf*, strategy

strategisch *adj*, *adv*, strategic; strategically

streichen *vb*, **1** (text), delete, cross out. **2** (order, plan, train), cancel. **3** (debts), write off. **4** (money), cut

Streichung *nf*, **1** (of text), deletion. **2** (of order, plan, train), cancellation. **3** (of debts), writing off. **4** (in money), cut

Streifbandzeitung *nf*, newspaper sent at printed paper rate

Streik *nm*, strike; **zum Streik aufrufen**, call out on strike; **in den Streik treten**, come out on strike, go on strike; **Streikaufruf** *nm*, strike call; **Streikbrecher(in)** *nm/f*, strike-breaker

streiken *vb*, be on strike, come out on strike

Streik-; **Streikgeld** *nn*, strike pay; **Streikposten** *nm*, picket; **Streikpostenkette** *nf*, picket line; **Streikwelle** *nf*, wave of strikes

Streit *nm*, argument, disagreement, dispute

streiten *vb*, argue, disagree

Streitgegenstand *nm* (law), matter in dispute

Streitigkeit *nf*, argument, disagreement, dispute

Streitpunkt *nm*, contentious issue

streng *adj*, *adv*, strict; strictly; **etwas streng befolgen**, keep strictly to something; **strenge Maßnahmen ergreifen**, take strict measures; **streng verboten**, strictly prohibited; **strenge Vorschriften**, strict regulations

strenggenommen *adv*, strictly speaking

Streß *nm*, stress

Streuung *nf*, diversification

Strohmann *nm*, nominee

Strom *nm* (electr), current, electricity, power; **Stromausfall** *nm*, power failure; **Stromspeicher** *nm*, storage battery; **Stromsperre** *nf*, power cut; **Stromverbrauch** *nm*, electricity consumption

Struktur *nf*, structure

strukturell *adj*, structural; **strukturelle Veränderungen** *nfpl*, structural changes

strukturieren *vb*, structure

Struktur-; **Strukturkrise** *nf*, structural crisis; **Strukturproblem** *nn*, structural problem; **Strukturwandel** *nm*, structural change

Stück *nn*, **1** (gen), piece. **2** (single product), unit; **Stückarbeit** *nf*, piecework; **Stückgut** *nn* (rail), parcel service; **Stückkosten** *npl*, unit cost; **Stücklohn** *nm*, piece rate; **Stückpreis** *nm*, unit price

stückweise *adv*, by the piece

Stückzahl *nf*, number of items, quantity

Stufe *nf* (gen), level, stage; **auf dieser Stufe**, at this level/stage

Stunde *nf*, hour; **eine halbe Stunde**, half an hour; **in einer dreiviertel Stunde**, in three quarters of an hour; **ein acht-Stunden-Tag**, an eight-hour day; **70 Meilen pro Stunde**, 70 miles per hour

stunden *vb* (comm), give extra time (to pay off debt)

Stundengeschwindigkeit *nf*, miles/km per hour

stundenlang *adj*, *adv*, lasting several hours

Stundenlohn *nm*, hourly wage

stündlich *adj*, *adv*, hourly

Stundung *nf* (comm), deferment of payment

Sturm *nm* (comm, fin), run; **ein Sturm auf die Aktien/Banken**, a run on the shares/banks

Sturz *nm* (in prices), drop, fall

stürzen *vb* (prices), drop, plummet

stützen *vb* (gen, fin), support

Stützung *nf* (gen, fin), support

Stützungsmaßnahme *nf*, supporting measure

Substanz *nf*, substance

subsumieren *vb*, subsume

subtrahieren *vb*, subtract

Subunternehmer *nm*, subcontractor

Subvention *nf*, subsidy

subventionieren *vb*, subsidise

Suche *nf*, search

Suchfunktion *nf* (comp), search function

Summe *nf*, sum, amount

Supermarkt *nm*, supermarket

supermodern *adj*, ultra-modern

superschnell *adj*, ultrafast

suspendieren *vb* (payments), suspend

synchronisieren *vb*, synchronise, phase

Synchronisierung *nf*, synchronisation, phasing

Syndikat *nn*, syndicate

Synthese *nf*, synthesis

synthetisch *adj*, synthetic

System *nn*, system; **Systemanalyse** *nf*, systems analysis; **Systemanalytiker(in)** *nm/f*, systems analyst

systematisch *adj*, *adv*, systematic; systematically

Systemberater(in) *nm/f*, systems analyst

T

tabellarisch *adj*, *adv*, in tabular form; **bitte fügen Sie einen tabellarischen Lebenslauf bei**, please let us have your CV in tabular form

Tabellarisierung *nf*, tabulation

Tabelle *nf*, table, chart

Tabellen-; **Tabellenform** *nf*, **in Tabellenform**, in tabular form, as a chart; **Tabellenführer** *nm*, **Tabellenführer sein**, be top of the chart; **Tabellenkalkulation** *nf* (comp), spreadsheet

Tacho *nm*, **Tachometer** *nm*, speedometer

Tafel *nf* (electr), control panel, console

Tag *nm*, day; **alle Tage/jeden Tag**, every day; **dieser Tage**, in the next few days; **zweimal am Tag**, twice a day; **Tagdienst** *nm*, day-duty

Tagegeld *nn*, daily (subsistence) allowance

tagelang *adj*, *adv*, lasting for days

tagen *vb* (meeting, conference), sit

Tages-; **Tagesarbeit** *nf*, day's work; **Tagesbedarf** *nm*, daily requirement; **Tageseinnahmen** *nfpl*, day's takings; **Tagesgeld** *nn*, overnight money; **Tageskurs** *nm*, daily rate of exchange; **Tageslichtprojektor** *nm*, overhead projector, OHP

Tagesordnung *nf*, agenda; **auf der Tagesordnung stehen**, be on the agenda; **etwas auf die Tagesordnung setzen**, put something on the agenda; **der**

nächste Punkt auf der Tagesordnung, (the) next item on the agenda; **zur Tagesordnung übergehen**, **1** proceed to the agenda. **2** get down to business. **3** carry on as usual

Tages-; **Tagespreis** *nm* (comm), current/yesterday's/today's etc price; **gestern betrug der Tagespreis . . .**, yesterday's price was . . .; **Tagespresse** *nf*, daily press; **Tagessatz** *nm*, daily rate; **Tageszeit** *nf*, time of day; **zu jeder Tageszeit**, at any time during the day; **Tageszeitung** *nf*, daily (paper)

täglich *adj*, *adv*, daily

tags *adv*, **tags darauf**, the day after, the next day; **tags zuvor**, the day before, the previous day

Tagschicht *nf*, day shift; **Tagschicht haben**, be on day shift

tagsüber *adv*, during the day

Tag- und Nachtdienst *nm*, 24-hour service

Tagung *nf* (gen), conference

Tagungsort *nm*, venue

Tagungsteilnehmer(in) *nm/f*, conference delegate

taktieren *vb*, manoeuvre

Taktik *nf*, tactics

Talentsuche *nf*, search for new talent

talentiert *adj*, talented, gifted

Talfahrt *nf* (fin), decline

Tangente *nf*, ring-road

tangieren *vb*, be tangential to, touch on

Tanker *nm* (naut), tanker

Tank-; **Tankfahrzeug** *nn*, tanker; **Tankinhalt** *nm*, tank contents; **Tanklaster** *nm*, **Tanklastzug** *nm*, tanker; **Tanksäule** *nf*, petrol pump; **Tankstelle** *nf*, petrol station; **Tankwagen** *nm*, tanker; **Tankwart** *nm*, petrol pump attendant

Tante-Emma-Laden *nm*, corner shop

Tantieme *nf*, **1** (of profit), percentage. **2** director's fee. **3** royalty

Tapet *nn*, **etwas aufs Tapet bringen**, raise an issue

tapfer *adj*, brave; **er hat sich tapfer geschlagen**, he has put on a brave show

Tara *nf* (comm), tare

Tarif *nm*, rate; **ermäßigter Tarif**, reduced rate; **üblicher Tarif**, market rate; **Tarifabschluß** *nm*, wage settlement; **Tarifautonomie** *nf*, free collective bargaining; **Tarifgehalt** *nn*, union rates; **Tarifgruppe** *nf*, grade; **Tarifkommission** *nf*, joint working party on pay

tariflich *adj*, agreed; **der tarifliche Mindestlohn**, the agreed minimum wage

Tarif-; **Tariflohn** *nm*, standard wage; **Tarifordnung** *nf*, wage/salary scale; **Tarifpartei** *nf*, **Tarifpartner** *nm*, party to a wage/salary agreement; **Tarifrunde** *nf*, pay round; **Tarifverhandlungen** *nfpl*, wage/salary negotiations; **autonome Tarifverhandlungen**, free collective bargaining; **Tarifvertrag** *nm*, union agreement

tarnen *vb*, camouflage, disguise

Taschen-; **Taschenformat** *nn*, pocket size; **Taschenlampe** *nf*, torch; **Taschenrechner** *nm*, pocket calculator; **Taschenwörterbuch** *nn*, pocket dictionary

Tastatur *nf* (comp, telec), keyboard

Taste *nf* (comp, telec), key

Tastentelefon *nn* push-button telephone

Tatbestand *nm* (law), the facts of the case

tatenlos *adj, adv*, idle; idly

tätig *adj*, active

tätigen *vb*, **1** (deal, business), conclude, effect; (business also), transact. **2** (phone call), make; **ich muß eben noch einen Anruf tätigen**, I just have to make a phone call

Tätigkeit *nf*, **1** (gen), activity. **2** (work), occupation, job; **er übt jetzt eine andere Tätigkeit aus**, he is now doing a different job

Tätigkeitsbericht *nm*, progress report

Tätigkeitsbeschreibung *nf*, job description

Tatsache *nf*, **1** fact; **das ist Tatsache**, that's a fact. **2 er hat mich vor vollendete Tatsachen gestellt**, he presented me with a fait accompli. **3 unter Vorspiegelung falscher Tatsachen**, under false pretences

Tatsachenmaterial *nn*, facts

tatsächlich *adj*, actual; **die tatsächliche Lage**, the actual situation

Tausch *nm*, **1** (money), exchange. **2** (goods), barter; **Tauschabkommen** *nn*, barter agreement

tauschen *vb*, **1** (money), exchange. **2** (goods), barter

täuschen *vb*, deceive

sich täuschen *vb*, be mistaken/wrong; **wenn mich nicht alles täuscht**, unless I am completely mistaken/wrong; **Sie haben sich getäuscht**, you are mistaken/wrong

Tauschhandel *nm*, barter; **Tauschhandel treiben** barter

Täuschung *nf*, deception

Taxator *nm* (comm), valuer

Taxi *nn*, taxi; **ich nehme mir ein Taxi**, I'll take a taxi

taxieren *vb* (price, value), estimate; **zu niedrig taxieren**, underestimate

Taxistand *nm*, taxi rank

Technik *nf*, **1** technology. **2** technique

Techniker(in) *nm/f*, technician

technisch *adj, adv*, **1** technological; **technischer Fortschritt**, technological progress. **2** technical; technically; **technischer Leiter**, technical director

Technologie *nf*, technology

technologisch *adj*, technological

Teer *nm*, tar

Teil *nm*, part; **zum Teil**, partly; **Teilbetrag** *nm*, **1** (gen), part (of an amount). **2** (on invoice), item. **3** (of payment), rate

teilen *vb*, divide; **die Meinungen sind geteilt**, opinions are divided

sich (etwas) teilen *vb*, share (something)

Teil-; **Teilerfolg** *nm*, partial success; **Teilergebnis** *nn*, partial/preliminary result; **Teilfabrikat** *nn*, component; **Teilhabe** *nf*, participation; **Teilhaber** *nm* (comm), associate, (co)partner; **tätiger Teilhaber**, active partner; **Teilhaberschaft** *nf* (comm), (co)partnership; **Teilkaskoversicherung** *nf*, third party, fire and theft; **Teillieferung** *nf*, part delivery

Teilnahme *nf*, **1** participation. **2** attendance

teilnahmeberechtigt *adj*, eligible

teil|nehmen *vb*, **1** participate. **2** attend

Teilnehmer(in) *nm/f*, **1** participant. **2** (on course, at conference), delegate. **3** (telec), subscriber; **Teilnehmerzahl** *nf*, attendance

teils *adv*, **teils . . . teils . . .**, partly . . . partly . . .

Teilverlust *nm*, partial loss

teilweise *adv*, partly

Teilzahlung *nf*, part payment, instalment; **als Teilzahlung**, on account; **auf Teilzahlung**, on hire-purchase

Teilzeitbeschäftigung *nf*, part-time employment

teilzeitbeschäftigt *adj*, working part-time

Teilzeitkraft *nf*, part-timer

Telefax *nn*, fax; **Telefax-Teilnehmer(in)** *nm/f*, fax subscriber

Telefon *nn*, (tele)phone; **ans Telefon gehen**, answer the phone; **das Telefon abnehmen**, pick up (the receiver)

Telefonanruf *nm*, (tele)phone call; **einen Telefonanruf annehmen**, take a call; **einen Telefonanruf beantworten**, answer a call; **einen Telefonanruf bekommen**, receive a call

Telefonat *nn*, (tele)phone call

Telefon-; **Telefonauskunft** *nf*, directory inquiries; **Telefonbeantworter** *nm*, answer phone; **Telefonbuch** *nn*, (tele)phone directory; **Telefongespräch** *nn*, (tele)phone call

telefonieren *vb*, (tele)phone

telefonisch *adj*, *adv*, telephonic, by (tele)phone; **telefonisch erreichen**, contact by phone; **telefonische Mitteilung** *nf*, (tele)phone message

Telefonist(in) *nm/f*, switchboard operator

Telefon-; **Telefonkarte** *nf*, phone card; **Telefonleitung** *nf*, telephone line; **Telefonnummer** *nf*, phone number; **Telefonrechnung** *nf*, telephone bill; **Telefonverbindung** *nf*, telephone line; **Telefonverzeichnis** *nn*, telephone directory; **Telefonzelle** *nf*, telephone booth; **Telefonzentrale** *nf*, switchboard

telegrafisch *adj*, telegraphic; **telegrafische Überweisung** *nf*, telegraphic transfer

Telemarketing *nn*, telemarketing

telexen *vb*, telex

Temperatur *nf*, temperature; **Temperaturregler** *nm*, thermostat

Tempo *nn*, speed; **Tempolimit** *nn*, speed limit; **Tempoüberschreitung** *nf*, speeding

Tendenz *nf* (gen), trend

tendenziell *adj*, **eine tendenzielle Veränderung**, a change in direction

tendieren *vb*, tend

Termin *nm*, **1** (gen), date. **2** (final date), deadline; **einen Termin einhalten**, keep to a deadline. **3** (with doctor, meeting), appointment; **sich einen Termin geben lassen**, make an appointment. **4** engagement; **ein dringender Termin**, a pressing engagement; **ich kann leider nicht kommen, ich habe schon einen anderen Termin**, I am afraid I won't be able to come due to a prior engagement

Termin-; **Terminbörse** *nf* (fin), futures market, forward exchange; **Termineinlage** *nf* (fin), time deposit; **Termingeld** *nn* (fin), fixed deposit

termingemäß *adv*, **termingerecht** *adv*, on schedule, according to schedule; **die Produktion läuft termingerecht**, production is running on schedule

Termin-; **Termingeschäfte** *nnpl* (fin), futures; **Terminkalender**

nm, (appointments) diary; **Terminmarkt** *nm* (fin), forward market; **Terminplanung** *nf*, (time) scheduling; **Terminprüfer** *nm*, progress chaser; **Terminschwierigkeiten** *nfpl*, scheduling difficulties; **Terminverkäufe** *nmpl* (fin), forward sales

Test *nm*, test; **sich einem Test unterwerfen**, undergo a test

testen *vb*, **1** (try), sample. **2** (examine), test

Test-; **Testfahrer** *nm*, test driver; **Testfall** *nm*, test case; **Testprogramm** *nn* (comp), test programme; **Testverfahren** *nn*, method of testing

teuer *adj*, *adv*, expensive; at a high price; **teuer erkaufen**, pay dearly for; **teurer werden**, go up in price

Teuerung *nf*, price rise, inflation

Teuerungsrate *nf*, inflation rate

Teuerungszuschlag *nm*, **1** surcharge. **2** cost-of-living bonus

Teufelskreis *nm*, vicious circle

Text *nm*, **1** (gen), text. **2** wording; **Texteingabe** *nf* (comp), text input

Textilarbeiter(in) *nm/f*, textile worker

Textilien *npl*, textiles

Textilindustrie *nf*, textile industry

Text-; **Textspeicher** *nm* (comp), memory; **Textverarbeiter** *nm*, word processor; **Textverarbeitung** *nf*, word processing

Textverarbeitungs-; **Textverarbeitungsanlage** *nf*, word processor; **Textverarbeitungsprogramm** *nn*, word processing program; **Textverarbeitungssoftware** *nf*, word processing software

TH *nf*, **Technische Hochschule** *nf*, technological university

Thema *nn*, subject (matter), topic; **das Thema wechseln**, change the subject; **das Thema ist erledigt**, the matter is closed

theoretisch *adv*, theoretically, in theory

Theorie *nf*, theory; **in der Theorie**, in theory

Thermodynamik *nf*, thermodynamics

Thermometer *nn*, thermometer

tief *adj*, *adv*, deep; deeply; underlying; **die tieferen Ursachen**, the underlying causes

Tiefbau *nm*, civil engineering

Tiefgarage *nf*, underground car park

tiefgefroren *adj*, frozen

tiefgekühlt *adj*, chilled, frozen

Tiefkühl-; **Tiefkühlfach** *nn*, freezer compartment; **Tiefkühlkost** *nf*, frozen food; **Tiefkühltruhe** *nf*, (chest-type) deep-freeze, freezer

Tief-; **Tieflader** *nm*, **Tiefladewagen** *nm*, low-loader; **Tiefpunkt** *nm*, **die Entwicklung hat einen Tiefpunkt erreicht**, developments have reached a low; **Tiefseefisch** *nm*, deep-sea fish

Tiefstpreis *nm*, rock-bottom price

Tiefstwert *nm*, lowest value

Tier *nn*, animal; **Tierversuch** *nm*, animal experiment; **Tierzucht** *nf*, stock breeding

tilgbar *adj* (fin), repayable

tilgen *vb* (fin), pay off, redeem

Tilgung *nf* (fin), discharge, redemption, repayment

Tilgungs-; **Tilgungserlös** *nm* (fin), redemption yield; **Tilgungsfonds** *nm* (fin), sinking fund; **(letzte) Tilgungsrate** *nf*, final discharge; **Tilgungssumme** *nf*, payoff; **Tilgungstermin** *nm*, redemption date; **Tilgungszeitraum** *nm*, payback period

timen *vb*, time

Tinte *nf*, ink

Tintenstrahldrucker *nm* (offce), ink-jet printer

tippen *vb* (offce), type; **können Sie tippen?**, can you type?

Tisch *nm*, **1** (gen), table. **2** (offce), desk; **Tischvorlage** *nf* (meeting), tabled paper

Titel *nm*, title

Tochtergesellschaft *nf*, subsidiary (company); **eine hundertprozentige Tochtergesellschaft**, a wholly-owned subsidiary; **eine Tochtergesellschaft ausgliedern**, spin off a subsidiary (company)

Toilette *nf*, toilet, lavatory, WC; **öffentliche Toilette**, public conveniences

Tokenring-Netzwerk *nn* (comp), token ring network

Toleranz *nf*, tolerance

tolerieren *vb*, tolerate

Ton *nm* (TV, radio), sound; **Tonband** *nn*, tape; **auf Tonband aufnehmen**, record on tape; **Tonbandansage** *nf*, recorded message; **Tonbandgerät** *nn*, tape recorder; **Toningenieur** *nm*, sound engineer

Tonnage *nf*, tonnage

Tonne *nf*, **1** (weight), (metric) ton (= 1.000 kg); **britische Tonne**, long ton (= 1016 kg). **2** (container), barrel; (metal), drum. **3** (large), dust bin

Tor *nn* (of factory), gate

total *adj*, *adv*, total; totally

Totalausverkauf *nm*, clearance sale

Totalschaden *nm* (ins), write-off

totschweigen *vb*, hush up

Tourismus *nm*, tourism

Tourist(in) *nm/f*, tourist

Tradition *nf*, tradition

traditionell *adj*, traditional

traditionellerweise *adv*, traditionally

traditionsbewußt *adj*, proud of a (long) tradition

traditionsreich *adj*, rich in tradition

tragen *vb*, **1** (weight), carry. **2** (title, costs), bear (the cost). **3** (risk, consequences), take; **zum Tragen kommen**, come to fruition

Trägheit *nf*, inertia

Trägheitsverkauf *nm*, inertia selling

Tragweite *nf*, possible consequences, implications; **eine Sache von großer Tragweite**, a matter of far-reaching consequences

Transaktion *nf*, transaction; **geschäftliche Transaktion**, business transaction

transatlantisch *adj*, transatlantic

Transfer *nm*, transfer

transferieren *vb*, transfer

Transformator *nm* (electr), transformer

Transit-; **Transitabkommen** *nn*, transit agreement; **Transitfracht** *nf*, transit freight; **Transithandel** *nm*, transit trade; **Transitverkehr** *nm*, transit traffic

Transport *nm*, **1** transport; **beim Transport**, in transit. **2** (of freight), consignment, shipment

transportabel *adj*, transportable

Transportarbeiter *nm*, transport worker

Transportbehälter *nm*, container

Transporter *nm*, **1** (ship), cargo ship, carrier. **2** (plane), transport plane. **3** (lorry), carrier

transportfähig *adj*, transportable

Transportflugzeug *nn*, cargo plane, freight plane

transportieren *vb*, ship, transport

Transport-; **Transportkosten** *npl*, carriage, freight costs, haulage; **Transportmittel** *nn*, means of transport; **Transportschaden** *nm*, damage in transit; **Transportschiff** *nn*, cargo ship; **Transportunternehmen** *nn*, carrier, haulier, haulage contractor; **Transportwesen** *nn*, transport (system)

Trassant *nm* (fin), drawer

Trassat *nm* (fin), drawee

Tratte *nf* (fin), bill, bill of exchange, draft

trauen *vb*, trust

treffen *vb*, **1** (people), meet; **treffen wir uns am Bahnhof!**, let's meet at the station. **2 Vorbereitungen treffen**, make preparations. **3 eine Maßnahme treffen**, take a measure

Treffen *nn*, meeting

Treffpunkt *nm*, meeting place; **einen Treffpunkt ausmachen**, arrange where to meet

treiben *vb*, **Geschäfte/Handel treiben mit** (+ dat), do business/trade with . . .

Trend *nm*, trend; **voll im Trend liegen**, follow the trend

trennen *vb*, separate

Trenn(ungs)wand *nf*, partition (wall)

Treppe *nf*, stairs; **drei Treppen hoch**, on the third floor

Tresor(raum) *nm*, strong room, vault

treten *vb*, **1 in den Ausstand/Streik treten**, go on strike. **2 in Kraft treten**, come into force. **3 in Verbindung treten**, get in touch

treu *adj*, faithful, loyal

Treue *nf*, loyalty; **die Treue halten**, remain loyal; **wir müssen unseren Kunden die Treue halten**, we must remain loyal to our customers; **Treueprämie** *nf*, long-service bonus

Treuhand *nf*, holding trust

Treuhänder *nm*, fiduciary, trustee

treuhänderisch *adj*, fiduciary

Treuhandfonds *nm*, trust fund

Treuhandvertrag *nm*, trust deed

triftig *adj*, valid; **er hatte keine triftige Entschuldigung**, he lacked a valid excuse; **ein triftiger Grund**, a valid reason

trinken *vb*, drink

Trinkgeld *nn*, (gratuity), tip; **wieviel Trinkgeld?**, how much of a tip?

trocken *adj*, dry; **trocken aufbewahren**, keep/store in a dry place; **ich trinke lieber trockenen Wein**, I prefer dry wine

Trockendock *nn*, dry dock

trocknen *vb*, dry

trotz (+ genitive) *prep*, in spite of; **trotz steigender Rohstoffpreise haben wir . . .**, in spite of price increases for raw materials we have . . .

trotzdem *adv*, nevertheless

trübe *adj, adv*, gloomy; gloomily; **trübe Aussichten**, gloomy prospects

trügen *vb*, deceive, be deceptive; **der erste Eindruck trügt**, the first impression is deceptive

tüchtig *adj*, competent, efficient

tunlichst *adv*, if possible; **wir sollten das tunlichst vermeiden**, we should avoid this if possible

Tür *nf*, door; **einen Fuß in der Tür haben**, have a foot in the door; **er hat mir die Tür vor der Nase zugemacht**, he shut the door in my face

Turnus *nm*, rota, rotation; **im (regelmäßigen) Turnus**, in rotation

Tüte *nf*, paper bag

TÜV *nm*, **Technischer Überwachungsverein** *nm*, ≈ MOT; **das Auto ist nicht durch den TÜV gekommen**, the car failed its MOT

typisch *adj*, typical, representative; **das ist typisch für ihn**, that's typical of him; **das ist kein typisches Beispiel**, that is not a representative example

U

u.a., **und anderes**, **unter anderem**, **unter anderen**, inter alia, amongst other things/people

U.A.w.g., **um Antwort wird gebeten**, RSVP

U-Bahn, *nf*, tube, underground; **U-Bahnhof** *nm*, tube station, underground station

über (+ acc, + dat) *prep*, over, above, via, about; **die Entscheidung fiel vor über 10 Tagen**, the decision was taken over 10 days ago; **besprechen wir die Sache über einem Glas Wein**, let's talk about that over a glass of wine; **10 Grad über Null**, 10 degrees above zero; **sind Sie über Stuttgart gekommen?**, have you come via Stuttgart?; **wir sprechen über die Leipziger Messe**, we are talking about the Leipzig Trade Fair

überall *adv*, everywhere

überarbeiten *vb* (text), revise

überbelegen *vb*, overbook; **leider ist das Hotel überbelegt**, unfortunately the hotel is overbooked

überbetrieblich *adj*, industry-wide

überbewerten *vb*, overrate

überbezahlt *adj*, overpaid

überbieten *vb*, **1** (at auction), outbid. **2** (record), beat

Überblick *nm*, overview, outline; **einen Überblick über . . . haben**, have an overview over . . . ; **ein kurzer Überblick über die Ereignisse**, a brief outline of developments; **den Überblick**

verlieren, lose track of things

überblicken *vb*, be able to assess; **ich überblicke die Lage noch nicht**, I still have difficulty assessing the situation

Überbringer *nm* (of cheque), bearer; **zahlbar an Überbringer**, payable to bearer

Überbrückungskredit *nm* (fin), bridging loan

überdies *adv*, furthermore, in any case

überdurchschnittlich *adj, adv*, above-average, exceptionally; **überdurchschnittlich hoch**, exceptionally high

übereilt *adj*, hasty

überein|kommen *vb*, agree; **wir sind übereingekommen, die Reise zu verschieben**, we (have) agreed to postpone the trip

Übereinkommen *nn*, **Übereinkunft** *nf*, arrangement, agreement

überein|stimmen *vb*, agree; **wir stimmen völlig überein**, we completely agree

Übereinstimmung *nf*, **1 es herrscht grundsätzliche Übereinstimmung darüber, daß . . .**, in principle there is agreement that . . . **2 in Übereinstimmung mit** (+ dat), in accordance with . . .

überfällig *adj*, overdue; **die Zahlungen sind seit dem 1. Dezember überfällig**, payments have been overdue since 1 December

Überflußgesellschaft *nf*, affluent society

überflüssig *adj*, redundant, spare

überfordern *vb*, overtax, expect too much; **wir haben ihn überfordert**, we expected too much of him

Überfracht *nf*, excess freight

überfüllt *adj*, overcrowded

Übergabe *nf*, **1** handover. **2** (of new building), opening

Übergangs-; **Übergangslösung** *nf*, interim/temporary solution; **Übergangsphase** *nf*, transitional phase; **Übergangsregelung** *nf*, interim/temporary measure

übergeben *vb*, hand over

übergeordnet *adj*, senior

Übergewicht *nn* (of luggage), excess weight

Übergröße *nf*, outsize

Überkapazität *nf*, excess capacity

überladen *vb* (transp), overload

überlastet *adj*, overburdened, overworked

überlegen *vb*, think about/over; **ich muß mir die Sache noch einmal genau überlegen**, I must think the matter over very carefully; **überlegen Sie sich meinen Vorschlag**, think about my suggestion

überlegen *adj*, superior, better

Übermaß *nn*, excess; **im Übermaß**, more than enough

übermitteln *vb* (message), transmit

übermorgen *adv*, the day after tomorrow

übernächste(r, s) *adj*, next but one

übernachten *vb*, stay the night

Übernachtung *nf*, overnight stay; **Übernachtung und Frühstück**, bed and breakfast, B&B

Übernachtungsmöglichkeit *nf*, overnight accommodation

Übernahme *nf*, **1** (of business), takeover. **2** (of job, costs), **er hat sich zur Übernahme der Kosten verpflichtet**, he has undertaken to pay the costs; **Übernahmeangebot** *nn*, takeover bid

übernational *adj*, supranational

übernehmen *vb*, **1** (business), take over. **2** (job, costs), take on; **sie hat diese Aufgabe übernommen**, she has taken on this task

Überproduktion *nf*, overproduction

überprüfen *vb*, check, inspect, examine

Überprüfung *nf*, check(ing), inspection, examination

überragend *adj* (achievement), outstanding

überraschen *vb*, surprise

überreagieren *vb*, overreact

überreden *vb*, persuade, talk into

überregional *adj*, national

überreichen *vb*, hand over, present

überrunden *vb*, outstrip

übersättigen *vb* (market), glut, oversaturate

Übersättigung *nf* (of market), glut, oversaturation

überschätzen *vb*, **1** (person, significance), overrate. **2** (figure, distance), overestimate

Überschau *nf*, overview

überschauen *vb* (situation), see at a glance

Überschicht *nf* (in factory), extra shift

Überschlag *nm* (calculation), rough estimate, computation

überschlagen *vb* (cost), estimate (roughly), compute

überschreiben *vb*, **1** (business), sign over to. **2** (comp), overwrite

Überschrift *nf*, heading

überschuldet *adj*, heavily in debt

Überschuldung *nf*, excessive debts

Überschuß *nm*, excess, surplus

überschüssig *adj*, excess, surplus

überschwemmen *vb* (the market with goods), swamp, inundate

Übersee, in/nach Übersee, overseas; **Überseehafen** *nm*, international port; **Überseehandel** *nm*, overseas trade; **Überseemärkte** *nmpl*, overseas markets

übersehbar *adj*, **1** (consequences), clear. **2** (damage, costs), assessable

übersehen *vb*, **1** (not notice), overlook; **das habe ich übersehen**, I overlooked that. **2** (consequences), see clearly. **3** (damage, costs), assess

übersenden *vb*, **1** (gen), send. **2** (corr), enclose; **hiermit übersende ich Ihnen . . .**, please find enclosed . . .

übersetzen *vb* (language), translate

Übersetzer(in) *nm/f*, translator

Übersetzung *nf* (language), translation

Übersetzungsdienst *nm*, translation service

überstehen *vb* (danger, crisis), come through, survive

übersteigert *adj* (demands), excessive

Überstunden *nfpl*, overtime; **Überstunden machen**, work overtime; **Überstundenlohn** *nm*, overtime pay; **Überstundenverbot** *nn*, overtime ban

überteuern *vb* (goods), overcharge for

Übertrag *nm* (fin), amount carried forward

übertragbar *adj*, **1** (gen), transferable. **2** (cheque), **nicht übertragbar**, not negotiable

übertragen *vb*, **1** (gen), switch,

transfer. **2** (function), assign. **3** (amount), carry forward

Übertragungsurkunde *nf*, conveyance

übertreffen *vb*, **1** (competitor), beat. **2** (record), break. **3** (expectations), surpass

übertrieben *adj* (claim), exaggerated

übervorsichtig *adj*, overcautious

überwachen *vb*, control, monitor, supervise

überweisen *vb* (fin), remit, transfer

Überweisung *nf* (fin), remittance, transfer

Überweisungsauftrag *nm* (fin), transfer order

Überweisungsformular *nn* (fin), transfer form

überwiegen *vb*, outweigh; **die Vorteile überwiegen die Nachteile**, the advantages outweigh the disadvantages

überwinden *vb* (problems), overcome

Überzahl *nf*, majority

überzeugen *vb*, persuade, convince

Überzeugung *nf*, conviction

überziehen *vb*, **1** (account), overdraw. **2** (time), overrun

Überziehung *nf* (fin), overdraft

Überziehungskredit *nm* (fin), overdraft provision

üblich *adj*, usual, normal

üblicherweise *adv*, usually, normally

übrig *adj*, remaining

übrig|behalten *vb*, have left over

übrig|bleiben *vb*, be left over, remain

übrigens *adv*, incidentally

Übung *nf*, practice

Uhr *nf*, **1** (clock), **wir arbeiten rund um die Uhr**, we work round the clock. **2** (time), **um wieviel Uhr?**, at what time?; **Uhrzeigersinn** *nm*, **im Uhrzeigersinn**, clockwise

Umfang *nm*, size, volume; **in großem Umfang**, on a large scale; **in vollem Umfang**, fully

umfangreich *adj*, extensive

umfassend *adj*, comprehensive, full-scale; **eine umfassende Untersuchung** *nf*, a full-scale investigation

Umfrage *nf* (mktg), survey; **eine Umfrage durchführen**, conduct a survey; **Umfrageergebnis** *nn* (mktg), survey results

umgehen *vb*, avoid; **wir können das Problem umgehen, indem wir . . .**, we can avoid the problem by . . .

um|gehen mit (+ dat) *vb*, handle; **er kann mit Geld nicht umgehen**, he is not good at handling money

umgehend *adj*, *adv*, immediate; immediately; **wir bitten um eine umgehende Antwort**, we would be grateful for a prompt reply; **mit umgehender Post**, by return of post

umgekehrt *adj*, **die umgekehrte Richtung**, the opposite direction; **die Sache war in Wirklichkeit umgekehrt**, in fact, things were the other way round

um|kehren *vb*, reverse, turn round

um|laden *vb* (naut), transship

Umlage *nf*, **eine Umlage machen**, split the cost

Umlauf *nm* (letter), circular; **in Umlauf bringen**, circulate; **Umlaufvermögen** *nn* (fin), current assets

um|legen *vb*, **1** (date), change; **leider müssen wir den Termin umlegen**, unfortunately, we have to change the date. **2** (fin), **die 1.000 DM wurden auf beide Partner zu gleichen Teilen**

umgelegt, each partner had to pay half of the 1,000 DM

um|ordnen *vb*, rearrange

um|organisieren *vb*, reorganise

um|packen *vb*, repack

um|räumen *vb*, rearrange

um|rechnen *vb* (fin), convert

Umrechnung *nf* (fin), conversion

Umrechnungskurs *nm* (fin), exchange rate

Umrechnungstabelle *nf* (fin), conversion table

Umriß *nm*, outline

Umsatz *nm* (comm), sales, turnover; **Umsatzanalyse** *nf*, sales analysis; **Umsatzanstieg** *nm*, increase in sales/turnover; **Umsatzdiagramm** *nn*, sales chart; **Umsatzrückgang** *nm*, drop in sales/turnover; **Umsatzsteuer** *nf*, sales/turnover tax; **Umsatzvolumen** *nn*, sales volume, volume of trade

Umschalttaste *nf* (comp), key shift

um|schichten *vb*, redistribute

Umschlag *nm*, **1** (of goods), handling. **2** (in goods handled), volume of traffic. **3** (reloading of goods, gen), transfer, (naut), transshipment

um|schlagen *vb*, **1** (goods), handle. **2** transfer, (naut), transship. **3** (trend, mood), change drastically

Umschlagspesen *npl*, handling charges

um|schreiben *vb*, **1** (text), rewrite. **2** (mortgage), transfer; **die Hypothek wird auf seinen Sohn umgeschrieben**, the mortgage is being transferred to his son

um|schulen *vb*, retrain

Umschulung *nf*, retraining

Umschwung *nm* (of trend), reversal, drastic change

umsonst *adv*, **1** gratis, free. **2** in vain

Umstand *nm*, **1** circumstance; **unter diesen Umständen**, under these circumstances. **2** trouble, fuss; **ohne große Umstände**, without much fuss

umständehalber *adv*, owing to circumstances

umständlich *adv*, in a roundabout way

um|steigen *vb* (bus, train etc), change

um|stellen *vb*, **1 auf Computer umstellen**, computerise. **2 auf Container umstellen**, containerise

um|stoßen *vb* (calculations), upset

um|strukturieren *vb*, reorganise, restructure

Umtausch *nm* (of money, goods), exchange

um|tauschen *vb*, **1** (goods), exchange. **2** (money), change

um|verteilen *vb*, redistribute

um|wechseln *vb* (money), change

Umweg *nm*, detour; **Umwegfinanzierung** *nf* (fin), indirect financing

Umwelt *nf*, environment; **Umweltauflage** *nf*, ecological requirement; **Umweltbehörde** *nf*, environmental authority

umweltbewußt *adj*, environmentally aware

Umweltbewußtsein *nn*, ecological awareness

Umweltbundesamt *nn*, Department of the Environment

umweltfeindlich *adj*, environmentally harmful, damaging to the environment

umweltgefährdend *adj*, harmful to the environment

Umwelt-; Umweltministerium *nn*, Ministry of the Environment; **Umweltpfennig** *nm*, levy on petrol for ecological purposes; **Umweltschaden** *nm*, damage to the environment

umweltschädlich *adj*, ecologically harmful

Umweltschutz *nm*, conservation, protection of the environment

Umweltschützer(in) *nm/f*, conservationist, environmentalist

Umweltschutz-; **Umweltschutzorganisation** *nf*, ecology group; **Umweltschutzpapier** *nn*, recycled paper; **Umweltschutztechnik** *nf*, conservation technology

Umwelt-; **Umweltsteuer** *nf*, ecology tax; **Umweltsünder** *nm*, polluter; **Umweltverschmutzung** *nf*, pollution; **Umweltverseuchung** *nf*, contamination of the environment

umweltverträglich *adj* (goods, substances), ecologically harmless

um|ziehen *vb* (firm, individual), move; **wir sind nach Berlin umgezogen**, we have moved to Berlin

Umzug *nm* (of firm, individual), move

unabhängig *adj*, *adv*, independent; independently; **unabhängig davon, was . . .**, irrespective/regardless of what . . .

unabsehbar *adj*, **1** (consequences), unforeseeable. **2** (damage), incalculable, immeasurable

unabsichtlich *adj*, unintentional

unangemeldet *adj*, unannounced, unexpected

Unannehmlichkeit *nf*, trouble; **ich hoffe, Sie bekommen dadurch keine Unannehmlichkeiten mit dem Zoll**, I do hope this doesn't get you into trouble at the customs

unauffällig *adj*, inconspicuous

unauffindbar *adj*, untraceable

unaufgefordert *adj* (comm), unsolicited; **unaufgefordert zugesandte Prospekte**, unsolicited brochures

unaufschiebbar *adj*, urgent

unausgefüllt *adj* (form), blank

unbeabsichtigt *adj*, unintentional

unbeachtet *adj*, unnoticed

unbeachtlich *adj*, insignificant

unbeanstandet *adj*, without any queries; **die Ladung kam unbeanstandet durch den Zoll**, the load passed through customs without any queries

unbeantwortet *adj*, unanswered

unbedenklich *adv*, **ich kann Ihnen diese Marke ganz unbedenklich empfehlen**, I can recommend this brand to you without the slightest hesitation

Unbedenklichkeitsbescheinigung *nf* (law), legal document confirming that there are no loans etc outstanding

unbedeutend *adj*, insignificant, minor; **es ist ein unbedeutender Rückgang zu verzeichnen**, there has been a minor decrease

unbedingt *adv*, absolutely; **das ist nicht unbedingt nötig**, that's not absolutely necessary

unbefriedigend *adj*, unsatisfactory

unbefristet *adj*, **1** (contract), open-ended, for an indefinite period. **2** (visa), permanent

unbefugt *adj*, unauthorised

unbegreiflich *adj*, inconceivable, inexplicable

unbegrenzt *adj*, **zeitlich unbegrenzt**, indefinite; **unbegrenzt haltbar** (goods), will keep indefinitely

unbegründet *adj*, **1** (doubts, fear), unfounded. **2** (measure), unwarranted

unbekannt *adj*, unknown; **aus unbekannter Ursache**, for some unknown reason

unbekannterweise *adv*, **bitte grüßen Sie Herrn Müller unbekannterweise**, please give Herr Müller my regards although we haven't (yet) met

unbeladen *adj*, unladen

unbemerkbar *adj*, imperceptible

unbemerkt *adj*, unnoticed

unbenutzbar *adj*, unusable

unbenutzt *adj*, unused

unberechenbar *adj*, unpredictable

unberechtigt *adj*, **1** (criticism), unwarranted. **2** (person), unauthorised

unberücksichtigt bleiben *vb*, fail to be considered

unbeschädigt *adj*, undamaged, intact

unbeschäftigt *adj*, idle

unbeschränkt *adj*, unrestricted; **unbeschränkte Vollmacht** *nf*, carte blanche

unbesetzt *adj*, vacant

unbesorgt sein *vb*, not to worry

unbestätigt *adj*, unconfirmed

unbestreitbar *adj*, **unbestritten** *adj*, (claim), indisputable

unbeweglich *adj*, immovable

unbewiesen *adj*, unproven

unbewohnt *adj* (accommodation), vacant

unbezahlt *adj*, **1** (debt), outstanding. **2** (leave), unpaid

unbezweifelbar *adj*, undeniable

unbrauchbar *adj*, **1** (product), unusable. **2** (equipment), unserviceable

undatiert *adj* (corr), undated

undenkbar *adj*, inconceivable

undeutlich *adj*, vague, unclear

unecht *adj*, false, fake

uneingeschränkt *adj*, *adv*, total; totally

uneinig *adj*, **sich uneinig sein**, fail to reach an agreement

Uneinigkeit *nf*, disagreement; **es herrscht Uneinigkeit**, there is disagreement

unempfindlich *adj*, **1** (gen), insensitive. **2** (product), **gegen Witterungseinflüsse unempfindlich sein**, weather well

unentbehrlich *adj*, indispensable

unentschieden *adj*, undecided

unerfahren *adj*, inexperienced

unerheblich *adj*, insignificant

unerhört *adj*, incredible

unerklärlich *adj*, inexplicable

unerläßlich *adj*, essential, imperative

unerlaubt *adj*, unauthorised, illicit; **unerlaubte Handlung** *nf* (law), tort

unerledigt *adj*, **1** (gen, task), unfinished. **2** (mail), unanswered. **3** (order), unfulfilled. **4** (file), **„unerledigt"**, "pending"

unerreichbar *adj* (telec), unobtainable

unerschwinglich *adj*, (price), exorbitant, prohibitive

unersetzbar *adj*, **unersetzlich** *adj*, irreplaceable

unerwartet *adj*, unexpected

unerwünscht *adj*, undesirable, not welcome

unfachmännisch *adj*, unprofessional

unfähig *adj*, incompetent

Unfähigkeit *nf*, incompetence

Unfall *nm*, accident; **Unfallgegner** *nm* (law), plaintiff for damages; **Unfallrente** *nf*, accident benefits; **Unfallversicherung** *nf*, accident insurance

unformatiert *adj* (comp), unformatted

unfrankiert *adj* (corr), unstamped

unfreiwillig *adj*, involuntary

ungeachtet (+ genitive) *prep*, in spite of, despite; **ungeachtet aller Warnungen**, despite all warnings

ungebraucht *adj*, unused

ungebührlich *adj*, improper

ungedeckt *adj* (cheque), uncovered

ungeduldig *adj*, impatient

ungefähr *adj*, *adv*, approximate; approximately, roughly; **die ungefähren Kosten**, approximate cost(s); **ungefähr um 8 Uhr**, at approximately/roughly 8 o'clock

ungelegen *adj*, inconvenient; **kommt Ihnen mein Besuch auch nicht ungelegen?**, I hope my visit isn't (going to be) inconvenient

Ungelegenheiten *nfpl*, inconvenience; **Ungelegenheiten machen**, cause inconvenience

ungelernt *adj* (worker), unskilled

ungenannt *adj*, anonymous

ungenau *adj*, inaccurate, inexact

ungeöffnet *adj* (corr), unopened

ungeprüft *adj*, unchecked

ungerechtfertigt *adj*, unjustified

ungern *adv*, reluctantly

ungesetzlich *adv*, unlawfully, illegally

ungesichert *adj*, unsecured

ungestört *adj*, undisturbed

ungetilgt *adj* (debts), uncleared

ungewiß *adj*, uncertain; **im ungewissen lassen**, leave in the dark

Ungewißheit *nf*, uncertainty

ungewöhnlich *adj*, *adv*, unusual, exceptional; unusually, exceptionally

ungewollt *adj*, unintentional

ungezeichnet *adj* (corr), unsigned

ungleich *adj*, *adv*, uneven; unevenly; **ungleich verteilt**, unevenly distributed

Ungleichbehandlung *nf* (law), discrimination

unglücklicherweise *adv*, unfortunately

ungültig *adj*, invalid; **für ungültig erklären** (law), declare null and void; **ungültig werden**, become invalid, expire

Ungültigkeit *nf*, invalidity

Ungültigkeitserklärung *nf*, invalidation

ungünstig *adj*, unfavourable

ungünstigstenfalls *adv*, if the worst comes to the worst

Unkenntnis *nf*, ignorance; **in Unkenntnis der Tatsachen**, in ignorance of the facts

unklar *adj*, unclear; **sich im unklaren sein über** (+ acc), be uncertain/in the dark about

unkollegial *adj*, uncooperative

unkorrigiert *adj*, uncorrected

Unkosten *npl*, cost(s), expense(s), overheads; **wer trägt die Unkosten?**, who bears the cost(s)?; **die Reise war mit großen Unkosten verbunden**, the journey involved considerable expense; **Unkosten werden erstattet**, expenses are reimbursed; **die allgemeinen Unkosten des Betriebs sind recht hoch**, the company has fairly high overheads; **Unkostenbeitrag** *nm*, contribution towards expenses; **Unkostenvergütung** *nf*, reimbursement of expenses

unkündbar *adj*, **1** (position), permanent. **2** (contract), binding, not terminable. **3** (loan), irredeemable

unmittelbar *adv*, directly, immediately

unmöglich *adj*, impossible

unnötig *adj, adv*, unnecessary; unnecessarily; **unnötig kompliziert**, unnecessarily complicated

unnötigerweise *adv*, unnecessarily

unökonomisch *adj*, uneconomical

unparteiisch *adj*, impartial

unpassend *adj* (time), inconvenient

unpünktlich *adj*, **1** (person), unpunctual. **2** (train), not on time

unqualifiziert *adj* (person), unqualified

unrationell *adj*, inefficient

unrealistisch *adj*, unrealistic

unrecht haben *vb*, be wrong; **Sie haben nicht ganz unrecht**, you are not entirely wrong

unredlich *adj*, dishonest

unregelmäßig *adj*, irregular

unrentabel *adj*, not commercially viable

unrichtig *adj*, incorrect

unsachgemäß *adj* (admin), improper; **bei unsachgemäßer Behandlung . . .**, if put to improper use . . .

unsachlich *adj*, lacking in objectivity; **unsachlich werden**, become personal

unschädlich *adj*, harmless, safe

unschätzbar *adj* (help), invaluable

Unselbständige(r) *nf/m* (fin), employed person

unsicher *adj*, **1** (doubtful), uncertain; **das Ergebnis ist noch unsicher**, the outcome is still uncertain. **2** (dangerous), unsafe, **auf unsicherem Boden**, on unsafe ground

Unsicherheit *nf*, uncertainty

Unsicherheitsfaktor *nm*, element of uncertainty

unsolide *adj* (person, company), unreliable

unstimmig sein *vb*, disagree

Unstimmigkeit *nf*, disagreement; **eine Unstimmigkeit beilegen**, settle a disagreement

Unsumme *nf*, vast sum; **der Umzug hat die Firma Unsummen gekostet**, the move cost the firm vast sums of money

untätig *adj*, inactive

unten *adv*, **1** (gen), at the bottom; **unten auf der Liste**, at the bottom of the list. **2** (of building) downstairs; **Sie finden das Büro unten (im Erdgeschoß)**, you'll find the office downstairs (on the ground floor)

untenerwähnt *adj*, **untengenannt** *adj*, **1** (gen), mentioned below. **2** (form) undermentioned

Unterabteilung *nf*, subdivision

Unterauftrag *nm*, subcontract

Unterausschuß *nm*, subcommittee

unterbelegt *adj*, **das Hotel ist stark unterbelegt**, the hotel has a lot of vacancies/is not very full

Unterbeschäftigung *nf*, underemployment

unterbesetzt *adj*, understaffed

Unterbesetzung *nf*, understaffing

unterbewerten *vb*, underrate

unterbezahlt *adj*, underpaid

Unterbezahlung *nf*, underpayment

unterbieten *vb*, undercut

unterbrechen *vb*, **1** (gen), interrupt; **entschuldigen Sie, wenn ich Sie unterbreche**, forgive me for interrupting. **2** (proceedings, law), suspend. **3** (journey), break. **4** (telec), disconnect

Unterbrechung *nf*, **1** (gen), interruption. **2** (of proceedings, law), suspension. **3** (of journey), break. **4** (telec), disconnection

Unterbringung *nf*, **1** (in hotel), accommodation. **2** (of student in company), placement

unterdessen *adv*, meanwhile

unterdurchschnittlich *adj*, below average

unterentwickelt *adj*, underdeveloped

Unterführung *nf*, underpass

Untergebene(r) *nf/m*, junior member of staff, subordinate

untergeordnet *adj* (position), junior, subordinate

Untergeschoß *nn*, basement

untergraben *vb*, undermine

Unterhalt *nm*, living; **seinen Unterhalt verdienen**, earn one's living

unterhalten *vb*, **1** (business), keep, run. **2** (account), have. **3** (building, vehicle, contacts), maintain. **4** (visitor), entertain

Unterhaltungselektronik *nf*, consumer electronics

Unterhändler *nm*, official mediator, negotiator

Unterkunft *nf*, accommodation, lodging; **möblierte Unterkunft**, furnished accommodation; **Unterkunft und Verpflegung**, board and lodging

Unterlagen *nfpl*, documents, papers; **bitte schicken Sie mir die Unterlagen zu**, would you kindly send me the documents

unterlassen *vb*, **1** refrain from. **2** fail to do; **er hat es leider unterlassen, mich zu benachrichtigen**, unfortunately he (has) failed to notify/inform me

Unterlassung *nf* (payment) (law), default

Unterlassungsfall *nm*, **im Unterlassungsfall**, in case of default

Unterlegenheit *nf*, inferiority

unterliegen (+ dat) *vb*, **1** (fee, tax), be liable to. **2 es unterliegt keinem Zweifel, daß . . .**, there can be no doubt that . . .

Untermiete *nf*, subtenancy; **zur Untermiete wohnen**, lodge

Untermieter(in) *nm/f*, lodger, subtenant

unternehmen *vb*, do, undertake

Unternehmen *nn*, **1** (firm), business, company, organisation; **exportorientiertes Unternehmen**, export-oriented company; **gemeinnütziges Unternehmen**, non profit-making organisation. **2** (action), undertaking, venture; **ein gewagtes Unternehmen**, a bold venture

Unternehmens-; **Unternehmensberater(in)** *nm/f*, management consultant; **Unternehmensbereich** *nm*, division; **Unternehmensforschung** *nf*, operational research; **Unternehmensführung** *nf*, management; **Unternehmensführung mit Zielvorgabe**, management by objectives; **Unternehmensgewinne** *nmpl*, corporate profits; **Unternehmensleitung** *nf*, management; **Unternehmensplanung** *nf*, operational planning; **Unternehmenspolitik** *nf*, company policy; **Unternehmenssanierung** *nf*, restructuring of a company; **Unternehmensspitze** *nf*, top management; **Unternehmensvorstand** *nm*, board of directors

Unternehmer(in) *nm/f*, employer, entrepreneur; **Unternehmerorganisation** *nf* employers' association

Unternehmertum *nn*, **freies Unternehmertum**, free enterprise

Unternehmerverband *nm*, employer's association

Unterpacht *nf*, subtenancy

unterrichten *vb*, **1** advise, brief, inform; **ich bin darüber gut unterrichtet**, I have been well briefed on that. **2** (in school), teach

unterschätzen *vb*, underestimate, underrate

unterscheiden *vb*, distinguish

sich unterscheiden von (+ dat) *vb*, differ from

Unterschied *nm*, difference; **es besteht ein Unterschied zwischen . . .**, there is a difference between . . .

unterschlagen *vb*, **1** (money), embezzle. misappropriate. **2** (information), withhold, suppress

Unterschlagung *nf*, **1** (of money), embezzlement, misappropriation. **2** (of information), withholding, suppression

unterschreiben *vb*. **1** (document), sign; **bitte hier unterschreiben**, please sign here. **2** (support point of view), subscribe to; **das unterschreibe ich!**, I support that!

Unterschrift *nf*, signature; **seine Unterschrift einlösen**, honour a signature; **eine Unterschrift leisten**, give one's signature; **seine Unterschrift unter etwas setzen**, put one's signature to something

Unterschriftenmappe *nf*, signature folder

unterschriftlich *adj*, *adv*, by signature

unterschriftsberechtigt *adj*, authorised to sign

Unterschriftsberechtigte(r) *nf/m*, authorised signatory

unterstehen *vb* (in hierarchy), be subordinate to, report to

unterstellen *vb*, **1** (department), put under the control of. **2** (pejorative), insinuate; **ihr wird Fahrlässigkeit unterstellt**, it is insinuated that she has been negligent

unterstützen *vb*, **1** (gen), assist, support. **2** (fin), back, sponsor. **3** (with public money), subsidise

Unterstützung *nf*, **1** (gen), assistance, support. **2 finanzielle Unterstützung**, (financial) backing. **3** (with public moneys), subsidy

untersuchen *vb*, investigate, check

Untersuchung *nf*, investigation, check

Untersuchungsausschuß *nm*, investigation committee, fact-finding committee

Untersuchungsergebnis *nn* (law), findings

untertreiben *vb*, understate

untervermieten *vb*, sublease, sublet

Unterweisung *nf*, instruction

unterworfen *adj*, **der Steuer unterworfen**, liable to tax

unterzeichnen *vb*, sign

Unterzeichner *nm*, signatory

Unterzeichnete(r) *nf/m*, undersigned; **wir, die Unterzeichneten, erklären, daß . . .**, we, the undersigned, declare that . . .

untragbar *adj*, (price), prohibitive

unüberbrückbar *adj*, irreconcilable

unumgänglich *adj*, unavoidable

unveränderlich *adj*, permanent

unverändert *adj*, unchanged, consistent

unverbindlich *adj* (offer, price), not binding

unverbürgt *adj*, unconfirmed

unvereinbar *adj*, incompatible

unverfälscht *adj*, unadulterated

unvergleichbar *adj*, incomparable

unverhältnismäßig *adv*, disproportionately

unverhofft *adj*, unexpected

unverkäuflich *adj*, not for sale

unvermeidlich *adj*, inevitable

unvermindert *adj*, undiminished

unvernünftig *adj*, unreasonable, irrational

unveröffentlicht *adj*, unpublished

unverpackt *adj*, loose

unverrichteterdinge *adv*, without having achieved anything

unversehens *adv*, all of a sudden

unversteuert *adj*, untaxed

unverzinslich *adj*, interest-free

unverzollt *adj*, *adv*, duty-free

unvorbereitet *adj*, unprepared, cold

unvoreingenommen *adj*, unbiased

unvorhergesehen *adj*, unforeseen

unvorteilhaft *adj*, unfavourable, disadvantageous

unwahr *adj*, untrue

unwesentlich *adj*, inessential, slight; **eine unwesentliche Änderung** *nf*, a slight change

unwichtig *adj*, unimportant, insignificant

unwiderruflich *adj*, irrevocable

unwirtschaftlich *adj*, uneconomical

unzählbar *adj*, **unzählig** *adj*, innumerable, countless

Unzeit *nf*, **zur Unzeit**, at the wrong moment, at an inopportune moment

unzufrieden *adj*, dissatisfied

Unzufriedenheit *nf*, dissatisfaction

unzulänglich *adj*, *adv*, insufficient, inadequate; insufficiently, inadequately

unzulässig *adj*, inadmissible, undue

unzumutbar *adj*, *adv*, unreasonable; unreasonably

unzustellbar *adj* (mail), undeliverable

unzutreffend *adj*, inappropriate; **Unzutreffendes bitte streichen**, delete as appropriate

unzuverlässig *adj*, unreliable

unzweideutig *adj*, *adv*, unambiguous; unambiguously

unzweifelhaft *adv*, undoubtedly

Urheberrecht *nn*, copyright

urheberrechtlich schützen *vb*, copyright

Urkunde *nf*, document

Urkundenfälschung *nf*, forgery

urkundlich *adj*, documentary

Urlaub *nm*, holiday, leave; **Herr Müller ist in/auf Urlaub**, Herr Müller is on leave

Urlaubsgeld *nn*, holiday pay

Urlaubsvertretung *nf*, temporary replacement

Ursache *nf*, cause, reason; **wir haben alle Ursache anzunehmen, daß . . .**, we have every reason to suppose that . . .

Ursprung *nm*, origin, source

Urteil *nn*, **1** (gen, court), judgment. **2** (of criminal), sentence

usw, und so weiter, and so on, etc.

vakuumverpackt *adj*, vacuum-sealed

Vakuumverpackung *nf*, **1** (object), vacuum pack. **2** (process), vacuum packaging

vakuumversiegelt *adj*, vacuum-sealed

Variable *nf*, variable

Variante *nf*, variant

variieren *vb*, vary

VB, Verhandlungsbasis *nf*, or near offer, o.n.o.

Vegetarier(in) *nm/f*, vegetarian

vegetarisch *adj*, vegetarian

verabreden *vb*, arrange, agree on; **am verabredeten Ort/zur verabredeten Zeit**, at the agreed venue/time; **sich verabreden mit** (+ dat), arrange an appointment/a meeting with

Verabredung *nf*, **1** (gen), arrangement, agreement. **2** (social), engagement. **3** (business), appointment, meeting

sich verabschieden von (+ dat) *vb*, say goodbye to

verallgemeinern *vb*, generalise

verändern *vb*, change; **hier müßte vieles verändert werden**, a lot of things have got to change here

Veränderung *nf*, change

veranlassen *vb*, **1** (gen), arrange (for something to be done); **ich werde sofort veranlassen, daß die Sendung heute noch an Sie abgeht**, I shall arrange immediately that the consignment is dispatched to you today. **2** (cause), give rise to

Veranlassung *nf*, cause, reason; **wir haben keine Veranlassung, unsere Strategie zu ändern**, we have no reason to change our strategy

veranschaulichen *vb* (presentation), illustrate

veranstalten *vb* (conference etc), organise, arrange

Veranstalter(in) *nm/f* (of conference etc), organiser

Veranstaltung *nf*, event

Veranstaltungskalender *nm*, calendar of events

Veranstaltungsprogramm *nn*, programme of events

verantworten *vb*, **etwas verantworten**, accept responsibility for something, be held accountable for something

verantwortlich *adj*, **1** (gen), responsible, accountable. **2** (law), liable

Verantwortlichkeit *nf*, **Verantwortung** *nf*, **1** (gen), responsibility, accountability. **2** (law), liability

verantwortungslos *adj*, irresponsible

verarbeiten *vb* (in industry), process

verarbeitende Industrie *nf*, processing industries

Verarbeitungskontrolle *nf*, process control

veräußern *vb*, **1** (gen), dispose of. **2** (assets), realise

Veräußerung *nf*, **1** (gen), disposal. **2** (of assets), realisation

Veräußerungsgewinne *nmpl*, capital gains

Veräußerungsgewinnsteuer *nf*, capital gains tax

Verband *nm* (professional),

association, federation

verbergen *vb*, conceal, hide

verbessern *vb*, **1** (make better), improve. **2** (remove errors), correct

Verbesserung *nf*, **1** (making better), improvement. **2** (removing errors), correction

Verbesserungsvorschlag *nm*, suggestion for improvement

verbieten *vb*, forbid; **ausdrücklich verbieten**, expressly forbid; **Rauchen verboten!**, no smoking

verbinden *vb*, **1** (telec), connect; **ich verbinde Sie**, trying to connect you. **2** involve; **mit diesem Projekt sind hohe Kosten verbunden**, this project involves high costs

verbindlich *adj*, **1** (participation, payment), obligatory, compulsory, **2** (acceptance, regulation), binding. **3** (information), reliable

Verbindlichkeit *nf* (fin), liability; **laufende Verbindlichkeit**, current liability; **äußere Verbindlichkeit**, external liability; **Verbindlichkeiten** (fin), obligations, debts, liabilities; **Verbindlichkeiten erfüllen**, meet/discharge liabilities; **gesicherte Verbindlichkeiten**, secured debts; **kurzfristige Verbindlichkeiten**, current liabilities; **langfristige Verbindlichkeiten**, long-term liabilities

Verbindung *nf*, **1** (gen, transport), connection; **in Duisburg haben Sie direkte Verbindung nach Koblenz**, there is a direct connection from Duisburg to Koblenz. **2** conjunction; **in Verbindung mit** (+ dat), in conjunction with. **3** contact, touch; **mit** (+ dat) **Verbindung aufnehmen** get in touch with. **4** (telec), **eine Verbindung nach München bekommen**, get through to Munich

verbleiben *vb*, **1** (formal corr), remain, ... **verbleibe ich Ihr ...**, ... I remain Yours sincerely ... **2 wie sind Sie verblieben?**, what did you agree on?

Verbot *nn*, ban, prohibition

verboten *adj*, forbidden; **Parken/Rauchen verboten**, no parking/smoking

Verbotsschild *nn*, **Verbotstafel** *nf*, prohibition sign or notice

Verbrauch *nm*, **1** (gen), use. **2** (of petrol, food), consumption. **3** (money), expenditure

verbrauchen *vb*, **1** (gen), use. **2** (petrol, food), consume. **3** (money), spend

Verbraucher *nm* (of goods), consumer; **Verbraucher-Abholmarkt** *nm*, cash-and-carry

verbraucherfeindlich *adj*, not consumer-friendly

verbraucherfreundlich *adj*, consumer-friendly

verbrauchergerecht *adj* (packaging), handy

Verbraucher-; **Verbraucher(groß)markt** *nm*, hypermarket; **Verbraucherpreis** *nm*, retail price; **Verbraucherpreisindex** *nm*, retail price index; **Verbraucherschutz** *nm*, consumer protection; **Verbraucherschutzgesetz** *nn*, Consumer Protection Act; **Verbraucherverband** *nm*, consumer council; **Verbraucherzentrale** *nf*, consumer advice centre

Verbrauchsgüter *nnpl*, consumer goods

Verbrauchssteuer *nf*, excise (duty)

verbreiten *vb*, **1** (ideas), spread, disseminate. **2** (journal), distribute, circulate

verbrennen *vb*, **1** (gen), burn. **2** (waste), incinerate

Verbrennung *nf*, **1** (gen), burning. **2** (of waste), incineration. **3** (of petrol), combustion

Verbrennungsmotor *nm*, internal combustion engine

verbringen *vb* (time), spend

verbuchen *vb* (fin), enter, credit; **wir haben den Betrag auf Ihr Konto verbucht**, we have credited the sum to your account

Verbund *nm*, **im Verbund arbeiten**, cooperate

Verbündete(r) *nf(m)*, ally

Verbund-; **Verbundfahrausweis** *nm*, travel pass (valid for all forms of public transport); **Verbundglas** *nn*, laminated glass; **Verbundstahl** *nm*, laminated steel; **Verbundwerbung** *nf*, joint advertising; **Verbundwerkstoff** *nm*, composite material; **Verbundwirtschaft** *nf*, integrated economy

verbürgen *vb*, confirm, guarantee; **sich verbürgen für** (+ acc), vouch for . . .

Verdacht *nm*, suspicion

verdächtig *adj*, suspicious

verdanken (+ dat) *vb*, owe; **ich verdanke ihm sehr viel**, I owe a lot to him

verderben *vb*, **1** (gen), spoil. **2** (food), go bad/off

verderblich *adj* (food), perishable

verdeutlichen *vb* (presentation), clarify, illustrate; **ich möchte das durch ein Beispiel verdeutlichen**, I would like to illustrate this by means of an example

verdienen *vb*, **1** (money, gen), earn. **2** (profit), make. **3** deserve

Verdiener *nm*, wage-earner

Verdienst *nm*, income, earnings; **Verdienstausfall** *nm*, loss of earnings

Verdienstausfallsentschädigung *nf*, compensation (for loss of earnings)

Verdienstspanne *nf*, profit margin

verdienstvoll *adj*, commendable

verdoppeln *vb*, **sich verdoppeln** *vb*, double

Verdoppelung *nf*, doubling

Verein *nm*, association, society; **wohltätiger Verein**, charity; **eingetragener Verein, e.V.**, registered society/charity

vereinbar *adj*, compatible

vereinbaren *vb*, **1** agree; **wir haben vereinbart, daß wir uns im März wieder treffen**, we have agreed to meet again in March. **2** reconcile; **diese beiden Standpunkte sind schwer (miteinander) zu vereinbaren**, these two points of view are difficult to reconcile (with each other)

Vereinbarung *nf*, agreement; **mündliche Vereinbarung**, verbal agreement; **eine Vereinbarung aushandeln**, hammer out an agreement; **eine Vereinbarung treffen**, reach an agreement

vereinbarungsgemäß *adv*, as agreed

vereinfachen *vb*, simplify

Vereinfachung *nf*, simplification

vereinheitlichen *vb*, standardise

vereinigen *vb*, **1** (gen), unite, combine. **2** (comm, firms), merge

Vereinigtes Königreich *nn*, United Kingdom, UK

Vereinigte Staaten von Amerika *npl*, United States of America

Vereinigung *nf*, **1** (gen, process), uniting, combining. **2** (comm, of firms), merging. **3** association, union

Vereinsmitglied *nn*, club/society member

verfahren *vb*, proceed

Verfahren *nn*, **1** (gen), method, procedure. **2** (techn), process. **3** (law), (legal) proceedings

verfallen *vb*, **1** (stamps, money), become invalid. **2** (ticket), expire. **3** (date), lapse

Verfallsdatum *nn* (food), best-before/eat-by date

verfärben *vb*, discolour

verfaulen *vb*, rot, decay

verfeinern *vb*, refine

verfertigen *vb*, manufacture, produce

verflechten *vb* (firms), integrate, combine

verfolgen *vb*, **1** (gen, idea, plan), pursue; **wir sollten diese Idee weiterverfolgen**, we ought to pursue/take this idea further. **2** (law), prosecute

verfrachten *vb*, **1** (gen, comm), transport, freight. **2** (naut), ship

verfügbar *adj*, available

verfügen über (+ acc) *vb*, have at one's disposal

Verfügung *nf* (gen), disposal; **ich stehe Ihnen jederzeit zur Verfügung**, I am always at your disposal; **jemandem etwas zur Verfügung stellen**, put something at someone's disposal

verführerisch *adj* (goods, display), appealing, tempting

Vergangenheit *nf*, past

vergeben *vb*, **1** (order), award. **2** (task), assign. **3** (post), fill

vergebens *adv*, in vain

vergeblich *adj*, *adv*, futile, in vain

vergehen *vb* (time), pass

vergessen *vb*, forget

vergeuden *vb*, waste

Vergleich *nm*, **1** (gen), comparison; **einen Vergleich ziehen**, draw a comparison. **2** (law), settlement; **einen gütlichen/außergerichtlichen Vergleich schließen**, reach an amicable/out-of-court settlement

vergleichen *vb*, **1** (gen), compare; **das läßt sich schwer vergleichen**, that's difficult to compare. **2** (law), settle

Vergleichsverfahren *nn*, (law), insolvency proceedings

vergleichsweise *adv*, comparatively

Vergnügen *nn*, pleasure, fun; **viel Vergnügen!**, have fun!, enjoy yourself!

vergrößern *vb*, **1** (business, market), expand. **2** (area, influence), extend. **3** (number, problems), increase

Vergrößerung *nf*, **1** (of business, market), expansion. **2** (of area, influence), extension. **3** (in number, problems), increase

Vergünstigung *nf*, **1** (price), concession, reduction. **2** (pers), perk

vergüten *vb*, **1** (expenses), reimburse. **2** (damage), compensate. **3** (work), pay, recompense

Vergütung *nf*, **1** (of expenses), reimbursement. **2** (for damage), compensation. **3** (for work), payment, recompense

verhalten *vb*, **wie verhält sich der Markt im Moment?**, what's the market situation like at the moment?; **damit verhält es sich ganz anders**, actually, things are very different; **wenn es sich so verhält, . . .**, if that's the case . . .

Verhältnis *nn*, proportion, ratio; **im Verhältnis 3:1**, at a ratio of 3:1

Verhältnisse *nnpl*, conditions, circumstances; **unter normalen Verhältnissen**, under normal circumstances

verhältnismäßig *adv*, relatively

verhandeln *vb*, **1** (gen), negotiate.

2 (law), hear (a case)

Verhandlung *nf*, **1** (gen), negotiation(s). **2** (law), (court) hearing

Verhandlungs-; **Verhandlungsausschuß** *nm*, negotiating committee; **Verhandlungsbasis** *nf*, basis for negotiation(s); **Verhandlungsbereitschaft** *nf*, readiness to negotiate; **Verhandlungsführer** *nm*, negotiator; **Verhandlungsgrundlage** *nf*, basis for negotiation(s); **Verhandlungsposition** *nf*, negotiating/bargaining position; **Verhandlungsstärke** *nf*, bargaining power; **Verhandlungstisch** *nm*, negotiating table

verhärten *vb*, harden

verhindern *vb*, prevent

verhindert sein *vb*, be unable to attend

verhüten *vb*, prevent

Verhütungsmaßnahme *nf*, preventive measure

verifizieren *vb*, verify

verjähren *vb* (claim), lapse

verkabeln *vb* (telec), link up (to the cable network)

verkalkulieren *vb*, miscalculate

Verkauf *nm*, selling, sale; **Verkauf auf Kommissionsbasis**, sale on commission; **Verkauf auf Kreditkarte**, credit card sale; **Verkauf mit Rückmietgarantie**, lease-back sale

verkaufen *vb*, sell

Verkäufer(in) *nm/f*, **1** shop assistant. **2** salesman, saleswoman; **Verkäufermarkt** *nm*, seller's market; **Verkäuferstab** *nm*, sales force

verkäuflich *adj*, marketable; **schwer verkäuflich** hard to sell

Verkaufs-; **Verkaufsabteilung** *nf*, sales department; **Verkaufsaktion** *nf*, sales campaign; **Verkaufsangebot** *nn*, offer; **einmaliges Verkaufsangebot**, unique offer; **Verkaufsbedingungen** *nfpl*, sales conditions; **Verkaufsbüro** *nn*, sales office; **Verkaufsförderung** *nf*, sales promotion; **Verkaufsgespräch** *nn*, sales pitch; **Verkaufsleiter(in)** *nm/f*, sales manager(ess); **Verkaufsmethoden** *nfpl*, sales techniques; **aggressive Verkaufsmethoden**, high-pressure sales techniques

verkaufsoffener Samstag *nm*, Saturday on which shops are open all day

Verkaufs-; **Verkaufspersonal** *nn*, sales personnel, sales staff; **Verkaufspreis** *nm*, selling price, retail price; **Verkaufsprognose** *nf*, projected sales; **Verkaufsprospekte** *nmpl*, sales literature; **Verkaufsschlager** *nm*, best-seller, big seller; **Verkaufsstab** *nm*, sales force; **Verkaufsstatistik** *nf*, sales chart; **Verkaufsstelle** *nf*, sales outlet, sales point; **Verkaufstechnik** *nf*, salesmanship; **Verkaufszahlen** *nfpl*, sales figures; **Verkaufsziel** *nn*, sales target

Verkehr *nm*, **1** (gen), traffic; **dichter Verkehr**, heavy traffic; **öffentlicher Verkehr**, public transport. **2** trade, business

verkehren *vb*, **1** (means of transport), operate, run; **das Flugzeug verkehrt einmal wöchentlich**, the flight operates once a week. **2** (pub, shop), frequent. **3** (formal), correspond with

Verkehrs-; **Verkehrsampel** *nf*, traffic lights; **Verkehrsaufkommen** *nn*, volume of traffic; **Verkehrsflugzeug** *nn*, commercial aircraft;

Verkehrskontrolle *nf*, traffic check; **Verkehrsmittel** *nn*, means of transport

verkehrssicher *adj* (vehicle), roadworthy

Verkehrs-; **Verkehrssicherheit** *nf*, road safety; **Verkehrsstau** *nm*, traffic jam; **Verkehrsstockung** *nf*, traffic hold-up; **Verkehrsteilnehmer(in)** *nm/f*, road user; **Verkehrsunfall** *nm*, road accident

verkennen *vb*, misjudge; **wir haben die Marktsituation verkannt**, we misjudged the market

verkleinern *vb*, reduce, scale down, decrease

verknüpfen *vb*, combine, link

Verladehafen *nm* (imp/exp), port of embarkation, POE

verladen *vb* (imp/exp), load

Verladerampe *nf*, loading platform

Verladung *nf* (imp/exp), loading

Verlag *nm*, publishing house

verlagern *vb*, shift, transfer, move

Verlagswirtschaft *nf*, publishing

verlangen *vb*, demand, require, want; **unsere Kunden verlangen, daß . . .**, our customers demand that . . . ; **Sie werden am Telefon verlangt**, you are wanted on the phone

verlängern *vb*, extend, lengthen

Verlängerung *nf*, extension, lengthening

Verlängerungskabel *nn* (electr), extension lead

verlangsamen *vb*, slow down

verlassen *vb*, **1** leave; **ich muß Sie leider verlassen**, I am afraid I'll have to leave you. **2** (comp), exit

sich verlassen auf (+ acc) *vb*, rely on; **Sie können sich darauf verlassen**, you can rely on it

verläßlich *adj*, reliable

Verlauf *nm*, course; **im Verlauf der Verhandlung**, in the course of the negotiations

verlaufen *vb*, go, take place; **der Tag verlief gut**, the day went well; **die Verhandlung verlief in angespannter Atmosphäre**, the negotiations took place in a tense atmosphere

verlautbaren *vb*, announce (publicly); **es wird amtlich verlautbart, daß . . .**, it is officially announced that . . .

Verlautbarung *nf*, public announcement

verlegen *vb*, **1** relocate; **die Produktion wird nach Bayern verlegt**, production is relocated to Bavaria. **2** (meeting), postpone; **die Sitzung wird auf Montagmorgen verlegt**, the meeting has been postponed until Monday morning

Verlegenheit *nf*, **finanziell in Verlegenheit sein**, be in financial difficulties

Verlegenheitslösung *nf*, stopgap

Verleih *nm*, rental

verleihen *vb*, **1** (both with and without fee), lend. **2** (against fee), rent (out), hire out

verlieren *vb*, lose; **Zeit verlieren**, lose time; **verlorene Zeit**, lost time

Verlust *nm*, loss; **mit Verlust verkaufen**, sell at a loss

verlustreich *adj* (comm), heavily loss-making

vermarkten *vb*, market, commercialise

vermeiden *vb*, avoid

vermieten *vb*, rent (out), let; **Zimmer zu vermieten**, room to let

Vermieter(in) *nm/f*, landlord,

landlady

vermindern *vb*, reduce

vermitteln *vb*, **1** (gen), arrange. **2** (telec), put through, connect. **3** (hotel room), find. **4** mediate

Vermittler(in) *nm/f* (comm), agent; **Vermittlergebühr** *nf*, commission

Vermittlung *nf*, **1** (comm), agency. **2** (telec), switchboard. **3** mediation

Vermögen *nn*, **1** (lots of money), fortune. **2** property. **3** (stocks and shares), assets

Vermögens-; **Vermögensabgabe** *nf*, property levy; **Vermögensbildung** *nf*, wealth creation; **Vermögenserklärung** *nf*, statement of property/assets; **Vermögenswerte** *nnpl*, assets

vermögenswirksam *adj*, profitable

vermuten *vb*, assume, suspect

Vermutung *nf*, assumption, supposition; **die Vermutung liegt nahe, daß . . .**, there are grounds for the assumption that . . .

vernachlässigen *vb*, neglect

verneinen *vb*, answer in the negative

vernetzen *vb* (comp), network

Venetzung *nf* (comp), networking

vernichten *vb*, destroy

vernünftig *adj*, sensible, reasonable

veröffentlichen *vb*, publish

verpachten *vb*, lease, rent out

Verpachter *nm*, lessor

verpacken *vb*, **1** (parcel), pack. **2** (goods), package

Verpackung *nf*, **1** (parcel), wrapping. **2** (of goods), packaging

Verpackungs-; **Verpackungsgewicht** *nn*, weight of packaging; **Verpackungsindustrie** *nf*, packaging industry; **Verpackungskosten** *npl*, packaging charges; **Verpackungsmaterial** *nn*, packaging; **Verpackungsmüll** *nm*, superfluous packaging

verpassen *vb* (train), miss

Verpflegung *nf*, catering

sich verpflichten *vb*, commit oneself

verpflichtet sein *vb*, be obliged

Verpflichtung *nf*, **1** (gen), obligation. **2** (fin), commitment

verrechnen *vb*, **1** (bill), settle. **2** (cheque), clear. **3** credit/debit an account. **4** (voucher), redeem. **5** (make a mistake), miscalculate

Verrechnungs-; **Verrechnungseinheit** *nf*, clearing unit; **Verrechnungspreise** *nmpl* (comm), internal prices; **Verrechnungsscheck** *nm*, crossed/non-negotiable cheque; **Verrechnungsstelle** *nf*, clearing house

Versand *nm*, **1** (gen), dispatch, shipping. **2** (transp), dispatch department. **3** mail order (firm); **Versandabteilung** *nf*, dispatch department; **Versandanweisungen** *nfpl*, shipping instructions; **Versandanzeige** *nf*, advice note, shipping note; **Versandbahnhof** *nm*, dispatch station

versandbereit *adj*, ready for dispatch

Versanddokument *nn*, shipping document

versandfertig *adj*, ready for dispatch

Versandgeschäft *nn*, **Versandhaus** *nn*, **Versandunternehmen** *nn*, mail-order business

versäumen *vb*, fail to . . .

verschärfen *vb* (regulations), tighten up

verschenken *vb*, give away

verschicken *vb*, send out

verschieben *vb* (event), postpone

verschieden *adj*, **1** different. **2** **verschiedene** (pl), several (pl)

verschiedentlich *adv*, on several occasions

verschiffen *vb*, ship

verschlechtern *vb*, make worse

sich verschlechtern *vb*, get worse, deteriorate

verschleudern *vb* (comm), dump

verschlimmern *vb*, make worse, aggravate

verschlossen *adj*, locked, closed, sealed; **gut verschlossen aufbewahren**, keep tightly closed

verschlüsseln *vb*, code, encode

Verschlüsselung *nf*, coding

verschrotten *vb* (ship, car), scrap

verschulden *vb*, **1** (accident), be responsible for, cause. **2** (fin), get into debt

verschuldet sein *vb*, be in debt

Verschuldung *nf*, **1** blame. **2** (fin), indebtedness

verschütten *vb*, spill

verschweigen *vb*, withhold information

verschwenden *vb*, waste; **Zeit verschwenden**, waste time

verschwenderisch *adj*, wasteful

verschwinden *vb*, disappear

Versehen *nn*, oversight, slip-up, mistake; **aus Versehen**, by mistake

versenden *vb* (catalogues), send (out)

Versendung *nf* (of catalogues), sending (out)

versichern *vb*, **1** (confirm), assure; **ich versichere Ihnen, daß . . .**, I assure you that . . . **2** (car, oneself), insure; **ich bin gegen Unfälle versichert**, I have taken out an accident insurance

Versicherte(r) *nf/m*, insured/assured party

Versicherung *nf*, **1** (confirmation), assurance. **2** (against payment), insurance/(life) assurance

Versicherungs-; **Versicherungsagent** *nm*, insurance agent; **Versicherungsbeitrag** *nm*, insurance premium; **Versicherungsgesellschaft** *nf*, insurance company; **Versicherungskarte** *nf*, insurance card; **die grüne Versicherungskarte** (car), the green card; **Versicherungsnehmer(in)** *nm/f*, policy holder; **Versicherungspolice** *nf*, insurance policy; **Versicherungsprämie** *nf*, insurance premium; **Versicherungssatz** *nm*, insurance rate; **Versicherungsschutz** *nm*, insurance cover; **Versicherungssumme** *nf*, sum insured; **Versicherungsträger** *nm*, insurer, assurer; **Versicherungsvertrag** *nm*, insurance contract; **Versicherungsvertreter** *nm*, insurance agent; **Versicherungszwang** *nm*, compulsory insurance

versiegeln *vb*, seal

versiegelt *adj*, sealed

versorgen *vb* (goods, electr), supply

Versorgung *nf* (goods, electr), supply

Versorgungs-; **Versorgungsengpaß** *nm*, supply shortage, bottleneck; **Versorgungsnetz** *nn* (for water, gas etc), (supply) grid; **Versorgungsschwierigkeiten** *nfpl*, supply problems; **Versorgungsweg** *nm*, supply channel

sich verspäten *vb*, be delayed, be late; **es tut mir leid, daß ich mich verspätet habe**, I am sorry I am late

Verspätung *nf*, **1** (of person), late arrival. **2** (of event), delay. **3 der Zug hat eine Stunde Verspätung**, the train will arrive one hour late

versprechen *vb*, promise

Versprechen *nn*, promise

Verständnis *nn*, understanding; **ich habe kein Verständnis dafür, daß . . .**, I cannot understand why . . .; **Sie haben mein volles Verständnis**, I fully understand

verstärken *vb*, **1** (gen), reinforce, strengthen. **2** (electr), amplify

Verstärker *nm* (electr), amplifier

verstehen *vb*, understand; **falsch verstehen**, misunderstand.

sich verstehen *vb*, **1 sich gut verstehen mit** (+ dat), get on well with. **2 das versteht sich von selbst**, that goes without saying. **3** (comm), **die Preise verstehen sich einschließlich Mehrwertsteuer**, prices include/are inclusive of VAT

versteigern *vb*, auction (off)

Versteigerung *nf*, auction

versteuern *vb*, pay tax on

Versteuerung *nf*, taxation

Verstoß gegen (+ acc) *nm* (law), violation of

Versuch *nm*, **1** (gen), attempt; **einen Versuch machen**, make an attempt. **2** (science), experiment. **3** test, trial

versuchen *vb*, **1** attempt, try. **2** (food), try, sample, taste

vertagen *vb*, adjourn, postpone

vertauschen *vb*, exchange

verteidigen *vb*, defend

Verteidigung *nf*, defence

verteilen *vb*, distribute, spread

Verteiler *nm*, **1** (comm), distributor. **2** (offce), list of people to receive a copy; **Verteilernetz** *nn* (comm), distribution network

Verteilung *nf*, shareout, sharing

verteuern *vb*, make more expensive, increase the price of

Vertrag *nm*, contract, agreement; **mündlicher Vertrag**, verbal/non-written agreement; **unter Vertrag stehen**, be under contract

vertraglich *adj*, contractual; **vertraglich zugesichertes Recht** *nn*, contractual right

Vertrags-; **Vertragsabschluß** *nm*, completion of a contract; **Vertragsbedingungen** *nfpl*, contractual terms; **Vertragsbruch** *nm*, breach of contract

vertragsbrüchig *adj*, in breach of contract

Vertrags-; **Vertragsgegenstand** *nm*, object of the contract/agreement; **Vertragshaftung** *nf*, contractual liability; **Vertragshändler** *nm*, appointed retailer; **Vertragspartner** *nm*, contracting party; **Vertragspflicht** *nf*, contractual obligation; **Vertragsrecht** *nn* (law), law of contract; **Vertragsunterzeichung** *nf*, exchange of contracts; **Vertragsverlängerung** *nf*, extension of a contract; **Vertragsverletzung** *nf*, breach of contract, default; **Vertragswerk** *nn*, contract; **Vertragswerkstätte** *nf*, authorised repair shop

vertrauen *vb*, trust

Vertrauen *nn*, trust, confidence; **im Vertrauen**, in strict confidence

vertrauenswürdig *adj*, trustworthy

vertraulich *adj*, confidential

Vertraulichkeit *nf*, confidentiality

vertreiben *vb* (comm), sell

vertreten *vb*, **1** (country, firm, interests), represent. **2** (comm, firm), be the agent for

Vertreter(in) *nm/f*, **1** (of country, firm, interests), representative. **2** (of firm, comm), agent; **zugelassener Vertreter**, recognised agent. **3** (employee), sales representative. **4** (law), **rechtlicher Vertreter**, attorney. **5** (during absence), replacement, substitute; **Vertreterbesuch** *nm*, **unangemeldeter Vertreterbesuch**, cold call(ing); **Vertreterprovision** *nf*, agent's commission

Vertrieb *nm*, distribution, sales

Vertriebs-; **Vertriebsabteilung** *nf*, sales department; **Vertriebskosten** *npl*, distribution costs, selling costs; **Vertriebsnetz** *nn*, distribution network; **Vertriebswege** *nmpl*, distribution channels

verursachen *vb*, cause

Verursacherprinzip *nn* (e.g. ecology), principle that those responsible are liable for the damages

verurteilen *vb*, condemn

vervielfältigen *vb*, duplicate, photocopy

Vervielfältigung *nf*, duplication, photocopying

Vervielfältigungsapparat *nm*, **Vervielfältigungsgerät** *nn*, **Vervielfältigungsmaschine** *nf*, photocopier

Verwahrung *nf*, safekeeping; **in Verwahrung geben**, deposit

verwalten *vb*, **1** (gen), manage, administer. **2** (office), hold

Verwaltung *nf*, management, administration

Verwaltungs-; **Verwaltungsapparat** *nm*, administrative machinery; **Verwaltungsbehörde** *nf*, administration; **Verwaltungsgebühr** *nf*, administrative charge; **Verwaltungskosten** *npl*, administrative expenses; **Verwaltungsweg** *nm*, **auf dem Verwaltungswege**, through the administrative channels

verwechseln mit (+ dat) *vb*, confuse with, mistake for

Verwechslung *nf*, confusion, mistake; **es muß sich um eine Verwechslung handeln**, there must be some mistake

verweigern *vb*, refuse

Verweigerung *nf* (gen), refusal

verwenden *vb*, utilise, make use of

Verwendung *nf*, use

verwerten *vb*, utilise, make use of

verzählen *vb*, miscount, count wrongly

Verzeichnis *nn*, **1** (of firms, names), register. **2** (of terms), index. **3** (of contents), table, list. **4** (comp, telec), directory

verzeihen *vb*, forgive; **verzeihen Sie!**, excuse me!

Verzeihung! *nf*, pardon!

Verzicht *nm*, **Verzichterklärung** *nf* (law), waiver

verzichten auf (+ acc) *vb*, **1** (gen), do without. **2** (law), waive

verzinsen *vb* (fin), pay interest on; **das Geld wird mit 4% verzinst**, 4% interest is paid on the money, the money bears 4% interest

verzinslich *adj* (fin), **fest verzinslich sein**, yield a fixed rate of interest; **nicht verzinslich**, free of interest; **Kapital verzinslich anlegen**, put capital out at interest

Verzinsung *nf* (fin), payment of interest

verzögern *vb*, delay, slow down

Verzögerung *nf*, delay, hold-up

verzollen *vb*, pay duty on; **haben Sie etwas zu verzollen?**, have you anything to declare?

Verzug *nm*, **1** (gen), delay; **ohne Verzug**, without delay. **2 im Verzug**, in arrears; **mit Zahlungen in Verzug geraten**, fall into arrears with payments

Veto *nn*, **sein Veto einlegen gegen** (+ acc), veto

vgl., vergleiche, cf., s., see

v.H., von Hundert, per cent

Video *nn*, **auf Video(band) aufnehmen**, record on video, video; **Videogerät** *nn*, video recorder; **Videokassette** *nf*, video cassette; **Videotechnik** *nf*, video technology

viel *adj*, a lot of, a great deal of; **viel Arbeit**, a lot of work; **viel Spaß!**, have fun!

vielbeschäftigt *adj*, very busy

vielerorts *adv*, in many places

vielfach *adj*, *adv*, multiple; frequently; **vielfach bewährt**, tried and tested many times

Vielfalt *nf*, (great) variety

vielleicht *adv*, perhaps

vielmals *adv*, **danke vielmals!**, many thanks!; **ich bitte vielmals um Entschuldigung!**, I do apologise!; **Frau Hinrich läßt vielmals grüßen**, Frau Hinrich sends her regards

Vierfachsteckdose *nf* (electr), four-socket plug

Vierradantrieb *nm* (car), four-wheel drive

Viertel *nn*, quarter; **Vierteljahr** *nn*, quarter; **pro Vierteljahr**, per quarter; **Viertelstunde** *nf*, quarter of an hour

vierwöchentlich *adj*, *adv*, four-weekly, every four weeks

Virusschutz *nm* (comp), virus protection

Visitenkarte *nf*, business card

Visum *nn*, visa; **ein Visum beantragen**, apply for a visa; **Visum mit Rückkehrberechtigung**, re-entry visa

Vitrine *nf*, display cabinet

Völkerrecht *nn* (law), international law

Volks-; **Volkseinkommen** *nn*, national income; **Volksentscheid** *nm*, referendum; **Volkshochschule** *nf*, **VHS**, adult education centre; **Volkswirt** *nm*, economist

vollautomatisch *adj*, fully automatic

Vollbeschäftigung *nf*, full employment

vollkaskoversichert *adj*, comprehensively insured

Vollkasko(versicherung) *nf*, fully comprehensive insurance

vollkommen *adj*, *adv*, complete; completely, fully

Vollmacht *nf* (law), power of attorney, proxy; **jemandem eine Vollmacht erteilen**, give someone power of attorney

Vollsichtregal *nn*, display stand

vollständig *adv*, completely; **vollständig abbezahlen**, pay off (completely); **vollständig abschreiben**, write off (completely)

Vollständigkeit *nf*, completeness

Vorabdruck *nm*, preprint

Vorabend *nm*, evening before, eve

voran|gehen *vb*, **die Arbeit geht gut voran**, the work is coming on/progressing well

Voranmeldung *nf*, (prior) appointment

Vorarbeit *nf*, preparatory work, groundwork

Vorarbeiter(in) *nm/f*, foreman, forewoman

voraus *adv*, ahead; **im voraus**, in advance

voraus|berechnen *vb* (costs), calculate in advance, estimate

vorausbezahlt *adj*, prepaid

Vorausbezahlung *nf*, advance payment

voraus|setzen *vb*, assume, presuppose, take for granted; **vorausgesetzt, daß . . .**, assuming that . . .

Voraussetzung *nf*, prerequisite, condition, requirement; **unter der Voraussetzung, daß . . .**, on condition that . . .

Vorbehalt *nm*, proviso

vor|behalten *vb*, **Änderungen vorbehalten**, subject to change

vorbehaltlos *adj*, unconditional

Vorbehaltsklausel *nf*, proviso

Vorbehaltspreis *nm*, reserve price

vor|bereiten *vb*, prepare

Vorbereitung *nf*, preparation

Vorbericht *nm*, preliminary report

Vorbesprechung *nf*, preliminary discussion, preliminary meeting

Vorbestellung *nf*, **1** (of goods), advance order. **2** (of hotel room), advance booking

vor|beugen *vb*, take preventive measures

Vorbild *nn*, model; **als Vorbild dienen**, serve as a model

vor|datieren *vb*, postdate

Vordergrund *nf* (priorities), fore(front); **in den Vordergrund treten**, come to the fore

vorderhand *adv*, for the time being

Vorderrad *nn*, front wheel

vordringlich *adj*, urgent

Vordruck *nm* (document), form

Vorentscheidung *nf*, preliminary decision

Vorfahrt *nf*, right of way; **Sie haben Vorfahrt**, you have right of way

Vorfall *nm*, incident, occurrence

vor|fallen *vb*, occur, happen

vor|fertigen *vb*, prefabricate

vor|fühlen *vb*, sound out

vor|führen *vb* (equipment), demonstrate

Vorführung *nf*, demonstration

Vorgang *nm*, **1** (gen), process. **2** (offce), file, dossier; **ich brauche den ganzen Vorgang**, I need the whole file

Vorgänger(in) *nm/f*, predecessor

Vorgehensweise *nf*, procedure

Vorgesetzte(r) *nf/m*, superior

vorgestern *adv*, the day before yesterday

vor|haben *vb*, intend, plan; **haben Sie für heute abend etwas vor?**, have you any plans for tonight?

vorhanden *adj*, available, in existence

vorher *adv*, before(hand); **am Tag vorher**, the day before

Vorhersage *nf*, forecast, projection

Vorjahr *nn*, previous year, year before

Vorjahresergebnis *nn*, previous year's result

Vorjahreswert *nm*, previous year's value

Vorkaufsrecht *nn*, option of purchase

Vorkehrung *nf*, precaution

Vorkenntnis *nf*, prior knowledge

vor|kommen *vb*, happen

Vorkommnis *nn*, incident

vor|laden *vb* (law), summon, issue a writ against, subpoena

Vorladung *nf* (law), summons

Vorlage *nf*, **1** (of cheque), presentation. **2** (of document), draft

vorläufig *adj*, *adv*, temporary; temporarily, provisionally

Vorliebe *nf*, prediliction, preference

vor|liegen *vb*, be available; **die Ergebnisse liegen jetzt vor**, the results are now available

vorliegend *adj*, **im vorliegenden Fall**, in the present case

vorm., **vormittags** *adv*, a.m.

Vormacht *nf*, supremacy

vormalig *adj*, former

Vorrang *nm*, priority; **Vorrang haben vor** (+ dat), take priority over

vorrangig *adj*, *adv*, of top priority

Vorrat *nm* (goods), stocks; **solange der Vorrat reicht**, subject to stock availability; **Vorräte anlegen**, stockpile

vorrätig *adj*, in stock, available

Vorrichtung *nf*, device

vor|schießen *vb* (money), advance

Vorschlag *nm*, proposal; **einen Vorschlag annehmen/ablehnen**, accept/reject a proposal

Vorschriften *nfpl*, regulations

Vorschuß *nm* (payment), advance

vor|sehen *vb*, earmark

Vorsicht *nf*, caution

Vorsichtsmaßnahme *nf*, precautionary measure, precaution; **Vorsichtsmaßnahmen ergreifen**, take precautions

Vorsitz *nm*, chair, chairmanship; **unter dem Vorsitz von . . .**, under the chairmanship of . . ., with . . . in the chair; **den Vorsitz übernehmen**, take the chair

vor|sitzen *vb*, chair

Vorsitzende(r) *nf/m*, chair(person)

Vorsprache *nf* (formal), visit

vor|sprechen bei (+ dat) *vb*, call at

Vorstadt *nf*, suburb

Vorstand *nm*, board (of directors)

Vorstandsmitglied *nn*, member of the board (of directors)

Vorstandssitzung *nf*, board meeting

vor|stehen *vb*, preside over

vor|stellen *vb*, **1** (e.g. results), present. **2** (person), introduce

sich vor|stellen *vb*, **1** imagine; **können Sie sich das vorstellen?**, can you imagine (this)? **2** (oneself), introduce; **darf ich mich vorstellen?**, may I introduce myself?

Vorstellungsgespräch *nn*, interview

vor|strecken *vb* (money), advance

Vorstufe *nf*, preliminary stage

Vortag *nm*, the day before, the eve

Vorteil *nm*, advantage

vorteilhaft *adj*, advantageous

vor|tragen *vb*, report (formally and orally), speak

Vortragende(r) *nf/m*, speaker

Vortritt *nm*, precedence; **Vortritt haben**, have/take precedence

vorübergehend *adj*, *adv*, temporary; temporarily

Vorurteil *nn*, prejudice

vorurteilsfrei *adj*, **vorurteilslos** *adj*, unprejudiced

vor|verlegen *vb* (date), bring forward

Vorwahl *nf* (telec), dialling code

vor|wählen *vb* (telec), dial first

Vorwahlnummer *nf* (telec), dialling code

Vorwand *nm*, pretext

vor|werfen *vb*, reproach

vorwiegend *adj*, predominant

Vorwort *nn*, foreword, preface

Vorwurf *nm*, reproach

vorzeitig *adj*, premature

vor|ziehen *vb*, **1** (gen), prefer. **2** (date), bring forward

Vorzimmerdame *nf*, receptionist

Vorzug *nm*, preference; **. . . den Vorzug geben**, give preference to . . .

vorzüglich *adj*, excellent, superb

Vorzugs-; **Vorzugsaktien** *nfpl*, preference shares; **Vorzugsbedingungen** *nfpl*, preferential terms; **Vorzugsbehandlung** *nf*, preferential treatment; **Vorzugspreis** *nm*, special discount price

Waage *nf*, scales; **eine Waage**, a pair of scales

wachsen *vb*, grow

Wachstum *nn*, growth

Wachstums-; **Wachstumsaktie** *nf*, growth stock; **Wachstumsbranche** *nf*, growth industry; **Wachstumsfonds** *nm*, growth fund

wachstumshemmend *adj*, *adv*, inhibiting growth

Wachstumsindex *nm*, growth index

Wächter *nm*, **1** (night) watchman. **2** (parking) attendant

wagen *vb*, **1** risk (something). **2** dare (do something)

Wagen *nm*, (motor) car; **mit dem Wagen**, by car; **Wagenladung** *nf*, lorry load; **Wagenpark** *nm*, fleet of cars

Waggon *nm*, goods wag(g)on

waggonweise *adv*, by the waggon load

Wahl *nf*, **1** (politics), election. **2** (from several things), choice. **3** (quality), **erste Wahl**, top quality; **zweite Wahl**, second(s), reject(s)

wählen *vb*, **1** (gen), choose, select. **2** (telec), dial. **3** (chairperson), elect

wählerisch *adj* (customer), discriminating

Wählscheibe *nf* (telec), dial

wahlweise *adv*, alternatively

Wählzeichen *nn* (telec), dialling tone; **bitte warten Sie auf das**

Wählzeichen, please wait for the dialling tone

wahr *adj*, true

wahren *vb* (claims, rights), look after, protect

während (+ genitive), *prep* **1** during; **während der ersten drei Monate**, during the first three months

während *conj*, **während die Produktion im Frühjahr anstieg, sank sie im Sommer wieder**, while production rose in the spring, it dropped again in the summer

wahrheitsgetreu *adj* (report), accurate, truthful

wahrscheinlich *adj*, *adv*, probable; probably

Wahrscheinlichkeit *nf*, probability; **aller Wahrscheinlichkeit nach**, in all probability

Währung *nf*, currency; **frei konvertierbare Währung**, convertible currency; **harte/weiche Währung**, hard/soft currency

Währungs-; **Währungsausgleich** *nm*, currency conversion compensation; **Währungseinheit** *nf*, currency unit; **(Internationaler) Währungsfond** *nm*, (International) Monetary Fund; **Währungsgarantie** *nf*, currency backing; **Währungskorb** *nm*, basket of currencies; **Währungsreserven** *nfpl*, currency reserves; **Währungssystem** *nn*, monetary system

Walzstahl *nm*, rolled steel

Wand *nf*, wall; **an der Wand**, on the wall

Wandel *nm* (significant), change; **Wandelanleihe** *nf*, convertible loan

wandeln *vb*, **sich wandeln** *vb*, change (significantly)

Ware *nf*, product; **Waren**, goods, products; **Warenangebot** *nn*, range of goods for sale; **Warenaufzug** *nm*, goods hoist; **Warenausfuhr** *nf*, export of goods; **Warenbegleitpapiere** *nnpl* (imp/exp), shipping documents; **Warenbeschreibung** *nf*, goods description; **Wareneinfuhr** *nf*, import of goods; **Warenexport** *nm*, export of goods; **Warenhaus** *nn*, (department) store; **Warenimport** *nm*, import of goods; **Warenlager** *nn*, **1** (building), warehouse. **2** (goods), stocks; **Warenmuster** *nn*, sample; **Warenprobe** *nf*, sample; **unverkäufliche Warenprobe**, no commercial value, NCV; **Warenterminbörse** *nf*, commodity futures exchange; **Warenumsatz** *nm*, turnover; **Warenumsatzsteuer** *nf*, value-added tax, VAT; **Warenzeichen** *nn*, trademark

warm *adj*, *adv*, warm; warmly; **er wird warm empfohlen**, he is being warmly recommended

Wärme *nf*, warmth; **Wärmeenergie** *nf*, thermal energy; **Wärmekraftwerk** *nn*, thermal power station; **Wärmemesser** *nm*, thermometer

Warnanlage *nf*, warning system

Warnblinkleuchte *nf*, **Warnblinklicht** *nn* (on car), flashing warning light

warnen *vb*, warn

Warnstreik *nm*, token strike

Warnung *nf*, warning

Wartefrist *nf*, **1** (gen), waiting period. **2** (of goods), delivery time

Wartehalle *nf*, **1** (gen), waiting room. **2** (at airport), departure lounge

warten *vb*, wait; **warten auf** (+ acc), wait for; **warten Sie mal!**, wait a minute!; **lange auf sich warten lassen**, be a long time in coming

Wartezeit *nf*, wait

Wartung *nf* (of car), servicing; (of machine), maintenance, servicing

Wartungs-; **Wartungsdienst** *nm*, (maintenance) service; **Wartungshandbuch** *nn*, service handbook, manual; **Wartungsvertrag** *nm*, maintenance contract, service contract

Wasch-; **Waschanlage** *nf*, car wash; **Waschanleitung** *nf*, washing instructions; **Waschautomat** *nm*, automatic washing machine

waschen *vb*, **1** (gen), wash. **2** (money), launder

Waschmittel *nn*, detergent

Wasser *nn*, water

wasserabstoßend *adj*, water-repellent

Wasserdampf *nm*, steam

wasserdicht *adj*, *adv*, waterproof; **wasserdicht machen**, waterproof

Wasserkraft *nf*, water-power

wasserlöslich *adj*, water-soluble

Wasser-; **Wasserstoff** *nm*, hydrogen; **Wasserverbrauch** *nm*, water consumption; **Wasserversorgung** *nf*, water supply; **Wasserverunreinigung** *nf*, water pollution

Watt *nn* (electr), watt; **Wattzahl** *nf*, wattage

Wechsel *nn*, **1** (gen), change. **2** (currency), exchange. **3** (fin), bill (of exchange); **einen Wechsel diskontieren**, discount a bill; **erstklassige Wechsel**, prime bills; **einen Wechsel indossieren**, endorse a bill; **kurzfristige/langfristige Wechsel**, short-dated/long-dated bills; **einen Wechsel unterzeichnen**, back a bill; **Wechselautomat** *nm*, change dispenser; **Wechselbürgschaft** *nf*, **eine Wechselbürgschaft leisten**, guarantee a bill of exchange; **Wechselforderungen** *nfpl*, bills receivable; **Wechselgarant** *nm*, backer of a bill; **Wechselgeld** *nn*, **1** (gen), change; **bitte behalten Sie das Wechselgeld**, do keep the change. **2** (to allow business to start), cash float; **Wechselkurs** *nm*, rate of exchange; **amtlicher Wechselkurs**, official rate of exchange

wechseln *vb*, **1** (gen, replace), change; **wir haben unseren Standort gewechselt**, we have changed our location; **könnten Sie mir 20 Mark wechseln?**, would you be able to change 20 marks for me? **2** (currency), exchange. **3 Briefe wechseln**, correspond

Wechsel-; **Wechselnehmer** *nm*, payee of a bill; **Wechselschalter** *nm* (in bank), counter for foreign currency exchange; **Wechselschuldner** *nm*, payer of a bill

wechselseitig *adj*, reciprocal

Wechsler *nm*, **1** (machine), change dispenser. **2** (person), money-changer

Weg *nm*, way, path; **auf dem Weg sein**, be on one's way; **im Wege stehen**, stand in the way; **auf dem Weg zum Flughafen**, on the way to the airport

weg|bleiben *vb*, stay away

wegen (+ genitive) *prep*, because of

weg|fallen *vb*, be discontinued, disappear

weg|gehen *vb*, leave; **sie geht von der Firma weg**, she is leaving the firm

weggeworfenes Geld *nn*, money down the drain

weg|lassen *vb*, leave out

weg|müssen *vb*, have to leave

weg|rationalisieren *vb* (jobs), rationalise away

weg|schicken *vb* (letter), send off

weg|weisend *adj* (deed, idea), pioneering, revolutionary

weg|werfen *vb*, throw away

Wegwerfgesellschaft *nf*, throwaway society

weich *adj*, soft; **weiche Währung**, soft currency

sich weigern *vb*, refuse

Weigerung *nf*, refusal
Weigerungsfall *nm*, **im Weigerungsfalle**, case of refusal

Weihnachten *nn*, Christmas, Xmas; **wir brauchen die Waren bis Weihnachten**, we need the goods by Christmas; **frohe Weihnachten!**, happy Christmas!

Weihnachtsgeld *nn*, Christmas bonus

weil *conj*, because

Weile *nf*, while; **bitte warten Sie eine Weile**, please wait a while; **vor einer Weile**, a while ago

Wein-; **Weinbauer** *nm*, wine grower; **Weinkarte** *nf* (catering), wine list; **Weinkenner(in)** *nm/f*, wine connoisseur; **Weinlokal** *nn*, wine bar; **Weinprobe** *nf*, wine tasting

weiß *adj*, white

Weisung *nf*, instruction; **auf Weisung von** (+ dat), on instructions of

weisungsgemäß *adj*, *adv*, as instructed

weit *adj* (distance), long, far

Weitblick *nm*, far-sightedness, vision

weiter *adj*, *adv*, further; **weiter nichts**, nothing else; **bis auf weiteres**, until further notice

weiter|arbeiten *vb*, carry on working

weiter|laufen *vb*, **1** (production), go on, continue. **2** (salary), continue to be paid

weiter|leiten *vb*, pass on, refer

Weiterreise *nf*, continuation of journey

weiter|schreiben *vb*, carry on writing

weiter|verarbeiten *vb*, process

Weiterverkauf *nm*, resale; **nicht zum Weiterverkauf bestimmt**, not for resale

weiter|verkaufen *vb*, resell

weiter|vermieten *vb*, sublet

weiter|zahlen *vb*, continue paying/to pay

weitreichend *adj*, far-reaching

weitsichtig *adj*, far-sighted

weitverbreitet *adj*, widespread, common

Welle *nf*, wave

Welt *nf*, world; **Weltbank** *nf*, World Bank; **Welthandel** *nm*, world trade, international trade; **Weltrang** *nm*, **von Weltrang**, world-famous; **Weltwährungsfonds** *nm*, International Monetary Fund

weltweit *adj*, *adv*, worldwide

Weltwirtschaft *nf*, world economy

wenden *vb*, turn; **bitte wenden, b.w.**, please turn over, p.t.o.

wenig *adj*, little

wenige *adj pl*, a few; **wenige Kunden wissen, daß . . .**, only a few customers are aware that . . .

wenigstens *adv*, at least

wenn *conj*, **1** (condition), if; **wenn Ihr Flugzeug pünktlich ist, . . .**, if your plane arrives on time, . . . **2** (time), when; **bitte sagen Sie uns Bescheid, wenn die Produktion beginnt**, please let us know when production starts

wenngleich *conj*, although

Werbe-; **Werbeabteilung** *nf*, publicity department; **Werbeagentur** *nf*, advertising agency; **Werbeaktion** *nf*, publicity/advertising campaign; **Werbeantwort** *nf*, business reply; **Werbeblatt** *nn*, free paper, giveaway paper; **Werbeetat** *nm*, advertising budget; **Werbefeldzug** *nm*, advertising/publicity campaign; **Werbefernsehen** *nn*, commercial TV; **Werbefunk** *nm*, radio commercials; **Werbegemeinschaft** *nf*, joint advertising arrangement; **Werbegrafiker(in)** *nm/f*, commercial artist; **Werbekampagne** *nf*, publicity/advertising campaign

werbekräftig *adj*, **ein werbekräftiger Slogan** *nm*, an effective publicity slogan

Werbematerial *nn*, advertising material, sales literature

werben *vb*, **1** (members, clients etc), recruit. **2** (publicity), **werben für** (+ acc), advertise, promote

Werbe-; **Werbeprospekt** *nm*, publicity leaflet; **Werbesätze** *nmpl*, advertising rates; **Werbeslogan** *nm*, publicity slogan; **Werbespot** *nm*, commercial; **Werbespruch** *nm*, slogan; **Werbetext** *nm* (gen), advertising copy; **Werbetexter(in)** *nm/f*, copy writer; **Werbeträger** *nm*, advertising medium; **Werbetrommel** *nf*, **die Werbetrommel rühren für** (+ acc), beat the big drum for; **Werbevideofilm** *nm* (mktg), promotional video

werbewirksam *adj*, effective

Werbung *nf*, advertising, publicity; **übertriebene Werbung**, hype; **Werbung machen für** (+ acc), publicise

Werbungsbranche *nf*, advertising (industry)

Werbungskosten *npl*, **1** (of individuals), professional outlay, expenses. **2** (of firm), business expenses

Werdegang *nm* (CV), career (background)

werfen *vb*, **1** (gen), throw. **2** (transp), **„nicht werfen!“**, “handle with care!” **3** (cheap goods on the market), dump

Werft *nf*, dockyard, shipyard; **ab Werft**, ex dockyard; **Werftarbeiter(in)** *nm/f*, shipyard worker

Werk *nn*, **1** (work, product), work. **2** (place), works, factory, plant; **ab Werk** (imp/exp), X-ml, X-mll, ex-mill, ex works

Werksangehörige(r) *nf/m*, factory employee

werkseigen *adj*, **werkseigen sein**, belong to the company

Werks-; **Werksgelände** *nn*, works/factory premises; **Werksleitung** *nf*, works/factory management; **Werksschließung** *nf*, plant closure; **Werksspionage** *nf*, industrial espionage

Werk-; **Werkstatt** *nf*, **Werkstätte** *nf*, **1** (gen), workshop. **2** (for car), garage; **Werkstoff** *nm*, material; **Werkstoffprüfer(in)** *nm/f*, materials tester; **Werktag** *nm*, work(ing) day

werktags *adv*, on working days

Werkzeug *nn*, tool; **Werkzeugmaschine** *nf*, machine tool

wert *adj*, worth

Wert *nm*, **1** (gen), value; **angegebener Wert**, declared value; **gegenwärtiger Wert**, present value. **2** (of people), worth. **3** (of bank notes), denomination; **Wertgegenstand** *nm*, object of value

wertlos *adj*, **1** (money), valueless.

2 (person), worthless

Wertmarke *nf* (to stick on), stamp

Wertminderung *nf*, depreciation

Wertpapier *nn* (fin), security, bond; **begebbares Wertpapier**, negotiable paper; **Wertpapiere** (fin), stocks and shares, securities; **Wertpapieranlage** *nf* (fin), investment; **sichere Wertpapieranlage**, blue-chip investment, blue-chip share; **Wertpapierbesitzer** *nm* (fin), stockholder; **Wertpapierbörse** *nf* (fin), stock exchange

Wert-; **Wertschöpfung** *nf* (fin), net product; **Wertsendung** *nf*, registered consignment; **Wertsteigerung** *nf*, appreciation; **Wertsteuer** *nf*, ad valorem duty

Wertung *nf*, evaluation, assessment

Wertverlust *nm*, depreciation

wertvoll *adj*, **1** (gen), valuable. **2** (person), worthy

Wertzuwachs *nm*, appreciation; **Wertzuwachssteuer** *nf*, capital gains tax

wesentlich *adj*, essential; **im wesentlichen**, essentially

Wettbewerb *nm*, competition; **freier Wettbewerb**, free competition; **mörderischer Wettbewerb**, cut-throat competition; **scharfer Wettbewerb**, keen competition; **unlauterer Wettbewerb**, unfair competition

Wettbewerbsbeschränkung *nf*, restraint of trade

wettbewerbsfähig *adj*, competitive

Wettbewerbsfähigkeit *nf*, competitiveness

Wettbewerbsfreiheit *nf*, free competition

Wette *nf*, bet

wetten *vb*, bet

wett|machen *vb*, **1** (gen), make up for. **2** (e.g. a loss), make good

Wettsteuer *nf*, betting tax

wichtig *adj*, important

Wichtigkeit *nf*, importance

Widerklage *nf* (law), counterclaim

widerlegen *vb*, refute

widerrechtlich *adj*, *adv*, unlawful; wrongfully

widerrufen *vb* (e.g. permission), withdraw

sich widersetzen *vb*, oppose

widersprechen *vb*, contradict

widersprechend *adj*, contradictory, conflicting

Widerspruch *nm*, **1** (gen), inconsistency, contradiction. **2** (protest), dissent, opposition; **auf Widerspruch stoßen**, meet with opposition

widersprüchlich *adj*, contradictory, inconsistent

widerspruchslos *adj*, *adv*, **1** (without protest), unopposed. **2** (free from contradiction), consistent

Widerstand *nm*, resistance

widerstandslos *adj*, *adv*, without resistance

Widerstreben *nn*, reluctance

widerwillig *adv*, reluctantly

sich widmen (+ dat) *vb*, devote oneself/apply oneself to

wiederauf|bereiten *vb*, **1** (waste), recycle. **2** (atomic waste), reprocess

Wiederaufbereitung *nf*, **1** (gen), recycling. **2** (of atomic waste), reprocessing

Wiederaufbereitungsanlage *nf*, **1** (gen), recycling plant. **2** (atomic waste), reprocessing plant

Wiederaufnahme *nf* (of negotiations, correspondence), resumption;

Wiederaufnahmeverfahren *nn* **1** (civil law), rehearing. **2** (criminal law), retrial

wiederauf|nehmen *vb* (negotiations, correspondence), resume

wiederaus|führen *vb* (comm), re-export

Wieder-; **Wiederausfuhrhafen** *nm*, entrepot port; **Wiederbeschaffungskosten** *npl* (comm), replacement cost; **Wiederbeschaffungswert** *nm*, replacement value

wieder|beschäftigen *vb*, reemploy

Wiederbeschäftigung *nf*, reemployment

wiederein|führen *vb* (comm), reimport

wiederein|stellen *vb* (pers), reinstate (after unfair dismissal)

Wiedereinstellungsklausel *nf* (law), reinstatement clause

wieder|ernennen *vb*, reappoint

wieder|eröffnen *vb*, reopen

wieder|erstatten *vb*, refund, reimburse

wiedergut|machen *vb*, **1** (damage), compensate for. **2** (mistake), rectify

wiederholen *vb*, **1** (say again), repeat, reiterate. **2** (learn again), revise

wiederholt *adj*, *adv*, repeated; repeatedly

Wiederholungskurs *nm*, refresher course

Wiedersehen *nn*, seeing . . . again, next meeting; **auf Wiedersehen!**, goodbye!; **auf baldiges Wiedersehen**, hoping to see you again soon

wieder|sehen *vb*, see again, meet again

Wiederverkauf *nm*, **1** resale. **2** retail

Wiederverkaufswert *nm*, resale value

wiederverwendbar *adj*, reusable

wieder|verwenden *vb*, reuse

wiederverwertbar *adj*, recyclable

wieder|verwerten *vb*, recycle

Wiederverwertung *nf*, recycling

wiegen *vb*, weigh

Wille *nm*, will; **der gute Wille**, goodwill

willens sein *vb*, be willing/prepared

willkommen *adj*, welcome; **eine willkommene Gelegenheit**, a welcome opportunity; **herzlich willkommen!**, welcome!

Willkommen *nn*, welcome

willkürlich *adj*, *adv*, arbitrary; arbitrarily

Wind *nm*, wind; **Windkraftwerk** *nn*, wind power station

Winterschlußverkauf *nm*, winter sale

Winzergenossenschaft *nf*, wine-growers' cooperative

wirken auf (+ acc) *vb*, have an effect on

wirklich *adj*, *adv*, real; really

Wirklichkeit *nf*, reality

Wirkung *nf*, effect; **Ursache und Wirkung**, cause and effect; **mit Wirkung vom 1. September**, with effect from 1 September

Wirkungsbereich *nm* (pers), domain, sphere of activity

Wirtschaft *nf*, **1** (national), economy. **2** industry and commerce. **3** (fin), business world

wirtschaftlich *adj*, **1** (concerning the economy), economic. **2** (careful with money), economical

Wirtschafts-; **Wirtschaftsaufschwung** *nm*, economic upswing or upturn; **Wirtschaftsausschuß** *nm*, economic committee;

Wirtschaftsberater(in) *nm/f*, business consultant; **Wirtschaftsbüro** *nn*, trade bureau; **Wirtschaftsflüchtling** *nm*, tax refugee; **Wirtschaftsform** *nf*, economic system; **Wirtschaftsführer** *nm*, leading businessman, leading industrialist; **Wirtschaftshilfe** *nf*, economic aid; **Wirtschaftskraft** *nf*, economic power; **Wirtschaftskriminalität** *nf*, white collar crime, industrial crime; **Wirtschaftskrise** *nf*, economic crisis; **Wirtschaftslage** *nf*, economic situation; **Wirtschaftsmacht** *nf*, economic power; **Wirtschaftsminister** *nm*, Minister for Economic Affairs; **Wirtschaftsordnung** *nf*, economic system; **Wirtschaftspolitik** *nf*, economic policy; **Wirtschaftsprüfer(in)** *nm/f*, **1** (gen), accountant; **beeidigter Wirtschaftsprüfer**, chartered accountant. **2** (checking books), auditor; **Wirtschaftsrecht** *nn* (law), commercial law; **Wirtschaftssanktionen** *nfpl*, economic sanctions; **Wirtschaftssanktionen verhängen**, impose economic sanctions; **Wirtschaftsspionage** *nf*, industrial espionage; **Wirtschaftswachstum** *nn*, economic growth; **Wirtschaftswissenschaftler(in)** *nm/f*, economist; **Wirtschaftszweig** *nm*, branch of industry

wissen *vb*, know

Wissen *nn*, knowledge; **nach bestem Wissen und Gewissen**, to the best of one's knowledge and belief

Wissenschaft *nf*, science

Wissenschaftler(in) *nm/f*, scientist

wissenschaftlich *adj*, scientific

wissenswert *adj*, worth knowing

woanders *adv*, somewhere else

Woche *nf*, week; **zweimal in der/pro Woche**, twice a week; **nächste Woche**, next week

Wochen-; **Wochenarbeitszeit** *nf*, working week; **Wochenbericht** *nm*, weekly report; **Wochenende** *nn*, weekend; **schönes Wochenende!**, have a nice weekend!; **Wochenkarte** *nf* (transp), weekly season ticket

wochenlang *adv*, for weeks

Wochentag *nm*, weekday

wöchentlich *adj*, *adv*, weekly; **wöchentliche Lieferung**, weekly delivery; **zweimal wöchentlich**, twice a week

Wochenzeitung *nf*, weekly (paper)

Wohl *nn*, well-being; **zum Wohl!**, cheers!; **auf Ihr Wohl!**, to your health!

wohlbehalten *adv*, safely; **wohlbehalten ankommen**, arrive safely

wohldurchdacht *adj*, carefully thought through

wohlerprobt *adj*, well-tested, well-tried

Wohlfahrt *nf*, welfare

wohlhabend *adj*, prosperous, well-to-do

Wohlstand *nm*, affluence, prosperity

Wohlstandsbürger *nm*, member of an affluent society

Wohlstandsgesellschaft *nf*, affluent society

wohlverdient *adj* (pension etc), well-earned

Wohlwollen *nn*, goodwill

wohlwollend *adj*, benevolent, kindly disposed

Wohnfläche *nf*, living space, size of flat/house (in sq m)

Wohngebiet *nn*, residential area

wohnhaft *adj*, resident

Wohn-; **Wohnküche** *nf*, kitchen-cum-living-room; **Wohnort** *nm*, place of residence; **Wohnsiedlung** *nf*, housing estate

Wohnung *nf*, apartment

Wohnungs-; **Wohnungsamt** *nn*, housing office; **Wohnungsbedarf** *nm*, housing requirements; **Wohnungssuche** *nf*, flat/house hunting; **Wohnungswechsel** *nm*, change of address

Wolle *nf*, wool; **aus Wolle**, woollen

Wort *nn*, word; **das gedruckte Wort**, the printed word; **ich werde Sie beim Wort nehmen**, I'll take you at your word; **in wenigen Worten**, in a few words; **ums Wort bitten**, ask to speak

Wörterbuch *nn*, dictionary

Wortgebühr *nf* (telec), rate per word

wortgetreu *adj*, *adv*, verbatim

Wortlaut *nm*, wording

Wortmeldung *nf*, request to speak; **gibt es noch weitere Wortmeldungen?**, does anyone else wish to speak?

Wuchermiete *nf*, exorbitant rent

wuchern *vb*, **1** (comm), profiteer. **2** (money lending), practise usury

Wucherpreis *nm*, exorbitant price; **Wucherpreise bezahlen**, pay through the nose

Wucherzins *nm*, exorbitant interest

Wühltisch *nm*, dump bin

Wunsch *nm*, wish; **alles geht nach Wunsch**, everything is going smoothly; **auf Wunsch**, by/on request; **auf Wunsch erhältlich** (features of product), optional; **haben Sie sonst noch einen Wunsch?** (in shop), is there anything else you would like?

wünschen *vb*, want, wish; **ich wünsche Ihnen alles Gute!**, I wish you all the best; **was wünschen Sie?**, what can I do for you?

wünschenswert *adj*, desirable

Wz, **Warenzeichen** *nn*, trademark

x-beliebig *adj*, any (old); **wir können uns an einem x-beliebigen Ort treffen**, we can meet anywhere you like

x-fach *adj*, umpteen

x-mal *adv*, umpteen times

Y

Yard *nn*, yard

Yuppie *nm*, yuppie

Z

z. A., zur Ansicht, for inspection

Zahl *nf*, **1** number; **die Zahl der Gäste**, the number of guests; **in großer Zahl**, in large numbers. **2** figure; **in einstelligen Zahlen**, in single figures; **Zahlen aufbereiten**, process figures

zahlbar *adj*, payable; **bei Lieferung zahlbar**, payable on delivery, POD; **nach Erhalt zahlbar**, payable on receipt

zahlen *vb*, pay; **einen hohen Preis zahlen**, pay a high price

zählen *vb*, count

Zahlenangabe *nf*, (statement of) figures; **ich hätte gern genauere Zahlenangaben**, I would like to see more precise figures

Zahler(in) *nm/f*, payer

Zähler *nm* (measuring device), meter; **Zählerstand** *nm*, meter reading

Zahlkarte *nf* (fin), giro transfer form

zahllos *adj*, countless, innumerable

zahlreich *adj*, numerous

Zahlstelle *nf*, payments office

Zahlung *nf*, payment; **eine einmalige Zahlung**, a lump-sum payment; **in Zahlung geben**, give in part exchange; **in Zahlung nehmen**, take in part exchange; **gegen eine Zahlung von . . .**, on payment of . . .; **pünktliche Zahlung**, prompt payment; **Zahlung in Sachleistungen**, payment in kind

Zahlungs-; **Zahlungsabkommen** *nn*, payments agreement; **Zahlungsanweisung** *nf*, giro transfer order; **Zahlungsart** *nf*, method/mode of payment; **Zahlungsaufforderung** *nf*, request for payment; **Zahlungsaufschub** *nm*, moratorium; **Zahlungsbedingungen** *nfpl*, terms of payment; **erleichterte Zahlungsbedingungen**, easy terms; **Zahlungsbilanz** *nf*, balance of payments; **Zahlungsbilanzdefizit** *nn*, balance of payments deficit; **Zahlungserleichterungen** *nfpl*, easy terms; **Zahlungsempfänger** *nm*, payee

zahlungsfähig *adj*, solvent

Zahlungsfrist *nf*, time allowed for payment

zahlungskräftig *adj*, wealthy

Zahlungs-; **Zahlungsmittel** *nn*, **1** means of payment. **2** currency; **gesetzliches Zahlungsmittel**, legal currency, legal tender; **Zahlungsschwierigkeiten** *nfpl*, financial difficulties; **Zahlungstermin** *nm*, date for payment; **letzter Zahlungstermin**, final date for payment

zahlungsunfähig *adj*, insolvent

Zahlungsunfähigkeit *nf*, insolvency

z.B., zum Beispiel, e.g., for example

Zehnerkarte *nf* (for bus), 10-journey ticket

Zehnerpackung *nf*, packet of ten

zehnmal *adv*, ten times

Zehntel *nn*, tenth

Zeichen *nn*, **1** (gen), sign, mark. **2** (corr), reference; **unser/Ihr Zeichen**, our/your reference. **3** (on goods), trademark; **Zeichenerklärung** *nf*, **1** (on timetable) key (to symbols). **2** (on map) legend

zeichnen *vb*, **1** (picture), draw.

2 (document), sign; **ich zeichne für diese Entscheidung verantwortlich**, I take responsibility for this decision. **3** (fin, shares), subscribe

Zeichnung *nf*, drawing

zeichnungsberechtigt *adj*, authorised to sign

Zeichnungsberechtigte(r) *nf/m*, authorised signatory

zeigen *vb*, show

Zeile *nf* (of text), line; **zwischen den Zeilen**, between the lines

Zeit *nf*, time; **lassen Sie sich Zeit!**, take your time!; **mit der Zeit**, gradually; **zur Zeit**, at the moment, currently; **Zeitabschnitt** *nm*, period (of time); **Zeitangabe** *nf*, date; **Zeitarbeit** *nf*, temporary work; **Zeitaufwand** *nm*, time (needed); **Zeitdruck** *nm*, **unter Zeitdruck**, under pressure; **Zeitersparnis** *nf*, time saving

zeitgemäß *adj*, up-to-date

zeitig *adj*, *adv*, early

zeitlich *adj*, *adv*, **in kurzem zeitlichem Abstand**, at short intervals; **das kann ich zeitlich nicht einrichten**, I can't fit it in (timewise); **paßt Ihnen das zeitlich?**, is the time convenient for you?

Zeit-; **Zeitlohn** *nm*, hourly rate; **Zeitmangel** *nm*, lack of time; **Zeitplan** *nm*, schedule; **Zeitpunkt** *nm*, (point in) time

zeitraubend *adj*, time-consuming

Zeitraum *nm*, period (of time)

Zeitrechnung *nf*, calendar

Zeitschrift *nf*, **1** magazine. **2** (scientific) periodical, journal

Zeitung *nf*, (news)paper

Zeitungs-; **Zeitungsabonnement** *nn*, subscription to a (news)paper; **Zeitungsanzeige** *nf*, newspaper ad(vertisement); **Zeitungsausschnitt** *nm*, press cutting; **Zeitungsbeilage** *nf*, newspaper supplement; **Zeitungshändler(in)** *nm/f*, newspaper agent

Zeit-; **Zeitverlust** *nm*, loss of time; **Zeitverschwendung** *nf*, waste of time; **Zeitvertrag** *nm*, short-term contract

zeitweise *adv*, at times

zeitweilig ein|stellen *vb* (production), suspend

Zement *nm*, cement

Zentimeter *nm*, centimetre

Zentner *nm*, hundredweight

zentral *adj*, *adv*, central; centrally

Zentralbank *nf*, central bank

Zentrale *nf*, **1** (of firm), head office. **2** central control (office). **3** (telec), exchange, switchboard

Zentraleinkauf *nm*, central purchasing

zentralisieren *vb*, centralise

Zentralisierung *nf*, centralisation

Zentralrechner *nm* (comp), mainframe

Zentralspeicher *nm* (comp), central memory

Zentrum *nn*, centre

zerbrechlich *adj*, fragile

zerstören *vb*, destroy

Zettel *nm*, piece of paper, slip; **Zettelkartei** *nf*, card index; **Zettelkasten** *nm*, file-card box

Zeuge *nm*, **Zeugin** *nf* (law), witness; **als Zeuge/Zeugin auftreten**, act as witness

zeugen für/gegen (+ acc) *vb* (law), testify for/against

Zeugnis *nf*, **1** (exam), certificate. **2** (pers), testimonial, reference. **3** (law), evidence

z.H(d)., zu Händen, attn., for the

attention of

Ziel *nn*, **1** (travel), destination. **2** (of efforts), aim, target; **Zielgruppe** *nf* (mktg), target group; **Zielhafen** *nm*, port of destination

ziellos *adj*, *adv*, aimless; aimlessly

Zielmarkt *nm* (mktg), target market

Ziffer *nf*, **Ziff.**, digit, figure; **die Ziffer 7**, the figure 7

Zigarette *nf*, cigarette

Zimmer *nn*, room; **ein freies Zimmer**, a vacancy; **Zimmernachweis** *nm*, accommodation service

Zins *nm*, **Zinsen** *nmpl*, interest (no pl); **aufgelaufene Zinsen**, accrued interest; **einfache Zinsen**, simple interest; **feste Zinsen**, fixed interest; **Zinsen bringen/tragen**, earn interest; **Zinsenkonto** *nn*, interest account

Zinseszins *nm*, compound interest

Zins-; **Zinsgefälle** *nn*, interest differential; **Zinsniveau** *nn*, level of interest (rates); **Zinsrückstand** *nm*, back interest; **Zinssatz** *nm*, **1** (on capital), interest rate. **2** (on loans), lending rate; **Zinssenkung** *nf*, lowering of interest rate; **Zinstermin** *nm*, interest due date; **Zinswucher** *nm*, usury

Zitat *nn*, quotation

zitieren *vb*, quote

zögern *vb*, hesitate

Zögern *nn*, hesitation; **ohne Zögern**, without hesitation

Zoll *nm*, customs (duty); **Zoll bezahlen**, pay duty; **einem Zoll unterliegen**, carry duty; **Zollabfertigung** *nf*, **1** (process), customs clearance. **2** (office), customs post, checkpoint

Zollager *nn*, bonded warehouse

Zollamt *nn*, customs office

zollamtlich *adj*, *adv*, **zollamtlich abfertigen lassen**, effect customs clearance; **zollamtlich geöffnet**, opened by the customs

Zoll-; **Zollbeamter** *nm*, **Zollbeamtin** *nf*, customs officer; **Zollbehörde** *nf*, customs authorities; **Zollbestimmung** *nf*, customs regulation; **Zollerklärung** *nf*, customs declaration

zollfrei *adj*, *adv*, duty-free

Zoll-; **Zollgebühr** *nf*, duty, excise; **Zollinhaltserklärung** *nf*, customs declaration; **Zollpapiere** *nnpl*, customs documents; **Zollschranke** *nf*, customs barrier; **Zolltarif** *nm*, customs tariff; **Zollverschluß** *nm*, customs seal

z.T., **zum Teil** *adv*, partly

Zubehör *nn*, accessories

zuerst *adv*, firstly, to begin with

Zufall *nm*, accident; **durch Zufall**, by accident

zufällig *adj*, *adv*, accidental; at random

zufrieden *adj*, satisfied

Zufriedenheit *nf*, satisfaction; **zu Ihrer Zufriedenheit**, to your satisfaction

zufrieden|stellen *vb*, satisfy

zu|führen *vb*, **einem Geschäft Kunden zuführen**, bring customers to a business

Zug *nm*, train; **mit dem Zug fahren**, go by train

Zugabe *nf* (comm), free gift

Zugang *nm*, access

zugänglich *adj*, **1** (building), accessible. **2** (person), approachable

Zugänglichkeit *nf*, **1** (of building), accessibility. **2** (of person), approachability

zu|geben *vb*, admit, concede

zugegebenermaßen *adv*, admittedly

Zugeständnis *nf*, concession

zügig *adj, adv*, speedy; speedily

zugkräftig *adj* (advertisement), catchy, eye-catching

zugleich *adv*, at the same time

zu|greifen *vb*, **1** (customers), grab. **2** (meal), help oneself; **bitte greifen Sie zu!**, please help yourself/yourselves

zugunsten (+ genitive) *prep*, in favour of

zugute kommen *vb*, benefit

Zugverbindung *nf*, train connection

zu|haben *vb* (shop, museum), be closed; **sonntags haben alle Geschäfte zu**, on Sundays all the shops are closed

zuhause *adv*, at home

Zukunft *nf*, future; **in Zukunft**, in future

zukünftig *adj, adv*, future; in future

Zukunftsaussichten *nfpl*, future prospects

Zukunftspläne *nmpl*, plans for the future

Zulage *nf*, bonus (payment)

zulänglich *adj*, adequate

zu|lassen *vb*, **1** (gen), allow; **das lasse ich nicht zu**, I won't allow that. **2** (fin), **an der Börse zugelassen**, quoted on the stock exchange; **zugelassene Aktien**, listed securities

Zulauf *nm*, **großen Zulauf haben** (shop, restaurant), be very popular

zuletzt *adv*, in the end

Zulieferbetrieb *nm*, **Zulieferer** *nm*, supplier

Zulieferindustrie *nf*, supply industry

zu|machen *vb* (shop), **1** (temporarily), close. **2** (for good), close down

zumindest *adv*, at least

Zumutung *nf*, unreasonable demand

zunächst *adv*, first (of all)

Zunahme *nf*, increase

zu|nehmen *vb* (number of customers), increase

zunehmend *adv*, increasingly

Zunft *nf* (crafts), guild

Zurechnung *nf*, **unter Zurechnung aller Kosten**, inclusive of all charges

zurück *adv*, back; **einmal Hamburg und zurück**, a return ticket to Hamburg; **zurück|erstatten** *vb*, refund; **zurück|fallen** *vb* (turnover), drop; **zurück|fordern** *vb*, **wir fordern das Geld zurück**, we demand the money back; **zurück|geben** *vb* (goods), return; **zurück|nehmen** *vb* (order), cancel; **zurück|schicken** *vb*, **zurück|senden** *vb*, send back, return; **zurück|zahlen** *vb*, repay, pay back; **zurück|ziehen** *vb* (offer), withdraw

zur Zeit *adv*, **z. Zt.**, at the moment, pro tem

zusammen|fassen *vb*, summarise

Zusammenfassung *nf*, summary

Zusammenhang *nm*, connection

zusammen|heften *vb* (documents), staple

zusammen|kommen *vb* (debts), accumulate

zusammen|legen *vb*, **1** (resources), pool. **2** (shares), amalgamate

Zusammenlegung *nf* (of shares), amalgamation

zusammen|rechnen *vb*, add up, total up; **ich habe die Kosten noch nicht zusammengerechnet**, I haven't yet added up the cost

Zusatz- *adj*, supplementary; **Zusatzabkommen** *nn*, supplementary agreement; **Zusatzaktie** *nf* (fin), bonus share; **Zusatzbestimmung** *nf*, supplementary provision; **Zusatzgebühr** *nf*, supplementary charge; **Zusatzgerät** *nn*, attachment; **Zusatzklausel** *nf*, rider; **Zusatzmittel** *nn*, additive; **Zusatzsteuer** *nf*, surtax; **Zusatzversicherung** *nf*, supplementary insurance

Zuschauer(in) *nm/f* (TV), viewer; **Zuschauerbefragung** *nf*, **Zuschauerumfrage** *nf* (TV), audience survey

Zuschlag *nm*, **1** (rail), supplement, surcharge. **2** (at auction), acceptance of a bid. **3** (of contract), award

Zuschrift *nf* (to ad), reply

Zuschuß *nm* (state), subsidy, grant

Zuschußbetrieb *nm*, loss-making firm

Zuschußgeschäft *nn*, loss-making deal

zusehends *adv*, visibly

zu|sein *vb* (shop), be closed/shut; **sind die Läden samstags zu?**, are shops closed on Saturdays?

zu|sichern *vb*, assure; **wir sichern Ihnen zu, daß . . .**, we assure you that . . .

Zusicherung *nf*, assurance

Zustand *nm* (of goods, health), condition, state; **in schlechtem Zustand**, in poor condition

zustande bringen *vb*, manage (to bring about)

zustande kommen *vb*, come about

zuständig für (+ acc) *adj*, responsible for

Zuständigkeit *nf*, responsibility

Zuständigkeitsbereich *nm*, area of responsibility; **das fällt nicht in seinen Zuständigkeitsbereich**, that's not his responsibility

zu|stellen *vb*, **1** (letter, goods), deliver. **2** (law), serve (a writ)

Zustellgebühr *nf*, delivery charge

Zustellung *nf*, **1** (of letter, goods), delivery. **2** (law), service (of a writ)

zu|stimmen *vb*, agree; **wir stimmen Ihnen zu**, we agree with you; **wir stimmen Ihrem Vorschlag zu**, we agree to your proposal

Zustimmung *nf*, agreement, approval; **Zustimmung finden**, meet with approval

zutage *adj*, **zutage liegen**, be evident; **zutage treten**, come to light

zu|teilen *vb* (shares), allocate

zutiefst *adv*, deeply

zuträglich *adj*, beneficial, conducive

zu|treffen *vb*, be accurate/correct; **das trifft völlig zu**, that's perfectly correct; **sein Bericht traf nicht immer zu**, his report was not totally accurate

zutreffend *adj*, *adv*, accurate; accurately; **Zutreffendes bitte ankreuzen**, please tick as appropriate

Zutritt *nm*, **Zutritt verboten**, no admittance; **den Zutritt verweigern**, refuse admittance

zuverlässig *adj*, reliable; **aus zuverlässiger Quelle**, from a reliable source

Zuverlässigkeit *nf*, reliability

Zuversicht *nf*, confidence (in the future)

zuviel *adj*, *adv*, too much; **zu viele**, too many

zuvor *adv*, before; **das Jahr zuvor**, the year before/the previous year

Zuwachs *nm*, increase; **Zuwachsquote** *nf*, rate of increase

zu|wenden *vb* (money), give

Zuwendung *nf* (money), financial contribution, donation

zuwenig *adj, adv*, too little; **zu wenige**, too few

zuwider|handeln *vb* (law), contravene, violate

Zuwiderhandlung *nf* (law), contravention, violation

Zwang *nm*, **1** (necessity), compulsion. **2** (physical, moral), force. **3** (obstacles), constraint. **4** (duty), obligation

Zwangs-; **Zwangsabgabe** *nf* (fin), compulsory levy/charge; **Zwangsanleihe** *nf*, compulsory/forced loan; **Zwangslage** *nf*, predicament

zwangsläufig *adj*, inevitable

Zwangspensionierung *nf*, compulsory retirement

Zwangsverkauf *nm*, forced sale

Zwangsverwaltung *nf*, sequestration

zwangsvollstrecken *vb*, foreclose

Zwangsvollstreckung *nf*, foreclosure

Zweck *nm*, purpose; **einem Zweck dienen**, serve a purpose; **das hat keinen Zweck**, there is no point; **Zweckbau** *nm*, functional building

zwecks (+ genitive) *prep*, for the purpose of

zweideutig *adj*, ambiguous

zweifach *adj*, double; **in zweifacher Ausfertigung**, in duplicate

Zweifel *nm*, doubt

zweifeln *vb*, doubt

Zweifelsfall *nm*, case of doubt

Zweigstelle *nf* (of bank), branch

zweimal *adv*, twice; **zweimal so . . . wie . . .**, twice as . . . as . . .; **zweimal jährlich**, twice a year

zweiseitig *adj*, **1** (contract), bilateral. **2** (disk), double-sided

zweistellig *adj* (money), in double figures

zweite(r, s) *adj*, second; **zweite Wahl** *nf* (goods), reject

zweitägig *adj*, two-day, lasting two days

Zweithypothek *nf*, second mortgage

Zweitinserat *nn*, readvertisement

zweitklassig *adj*, **zweitrangig** *adj*, inferior, second-rate

Zweitschrift *nf*, duplicate

zwingen *vb*, force

zwischen (+ dat) *prep*, between

Zwischen-; **Zwischenaufenthalt** *nm*, stopover; **Zwischenbericht** *nm*, interim report; **Zwischenbilanz** *nf* (fin), interim balance; **Zwischendividende** *nf*, interim dividend; **Zwischenergebnis** *nn*, interim result; **Zwischenfinanzierung** *nf*, bridging/interim financing; **Zwischenhändler** *nm*, middleman; **Zwischenlagerung** *nf*, temporary storage; **Zwischenlandung** *nf* (in plane journey), stopover; **Zwischenstecker** *nm* (electr), adaptor (plug); **Zwischensumme** *nf*, sub-total; **Zwischenzeit** *nf*, **in der Zwischenzeit**, in the interim (period)

zwischenzeitlich *adv*, (in the) meantime

Zwischenzins *nm*, interim interest

zwo (number), (= **zwei**) (esp telec), two

zyklisch *adj*, cyclical

z.Zt. *adv*, **zur Zeit**, pro tem, at the moment

ENGLISH — GERMAN

able, be able to *vb*, können; **we are able to deliver promptly**, wir können prompt liefern

aboard *adv*, an Bord

about *adv*, (approximately), ungefähr; **at about 5 o'clock**, ungefähr um 5 Uhr

about *prep*, (on the subject of), über (+ acc); **he wants to talk about his trip**, er möchte über seine Reise sprechen

above *adv*, darüber; **the figure above**, die Ziffer darüber

above *prep*, über (+ dat); **above the main entrance**, über dem Haupteingang; **above 5%** über 5%

above *adj*, obig; **the above address**, die obige Adresse

abroad *adv*, im/ins Ausland; **I live abroad**, ich lebe im Ausland; **I am going abroad**, ich fahre ins Ausland

absenteeism *n* (pers), Krankfeiern *nn*

abuse *n*, **1** (insults), Beschimpfungen *nfpl*. **2** (misuse), Mißbrauch *nm*; **abuse of confidence**, Vertrauensmißbrauch *nm*

accept *vb* (gen), akzeptieren; **I accept the invitation**, ich akzeptiere die Einladung; **please accept our apologies for our absence**, bitte entschuldigen Sie unsere Abwesenheit

acceptable *adj*, akzeptabel

acceptance *n*, Annahme *nf*

access *vb* (comp), zugreifen auf (+ acc)

access to *n*, **1** (gen), Zugang *nm* zu (+ dat). **2** (comp), Zugriff *nm* auf (+ acc); **access time** (comp), Zugriffszeit *nf*

accident *n* (pers), Unfall *nm*

accommodation *n* (hotel etc), Unterbringung *nf*

according to *prep*, nach (+ dat)

account *n* (fin), **1** Konto *nn*; **advertising account**, Werbekonto *nn*; **current account**, laufendes Konto; **expense account**, Spesenkonto *nn*; **pay money into an account**, Geld auf ein Konto einzahlen. **2** (bill), Rechnung *nf*; **account executive**, Kundenbetreuer(in) *nm/f*; **accounts clerk**, Buchhalter(in) *nm/f*; **accounts receivable**, Außenstände *nmpl*

account for *vb*, Rechenschaft ablegen über (+ acc)

accountant *n*, Bilanzbuchhalter(in) *nm/f*

accounting *n*, Buchführung *nf*, Buchhaltung *nf*; **accounting period**, Abrechnungszeitraum *nm*

achieve *vb*, (a result), erzielen; **they achieved a 30 per cent increase in turnover**, sie erzielten einen Umsatzzuwachs von 30 Prozent

achievement *n*, Leistung *nf*

acid test *n*, Feuerprobe *nf*, Härtetest *nm*; **acid test ratio** (fin), Liquiditätsgrad *nm*

acknowledge *vb*, **1** (someone's achievement), (an)erkennen. **2** (receipt of letter), bestätigen

acronym *n*, Akronym *nn*

ad *n* (mktg, sales), Anzeige *nf*; **put an ad in the paper**, eine Anzeige in der Zeitung aufgeben

adapt to *vb*, anpassen; **we are very happy to adapt to your needs**, wir passen uns gern Ihren Erfordernissen an

add to *vb*, hinzufügen; **please add . . . to our order**, bitte fügen Sie unserer Bestellung . . . hinzu

add up *vb*, **1** (maths), addieren. **2 the figures don't add up**, die Zahlen stimmen nicht. **3 add up to . . .**, sich belaufen auf (+ acc); **total expenditure adds up to £30,000**, die Gesamtausgaben belaufen sich auf £30.000

additional *adj*, zusätzlich; **additional charge**, Aufpreis *nm*

address *n* Adresse *nf*, Anschrift *nf*; **wrong address**, falsche Adresse/Anschrift; **not known at this address**, Empfänger unbekannt

address *vb*, **1** (letter), adressieren; **the letter is addressed to him**, der Brief ist an ihn adressiert. **2 address your CV for the attention of . . .**, senden Sie Ihren Lebenslauf zu Händen von . . . . **3 address a problem**, ein Problem in Angriff nehmen. **4 address an audience**, einen Vortrag halten

addressee *n*, Adressat(in) *nm/f*

adjust *vb*, **1** (machine), einstellen. **2** (production), regulieren. **3** (account), bereinigen

adjustment *n*, **1** (of machine), Einstellung *nf*. **2** (of production), Regulierung *nf*. **3** (of account), Bereinigung *nf*

administration *n*, Verwaltung *nf*

admit *vb*, **1** (error), zugeben; **I am the first to admit that I made a mistake**, ich gebe gern zu, daß ich einen Fehler gemacht habe. **2** (business partner), aufnehmen. **3** (to profession, meeting etc), zulassen; **be admitted to the Bar**, bei Gericht zugelassen werden

admittance *n*, Zutritt *nm*; **no admittance**, Zutritt verboten

ad val, **ad valorem** (fin), dem Wert nach; **ad valorem duty/tax** Wertsteuer *nf*

advance *n*, **1** (progress), Fortschritt *nm*. **2** (money), Vorschuß *nm*. **3 in advance** im voraus

advance *adj*, vorherig; **advance booking**, vorherige Buchung *nf*

advantage *n*, Vorteil *nm*; **to our advantage**, zu unserem Vorteil

advertise *vb*, **1** (a post), ausschreiben. **2** (product), werben für (+ acc). **3** (in paper), annoncieren

advertisement *n*, **1** (of post), Ausschreibung *nf*. **2** (of product), Werbung *nf*. **3** (small ad), Anzeige *nf*; **place an advertisement**, eine Anzeige aufgeben; **reply to a (job) advertisement**, sich auf eine (Stellen-)Anzeige hin bewerben

advertiser *n*, **1** (in paper), Inserent *nm*. **2 TV advertisers**, Firmen, die im Fernsehen werben

advertising *n*, Werbung *nf*; **advertising account**, Werbekonto *nn*; **advertising agent**, Werbeagent *nm*; **advertising campaign**, Werbefeldzug *nm*; **advertising manager**, Werbeleiter *nm*; **advertising rates**, **1** (press), Anzeigenpreise *nmpl*. **2** (on radio, TV), Preise für Werbespots

advertorial *n* (mktg, sales), redaktionell aufgemachte Werbung *nf*

advice *n* (comm), Mitteilung *nf*; **advice note**, Versandanzeige *nf*, Avis *nn* or *nm*

advise *vb*, **1** (give advice), raten. **2** (inform), mitteilen; **please advise us of the delivery date**, bitten teilen Sie uns den Liefertermin mit

advocate *vb*, befürworten; **he is advocating the introduction of a new marketing strategy**, er befürwortet die Einführung einer neuen Marketingstrategie

affect *vb*, **1** (have significance for),

betreffen. **2** (have an impact on), sich auswirken auf (+ acc); **rising inflation has affected consumer demand**, die steigende Inflation hat sich auf die Nachfrage ausgewirkt

after *prep* (time), nach (+ dat); **after her departure**, nach ihrer Abreise; **after sight**, nach Sicht; **90 days after date**, 90 Tage nach dem Verfallsdatum

after *adv*, nachher, danach; **weeks after**, Woche danach

after *conj*, nachdem; **after we had tested the samples, . . .,** nachdem wir die Proben geprüft hatten, . . .

after sales service *n*, Kundendienst *nm*

against *adv*, gegen (+ acc); **against his will**, gegen seinen Willen; **the board has decided against the project**, der Vorstand hat sich gegen das Projekt entschieden; **against all risks** (ins), gegen alle Risiken

agency *n*, **1** (sales), Agentur *nf*. **2** (garage), Vertragswerkstätte *nf*; **Opel agency**, Opel-Vertragswerkstätte

agenda *n*, Tagesordnung *nf*; **on the agenda**, auf der Tagesordnung

agent *n* (comm), Vertreter(in) *nm/f*

AGM, Annual General Meeting, Jahreshauptversammlung *nf*

agree *vb* (figure, time), vereinbaren; **agree with**, übereinstimmen mit; **I agree with him**, ich stimme mit ihm überein; **we agree with your assessment of the situation**, wir stimmen mit Ihrer Beurteilung der Lage überein

agree to *vb*, zustimmen; **he agreed to my proposal**, er hat meinem Vorschlag zugestimmt; **we agree to the terms of the contract**, wir stimmen den Vertragsbedingungen zu; **agree to do something**, vereinbaren, etwas zu tun; **at our last meeting we agreed to write to the producer**, bei unserem letzten Treffen haben wir vereinbart, dem Hersteller zu schreiben

agreed *adj*, vereinbart; **the agreed date**, der vereinbarte Termin

agreement *n*, **1** (same opinion), Übereinstimmung *nf*; **there is general agreement that . . .,** es herrscht allgemein Übereinstimmung, daß . . .; **reach agreement**, Übereinstimmung erzielen. **2** (business agreement), Vereinbarung *nf*; **exclusive agreement**, Allleinvertretungsvereinbarung *nf*. **3** (consent), Zustimmung *nf*

aid *n*, **1** (help), Hilfe *nf*; **foreign aid**, Entwicklungshilfe *nf*. **2** (support), Unterstützung *nf*. **3** (assistance), Beistand *nm*

aim *n*, Ziel *nn*

aim to *vb*, beabsichtigen, zu

air *n*, Luft *nf*

air cargo *n*, Luftfracht *nf*

air-conditioned room *n*, Zimmer *nn* mit Klimaanlage

air conditioning *n*, Klimaanlage *nf*

air consignment note *n* (imp/exp), Luftffrachtbrief *nm*

airfreight *n* (imp/exp), Luftfracht *nf*; **send by airfreight**, per Luftfracht senden; **airfreight collect** (imp/exp), Luftfrachtnachnahme *nf*

air mail *n*, Luftpost *nf*; **air mail transfer**, Luftpostüberweisung *nf*

airport *n*, Flughafen *nm*; **airport terminal**, Terminal *nm*

airtight *adj*, luftdicht

air waybill *n* (imp/exp), Luftfrachtbrief *nm*

A Level, advanced level *n* (educ), ≈ Abitur *nm*

all-day meeting *n*, ganztägige Sitzung *nf*

all-in-price *n*, Pauschalpreis *nm*

allow for *vb* (fin), einrechnen, vergüten

all risks *npl* (fin, ins), alle Risiken; **all risks insurance policy**, kombinierte Haftpflicht- und Vollkaskoversicherung *nf*

almost *adv*, fast; **inflation has reached almost 9%**, die Inflation hat fast 9% erreicht; **your order is almost ready**, Ihre Bestellung ist fast lieferungsbereit

alter *vb*, ändern, verändern; **alter the wording of the letter**, den Wortlaut des Briefes (ver)ändern

alteration *n*, Änderung *nf*

alternating current *n*, Wechselstrom *nm*

alternative *n*, Alternative *nf*

a.m., ante meridian, morgens, vormittags; **at 6 a.m.**, um 6 Uhr morgens

amt, amount *n* (fin), Betrag *nm*; **the final amount is £321**, der Endbetrag ist £321

analyse *vb*, analysieren

analysis *n*, Analyse *nf*; **an analysis of the figures indicates that . . .**, eine Analyse der Zahlen ergibt, daß . . .

analyst *n*, Analytiker(in) *nm/f*

annual *adj*, jährlich, Jahres-; **annual bonus**, (pers), Jahresprämie *nf*; **annual report**, Geschäftsbericht *nm*

ansaphone/answerphone *n* (telec), Anrufbeantworter *nm*

answer *n*, Antwort *nf*; **in answer to your letter of . . .**, in Antwort auf Ihren Brief vom . . .

answer *vb*, **1** (somebody), antworten; **he did not answer her**, er antwortete ihr nicht. **2** (a letter), beantworten; **I must answer his letter**, ich muß seinen Brief beantworten

A/P, Additional Premium (ins), Prämienzuschlag *nm*

apologise *vb*, sich entschuldigen; **we apologise for the delay**, wir entschuldigen uns für die Verzögerung

apology *n*, Entschuldigung *nf*

appeal *vb*, **1** (law), **he appealed against the sentence**, er legte gegen das Urteil Berufung ein. **2 appeal to**, zusagen; **this will appeal to our customers**, das wird unseren Kunden zusagen

application *n*, **1** (for job), Bewerbung *nf*. **2** (for visa, reservation etc), Antrag *nm*. **3** (use of product), Verwendung(smöglichkeit) *nf*; **our new product has many applications**, unser neues Produkt hat viele Verwendungsmöglichkeiten. **4** (comp), Anwendung *nf*

application form *n*, **1** (for job), Bewerbungsformular *nn*. **2** (for visa, reservation etc), Antragsformular *nn*; **please complete the enclosed application form for a stand**, bitte füllen Sie beiliegendes Antragsformular für einen Stand aus

apply *vb*, **1** (for a job), sich um eine Stelle bewerben. **2** (skills, information), anwenden

appoint *vb*, **1** (to a job, gen), einstellen; **we need to appoint at least three more secretaries**, wir müssen mindestens noch drei Sekretärinnen einstellen. **2** (to a post), ernennen zu . . .; **she was appointed Head of Department**, sie wurde zur Abteilungsleiterin ernannt

appointment *n*, **1** (of job, gen), Einstellung *nf*. **2** (to a post), Ernennung *nf*. **3** (to see someone), Termin *nm*; **make an appointment**, einen Termin vereinbaren

appraisal *n* (pers), Beurteilung *nf*

appreciate *vb*, **1** (understand),

verstehen; **we appreciate your situation**, wir verstehen Ihre Lage. **2** (be grateful for), dankbar sein für (+ acc); **we appreciate your advice**, wir sind Ihnen für Ihren Rat dankbar

appreciation *n*, **1** (gratitude), Dankbarkeit *nf*. **2** (fin) (increase in value), Wertsteigerung *nf*, Wertzuwachs *nm*

approach *n*, **1** (way of tackling), Ansatz *nm*. **2** (to person, committee etc), Herantreten *nn* an (+ acc)

approach *vb*, **1** (come near), sich nähern (+ dat); **the inflation rate is approaching the 3% mark**, die Inflationsrate nähert sich der 3%-Grenze. **2** (tackle), angehen; **the problem must be approached from a different angle**, das Problem muß aus einer anderen Richtung angegangen werden. **3** (person, committee etc), sich wenden an (+ acc); **might I approach you with a problem?**, dürfte ich mich mit einem Problem an Sie wenden?

appropriation *n* (balance sheet), Zuweisung *nf*

approval *n*, Zustimmung *nf*; **we have the approval of X**, wir haben die Zustimmung von X; **on approval**, auf Probe, zur Ansicht

approved *adj*, **1** (agreed), gebilligt. **2** (authorised), genehmigt

AR, advice of receipt (imp/exp), Empfangsbescheinigung *nf*

arbitration *n* (pers), Schlichtung *nf*

arcade *n* (mktg, sales), Arkade *nf*, Passage *nf*; **shopping arcade**, Einkaufspassage *nf*

area *n*, **1** (admin), Bezirk *nm*. **2** (sales, interest), Gebiet *nn*, Bereich *nm*; **sales area**, Verkaufsgebiet *nn*, Verkaufsbereich *nm*; **area manager(ess)**, Bereichsleiter(in) *nm/f*, Gebietsleiter(in) *nm/f*

argument *n*, **1** (reason), Argument *nn*. **2** (quarrel), Streit *nm*, Streitigkeit *nf*

armchair *n* (offce), Bürosessel *nm*

around *adv* (roughly), etwa; **the price is around £ 5000**, der Preis liegt bei etwa £5.000

arr, arrival, Ank., Ankunft *nf*

arrange for *vb*, **1** (see to), sorgen für; **I'll arrange for you to meet Mr X**, ich werde dafür sorgen, daß Sie Herrn X kennenlernen. **2** (plan), vorsehen; **it has been arranged for the goods to reach you tomorrow**, es ist vorgesehen, daß die Waren morgen bei Ihnen ankommen

arrangements *npl*, **1** (preparations), Vorbereitungen *nfpl*; **we have made careful arrangements**, wir haben sorgfältige Vorbereitungen getroffen. **2** (plans), Pläne *nmpl*; **our arrangements haven't been finalised as yet**, unsere Pläne sind noch nicht endgültig

arrears *npl* (fin), Rückstände *nmpl*; **your payments are three months in arrears**, Sie sind mit Ihren Zahlungen drei Monate im Rückstand

arrival *n*, Ankunft *nf*, Ank.; **their arrival is imminent**, ihre Ankunft steht kurz bevor

arrive *vb*, ankommen; **have the goods arrived yet?**, sind die Waren schon angekommen?

articulated lorry *n*, Sattelschlepper *nm*

artwork *n* (mktg, sales), Bildmaterial *nn*

A/S, Account Sales Verkaufsabrechnung *nf*

a/s, after sight (fin), nach Sicht

assemble *vb*, **1** (fit together, kits), zusammensetzen. **2** (machines, cars), montieren. **3** (meet), sich versammeln; **please assemble in**

Room 5, bitte versammeln Sie sich in Raum 5

assembled *adj* (pers), versammelt

assembler *n* (comp), Assembler *nm*

assembly *n*, **1** (fitting together), Zusammensetzen *nn*, Zusammenbau *nm*. **2** (of machines, cars), Montage *nf*. **3** (gathering), Versammlung *nf*; **assembly line**, Montageband *nn*

assess *vb*, **1** (pers), beurteilen. **2** (quality), bewerten. **3** (ins, tax), taxieren, veranlagen

assessment *n* (pers), Beurteilung *nf*; **staff assessment**, Personalbeurteilung *nf*

assessor *n* (ins), Veranlagungsbeamter *nm*, Veranlagungsbeamtin *nf*

asset(s) *n(pl)*, **1** (fin), Vermögen *nn*, Kapital *nn*; **his main asset is . . .**, sein größtes Kapital ist . . .; **fixed assets**, Anlagekapital *nn*. **2** (balance sheet). Aktivposten *nm(pl)*

assistant *n*, **1** Assistent(in) *nm/f*; **manager's assistant**, Assistent(in) des Geschäftsführers. **2** (deputy), Stellvertreter(in) *nm/f*; **assistant manager(ess)**, stellvertretender Geschäftsführer *nm*, stellvertretende Geschäftsführerin *nf*

ATM, **Automatic Teller Machine** (fin), Geldautomat *nm*

attach *vb*, **1** (gen), befestigen. **2** (corr), beiheften; **we attach a copy**, wir heften eine Kopie bei

auction *n*, Auktion *nf*

audiotypist *n*, Phonotypist(in) *nm/f*

audit *n*, **1** (gen), Prüfung *nf*. **2** (fin), Rechnungsprüfung *nf*

audit *vb*, **1** (gen), überprüfen; **audit the computer system**, das Computersystem überprüfen. **2** (fin), eine Rechnungsprüfung durchführen; **the books are just being audited**, es wird gerade eine Rechnungsprüfung vorgenommen

auditor *n* (fin), Rechnungsprüfer(in) *nm/f*

authorise *vb*, **1** (someone to do something), autorisieren, ermächtigen, bevollmächtigen; **he was authorised to sign the letter**, er war bevollmächtigt, den Brief zu unterschreiben. **2** (something), bewilligen, genehmigen; **the sale hasn't yet been authorised**, der Verkauf ist noch nicht bewilligt

authorised capital *n* (fin), genehmigtes Grundkapital *nn*

av, **average** *n*, **1** Durchschnitt *nm*; **on average**, im Durchschnitt; **calculate the average**, den Durchschnitt berechnen; **sales reached an average of £ 1,000 per month**, der Absatz lag bei einem monatlichen Durchschnitt von £ 1.000. **2** (ins), Havarie *nf*; **general average**, große Havarie; **with particular average**, mit besonderer Havarie

avoid *vb*, vermeiden

aware *adj*, **1 be aware of . . .**, sich . . . bewußt sein; **I am aware of this**, ich bin mir dessen bewußt. **2 make someone aware of something**, jemanden auf etwas aufmerksam machen; **make customers aware of price reductions** (mktg, sales), die Kunden auf Preissenkungen aufmerksam machen

B

B.A., Bachelor of Arts *n*, ~ Magister *nm* (der philosophischen/ naturwissenschaftlichen Fakultät) (however: initial German university qualification tends to be at Master's level)

back *adv*, zurück; **when are you coming back?**, wann kommen Sie zurück?

back *vb*, **1** (support), unterstützen. **2** (fin), indossieren; **the bill has been backed by . . .**, der Wechsel wurde von . . . indossiert

back up *vb*, **1** (support), unterstützen. **2** (comp), sichern

backer *n* (fin), **1** (of a person), Sponsor *nm*. **2** (of a bill), Wechselgarant *nm*

backing *n* (fin), Unterstützung *nf*

back-to-back credit *n* (fin), Gegenakkreditiv *nn*

badge *n*, **1** (with pin), Abzeichen *nn*. **2** (sticker), Aufkleber *nm*

bail *n* (law), Kaution *nf*; **release on bail**, gegen Kaution freilassen

bailiff *n* (law) (for property), Gerichtsvollzieher(in) *nm/f*

bal, balance *n*, **1** (balance of payments, trade), Bilanz *nf* **balance of payments**, Zahlungsbilanz *nf*; **balance of trade**, Handelsbilanz *nf*; **balance sheet**, Bilanz(aufstellung) *nf*. **2** (account), Saldo *nm*; **credit balance**, Kreditsaldo *nm*; **balance carried forward**, Saldovortrag *nm*. **3** (rest of amount owed), Restbetrag *nm*; **balance due**, fälliger Rechnungsbetrag *nm*

balance *vb* (gen), **1** (equalise difference), ausgleichen. **2** (account), saldieren. **3 balance the books**, die Bilanz ziehen;

bale *n* (imp/exp), Ballen *nm*

ban *n*, **1** (gen), Verbot *nn*; **ban on smoking**, Rauchverbot *nn*. **2** (imp/exp), Embargo *nn*, Verbot *nn*

ban *vb*, verbieten

bank *n* (fin), Bank *nf*; **bank balance**, Kontostand *nm*; **bank charges**, (in particular transaction), Bankgebühr *nf*; **bank deposit**, Bankeinlage *nf*; **bank draft**, Banktratte *nf*, Bankwechsel *nm*; **Bank for International Settlements, BIS**, Internationale Vergleichsbank *nf*; **bank note**, Banknote *nf*; **bank rate**, Diskontsatz *nm*; **bank statement**, Kontoauszug *nm*

bank on *vb*, sich verlassen auf (+ acc); **I am banking on him**, ich verlasse mich auf ihn

bankrupt *adj*, bankrott; **go bankrupt**, bankrott machen

bar chart *n*, Balkendiagramm *nn*

bar code *n* (gen, comp), Barkodierung *nf*

bargain *n*, **1** (gen), Handel *nm*. **2** (mktg, sales), Schnäppchen *nn*, Gelegenheitskauf *nm*; **bargain offer**, Sonderangebot *nn*; **bargain price**, Sonderpreis *nm*

bargain *vb*, handeln

bargaining *n*, Verhandlung(en) *nf(pl)*; **collective bargaining**, Tarifverhandlungen *nfpl*; **bargaining position**, Verhandlungsposition *nf*

barge *n* (transp), Schleppkahn *nm*

barrel *n*, **1** (gen), Faß *nn*. **2** (for oil), Barrel *nn*

barrister *n* (law), Rechtsanwalt *nm*, Rechtsanwältin *nf*

barter *n*, **barter trade** *n* (imp/exp), Tauschhandel *nm*

barter *vb* (gen), tauschen

based *adj*, **be based in . . .**, seinen Standort/Sitz in . . . haben; **be based on . . .**, beruhen auf (+ acc); **the calculation is based on the following figures**, die Berechnung beruht auf folgenden Zahlen

base rate *n* (fin), Eckzins *nm*

basic *adj*, Grund-, Haupt-; **basic equipment**, Grundausstattung *nf*; **basic point**, Hauptpunkt *nm*

batch *n* (gen, comp), Stapel *nm*; **batch processing** (comp), Stapelverarbeitung *nf*

battery *n*, Batterie *nf*

B/D, bank draft (fin), Bankwechsel *nm*

bd, b/d, brought down, balance brought down (fin), Saldo *nm*

B/E, 1 bill of entry (imp/exp), Einreisebescheinigung *nf*. **2 bill of exchange** (fin), Wechsel *nm*

bear *n* (stock market), Baissier *nm*

bearer *n* (of document), Überbringer *nm*; **bearer securities**, Inhaberschuldverschreibung *nf*

before *prep* (time), vor (+ dat); **before breakfast**, vor dem Frühstück

before *adv* vorher; **he has said so before**, er hat das schon vorher gesagt

before *conj*, bevor; **before he came**, bevor er kam

behalf *n*, **on behalf of**, im Namen von (+ dat), im Auftrag von (+ dat)

below *prep*, unter (+ dat or + acc); **below 3%**, unter 3%

below *adv*, unten; **please read the notes below**, bitte die Anmerkungen unten lesen

benefit *n*, Vorteil *nm*

benefit from *vb*, profitieren von (+ dat); **he has benefited from this change of career**, er hat von dieser Laufbahnveränderung profitiert

berth *n*, **1** (harbour), Liegeplatz *nm*. **2** (in trains), Bett *nn*

berth *vb* (shipping), anlegen

between *prep*, zwischen (+ dat or + acc); **between these dates**, zwischen diesen Terminen

bf, b/f, brought forward (fin), Übertrag *nm*

bid *n* (fin), Angebot *nn*

bid for *vb* (fin), bieten für/auf (+ acc)

bill *n*, **1** (to be paid), Rechnung *nf*. **2** (banknote), Banknote *nf*. **3** (poster), Plakat *nn*. **4** (politics), Gesetzentwurf *nm*. **5 bill of entry**, Einreisebescheinigung *nf*; **bill of lading, BL**, (imp/exp), Konnossement *nn*; **clean bill of lading**, einwandfreies Konnossement; **bill of sale, B/S**, Verkaufsurkunde *nf*

billboard *n* (mktg, sales), Reklametafel *nf*

binding *adj* (law), bindend; **binding agreement**, bindende Vereinbarung *nf*

biro *n*, Kugelschreiber *nm*

BIS, Bank for International Settlements *n*, Internationale Vergleichsbank *nf*

Bk, bank (fin), Bank *nf*

blister pack *n* (mktg, sales), Schrumpffolienpackung *nf*

blue-chip *adj*, erstklassig; **blue-chip company**, erstklassiges Unternehmen *nn*; **blue-chip shares**, erstklassige Wertpapiere *nnpl*

blue-collar worker *n*, Arbeiter(in) *nm/f*

blurb *n* (mktg, sales), Werbematerial *nn*

board *n*, **1** (committee), Ausschuß *nm*. **2** (authority), Behörde *nf*;

board of directors 1 (executive), Vorstand *nm*. **2** (supervisory board), Aufsichtsrat *nm*. **3** (British/American company), Verwaltungsrat *nm*

bolt *vb* (eng), verschrauben

bolted *adj* (eng), verschraubt, Schrauben-

bond *n*, **1** (stock market), Pfandbrief *nm*. **2** (comm) (custody of goods), Zollverschluß *nm*

bonded warehouse *n*, Zolldepot *nn*

bonus *n* (ins, extra payment), Prämie *nf*; **incentive bonus**, Leistungsprämie *nf*; **productivity bonus**, Produktivitätsprämie *nf*

book *vb*, **1** (accommodation, stand), buchen. **2 book an order**, einen Auftrag annehmen

booking *n* (of accommodation, stand), Buchung *nf*; **double booking**, Doppelbuchung *nf*; **booking form**, Buchungsformular *nn*

book value *n* (acc, ins), Buchwert *nm*

boom *n* (mktg, sales, fin), Boom *nm*; **we have seen a boom in sales**, wir hatten einen Verkaufsboom; **boom industry**, Konjunkturindustrie *nf*

booming *adj*, florierend; **a booming business**, ein florierendes Geschäft

boot up *vb* (comp), laden

born *adj* (pers), geboren; **born 12 August 1969**, geb./geboren am 12. August 1969

borrow *vb*, Kredit *nm* aufnehmen

borrowings *npl* (fin), Fremdkapital *nn*

box *n*, **1** (gen), Schachtel *nf*. **2** (on a form), **tick the appropriate box**, Zutreffendes bitte ankreuzen

brainstorming *n*, Brainstorming *nn*

branch *n* (comm), Filiale *nf*

brand *n* (mktg, sales), Marke *nf*; **brand image**, Markenprofil *nn*; **brand loyalty**, Markentreue *nf*; **brand name**, Markenbezeichnung *nf*

breach of an agreement *n*, Verstoß *nm* gegen eine Vereinbarung

breach of contract *n*, Vertragsbruch *nm*

break *n*, Pause *nf*; **coffee break**, Kaffeepause *nf*

break *vb*, **1** kaputtmachen. **2** (agreement), verletzen. **3 break the law**, gegen das Gesetz verstoßen

break bulk *vb* (transp), mit Entladen anfangen

break down *vb*, **1** (car), eine Panne haben. **2** (machine), ausfallen. **3** (figures), aufschlüsseln

break even *vb*, seine Kosten decken; **we managed to break even**, wir haben unsere Kosten gedeckt

break in *vb*, einbrechen

breakdown *n*, **1** (car), Panne *nf*. **2** (of machine), Ausfall *nm*. **3** (of figures), Aufschlüsselung *nf*

break-even point *n*, Break-even-Point *nm*

bridge *vb*, (gap, difference), überbrücken

brief on/about *vb*, instruieren über (+ acc), informieren über (+ acc)

briefing *n*, Besprechung *nf*, Briefing *nn*; **briefing session**, Einsatzbesprechung *nf*

bring out *vb* (new model), herausbringen

broadcast *vb* (radio, TV), senden

brochure *n* (mktg, sales), Broschüre *nf*

broken *adj*, kaputt

broker *n* (fin), Händler *nm*

bros, brothers *npl*, Gebr., Gebrüder *nmpl*

B/S, **1** (fin), **balance sheet**, Bilanz *nf*.

2 (fin, imp/exp), **bill of sale**, Kaufvertrag *nm*

BS 5750 *nm*, BS 5750

bt fwd, brought forward (fin), übertragen

budget *n* (fin), Budget *nn*

budget for *vb* (fin), in das Budget einplanen; **we hadn't budgeted for this**, das hatten wir in unser Budget nicht eingeplant

build *vb*, bauen

building *n*, **1** (e.g. office block), Gebäude *nn*. **2** (activity), Bauen *nn*; **building industry**, Bauwirtschaft *nf*; **building site**, Baustelle *nf*

bulk *n*, **1** (quantity, volume), Masse *nf*, Menge *nf*; **bulk buying**, Mengeneinkauf *nm*; **bulk carrier**, (shipping), Massengutfrachter *nm*; **bulk storage, 1** (transp), Großlager *nn*. **2** (comp), Massenspeicher *nm*

bull *n* (stock market), Haussier *nm*

buoyant *adj* (mktg, sales), rege; **buoyant sales**, reger Absatz *nm*

business *n* (gen), Geschäft *nn*; **do business with, 1** (be doing business), mit . . . in Geschäftsverbindung stehen; **we have been doing business with them for many years**, wir stehen seit vielen Jahren mit ihnen in Geschäftsverbindung. **2** (plan/hope to be doing business with), mit jemandem in Geschäftsverbindung treten; **we are looking forward to doing business with you**, wir freuen uns darauf, mit Ihnen in Geschäftsverbindung zu treten; **business address**, Geschäftsadresse *nf*; **business card**, Visitenkarte *nf*; **businessman**, Geschäftsmann *nm*; **business trip**, Geschäftsreise *nf*; **business woman**, Geschäftsfrau *nf*; **business year**, Geschäftsjahr *nn*

bust, go bust *vb* (fin), bankrott machen

busy *adj*, **1** (telephone), besetzt; **the line is busy**, die Leitung ist besetzt. **2** (person), beschäftigt; **I am very busy at the moment**, ich bin im Moment sehr beschäftigt

buy *vb*, kaufen

buy out *vb*, **1** aufkaufen. **2** (take over), übernehmen

buyer *n*, **1** (gen), Käufer *nm*. **2** (in charge of purchasing), Einkäufer *nm*

by-product *n*, **1** (still useful for something), Nebenprodukt *nn*. **2** (waste), Abfallprodukt *nn*

C

C & F, cost and freight (imp/exp), Kosten *npl* und Fracht *nf*

CA, chartered accountant, Wirtschaftsprüfer *nm*, Wirtschaftsprüferin *nf*

CAD, Computer Assisted Design (comp), CAD, computergestützter Entwurf *nm*

CAD/CAM, Computer Assisted Design and Manufacture, CAD/CAM, computergestützte Entwurf und Fertigung

calculate *vb* (fin), berechnen

calculator *n* (offce), Rechner *nm*

calendar *n*, Kalender *nm*; **calendar year**, Kalenderjahr *nn*

call *n*, **1** (gen), Ruf *nm*. **2** (telec), Anruf *nm*. **3** (visit), Besuch *nm*

call *vb*, **1** (gen), rufen. **2** (telephone), anrufen. **3** (visit), besuchen. **4** (meeting), einberufen. **5** (give name), nennen. **6** (be called), heißen; **the new product is called "Luxus"**, das neue Produkt heißt „Luxus"

call back *vb* (telec), zurückrufen; **when can I call you back?**, wann kann ich Sie zurückrufen?

call for *vb*, **1** (load, person), abholen. **2** (a change), verlangen. **3** (strike), zum Streik aufrufen

call on *vb*, **1** (visit), vorsprechen bei (+ dat). **2** (request support), sich wenden an (+ acc)

camera *n*, Kamera *nf*

campaign for *vb*, **1** (fight), kämpfen für (+ acc). **2** (advert), werben für (+ acc)

can *n*, **1** (tin can), Dose *nf* **2** (container), Container *nm*

can *vb*, können; **can I talk to you?**, kann ich mit Ihnen sprechen?

cancel *vb*, **1** (call off), absagen. **2** (contract), kündigen. **3** (debt), streichen. **4** (reservation), rückgängig machen

cancellation *n*, **1** (calling off), Absage *nf*. **2** (of contract), Kündigung *nf*. **3** (of debt), Streichung *nf*. **4** (of reservation), Rückgängigmachung *nf*

canvass *vb* (mktg, sales), befragen; **500 clients were canvassed**, 500 Kunden wurden befragt

capacity *n*, **1** (cubic content), Kapazität *nf*. **2** (ability), Fähigkeit *nf*. **3** (role, position), Funktion *nf*

capital *n* (fin), Kapital *nn*; **capital assets**, Kapitalvermögen *nn*; **capital gains tax**, Kapitalertragssteuer *nf*; **capital investment**, Kapitalanlage *nf*; **capital outlay**, Kapitalaufwand *nm*

car *n*, Auto *nn*; **car hire**, Autoverleih *nm*; **car parking**, **1** (parking place), Parkplatz *nm*. **2** (parking facilities), Parkmöglichkeiten *nfpl*

card *n*, Karte *nf*; **business card**, Visitenkarte *nf*; **file card**, Karteikarte *nf*

cardboard box *n*, Karton *nm*

care, take care of *vb*, sich kümmern um (+ acc); **our agent will take care of the repairs**, unser Vertreter wird sich um die Reparaturen kümmern

care of, c/o, (transp, corr), bei (+ dat)

career *n* (pers), **1** Karriere *nf*. **2** (occupation), Beruf *nm*; **career objective**, Berufsziel *nn*. **3** (professional life), Laufbahn *nf*

cargo *n* (transp), Fracht *nf*; **cargo handling** (transp), Güterumschlag *nm*

carphone *n*, Autotelefon *nn*

carriage *n* (transp), **1** (process), Transport *nm*. **2** (cost), Transportkosten *npl*; **carriage free**, frachtfrei; **carriage paid** (mktg, sales), frachtfrei

carried forward, **cf** (acct), vorgetragen

carrier *n* (transp), Spedition *nf*

carry *vb*, **1** (on vehicle), befördern, transportieren. **2** (stock), führen, auf Lager haben

carry forward *vb* (acct), vortragen

carry out *vb*, ausführen; **the director carried out his plan**, der Direktor führte seinen Plan aus

carton *n* (imp/exp), Karton *nm*

case *n*, **1** (gen, crime, problem), Fall *nm*. **2** (suitcase), Koffer *nm*. **3** (crate), Kiste *nf*

cash *n*, Bargeld *nn*; **in cash** bar; **pay cash**, bar bezahlen; **cash on delivery**, **COD**, Zahlung bei Lieferung; **cash on shipment**, **COS**, Zahlung bei Versand; **cash with order**, **CWO**, **cwo**, bar bei Bestellung; **cash and carry**, Cash and Carry *nn*; **cash desk**, Kasse *nf*; **pay at the cash desk**, an der Kasse zahlen; **cash discount**, Diskont *nm*; **cash dispenser**, Geldautomat *nm*; **cash flow**, Cashflow *nm*; **cash receipt**, Kassenquittung *nf*

cash *vb*, (a cheque), (einen Scheck) einlösen

cashier *n*, Kassierer *nm*, Kassiererin *nf*

cast iron *n*, Gußeisen *nn*

catalogue *n*, Katalog *nm*

catch *vb* (train/plane), erreichen

catch up with *vb*, (gen), einholen

cater for *vb* (take into account), ausgerichtet sein auf (+ acc); **the plan caters for disabled persons**, der Plan ist auf Behinderte ausgerichtet

catering *n* (industry), Gaststättengewerbe *nn*

cause *n*, Ursache *nf*

cause *vb*, verursachen

CBD, **cash before delivery** (mktg, sales), Zahlung *nf* vor Lieferung

CBI, **Confederation of British Industry** *n*, ~ BDI, Bundesverband *nm* der Deutschen Industrie

cc, **carbon copy**, Kopie *nf*

cc, **charges collect** (imp/exp), Zahlung *nf* bei Lieferung

cc, **cubic centimetre** ccm, Kubikzentimeter *nm*

CCTV, **closed circuit television**, interne Fernsehanlage *nf*

CD-ROM *n*, CD-ROM *nn*

cease *vb*, einstellen; **we had to cease production**, wir mußten die Produktion einstellen

ceiling *n* (maximum), Höchstgrenze *nf*; **go through the ceiling**, die Höchstgrenze durchbrechen

central *adj*, zentral; **central processing unit** (comp), Zentraleinheit *nf*, CPU

centralise *vb*, zentralisieren

CEO, **Chief Executive Officer**, geschäftsführender Direktor *nm*, geschäftsführende Direktorin *nf*

certificate *n*, Zertifikat *nn*; **certificate of origin** (imp/exp), Herkunftszertifikat *nn*

certified *adj*, **1** (ins), beglaubigt; **certified copy**, beglaubigte Abschrift *nf*. **2 certified cheque**, bestätigter Scheck *nm*

cf, **carried forward** *adj*, (acct), vorgetragen

chain *n*, Kette *nf*; **chain store**, Kettenladen *nm*, Filiale *nf*

chair *vb* (meeting), (eine Sitzung) leiten

chair, chairman, chairperson *n*, Diskussionsleiter(in) *nm/f*, Vorsitzende(r) *nf/m*

challenge *n*, Herausforderung *nf*

chamber *n*, Kammer *nf*; **Chamber of Industry and Commerce**, Industrie- und Handelskammer *nf* (IHK); **Chamber of Crafts**, Handwerkskammer *nf*

change *n*, Wechselgeld *nn*; **please keep the change**, bitte behalten Sie das Wechselgeld

change *vb*, **1** (gen), ändern, verändern; **we have changed the product mix**, wir haben den Produkt-Mix verändert. **2** (trains), umsteigen. **3** (money), wechseln. **4** (plan), ändern

channel *n*, Kanal *nm*; **the English Channel**, der Ärmelkanal; **distribution channel**, Vertriebskanal *nm*

channel *vb*, steuern

character *n*, **1** (gen), Charakter *nm*. **2** (comp), Zeichen *nn*

charge *n*, **1** (fee), Gebühr *nf*. **2** (law), Anklage *nf*

charge *vb*, **1** (money), berechnen. **2** (law), anklagen

chart *n*, Diagramm *nn*

chart *vb* (results), auswerten

charter *vb* (transp), chartern

chartered accountant *n*, **CA**, Wirtschaftsprüfer *nm*, Wirtschaftsprüferin *nf*

chartered flight *n*, Charterflug *nm*

charter-party *n*, **CP** (imp/exp), Chartergesellschaft *nf*

cheap *adj*, billig

check *vb*, **1** (monitor regularly), kontrollieren, überprüfen. **2** (make sure), sicherstellen. **3** (stop), stoppen

check in *vb*, **1** (at hotel), sich anmelden. **2** (at airport), einchecken

check out *vb* (of hotel), abreisen, das Zimmer räumen

check-in desk *n* (at airport), Abflugschalter *nm*

chemicals *npl*, Chemikalien *nfpl*

cheque *n*, Scheck *nm*; **blank cheque**, Blankoscheck *nm*; **crossed cheque**, Verrechnungsscheck *nm*; **uncrossed cheque**, Barscheck *nm*; **cheque book**, Scheckbuch *nn*

children *npl* (CV), Kinder *nnpl*

choose *vb*, wählen

CIA, cash in advance (mktg, sales), Barvorschuß *nm*

CIF, cost, insurance, freight (imp/exp), Kosten, Versicherung, Fracht

CIF E, cost, insurance, freight and exchange variations/or banker's charges (imp/exp), Kosten, Versicherung, Fracht und Währungsschwankungen/oder Bankgebühren

circuit *n* (comp), Schaltkreis *nm*

circulate *vb* (document), zirkulieren lassen, in Umlauf bringen

circumstances *npl*, Umstände *nmpl*, Verhältnisse *nnpl*; **under the circumstances**, unter diesen Umständen

claim *n* (ins), Anspruch *nm*

claim *vb*, **1** (state), behaupten. **2** (demand), fordern, beanspruchen. **3** (responsibility), übernehmen. **4** (ins), Ansprüche *nmpl* geltend machen

claims department *n* (ins), Schadenabteilung *nf*

clause *n*, Klausel *nf*

clean bill of lading *n*, einwandfreies Konnossement *nn*

clear *vb* **customs** (imp/exp), den Zoll passieren; **cleared customs**, zollamtlich abgefertigt

clearance *n* (customs),

Zollabfertigung *nf*

clearance sale *n* (comm), Ausverkauf *nm*

cleared without examination, CWE (imp/exp), nicht zollamtlich geprüft

clerical assistant *n* (offce), Büroangestellte(r) *nf/m*

client *n*, Kunde *nm*, Kundin *nf*; **client database**, Kundendatenbank *nf*

clip *vb* **the coupon** (mktg, sales), **just clip the coupon and return to the address at the top of the advertisement**, Coupon abtrennen und an die oben angegebene Adresse zurücksenden

clone *n* (comp), Klon *nm*

close down *vb* (comp, company), schließen

closing date *n*, **1** (of business), Schließungstag *nm*. **2** (registration, booking), **closing date for registration: 9 June**, letzter Anmeldetermin: 9. Juni

closing down sale *n*, Räumungsverkauf *nm*

closing time *n* (shops), Ladenschluß *nm*

Co, company, Firma *nf*, Gesellschaft *nf*

COD, cash on delivery (mktg, sales), Zahlung *nf* bei Lieferung

code *n*, **1** (rules), Kodex *nm*, Regeln *nfpl*; **code of practice**, Verfahrensregeln *nfpl*. **2** (software, security), Kode *nm*, Code *nm*; **bar code**, Bar-Code *nm*. **3** (post), Postleitzahl *nf*. **4** (telec), Vorwahl *nf*

code *vb*, kodieren

cold calling *n* (mktg, sales), **1** (telephone), unangemeldeter Vertreteranruf *nm*. **2** (at the door), unangemeldeter Vertreterbesuch *nm*

cold storage *n* (transp), Kühlhaus *nn*

collapse *n* (gen, mktg, sales), Zusammenbruch *nm*

collapse *vb* (gen, mktg, sales), zusammenbrechen

collateral *n* (fin), Sicherheit *nf*, Deckung *nf*

collect *vb*, **1** (a load), abholen. **2** (debts), einziehen

collection *n*, **1** (of a load), Abholung *nf*. **2** (of debts), Einziehung *nf*

column *n*, **1** (of figures), Kolonne *nf*. **2** (bar chart), Säule *nf*

combine *vb*, kombinieren; **combined**, kombiniert

come out *vb* (product), herauskommen; **the new model will come out next month**, das neue Modell wird nächsten Monat herauskommen

command *n* (comp), Befehl *nm*

commerce *n*, Handel *nm*

commercial *adj*, kommerziell

commercial *n* (on TV, radio), Werbespot *nm*

commission *n* (sales, fin), Kommission *nf*, Provision *nf*; **charge commission on**, Provision erheben für (+ acc)

commodity *n*, Ware *nf*

compact disc *n*, **CD**, Compact Disk *nf*, CD *nf*

company *n* (comm), Firma *nf*, Gesellschaft *nf*; **company car**, Firmenwagen *nm*; **company secretary**, Manager *nm* (mit Aufgabenbereich Finanzen und Verwaltung)

comparatively *adv*, vergleichsweise

comparison *n*, Vergleich *nm*; **in comparison with**, im Vergleich mit (+ dat)

compensate *vb* (gen, ins), entschädigen; **we would like to compensate you for the loss**, wir möchten Sie für den Verlust entschädigen

compensation *n* (law), Entschädigung *nf*; **compensation for damage** (law), Schadenersatz *nm*

competition *n* (mktg, sales), Konkurrenz *nf*

competitive *adj*, konkurrenzfähig

competitor *n*, Konkurrent(in) *nm/f*

complain *vb*, **1** (put in an official complaint), sich beschweren über (+ acc). **2** (customers), reklamieren

complaint *n* (mktg, sales), **1** (official), Beschwerde *nf*; **make a complaint**, Beschwerde einlegen. **2** (customers), Reklamation *nf*

complimentary ticket *n*, Freikarte *nf*

component *n*, Bestandteil *nm*; **components factory**, Zulieferant *nm*, Zulieferer *nm*

composed of, be composed of *vb*, bestehen aus (+ dat)

comprehensive *adj*, umfassend; **comprehensive insurance**, kombinierte Haftpflicht- und Vollkaskoversicherung *nf*

computer *n*, Computer *nm*; **computer-literate**, computersachverständig; **computer manager** (pers), Computerverwalter *nm*; **computer operator**, Computeroperator *nm*

computing *n*, Computing *nn*; **computing speed**, Rechengeschwindigkeit *nf*

concessionaire *n*, Konzessionär *nm*

condition *n*, **1** (general state), Zustand *nm*; **the machinery is in good condition**, die Maschinen sind in gutem Zustand. **2** (to be satisfied), Bedingung *nf*; **conditions of sale**, Verkaufsbedingungen *nfpl*; **on condition that . . .**, unter der Bedingung, daß . . .; **market conditions**, Marktbedingungen *nfpl*

conduct *vb* (survey), (eine Umfrage) durchführen

conference *n*, Konferenz *nf*; **conference hall**, Konferenzraum *nm*

confidence *n*, **1** Vertrauen *nn*; **have confidence in**, Vertrauen haben zu (+ dat). **2** (confidentiality), **in confidence**, vertraulich

confidential *adj*, vertraulich

confidentiality *n*, Vertraulichkeit *nf*

confirm *vb*, bestätigen

confirmation *n*, Bestätigung *nf*

confiscate *vb* (law), konfiszieren, beschlagnahmen

congratulate *vb*, gratulieren; **I would like to congratulate you on your promotion**, ich möchte Ihnen zu Ihrer Beförderung gratulieren

congratulations *npl*, Glückwünsche *nmpl*

connection *n*, **1** (gen, train), Verbindung *nf*. **2** (context), Zusammenhang *nm*

consider *vb*, **1** (reflect), nachdenken. **2** (take into account), bedenken.

considerably *adv*, beträchtlich

consignee *n* (imp/exp), Empfänger(in) *nm/f*

consignment *n* (transp), Sendung *nf*

consignor *n* (transp), Absender *nm*, Versender *nm*

construction industry *n*, Bauindustrie *nf*

consular *adj*, konsularisch

consult *vb*, konsultieren

consultancy *n*, Beratung *nf*

consultant *n*, Berater(in) *nm/f*; **a firm of consultants**, Beratungsunternehmen *nn*

consumer *n*, Verbraucher *nm*; **consumer goods**, Verbrauchsgüter *nnpl*, Konsumgüter *nnpl*; **consumer protection**, Verbraucherschutz *nm*

cont, to be continued, Forts. folgt, Fortsetzung folgt

contact *vb*, kontaktieren

contain *vb*, enthalten; **the file contains . . .**, die Akte enthält . . .

container *n* **1** (gen), Behälter *nm*. **2** (transp), Container *nm*; **refrigerated container**, Kühlcontainer *nm*; **sealed container**, versiegelter Container *nm*; **container lorry** (transp), Containerlastwagen *nm*, Container-Lkw *nm*

containerise *vb* (transp), auf Container umstellen

content(s) *n(p)*, Inhalt *nm*

continuous paper *n* (comp), Endlospapier *nn*

contract *n*, **1** (legal agreement), Vertrag *nm*; **contract of employment**, Arbeitsvertrag *nm*; **fixed-term contract**, Zeitvertrag *nm*. **2** (agreement for supply of goods/services), Auftrag *nm*

contract out *vb*, außer Haus machen lassen, vergeben; **the company intends to contract out assembly work**, die Firma beabsichtigt, Montagearbeit zu vergeben

contractor *n*, **1** Auftragnehmer *nm*, Beauftragter *nm*. **2** (building), Bauunternehmer *nm*

control *vb*, **1** (check), kontrollieren. **2** (dominate), beherrschen. **3** (supervise), beaufsichtigen

convenient *adj*, **1** (suitable), passend. **2** (favourable), günstig

cooling off period *n*, **1** (before signing contract), Überlegungsfrist *nf*. **2** (in strike), Friedenspflicht *nf*

copy *n*, **1** (of book), Exemplar *nn*. **2** (photocopy etc), Kopie *nf*. **3** (advertising text), Werbetextentwurf *nm*

copy *vb* (document), kopieren; **copy this to . . .**, bitte senden Sie eine Kopie an . . .

copyright *n*, Copyright *nn*

copywriter *n*, Werbetexter(in) *nm/f*

cordless telephone *n*, drahtloses Telefon *nn*

corporate *adj*, Firmen-, Unternehmens-; **corporate identity**, Firmenimage *nn*

corporation tax *n*, Körperschaftssteuer *nf*

correspond to *vb*, entsprechen (+ dat); **this corresponds to my expectations**, das entspricht meinen Erwartungen

COS, cash on shipment, (imp/exp), Zahlung *nf* bei Versand

cost *n*, Kosten *npl*; **cost and freight** (imp/exp), Kosten und Fracht; **cost, insurance, freight** (imp/exp), Kosten, Versicherung, Fracht; **cost-effective**, kosteneffektiv; **cost of living**, Lebenshaltungskosten *npl*; **cost of living index**, Lebenshaltungsindex *nm*; **cost price**, Selbstkostenpreis *nm*; **cost savings**, Kostenersparnis *nf*; **achieve cost savings**, Kosten einsparen

cost *vb*, **1** (calculate cost), die Kosten kalkulieren; **the project has been costed at £ 200,000**, die Kosten des Projekts werden auf £ 200.000 kalkuliert. **2 the machinery cost £ 40,000**, die Maschinen haben £ 40.000 gekostet

costly *adj*, teuer

count *vb*, zählen

counter-claim *n*, Gegenforderung *nf*

counter-offer *n*, Gegenangebot *nn*

counterproductive *adj*, kontraproduktiv

countersign *vb*, gegenzeichnen

country *n*, Land *nn*; **country of origin**, Ursprungsland *nn*

coupon *n* (mktg, sales, fin), Coupon

nm, Kupon *nm*; **reply coupon**, Antwortcoupon *nm*

court *n* (law), Gericht *nn*

cover *n* (fin, ins), Schutz *nm*; **insurance cover**, Versicherungsschutz *nm*; **cover note** (ins), vorläufiger Versicherungsschein *nm*

cover *vb*, **1** (fin), decken. **2** (ins), versichern

CP, **carriage paid** (mktg, sales), frachtfrei

CPA, **critical path analysis** kritische Pfadanalyse *nf*

CPT, **cost per thousand** (mktg, sales), Kosten *npl* pro Tausend

CPU, **central processing unit** (comp), Zentraleinheit *nf*, CPU

CR, **current rate** (fin), Tageskurs *nm*

craftsman *n*, Handwerker *nm*

crane *n* (transp), Kran *nm*

crash *n*, **1** (of vehicle), Kollision *nf*. **2** (comp) Absturz *nm*

crash *vb*, **1** (vehicle), verunglücken, einen Unfall haben. **2** (comp), abstürzen

crate *n* (transp, imp/exp), Kiste *nf*

create *vb* (company), gründen;

credit *n*, (fin), Kredit *nm*; **on credit**, auf Kredit; **credit account**, Kreditkonto *nn*; **credit balance**, Kontostand *nm*; **credit note** (mktg, sales), Gutschrift *nf*; **credit terms**, Kreditbedingungen *nfpl*; **credit transfer**, Kredittransfer *nm*

credit *vb* (fin), gutschreiben; **this will be credited to your account**, das wird Ihrem Konto gutgeschrieben

creditor *n*, (fin), Kreditgeber *nm*

crew *n*, Mannschaft *nf*

crime *n* (law), **1** (minor), Vergehen *nn*, Delikt *nn*. **2** (serious), Verbrechen *nn*

crisis *n*, Krise *nf*; **be in a crisis**, in einer Krise sein; **go through a crisis**, eine Krise durchmachen

critical path *n*, kritischer Pfad *nm*; **critical path analysis**, kritische Pfadanalyse *nf*

criticise *vb*, kritisieren

criticism *n*, Kritik *nf*

cross *vb*, **1** (in documents), ankreuzen. **2** (frontier), überqueren. **3** (cheque), zur Verrechnung ausstellen

cross out *vb*, (durch)streichen; **please cross out the parts that do not apply**, Unzutreffendes bitte streichen

cu ft, **cubic foot**, Kubikfuß *nm*

curr, **currt**, **current** *adj*, laufend

currency *n*, **1** (gen), Währung *nf*. **2** (foreign), Devisen *nfpl*; **currency dealer**, Devisenhändler *nm*

current account *n*, laufendes Konto *nn*

current affairs *npl*, Tagespolitik *nf*

currently *adv*, gegenwärtig

customer *n*, Kunde *nm*, Kundin *nf*; **customer loyalty**, Kundentreue *nf*; **customer service**, Kundendienst *nm*

customised *adj*, den Kundenwünschen angepaßt, individuell gestaltet

customs *npl* (imp/exp), Zoll *nm*; **customs clearance**, Zollabfertigung *nf*; **customs officer**, Zollbeamter *nm*, Zollbeamtin *nf*

cut *n* (reduction), Reduzierung *nf*

cut *vb* (prices etc), reduzieren

cut and paste *vb* (comp), Text umstellen

cutback *n*, Kürzung *nf*

cut-off date *n*, letztmöglicher Termin *nm*

CV, curriculum vitae (pers), Lebenslauf *nm*

CWO, cwo, cash with order (mktg, sales), bar bei Bestellung

cwt, hundredweight (50.7kg), (englischer) Zentner *nm*

cycle *n*, Kreis *nm*, Zyklus *nm*

DA, deposit account (fin), Sparkonto *nn*

D/A, documents against acceptance (imp/exp), Dokumente gegen Akzept

DAF, delivered at frontier (imp/exp), Lieferung frei (ab) Grenze

daily *adj*, täglich, Tages-; **daily newspaper**, Tageszeitung *nf*

dairy products *npl*, Milchprodukte *nnpl*

damage *n* (gen), Schaden *nm*

damaged *adj* (gen), beschädigt

damages *npl* (law), Schadenersatz *nm*

damp *n* (gen), Feuchtigkeit *nf*

damp-proof *adj*, feuchtigkeitsbeständig

danger *n*, Gefahr *nf*; **there is a danger that . . .**, es besteht die Gefahr, daß . . .

dangerous *adj*, gefährlich

data *npl* (gen, comp), Daten *nnpl*; **data capture** (comp), Datenerfassung *nf*; **data processing** (comp), Datenverarbeitung *nf*; **data protection**, Datenschutz *nm*; **data transmission** (comp), Datenübertragung *nf*

database *n* (comp), Datenbank *nf*; **database software** (comp), Datenbank-Software *nf*

date *n*, Datum *nn*; **date of birth** CV, Geburtsdatum *nn*; **date stamp** (offce), Datumsstempel *nm*

date *vb* (e.g. document), datieren

day *n*, Tag *nm*; **at . . . days after sight** (fin), . . . Tage nach Sicht; **day book** (acct), Journal *nn*; **day by day**, Tag für Tag; **day-to-day** (usual, every day), täglich, Tages-; **day-to-day routine**, tägliche Routine *nf*

DC, **direct current**, Gleichstrom *nm*

dd, **d/d**, **del'd**, **delivered** (imp/exp, transp), geliefert

DDP, **delivered duty paid** (imp/exp), Lieferung verzollt

deadline *n*, (letzter) Termin *nm*; **deadline for delivery**, letzter Lieferungstermin; **meet a deadline**, einen Termin einhalten

deal *n* (comm), Geschäft *nn*

deal in *vb* (comm), handeln mit (+ dat)

deal with *vb*, **1** (e.g. a topic), sich befassen mit (+ dat); **the report deals with . . .** der Bericht befaßt sich mit . . . **2** (do business with), in Geschäftsverbindung stehen mit (+ dat)

dealer *n*, Händler *nm*, Händlerin *nf*

dear *adj*, **1** (cost), teuer. **2** (corr), **Dear Mr Smith, . . . Yours sincerely**, Sehr geehrter Herr Smith, . . . Mit freundlichen Grüßen; **Dear Sir or Madam, . . . Yours faithfully**, Sehr geehrte Damen und Herren, . . . Mit freundlichen Grüßen

debit *n*, Debet *nn*; **debit note**, Lastschriftanzeige *nf*

debit *vb* **an account** (fin), ein Konto belasten

debt *n*, Schulden *nfpl*; **be in debt**, Schulden haben; **pay off debts**, Schulden begleichen; **debts due**, fällige Schulden

debtor *n*, Schuldner *nm*

debug *vb* (comp), entwanzen

decide *vb* (decide to), beschließen; **we have decided to cancel the order**, wir haben beschlossen, den Auftrag zu stornieren

decision *n*, Beschluß *nm*

deck cargo *n* (transp), Deckladung *nf*

declaration *n*, Erklärung *nf*; **customs declaration**, Zollerklärung *nf*

decline *n*, Rückgang *nm*

decline *vb*, **1** (an offer), ablehnen. **2** (sales), sinken

decrease *n*, **1** (drop), Sinken *nn*. **2** (reduction), Senkung *nf*

decrease *vb*, sinken; **prices have decreased**, die Preise sind gesunken; **we have decreased our prices**, wir haben unsere Preise gesenkt

dedicated *adj* (comp), dediziert

deduct *vb* (gen), abziehen; **please deduct £10 from the price quoted**, bitte ziehen Sie £10 von dem angegebenen Preis ab

deductible *adj* (gen), abziehbar

deduction *n* (fin), Abzug *nm*

defect *n*, Defekt *nm*; **hidden defect**, versteckter Defekt

defective *adj*, defekt

defence *n*, Verteidigung *nf*

defend against *vb* (gen, law), verteidigen gegen (+ acc)

defer *vb* (put off), vertagen

deferred *adj*, vertagt

definite *adj*, fest

definitely *adv*, bestimmt

delay *n*, Verzögerung *nf*

delay *vb* (consignment etc), verzögern; **payment was delayed**, die Zahlung wurde verzögert

delete *vb*, **1** (text), streichen. **2** (comp), löschen

deliver *vb* (transp), liefern; **delivered duty paid**, Lieferung verzollt

delivered at frontier, DAF (imp/exp), Lieferung frei (ab) Grenze

delivery *n* (transp), Lieferung *nf*; **delivery arrangements**, Lieferungsbedingungen *nfpl*; **delivery date**, Lieferdatum *nn*; **delivery deadline**, Liefertermin *nm*; **delivery note**, Lieferschein *nm*

demand *n* (comm), Nachfrage *nf*; **demand has risen steeply**, die Nachfrage ist steil angestiegen; **note payable on demand** (fin), Zahlungsaufforderung *nf*

demand *vb*, fordern

demonstrate *vb*, demonstrieren

demonstration *n* (mktg), Demonstration *nf*

demurrage *n* (transp), Liegegeld *nn*

depart *vb*, **1** (bus, train), abfahren. **2** (ships), ablegen

department *n*, Abteilung *nf*; **department store**, Kaufhaus *nn*

departmental *adj*, Abteilungs-; **departmental manager**, Abteilungsleiter *nm*

depend on *vb*, **1** (be dependent on), abhängen von (+ dat). **2** (rely on), sich verlassen auf (+ acc)

deposit *n*, **1** (advance payment), Anzahlung *nf*; **pay a deposit**, eine Anzahlung machen. **2** (in bank), Einzahlung *nf*; **deposit account** (fin), Sparkonto *nn*

deposit *vb*, **1** (part of payment), anzahlen. **2** (into bank account), einzahlen

depreciation *n* (acct), Abschreibung *nf*

deputy *adj*, stellvertretend; **deputy manager**, stellvertretender Leiter *nm*

description of goods *n* (imp/exp), Warenbeschreibung *nf*

design *n*, Design *nn*

designed for *adj*, bestimmt für (+ acc)

designer *n*, Designer(in) *nm/f*

desk *n* (offce), Schreibtisch *nm*

desktop publishing *n* (comp), Desktop Publishing *nn*

despatch *vb* (imp/exp), versenden

detail *n*, Detail *nn*, Einzelheit *nf*

detailed *adj*, detailliert

details *npl*, **1** (CV), Angaben *nfpl*. **2 customer details** (mktg, sales), Kundendaten *nnpl*. **3** (of event, company), Einzelheiten *nfpl*

develop *vb* (gen), entwickeln

developing countries, *npl*, Entwicklungsländer *nnpl*

development *n* (gen), Entwicklung *nf*; **development area**, Förderungsgebiet *nn*

deviation *n*, Abweichung *nf*

device *n* (equipment), Gerät *nn*

dial *vb* (telec), wählen; **dial a number**, eine Nummer wählen

diary *n* (offce), Kalender *nm*; **desk diary**, Terminkalender *nm*

dictaphone *n*, Diktiergerät *nn*

dictate *vb* (offce), diktieren

dictation *n*, Diktat *nn*

diesel engine *n*, Dieselmotor *nm*

diesel oil *n*, Dieselöl *nn*

difference *n*, **1** (gen), Unterschied *nm*. **2** (fin), Differenz *nf*; **by my calculations the difference is . . .**, nach meinen Berechnungen beträgt die Differenz . . .

digital computer *n* (comp), Digitalcomputer *nm*

digitise *vb* (comp), digitalisieren

dimensions *npl*, Abmessungen *nfpl*

direct *adj*, direkt, Direkt-; **direct**

debit, Direktabbuchung *nf*; **direct line**, (telec), direkte Verbindung *nf*; **direct marketing**, Direktmarketing *nn*; **direct sales**, Direktverkauf *nm*

directions *npl*, **1** (for driving), Fahranweisungen *nfpl*. **2** (for use), Gebrauchsanweisungen *nfpl*

director *n* (pers), Direktor(in) *nm/f*; **director of communication**, Kommunikationsdirektor *nm*; **marketing director**, Marketingdirektor *nm*

disadvantage *n*, Nachteil *nm*

disagree with *vb*, nicht zustimmen; **we disagree with your analysis**, wir stimmen Ihrer Analyse nicht zu

discharge *vb* (transp), entladen

discontinue *vb* **production**, die Produktion einstellen

discontinued line *n*, ausgelaufene Serie *nf*

discount *n* (fin), Diskont *nm*, Rabatt *nm*; **give discount**, Diskont/Rabatt gewähren

discounted *adj* (fin), diskontiert

discrepancy *n* (gen), Diskrepanz *nf*

discuss *vb* (gen), diskutieren

discussion *n* (gen), Diskussion *nf*

dishonour a bill *vb*, eine Rechnung nicht bezahlen

disk *n* (comp), **hard disk**, Festplatte *nf*; **floppy disk**, Floppy Disk *nf*, Diskette *nf*

dismiss *vb* (pers), entlassen

dispatch *vb*, senden

display *n* (of goods), Auslage *nf*

display *vb*, ausstellen

distribute *vb*, **1** (gen), verteilen. **2** (comm), vertreiben. **3** (dividends), ausschütten

distribution *n*, **1** (gen), Verteilung *nf*. **2** (comm), Vertrieb *nm*. **distribution network**, Vertriebsnetz *nn*; **distribution problems**, Vertriebsprobleme *nnpl*. **3** (of dividends), Ausschüttung *nf*

distributor *n*, Verteiler *nm*, Händler *nm*

diversify *vb*, diversifizieren

divide *vb*, **1** (into), (zer)teilen. **2** (among), verteilen

dividend *n* (fin), Dividende *nf*

division *n*, Teilung *nf*

DIY, **do-it-yourself** (mktg, sales), Do-it-yourself

do *vb* **business with**, geschäftlich zu tun haben mit (+ dat)

dock *vb* (shipping), anlegen

dockyard *n*, Werft *nf*

document *n*, **1** (offce), Akte *nf*. **2** **documents** (imp/exp), Papiere *nnpl*; **documents against acceptance**, **D/A** (imp/exp), Dokumente gegen Akzept

domestic *adj*, **1** (household), Haus-, Haushalts-; **domestic appliance**, Haushaltsgerät *nn*; **domestic trade**, Binnenhandel *nm*. **2** (country), Binnen-

dominant *adj* (market position), dominierend

dominate the market *vb*, den Markt dominieren

door-to-door *adj*, von Tür zu Tür; **door-to-door sales**, Verkauf *nm* durch Vertreter; **door-to-door salesman**, Vertreter *nm*

double *vb*, (sich) verdoppeln; **I have doubled my income**, ich habe mein Einkommen verdoppelt; **profits have doubled**, der Gewinn hat sich verdoppelt

Dow Jones Average *n* (fin), Dow-Jones Aktienindex *nm*

down, be down *vb* (fin, results), gesunken sein; **sales are down by . . .**, der Umsatz ist um . . . gesunken

download *vb* (comp), **1** (via telephone), fernladen. **2** (from mainframe to small computer), hinunterladen. **3** (software), Zeichensätze laden

down-time *n*, Ausfallzeit *nf*

downturn *n* (fin, mktg, sales), Flaute *nf*

downward trend *n* (gen, fin), rückläufiger Trend *nm*

dozen *n*, (ein) Dutzend *nn*; **a dozen bottles**, ein Dutzend Flaschen; **by the dozen**, im Dutzend

D/P, **documents against payment** (imp/exp), Papiere gegen Zahlung

DP Manager, **data processing manager** *n* (comp), Datenverarbeitungsmanager *nm*

Dr to, **draw on** (fin), ausgestellt auf (+ acc)

draft *n*, **1** (of letters, reports), Entwurf *nm*; **draft contract**, Vertragsentwurf *nm*. **2** (fin), Wechsel *nm*; **bank draft**, Bankwechsel *nm*

draft *vb* (report, letter), entwerfen

draw up *vb* (agreement, contract), entwerfen

drawback *n*, **1** (disadvantage), Nachteil *nm*. **2** (imp/exp), Zollrückvergütung *nf*

drawee *n* (fin), Bezogener *nm*

drawer *n* (fin), Aussteller *nm*

drive *n*, **1** (campaign), Kampagne *nf*. **2** (in vehicle), Fahrt *nf*. **3** (personality), Elan *nm*; **plenty of drive**, voller Elan. **4** (propulsion), Antrieb *nm*; **rear-wheel drive**, Hinterradsantrieb *nm*. **5 left-hand drive**, Linkssteuerung *nf*

drive *vb* (car), fahren

driver *n* (of vehicle), Fahrer(in) *nm/f*

driving licence *n*, Führerschein *nm*

drop *vb*, **1** (prices, interests), fallen; **interest rates have dropped**, die Zinsen sind gefallen. **2** (drop something), fallenlassen; **he dropped the idea**, er ließ die Idee fallen

dry-run *n*, Probelauf *nm*

DTI, **Department of Trade and Industry**, ≈ Wirtschaftsministerium *nn*

DTP, **desktop publishing** (comp), Desktop Publishing *nn*

due *adj*, **1** (fin), fällig; **amount due**, fälliger Betrag *nm*. **2** (expected, scheduled), sollen; **the plane is due to land at 17 hrs**, das Flugzeug soll um 17 Uhr landen

dump *vb* (sell at a loss), billig auf den Markt werfen

dumping *n*, Dumping *nn*

duplicate *n* (second copy), Duplikat *nn*, doppelte Ausführung *nf*; **receipt in duplicate**, Quittung *nf* in doppelter Ausführung

duplicate *vb* (make copy), kopieren

durable *adj*, **1** (goods), langlebig. **2** (material), haltbar. **3** (metal), widerstandsfähig

durables *npl*, langlebige Güter *nnpl*

duration *n*, Dauer *nf*

duty *n* (customs), Zoll *nm*; **duty paid** (imp/exp), verzollt

E

E + O E, errors and omissions excepted, Irrtümer und Auslassungen vorbehalten

early *adv*, **1** früh(zeitig). **2** (before time), vorzeitig

early *adj*, früh, baldig: **we can guarantee early delivery**, wir garantieren baldige Lieferung; **early repayment**, baldige Rückzahlung; **early reply**, baldige Antwort

earn *vb*, verdienen

earnings *npl*, **1** Einkünfte *npl*. **2** (fin), Rendite *nf*; **earnings per share**, Gewinnrendite *nf*

ease *vb*, **1** (make easier), erleichtern. **2** (drop in rates, prices), nachlassen

ECGD, export credit guarantee department, ≈ Hermes Kreditversicherung *nf*

economic *adj*, wirtschaftlich; **economic problems**, wirtschaftliche Probleme *nnpl*

economical *adj*, sparsam; **economical car**, benzinsparendes Auto *nn*

economics *n* (subject, study of), Wirtschaftswissenschaften *nfpl*

economise *vb*, sparen

economy *n*, Wirtschaft *nf*; **the German economy**, die deutsche Wirtschaft

EDI, electronic data interchange (comp), elektronischer Datenaustausch *nm*

editor *n* (of a newspaper), Herausgeber(in) *nm/f*

education *n*, **1** (gen, teaching), Erziehung *nf*. **2** (section of CV), Bildungsweg *nm*

EE, errors excepted, Irrtümer *nmpl* vorbehalten

effect *n* **of/on**, Wirkung *nf* von (+ dat)/auf (+ acc)

effective *adj*, effektiv

efficiency *n*, Effizienz *nf*

efficient *adj*, effizient

electrical *adj*, elektrisch, Elektro-; **electrical equipment**, Elektrogeräte *nnpl*

electronic *adj*, elektronisch

electronics *n*, Elektronik *nf*

eligible *adj*, **1** (for membership), wählbar. **2** (for rights), wahlberechtigt

E-mail, electronic mail *n* (comp), E-Mail, elektronische Post *nf*

embargo *n*, Embargo *nn*; **lift an embargo**, ein Embargo aufheben; **place an embargo on**, ein Embargo über (+ acc) verhängen

embark on *vb*, **1** (gen, a venture), sich auf (+ acc) einlassen. **2** (take cargo onto ship), verladen

emphasise *vb*, betonen

employ *vb*, beschäftigen; **we employ 52 people**, wir beschäftigen 52 Leute

employee *n*, **1** (gen), Beschäftigte(r) *nf/m*; **number of employees**, Zahl *nf* der Beschäftigten. **2** (white-collar), Angestellte(r) *nf/m*

employer *n*, Arbeitgeber *nm*

employment *n*, Beschäftigung *nf*; **he found employment with . . .**, er fand Beschäftigung bei . . .; **employment history** (CV), beruflicher Werdegang *nm*

empty *adj*, leer

Enc, Encl, enclosure(s) (corr), Anlage *nf*, Anl.

enclose *vb* (corr), beilegen; **I enclose a copy of our brochure**, ich lege ein Exemplar unserer Broschüre bei; **please find enclosed . . .**, in der Anlage finden Sie . . .

endorse *vb*, **1** (cheque), indossieren. **2** (idea), beipflichten; **he has endorsed the plan**, er hat diesem Plan beigepflichtet

engine *n*, Motor *nm*

engineer *n*, **1** (graduate), Ingenieur(in) *nm(f)*. **2** (technician), Techniker(in) *nm(f)*

enquiry *n*, Untersuchung *nf*

enter *vb*, **1** (bookkeeping etc), eintragen. **2** (comp), eingeben

enterprise *n* (firm), Unternehmen *nn*

entrance *n*, Eingang *nm*

entry *n* (bookkeeping etc), Eintragung *nf*

envelope *n*, Umschlag *nm*

equal *vb*, gleichen

equal *adj*, gleich

equity *n* (ordinary share), Eigenkapital *nn*

error *n*, Irrtum *nm*

establish *vb*, **1** (in location), **the company is established in Sussex**, die Firma ist in Sussex ansässig. **2** (date), **the company was established in 1954**, die Firma wurde 1954 gegründet

estate agent *n*, Grundstücksmakler(in) *nm/f*

estimate *n*, **1** (quotation), Kostenvoranschlag *nm*. **2** (rough calculation), Schätzung *nf*

estimate *vb*, schätzen; **estimated cost**, geschätzte Kosten *npl*; **estimated (time of) arrival**, voraussichtliche Ankunft *nf*

EU, **European Union**, EG, Europäische Gemeinschaft *nf*

event *n*, **1** (gen), Ereignis *nn*; **be overtaken by events**, von den Ereignissen überholt werden; **in the normal course of events**, normalerweise. **2** (organised function), Veranstaltung *nf*. **3** (case), Fall *nm*; **in the event of her arrival**, im Falle ihrer Ankunft

eventual *adj*, letztlich

examine *vb*, prüfen

exceed *vb*, überschreiten

exceptional items *npl* (acct), Sonderposten *nmpl*

excess *n* (fin), Überschuß *nm*; **excess capacity**, Überkapazität *nf*

exchange for *vb* (gen), (aus)tauschen für (+ acc)

exchange rate *n*, Wechselkurs *nm*

exclusive *adj* (role), Allein-; **exclusive agreement** (comm), Alleinvertretungsvereinbarung *nf*; **exclusive right to market a product**, Alleinvertriebsrechte *nnpl*

excuse *n*, Entschuldigung *nf*

executive *adj* (in company), geschäftsführend, leitend; **executive director** (managing director), **1** geschäftsführender Direktor *nm*, geschäftsführende Direktorin *nf*. **2** (member of executive committee), Vorstandsmitglied *nn*

exhibit *vb* (mktg, sales), ausstellen

exhibition *n* (mktg, sales), Ausstellung *nf*; **exhibition centre**, Ausstellungszentrum *nn*

exhibitor *n* (mktg, sales), Aussteller(in) *nm/f*

expand *vb*, expandieren; **expanding company**, expandierendes Unternehmen *nn*; **expanding market**, expandierender Markt *nm*

expansion *n*, Expansion *nf*

expect *vb*, erwarten; **we expect to sign the contract with . . .**, wir erwarten, daß wir den Vertrag mit . . . unterzeichnen; **we are**

expecting your reply, wir erwarten Ihre Antwort; **we expect you at the hotel at 7 p.m.**, wir erwarten Sie um 19 Uhr am Hotel

expenditure *n*, Ausgaben *nfpl*

expenses *npl*, Unkosten *npl*; **travelling expenses**, Reiseunkosten *npl*

experience *n*, Erfahrung *nf*; **gain experience in marketing**, Erfahrung(en) im Marketing sammeln

experienced *adj*, erfahren; **we are looking for an experienced manager**, wir suchen einen erfahrenen Manager

expert *n*, Experte *nm*, Expertin *nf*

export *n*, Export *nm*; **export manager**, Exportmanager(in) *nm/f*

exporter *n*, Exporteur *nm*

express *n*, **1** (train), Schnellzug *nm*. **2** (letter, goods), Expreßsendung *nf*

ExQ, **Exq**, **Ex Quay** (imp/exp), ab Kai

ExS, **Exs**, **Ex Ship** (imp/exp), ab Schiff

external disc drive *n*, externes Plattenlaufwerk *nn*

extra charge *n* (fin), zusätzliche Kosten *npl*

extrude *vb*, ausstoßen

EXW, **Ex Works** (imp/exp), ab Fabrik

F

FAA, **faa**, **free of all average** (ins), frei von jeder Havarie

face *vb*, **1 the company is faced with great problems**, das Unternehmen steht vor großen Problemen. **2** (meet confidently), **problems will be faced and solved**, die Probleme werden in Angriff genommen und gelöst

face value *n* (fin), Nominalwert *nm*

facilitate *vb*, ermöglichen

facilities *npl* (of a hotel), Einrichtung *nf*; **facilities for the disabled**, Einrichtungen für Behinderte

factor *n* (gen, maths), Faktor *nm*; **decisive, major, crucial factor**, entscheidender, wichtiger, ausschlaggebender Faktor; **. . . has increased by a factor of 2**, . . . hat sich um einen Faktor von 2 erhöht

factory *n*, Fabrik *nf*, Werk *nn*; **factory gate price**, Fabrikpreis *nm*, Preis *nm* ab Werk; **factory worker**, Fabrikarbeiter(in) *nm/f*

fail *vb* (fin), **1** (go bust), bankrott gehen. **2** (not succeed), **the division failed to reach its target for the quarter**, der Unternehmensbereich hat sein Ziel/Plansoll für das Quartal nicht erreicht/erfüllt; **they failed to deliver by the agreed date**, sie haben das vereinbarte Lieferdatum nicht eingehalten

failure *n*, **1** (gen, mechanics), Versagen *nn*. **2** (business), Bankrott *nm*; **failure to pay**, Nichtbezahlen *nn*

fair *n* (comm), Messe *nf*; **international trade fair**, internationale Handelsmesse *nf*

fair *adj*, fair; **a fair price**, ein fairer Preis

fall *n*, Rückgang *nm*, Sinken *nn*; **a fall in prices**, ein Sinken der Preise; **a steady fall in sales**, ein stetiger Absatzrückgang

fall *vb*, fallen; **prices have fallen this year**, die Preise sind dieses Jahr gefallen; **sales have fallen by 15%**, der Absatz ist um 15% gefallen

fall due *vb*, (payment), fällig sein

fall off *vb*, nachlassen; **demand is beginning to fall off**, die Nachfrage läßt allmählich nach

fall through *vb*, scheitern; **the negotiations fell through because of . . .**, die Verhandlungen scheiterten an (+ dat)

fall-off *n* (reduction, slackening), Nachlassen *nn*; **a fall-off in orders**, ein Nachlassen der Aufträge

FAQ, faq, 1 free alongside quay (imp/exp), frei ab Kai. **2 fair average quality** (mktg, sales), gute Durchschnittsqualität *nf*

fare *n*, Fahrpreis *nm*; **concessionary fare**, Vorzugsfahrpreis *nm*; **half fare**, halber Fahrpreis; **return fare**, Hin- und Rückfahrpreis *nm*; **second-class fare**, Fahrpreis zweiter Klasse; **single fare**, einfacher Fahrpreis

farmer *n*, Landwirt(in) *nm/f*

farming *n*, Landwirtschaft *nf*

FAS, fas, free alongside ship (imp/exp), frei ab Schiff

fast *adv*, schnell; **work fast**, schnell arbeiten

fast *adj* schnell; **fast delivery guaranteed**, garantiert schnelle Lieferung; **fast food industry**, Fast-Food-Industrie *nf*

fault *n*, Defekt *nm*, Fehler *nm*; **we believe that the problem is due to a fault in the system**, wir führen das Problem auf einen Systemdefekt zurück; **we must apologise, the fault was ours**, wir bitten um Entschuldigung, der Fehler lag bei uns

faulty *adj*, fehlerhaft

fax *n*, (Tele-)Fax *nn*; **fax machine**, (Tele-)Faxmaschine *nf*; **fax number**, (Tele-)Faxnummer *nf*

fax *vb*, (tele)faxen

FCL, fcl, full container load (imp/exp), volle Containerladung *nm*

feasibility study *n*, Durchführbarkeitsstudie *nf*

feasible *adj*, durchführbar

feature *n* (of a product), Merkmal *nn*; **a key feature**, ein wesentliches Merkmal

feature *vb* (mktg, sales), **1** (programme, article), bringen; **the magazine will feature an article about our company**, die Zeitschrift bringt einen Artikel über unser Unternehmen. **2** (product), **the product features the latest technology**, das Produkt entspricht dem neusten technischen Standard

fee *n*, **1** (cost of professional service), Gebühr *nf*; **there will be a fee of £25 payable**, eine Gebühr von £25 ist zahlbar. **2** (regular contribution), Beitrag *nm*; **annual membership fee**, Jahresmitgliedsbeitrag *nm*

female connector *n* (electr), Anschlußbuchse *nf*

female socke *n* (electr), Steckdose *nf*

ferry *n*, Fähre *nf*

fga, free of general average (ins), frei von großer Havarie

field *n*, **1** (gen), Feld *nn*; **field work**, Felduntersuchung *nf*. **2** (mktg, sales), **in the field**, im Außendienst *nm*. **3** (subject), **a specialist in the**

field of . . ., ein Spezialist im Bereich . . .

fight *vb* (oppose), bekämpfen

figure *n* (1, 2, 3, etc), Ziffer *nf*

file *n*, **1** (single card), Karteikarte *nf*. **2** (collection of information on a subject), Kartei *nf*. **3** (container for storage files), Aktenordner *nm*. **4** (binder to hold documents), Aktenhefter *nm*. **5** (comp), Datei *nf*; **file management** (comp), Dateimanagement *nn*; **file server** (comp), Controller *nm* für Speicherzugriff

file *vb* (offce), ablegen

filing cabinet *n* (offce), Aktenschrank *nm*

filing clerk *n* (offce), Registraturangestellte(r) *nf/m*

fill in *vb* (a form), ausfüllen

fill up *vb*, **1** (gen), (aus)füllen. **2** (petrol tank), vollmachen

film-wrapped *adj* (mktg, sales), folienverpackt

finalise *vb*, **1** (decide on final shape), endgültig formulieren. **2** (complete), abschließen

finance *vb*, finanzieren

finance(s) *n(pl)*, Finanzmittel *nnpl*

financial *adj*, finanziell, Finanz-; **financial arrangements**, Finanzvereinbarungen *nfpl*; **financial director**, Finanzdirektor(in) *nm/f*; **financial manager**, Finanzmanager *nm*; **financial planning**, Finanzplanung *nf*; **financial year**, Finanzjahr *nn*

financier *n*, Geldgeber *nm*

financing *n*, Finanzierung *nf*

findings *npl* (of inquiry), Ergebnisse *nnpl*

fine *n* (law), Geldstrafe *nf*; **impose a fine**, eine Geldstrafe verhängen; **pay a fine**, eine Geldstrafe zahlen

fine *vb*, mit einer Geldstrafe belegen

finish *n* (on a product), Verarbeitung *nf*

finished *adj* (completed), fertig; **finished goods/products** (fin), Fertigwaren *nfpl*

fire *n* (accidental), Brand *nm*

firm *adj*, fest; **a firm order**, ein fester Auftrag

firm *n* (business), Firma *nf*

first *adj*, erst; **first quarter**, erstes Quartal *nn*; **for the first time**, zum ersten Mal

fit *vb*, **1** (be the right size), passen. **2** (fix on), einbauen, anbauen. **3** (adjust, assemble), zusammenbauen

fix *vb*, **1** (make arrangements), festsetzen; **fix an appointment**, einen Termin festsetzen. **2** (repair), reparieren

fixed assets *npl* (fin), Anlagevermögen *nn*

fixed expenses *npl*, Festkosten *npl*

fixed-interest investments *npl* (fin), festverzinsliche Kapitalanlagen *nfpl*

fixed rate *n* (fin), fester Satz *nm*

fixed-term contract *n* (pers), Zeitvertrag *nm*

flat rate *n*, Einheitssatz *nm*

flatten out *vb* (trends, figures), sich abflachen

flaw *n*, Fehler *nm*

flexible *adj*, flexibel; **flexible working hours**, gleitende Arbeitszeit *nf*, Gleitzeit *nf*

flier/flyer *n* (leaflet), Handzettel *nm*

flip chart *n*, Flip-Chart *nf*

float *vb* **a company** (fin), eine Gesellschaft durch Aktienemissionen an der Börse gründen

float *vb* **a loan** (fin), eine Anleihe aufnehmen

flow chart *n* (fin), Flußdiagramm *nn*

fluctuate *vb*, fluktuieren

fluctuations *npl*, Fluktuationen *nfpl*; **fluctuations in the exchange rate**, Wechselkursfluktuationen *nfpl*

fly *vb*, fliegen

FM, **frequency modulation**, Frequenzmodulation *nf*

FMCG, **fast-moving consumer goods** (mktg, sales), schnell verkäufliche Verbrauchsgüter *nnpl*

FOB, **fob**, **free on board** (imp/exp), frei an Bord

focus on *vb* (gen), sich konzentrieren auf (+ acc)

fold *vb* (documents), falten

folder *n*, **1** (product information), Mappe *nf*. **2** (documents), Aktenmappe *nf*

follow up *vb* (contact, point, lead etc), nachgehen (+ dat)

food *n*, Nahrungsmittel *nnpl*; **food analyst**, Lebensmittelchemiker(in) *nm/f*; **food industry**, Nahrungsmittelindustrie *nf*; **food products** (groceries), Lebensmittel *nnpl*

forecast *n* (gen, fin), Vorhersage *nf*; **weather forecast**, Wettervorhersage *nf*

forecast *vb* (gen, fin), vorhersagen

foreign *adj*, Auslands-; **foreign currency**, Devisen *nfpl*; **foreign goods**, Auslandswaren *nfpl*; **foreign investments**, Auslandsinvestionen *nfpl*; **foreign trade**, Außenhandel *nm*

foreman *n*, Vorarbeiter *nm*

FOR/FOT, **for/fot**, **free on rail/free on truck** (imp/exp), frei Waggon (oder offene Güterwagen)

forklift *n* (truck), Gabelstapler *nm*

form *n* (imp/exp), Formular *nn*; **fill in a form**, ein Formular ausfüllen

forward *vb* (imp/exp), nachsenden; **please forward to the above address**, bitte an obige Adresse nachsenden

forwarding agent *n* (transp), Spediteur *nm*

four-colour *adj* (mktg, sales), Vierfarben-; **four-colour advertisement**, Vierfarbenreklame *nf*

FPA, **fpa**, **free of particular average** (imp/exp), frei von besonderer Havarie

FPAD, **fpad**, **freight payable at destination** (imp/exp), Fracht zahlbar am Bestimmungsort

franchise *n* (mktg, sales), Franchise *nf*

franchise *vb* (mktg, sales), auf Franchise-Basis vergeben

franchiser *n* (mktg, sales), Franchisegeber *nm*

frank *vb* (corr), frankieren

franking machine *n* (offce), Frankiermaschine *nf*

FRC, **frc**, **free carrier** (imp/exp), Transport frei

free *adj* **1** (gen), frei; **free admission**, Eintritt frei; **free gift** (mktg, sales), Werbegeschenk *nn*; **free choice**, freie Wahl *nf*. **2** (imp/exp), **free alongside quay**, **FAQ**, frei ab Kai; **free alongside ship**, **FAS**, frei ab Schiff; **free carrier/free delivery**, Transport frei/Lieferung frei Haus; **free on board**, frei an Bord; **free on rail/free on truck**, **FOR/FOT**, frei Waggon (oder offene Güterwagen). **3** (ins), **free of all average**, **faa**, frei von aller Havarie; **free of general average**, **fga**, frei von großer Havarie; **free of particular average**, **fpa**, frei von besonderer Havarie

freebie *n* (mktg, sales), Gratisprobe *nf*

freephone number *n* (mktg, sales), ≈ SERVICE 130 *nm*

freepost *n*, Gebühr *nf* bezahlt Empfänger

freesheet *n* (mktg, sales), Anzeigenblatt *nn*

freeze *n*, **1** (credit), Einfrieren *nn*. **2** **freeze on wages and prices**, Lohn- und Preisstopp *nm*

freight *n* (imp/exp), **1** (load), Fracht *nf*. **2** (transp), Transport *nm*. **3** (freight cost), Frachtgebühren *nfpl*, Transportgebühren *nfpl*; **freight paid**, frachtfrei; **freight payable at destination, FPAD**, Fracht zahlbar am Bestimmungsort; **freight car**, Güterwagen *nm*; **freight handling** (transp), Güterabfertigung *nf*; **freight train**, Güterzug *nm*

frequency *n*, Frequenz *nf*

frequent *adj*, häufig

fringe benefits *npl*, Leistungsanreize *nmpl*

fuel *n*, Brennstoff *nm*; **fuel oil**, Heizöl *nn*

full *adj*, **1** (trains, aeroplanes, hotels), (voll) besetzt, ausgebucht. **2 full container load** (transp), volle Containerladung *nf*

full-time *adj* (pers), ganztägig, Ganztags-; **a full-time job/position**, Ganztagsarbeit *nf*

fund *n*, Fonds *nm*

fund *vb*, finanzieren

future *n*, Zukunft *nf*; **in the future**, in Zukunft

future *adj*, zukünftig; **future developments**, zukünftige Entwicklungen

futures market *n* (fin), Futures-Markt *nm*

G

gadget *n*, **1** (unflattering), nutzlose Zutat *nf*. **2** (small piece of equipment), Gerät *nn*

gain *n* (gen, fin), Gewinn *nm*, Profit *nm*

gain *vb*, gewinnen; **gain in value**, an Wert gewinnen; **gain experience**, (an) Erfahrung gewinnen

gap *n*, **1** (distance), Abstand *nm*; **the gap between . . . and . . . is widening**, der Abstand zwischen . . . und . . . wächst. **2** (vacuum, hole), Lücke *nf*; **market gap**, Marktlücke *nf*

gas *n*, Gas *nn*

gather *vb* (gen, also information), sammeln

GDP, gross domestic product, Bruttoinlandsprodukt *nn*

gearing *n* (fin), Verhältnis *nn* zwischen Fremdkapital/Eigenkapital/ Verschuldungsgrad

general *adj*, allgemein; **general cargo rates, GCR, gcr** (transp), allgemeine Frachtgebührensätze *nmpl*; **general expenses**, allgemeine Unkosten *npl*; **general manager**, geschäftsführender Direktor *nm*

get *vb* **in touch with**, sich in Verbindung setzen mit (+ dat)

gift *n*, Geschenk *nn*

gift wrap *n*, Geschenkpapier *nn*

giro cheque *n*, Giroscheck *nm*

give *vb*, **1** (gen), geben; **give credit** (fin), Kredit geben. **2 give a talk**, eine Rede halten. **3 give notice**, kündigen

giveaway *n* (mktg, sales), Werbegeschenk *nn*

gloomy *adj* (financial outlook), düster

glossy *n* (magazine), Hochglanzmagazin *nn*

glut *n*, Überangebot *nn*

GNP, gross national product, Bruttosozialprodukt *nn*

go-ahead *n*, grünes Licht *nn*; **get the go-ahead**, grünes Licht bekommen

go ahead *vb*, **1** (go before), vorangehen. **2** (start), anfangen

go down *vb* (rates, prices), sinken; **sales have gone down by 2%**, der Absatz ist um 2% gesunken; **inflation will go down to 5%**, die Inflation wird auf 5% sinken

go *vb* **public** (fin, stock market), sein Unternehmen in eine Aktiengesellschaft umwandeln

go up *vb*, steigen; **prices have gone up by 10%**, die Preise sind um 10% gestiegen

goods *npl*, Güter *nnpl*, Waren *nfpl*; **imported goods**, Importwaren *nfpl*; **luxury goods**, Luxuswaren *nfpl*; **manufactured goods**, Fertigwaren *nfpl*; **goods wagon** (transp), Güterwagen *nm*; **goods in transit** (transp), Transitgüter *nnpl*

goodwill *n* (acct), Firmenansehen *nn*, Goodwill *nm*

go-slow *n* (pers), Bummelstreik *nm*

grade *n* (quality), Qualitätsstufe *nf*

grade *vb* (quality of goods), in Qualitätsstufen einteilen

graph *n* (chart showing axes), Schaubild *nn*; **graph paper**, Millimeterpapier *nn*; **graph plotter** (comp), Plotter *nm*

graphic artist *n*, Graphiker(in) *nm/f*

graphics *npl*, Graphik *nf*; **computer graphics**, Computergraphik *nf*

green *adj*, grün; **Green Card** (ins), Grüne Karte *nf*; **Green Party**, Grüne Partei *nf*

grievance procedure *n* (pers), Beschwerdeweg *nm*

gross *adj* (fin), Brutto-; **gross earnings**, Bruttoverdienst *nm*; **gross profit**, Bruttogewinn *nm*; **gross revenue**, Bruttoeinnahmen *nfpl*; **gross weight**, Bruttogewicht *nn*

gross *n* (12 dozen), Gros *nn*

gross *vb* (fin), brutto einnehmen; **the company grossed 50 million last year**, die Firma hat letztes Jahr 50 Millionen eingenommen

grow *vb*, **1** (become bigger), wachsen; **the firm has grown a lot**, die Firma ist sehr gewachsen. **2** (cultivate), anbauen

growth *n*, Wachstum *nn*

guarantee *n*, Garantie *nf*; **the product comes with a 2-year guarantee**, auf dem Produkt sind 2 Jahre Garantie

guarantee *vb*, garantieren; **we can guarantee that . . .**, wir können garantieren, daß . . .

guaranteed *adj*, garantiert, echt; **guaranteed pure gold**, echt Gold

guest *n*, Gast *nm*

H

half *n*, Hälfte *nf*

half *adj*, halb; **half-time employment** (pers), halbe Stelle; **at half price**, zu halbem Preis

half year *n*, Halbjahr *nn*; **half-year results**, Halbjahresergebnisse *nnpl*

half-yearly *adj*, *adv*, halbjährlich

hall *n*, Halle *nf*; **exhibition hall**, Ausstellungshalle *nf*; **main hall**, Haupthalle *nf*

hallmark *n* (silver), Feingehaltsstempel *nm*

halve *vb* (reduce by half), halbieren

handbook *n*, Handbuch *nn*

handle *vb*, **1** (see to), erledigen; **we can handle it for you**, wir können es für Sie erledigen. **2** (move goods) (transp), befördern; **handle with care!** (transp), Vorsicht! Zerbrechlich! **3** (work on document), bearbeiten. **4** (stock, sell), führen; **we do not handle foreign makes**, wir führen keine ausländischen Marken

handling *n*, **1** (dealing with), Erledigung *nf*. **2** (transp), Straßenbeförderung *nf*. **3** (goods handling), Warenbehandlung *nf*; **handling charges/costs**, **1** (work on documents), Bearbeitungsgebühr *nf*. **2** (warehouse, transp), Umschlagspesen *npl*

handout *n* (printed information), Werbeprospekt *nm*

hard *adj*, **1** (materials), hart. **2** (task), schwer. **3** (comp) **hard copy**, Ausdruck *nm*; **hard disc**, Festplatte *nf*

hardware *n*, **1** (in shop), Haushaltswaren *nfpl*. **2** (comp), Hardware *nf*

haulage *n*, **1** (transp, road), Güterkraftverkehr *nm*, Transport *nm*. **2** (cost), Transportkosten *npl*; **haulage contractor** (transp), Spediteur *nm*; **haulage firm** (transp), Spedition *nf*

haulier *n* (transp), Spediteur *nm*

head *n* (leader), Leiter(in) *nm/f*, Manager(in) *nm/f*; **head of department**, Abteilungsleiter(in) *nm(f)*; **Head of Marketing**, Marketingmanager *nm*

headed paper *n* (offce), Firmenbogen *nm*; **we require official notification by letter on headed paper**, wir erbitten offiziellen schriftlichen Bescheid auf Firmenbogen

headhunter *n*, Headhunter *nm*

headline *n*, Überschrift *nf*

headquarters *npl*, Hauptgeschäftsstelle *nf*

health *n*, Gesundheit *nf*; **health and safety at work**, Gesundheit und Unfallverhütung am Arbeitsplatz

healthy *adj*, gesund; **a healthy balance sheet**, eine gesunde Bilanz

heat *n*, Hitze *nf*

heating *n*, Heizung *nf*; **central heating**, Zentralheizung *nf*

heavy *adj*, **1** (weight), schwer; **heavy industry**, Schwerindustrie *nf*. **2** (quantity), groß; **heavy expenditure**, große Ausgaben; **heavy orders**, große Aufträge; **heavy buyer**, Großabnehmer *nm*

heavy-duty *adj*, **1** (clothes), strapazierfähig. **2** (machine), Hochleistungs-

height *n*, **1** (of people), Körpergröße *nf*. **2** (of buildings), Höhe *nf*

help *n*, Hilfe *nf*; **thank you for your help**, ich danke Ihnen für Ihre Hilfe

help *vb*, helfen (+ dat); **our agent in . . . will be able to help you**, unser Vertreter in . . . wird Ihnen helfen können

hereafter *adv* (document), im folgenden

hesitate *vb*, zögern

HGV, **heavy goods vehicle**, Last(kraft)wagen *nm*, Lkw *nm*

hidden *adj* (gen), versteckt; **hidden defect**, versteckter Fehler *nm*; **hidden reserves** (fin), stille Reserven *nfpl*

hi fi *n* (mktg, sales), Hi-Fi *nn*; **hi fi equipment** (mktg, sales), Hi-Fi-Gerät *nn*

high *adj*, hoch; **the price is too high**, der Preis ist zu hoch; **a high price**, ein hoher Preis

high-grade *adj*, hochwertig

highlighter *n* (offce), Textmarker *nm*

high-quality *adj*, hochwertig; **high-quality goods**, hochwertige Güter *nnpl*

hire *n* (of goods), Mieten *nn*

hire *vb*, **1** (people), einstellen. **2** (objects), mieten

hired car *n*, Mietwagen *nm*

hire purchase *n*, Ratenkauf *nm*; **hire purchase terms**, Teilzahlungsbedingungen *nfpl*

hit, be hit by *vb* (affected), getroffen von (+ dat); **we have been hit by the high price of fuel**, wir sind von dem hohen Brennstoffpreis getroffen worden

hoarding *n* (mktg, sales), Plakatwand *nf*

hobbies *npl* (CV), Hobbies *nnpl*

hold *n* (of ship), Laderaum *nm*

hold *vb* (stocks), **1** (have room for), fassen; **our warehouse holds considerable stocks of . . .**, unser Lagerhaus faßt beträchtliche Mengen . . . **2** (have available), vorrätig haben

holding *n* (shares), Beteiligung *nf*; **the company has a holding in . . .**, die Firma hat eine Beteiligung bei . . .; **holding company**, Holdinggesellschaft *nf*

hold-up *n*, Verzögerung *nf*; **we are sorry that there has been a hold-up in production**, wir bedauern die Verzögerung in der Produktion

hole puncher *n* (offce), Locher *nm*

holiday *n*, Urlaub *nm*; **on holiday** (from work), auf Urlaub; **holiday period/season**, Urlaubszeit *nf*

home *n*, (Privat-)Wohnung *nf*; **home address**, Privatadresse *nf*; **home market**, Inlandsmarkt *nm*; **home-produced goods**, heimische Erzeugnisse *nnpl*

honest *adj*, ehrlich

horse power *n*, Pferdestärke *nf*, PS

hospitality *n*, Gastfreundlichkeit *nf*

hotel *n*, Hotel *nn*; **hotel chain**, Hotelkette *nf*

hour *n*, Stunde *nf*; **at this early hour**, zu dieser frühen Stunde; **it takes 3 hours**, es dauert 3 Stunden

hourly *adj*, *adv* (every hour), stündlich; (per hour), Stunden-; **hourly flights**, stündliche Flüge; **hourly rate/hourly wage**, Stundenlohn *nm*

household *n*, Haushalt *nm*; **household goods**, Haushaltswaren *nfpl*

house-to-house selling *n*, Direktverkauf *nm*

hovercraft *n* (transp), Hovercraft *nn*

huge *adj*, riesig

human resources *npl*, Arbeitskräfte *nfpl*

hurry *n*, Eile *nf*

hypermarket *n* (mktg, sales), Hypermarkt *nm*

I

ignore *vb*, ignorieren

illegible *adj*, unleserlich; **page 2 of the fax is illegible**, Seite 2 des Telefaxes ist unleserlich

import *n*, Import *nm*; **import permit** Importgenehmigung *nf*

import *vb*, importieren

importance *n*, Bedeutung *nf*

important *adj*, bedeutend

imported goods *npl*, Importwaren *nfpl*

impound *vb* (imp/exp), beschlagnahmen

incentive *n* (mktg, sales), Anreiz *nm*; **incentive to buy**, Kaufanreiz *nm*; **sales incentive**, Verkaufsanreiz *nm*

include *vb*, **1** (corr, enclose), beilegen; **please include . . .**, bitte legen Sie . . . bei. **2** (gen) (contain, comprise), enthalten; **the contract includes a clause on . . .**, der Vertrag enthält eine Klausel über (+ acc)

inclusive *adj* **(of)**, inklusive; **inclusive of delivery**, inklusive Lieferung; **inclusive price**, Pauschalpreis *nm*

income *n*, Einkommen *nn*; **personal income**, persönliches Einkommen; **regular income**, regelmäßiges Einkommen; **income bracket**, Einkommensstufe *nf*; **income tax**, Einkommenssteuer *nf*

incoming mail *n* (offce), Posteingang *nm*

incorrect *adj*, inkorrekt

increase *n*, Steigerung *nf*; **increase in value**, Wertsteigerung *nf*; **wage increase**, Lohnsteigerung *nf*

increase *vb*, **1** (grow), steigen; **production has increased by 10%**, die Produktion ist um 10% gestiegen; **inflation has increased to 3%**, die Inflation ist auf 3% gestiegen. **2** (raise), erhöhen; **we have had to increase all prices by 2%**, wir mußten alle Preise um 2% erhöhen

independence *n*, Unabhängigkeit *nf*

independent *adj*, unabhängig

indication *n*, Hinweis *nm*

indirect *adj*, indirekt; **indirect taxation**, indirekte Besteuerung *nf*

indispensable *adj*, unentbehrlich

industrial *adj*, industriell; **industrial accident**, Arbeitsunfall *nm*; **industrial dispute**, Arbeitskampf *nm*; **industrial estate**, Gewerbegebiet *nn*; **industrial injury**, Berufsschaden *nm*; **industrial relations**, Beziehungen *nfpl* zwischen Arbeitgebern und Arbeitnehmern; **industrial training**, betriebliche Ausbildung *nf*

industrialist *n*, Industrieller *nm*

industry *n*, Industrie *nf*; **basic industry**, Grundstoffindustrie *nf*; **domestic industry**, einheimische Industrie; **heavy industry**, Schwerindustrie *nf*; **light industry**, Leichtindustrie *nf*

inexpensive *adj*, preiswert

inflated price *n*, überhöhter Preis *nm*

inflation *n*, Inflation *nf*

influence *n*, Einfluß *nm*; **have an influence on**, Einfluß auf (+ acc) haben

influence *vb*, beeinflussen

inform *vb*, informieren; **I have to inform you that . . .**, ich muß Sie informieren, daß . . .

informal *adj*, informell; **an informal**

discussion, ein informelles Gespräch

information *n*, Information *nf*, Informationen *nfpl*; **some information about . . .**, einige Informationen über (+ acc); **information flow**, Informationsfluß *nm*; **information management systems** (comp), Informationsverwaltungssystem *nn*

infrared control *n*, Infrarotüberwachung *nf*

infrastructure *n*, Infrastruktur *nf*

infringe *vb* (law), verletzen; **infringe a patent**, ein Patent verletzen

in-house magazine *n*, Firmenzeitschrift *nf*

initial *adj*, Anfangs-; **initial sales**, Anfangsverkauf *nm*

initials *npl* (pers), Initialen *nfpl*

Inland Revenue *n* (fin), ~ Finanzamt *nn*

innovate *vb*, Innovationen einführen

innovation *n*, Innovation *nf*

input *n* (comp), Dateneingabe *nf*

input *vb* (comp), eingeben

inquiry *n*, **1** (investigation), Untersuchung *nf*; **make an inquiry into . . .**, eine Untersuchung über (+ acc) durchführen. **2** (police), Ermittlung *nf*; **carry out an inquiry**, eine Ermittlung durchführen. **3** (request for information), Anfrage *nf*; **thank you for your inquiry about . . .**, wir danken Ihnen für Ihre Anfrage bezüglich (+ genitive)

insert *n* (mktg, sales), Beilage *nf*

insert *vb* (mktg, sales), einfügen; **insert an ad in . . .**, eine Anzeige in . . . einfügen

insider trading *n* (fin), Insiderhandel *nm*

insist on *vb*, bestehen auf (+ acc); **he insisted on his rights**, er bestand auf seinen Rechten

inspect *vb*, **1** (check), kontrollieren. **2** (investigate), untersuchen

inspection *n*, Inspektion *nf*

inst, instant, your letter of the 5th inst, Ihr Brief vom 5. d.M.

install *vb*, **1** (gen), installieren. **2** (machine), aufstellen

installation *n*, **1** (gen), Installation *nf*. **2** (of machine), Aufstellen *nn*

instalment *n* (fin), Rate *nf*; **the first instalment is due on 1 June**, die erste Rate ist am 1. Juni fällig; **pay by instalments**, in Raten zahlen

institute *vb* **proceedings against** (law), ein Verfahren gegen (+ acc) einleiten

instruct *vb*, instruieren; **he was instructed to . . .**, er wurde instruiert, zu . . .

instructions *npl*, Anweisungen *nfpl*; **give instructions**, Anweisungen geben; **instructions for use**, Gebrauchsanweisungen *nfpl*

insulation *n* (electr, heat), Isolierung *nf*

insurance *n*, Versicherung *nf*; **insurance policy**, Versicherungspolice *nf*

insure against *vb*, versichern gegen (+ acc)

insured *n*, Versicherungsnehmer *nm*

insurer *n*, Versicherungsträger *nm*

intangible *adj* (acct), immateriell; **intangible assets**, immaterielle Vermögenswerte *nnpl*

intend *vb*, beabsichtigen

interest *n*, **1** (financial interest), Interesse *nf*. **2** (shares in), Beteiligung *nf* an (+ dat); **a 10% interest in**, eine 10%ige Beteiligung an. **3** (return on capital), Zinsen *nmpl*

interested, be interested in *vb*, **1** (intellectual, emotional interest), sich interessieren für (+ acc). **2** (keen to own, implement), interessiert sein an (+ acc)

interests *npl* (CV), Interessen *nfpl*

interface *n* (comp), Schnittstelle *nf*

intervene *vb*, intervenieren

intervention *n*, Intervention *nf*

interview *n* (pers), Interview *nn*

interview *vb* **an applicant** (pers), ein Vorstellungsgespräch *nn* (mit einem Bewerber/einer Bewerberin) führen

in tray *n* (offce), Eingänge *nmpl*

introduce *vb*, **1** (pers), vorstellen; **may I introduce myself?**, darf ich mich vorstellen?; **I would like to introduce you to Mr Smith**, ich möchte Sie Herrn Smith vorstellen. **2** (product, idea, policy), einführen; **introduce a new product**, ein neues Produkt einführen

introductory price *n* (comm), Einführungspreis *nm*

invalid *adj*, ungültig

invent *vb*, erfinden

inventory *n*, **1** (goods in warehouse), Warenbestände *nmpl*. **2** (list of goods), Inventarliste *nf*; **make an inventory**, eine Inventarliste machen; **inventory control**, Bestandskontrolle *nf*; **inventory turnover**, Lagerumschlag *nm*

invest *vb* **in**, investieren in (+ dat or acc)

investigate *vb* (law), ermitteln

investment *n* (fin), Investition *nf*

invisible *adj*, unsichtbar; **invisible assets**, unsichtbare Vermögenswerte *nmpl*

invitation *n*, **1** (to dinner), Einladung *nf*; **thank you for your invitation**, vielen Dank für Ihre Einladung. **2** (to act), Aufforderung *nf*; **invitation to tender** (mktg, sales), Aufforderung, ein Angebot zu machen

invoice *n*, Rechnung *nf*; **pro forma invoice**, Proforma-Rechnung; **invoice value** (fin, mktg, sales), Rechnungsbetrag *nm*

invoice *vb* (someone), belasten

invoicing *n* (fin), Abrechnung *nf*

involve *vb*, beinhalten; **what does this job involve?**, was beinhaltet diese Stelle?

involved, be involved in *vb*, **1** (be active in), tätig sein in (+ dat). **2** (be part of a scandal), verwickelt sein in (+ acc)

inward bill *n* (imp/exp), Importkonnossement *nn*

IQ, intelligence quotient, IQ, Intelligenzquotient *nm*

iron *n*, Eisen *nn*

irregular *adj*, **1** (not regular), unregelmäßig. **2** (not done in the correct way), nicht ordnungsgemäß

irrevocable letter of credit *n* (fin), unwiderrufliches Akkreditiv *nn*

issue *n*, **1** (of magazine), Nummer *nf*. **2** (of new shares), Emission *nf*. **3** (subject of discussion), Problem *nn*; **we must discuss the issue of site maintenance**, wir müssen das Problem der Grundstückswartung erörtern

issue *vb*, **1** (magazine, press release), veröffentlichen. **2** (fin, shares), emittieren

item *n*, **1** (goods etc), Artikel *nm*; **luxury item**, Luxusartikel *nm*; **missing items**, fehlende Artikel *nmpl*. **2** (part of a list), Punkt *nm*; **an item on the agenda**, ein Punkt auf der Tagesordnung

itemised bill/invoice *n* (fin, mktg, sales), aufgegliederte Rechnung *nf*

itinerary *n*, Reiseroute *nf*

J

jam *vb* (mechanical), klemmen

jeopardise *vb*, in Gefahr bringen; **this jeopardised the whole enterprise**, das brachte das ganze Unternehmen in Gefahr

jingle *n* (mktg, sales), Jingle *nn*

JIT, just in time (production), Just-in-Time (Produktion)

job *n*, **1** (pers), Stelle *nf*; **find a job**, eine Stelle finden. **2** (piece of work to do), Aufgabe *nf*; **his job is to . . .**, es ist seine Aufgabe, zu . . .; **job advertisement**, Stellenanzeige *nf*; **job description**, Stellenbeschreibung *nf*

joint *adj*, gemeinsam; **joint account**, gemeinsames Konto *nn*; **joint decision**, gemeinsame Entscheidung *nf*; **joint stock company**, Aktiengesellschaft *nf*; **joint venture**, Joint Venture *nn*

journey *n*, Reise *nf*

judge *n* (law), Richter(in) *nm/f*

judge *vb*, **1** (assess), beurteilen; **judge the quality of a product**, die Qualität eines Produkts beurteilen. **2** (decide), entscheiden. **3** (law), urteilen

judg(e)ment *n* (law), Urteil *nn*

junior *adj*, **1** (subordinate), untergeordnet. **2** (up and coming), Nachwuchs-; **junior manager**, Nachwuchsmanager *nm*; **junior partner**, Juniorpartner *nm*; **junior staff**, Nachwuchs *nm*; **we lack qualified junior staff**, es fehlt uns an qualifiziertem Nachwuchs

junk mail *n*, Reklamesendungen *nfpl*

just *adv*, **1** (barely), knapp; **just over**, knapp über; **just under**, knapp unter; **they just managed to . . .**, sie schafften es knapp, zu . . . **2** (a short while ago), gerade; **they have just merged with XYZ Plc**, sie haben gerade mit XYZ Plc fusioniert

justify *vb*, rechtfertigen

K

keep *vb*, **1** (as one's own), behalten. **2** (preserve), aufbewahren; **please keep the receipt**, bitte bewahren Sie die Quittung auf; **keep in a dry place**, trocken aufbewahren

keep *vb* **ahead of**, einen Vorsprung vor (+ dat) behalten

keep *vb* **to a deadline**, einen Termin einhalten

keep up with *vb*, **1** (stay informed), auf dem Laufenden bleiben mit (+ dat). **2** (maintain the same level, price, rate), halten; **we are unable to keep our current price levels much longer**, wir können unser gegenwärtiges Preisniveau nicht mehr lange halten

key *n*, **1** (comp), Drucktaste *nf*. **2** (for lock, security), Schlüssel *nm*

key *adj*, wichtig, Schlüssel-; **a key part**, ein wichtiger Teil; **a key feature**, ein wichtiges Merkmal; **a key factor**, ein Schlüsselfaktor *nm*

key in *vb* (comp), eingeben; **key in the date**, geben Sie das Datum ein

keyboard *n* (comp), Tastatur *nf*; **keyboard operator** (comp), Datentypist(in) *nm/f*

keyboard *vb*, Daten eingeben

kind *n*, **payment in kind**, Zahlung *nf* in Sachleistungen

kit *n* (mktg, sales), Ausrüstung *nf*; **in kit form**, als komplette Ausrüstung

know *vb*, **1** (facts), wissen; **did you know that . . .?**, wußten Sie, daß . . .? **2** (people, places etc), kennen; **do you know Bonn?**, kennen Sie Bonn?

know-how *n*, Knowhow *nm*

knowledge *n*. **1** (familiarity with). Kenntnis *nf*; **a good knowledge of the market**, gute Marktkenntnis *nf*. **2** (body of knowledge), Wissen *nn*

label *n*, **1** (on goods), Etikett *nn*. **2** (name, make), Markenzeichen *nn*

label *vb* (goods), beschriften; **please label clearly**, bitte lesbar beschriften

labour *n*, **1** (hard work), Arbeit *nf*. **2** (pers), Arbeitskräfte *nfpl*; **labour costs**, Lohnkosten *npl*; **labour force** (pers), Arbeitskräfte *nfpl*, Belegschaft *nf*; **labour market**, Arbeitsmarkt *nm*; **labour shortage**, Arbeitskräftemangel *nm*

lack *n*, Mangel *nm*; **lack of materials**, Materialmangel *nm*

lack *vb*, fehlen (+ dat); **the report lacks detail**, dem Bericht fehlen Einzelheiten; **he lacks enthusiasm**, ihm fehlt Begeisterung

laminate *vb*, laminieren

LAN, local area network, LAN, Lokalnetz *nn*

land *n*, **1** (country, rural area), Land *nn*. **2** (landed property), Grundbesitz *nm*. **3** (piece of land), Grundstück *nn*; **acquire a piece of land**, ein Grundstück erwerben

land *vb*, **1** (plane), landen. **2** (cargo), ausladen

landing charges *npl* (transp), Löschungskosten *npl*

language *n*, Sprache *nf*; **foreign language**, Fremdsprache *nf*; **programming language**, Programmiersprache *nf*; **languages spoken** (CV), Fremdsprachenkenntnisse

laptop (computer) *n* (comp), Laptop(-Computer) *nm*

large-scale producer *n*, Großhersteller *nm*

last *adj*, letzt; **the last time**, das letzte Mal

last *vb*, **1** (continue), dauern; **it won't last long**, es wird nicht lange dauern. **2** (keep), (lange) haltbar sein; **the material will not last**, das Material ist nicht lange haltbar

late *adj*, *adv*, **1** (time), spät. **2** (to be late), (zu)spät, verspätet; **arrive/be late**, zu spät/verspätet kommen

latest *adj* (model, figures), neust; **the very latest model**, das neuste Modell; **the latest results**, die neusten Ergebnisse

launch *n*, Einführung *nf*; **product launch**, Produkteinführung *nf*; **launch price**, Einführungspreis *nm*

launch *vb* (product), (ein Produkt) auf den Markt bringen

law *n*, **1** (rule), Gesetz *nn*. **2** (legal system), Recht *nn*

lawyer *n*, Rechtsanwalt *nm*, Rechtsanwältin *nf*

lay day *n* (transp), Liegetag *nm*

lay off *vb* (pers), **1** (permanently), entlassen. **2** (temporarily), vorübergehend entlassen

layoffs *npl* (pers), Feierschicht *nf*

LBO, leveraged buyout (fin), Leveraged Buyout *nm*

LC, L/C, letter of credit (fin), Akkreditiv *nn*

LCL, less than container load (transp), weniger als Containerladung

lead *n*, **have a lead**, führen

leader *n*, Führer *nm*; **market leader**, Marktführer *nm*

leading *adj*, führend; **leading producer of . . .**, *nm* führender Hersteller *nm* von (+ dat); **leading-edge technology**, bahnbrechende Technologie *nf*

lead time *n* (comm), Lieferzeit *nf*

leaflet *n* (mktg, sales), Handzettel *nm*

leakage *n*, **1** (of fluids), Auslaufen *nn*. **2** (of information), Durchsickern *nn*

learn *vb*, **1** (acquire knowledge), lernen. **2** (acquire information), erfahren; **we have just learned that . . .**, wir haben gerade erfahren, daß . . .

lease *n*, **1** (of land), Pacht *nf*. **2** (contract), Pachtvertrag *nm*

lease *vb*, **1** (to someone), an (+ acc) verpachten. **2** (from someone), von (+ dat) pachten

leaseback *n*, Verkauf *nm* und Rückmiete *nf*

leasing *n*, Leasing *nn*

leave *vb*, **1** (a place), verlassen; **the lorry left the factory at 5 a.m.**, der Lastwagen hat die Fabrik um 5 Uhr morgens verlassen. **2** (forget to take), liegenlassen; **he left his keys in the hotel**, er hat seine Schlüssel im Hotel liegengelassen. **3** (leave behind on purpose), hinterlegen; **please leave a copy of the report at our office**, bitte hinterlegen Sie ein Berichtexemplar in unserem Büro

leave *n*, Urlaub *nm*; **be on leave**, auf Urlaub sein

ledger *n* (offce), Hauptbuch *nn*

left *adv* (direction), links; **turn left**, biegen Sie (nach) links ab

left *adj*, linke(r, s); **the left side**, die linke Seite

left-luggage office *n* (gen), Gepäckaufbewahrung *nf*

legal *adj*, Rechts-; **legal position**, Rechtslage *nf*; **legal adviser**, Rechtsberater *nm*; **legal claim**, Rechtsanspruch *nm*; **legal costs**, Anwaltskosten *npl*; **legal department**, Rechtsabteilung *nf*; **legal tender**, gesetzliches Zahlungsmittel *nn*

legislation *n*, Gesetzgebung *nf*

leisure *n* (gen, mktg, sales), Freizeit *nf*

leisure centre *n* (mktg, sales), Freizeitzentrum *nn*

lend *vb*, leihen

lender *n*, Gläubiger *nm*

lending limit *n*, Kreditlimit *nn*

length *n*, Länge *nf*

lessee *n*, Pächter *nm*

lessor *n*, Verpächter *nm*

let *vb* (property to someone), vermieten

letter *n*, **1** (of alphabet), Buchstabe *nm*. **2** (document) Brief *nm*, Schreiben *nn*; **letter of application** (pers), Bewerbungsschreiben *nn*; **letter of complaint**, Beschwerdebrief *nm*; **letter of credit**, **LC**, **L/C** (fin), Akkreditiv *nn*; **letter of intent**, Absichtserklärung *nf*

letterhead *n*, Briefkopf *nm*

level *n*, Ebene *nf*, Niveau *nn*, Stand *nm*; **decision at high level**, Entscheidung *nf* auf hoher Ebene; **level of investment**, Investitionsstand *nm*; **staffing levels**, Personalstand *nm*

level out *vb* (gen, fin), ausgleichen

liabilities *npl* (gen, fin, acct), Verbindlichkeiten *nfpl*

liability *n* (law), Haftung *nf*

liable *adj*, **1** (likely to), wahrscheinlich; **he is liable to arrive late**, er kommt wahrscheinlich verspätet an. **2 be liable for**, haften für (+ acc); **be liable for damages**, für Schaden haften

library *n*, Bibliothek *nf*

licence *n*, Genehmigung *nf*; **import licence**, Einfuhrgenehmigung *nf*; **driving licence**, *n* (driving), Führerschein *nm*

license *vb* (e.g. a process), genehmigen

life *n*, Leben *nn*

life insurance *n*, Lebensversicherung *nf*

lift *vb* (gen, transp), heben

light *adj*, **1** (weight, difficulty), leicht. **2** (colour), hell

lighten *vb*, **1** (reduce weight, difficulty), erleichtern. **2** (make less dark), erhellen

lighting *n* (mktg, sales), Beleuchtung *nf*

limit *n*, Grenze *nf*, Limit *nn*; **there are limits**, es gibt Grenzen; **credit limit**, Kreditlimit *nn*

limit *vb*, beschränken

limited liability company *n*, Gesellschaft *nf* mit beschränkter Haftung, GmbH *nf*

limited market *n*, begrenzter Absatzmarkt *nm*

line *n*, **1** (long mark), Linie *nf*. **2** (row of letters on page), Zeile *nf*. **3** (telec), Leitung *nf*, Verbindung *nf*, Anschluß *nm*; **the line is bad**, die Verbindung ist schlecht; **the line is engaged**, der Anschluß ist besetzt. **4 line management**, Linienmanagement *nn*. **5 line of business**, Branche *nf*

liner *n* (shipping), Linienschiff *nn*

liquid *adj*, flüssig

liquidate *vb*, liquidieren

liquidation *n* (fin), Liquidation *nf*; **go into liquidation**, in Liquidation gehen; **voluntary liquidation**, freiwillige Liquidation

liquidity *n*, Liquidität *nf*; **liquidity problems** (fin), Liquiditätsprobleme *nnpl*

list *vb*, **1** (gen), auflisten. **2** (on stock exchange), an der Börse notieren

listing *n*, **Stock Exchange listing**, amtliche Notierung *nf* an der Börse

listing paper *n* (comp), Tabellierpapier *nf*

list price *n*, Listenpreis *nm*

literature *n* (mktg, sales), Prospekte *nmpl*

litigation *n* (law), Prozeß *nm*

live *adj*, **1** (TV), live; **live programme**, Livesendung *nf*. **2** (electrical instrument), elektrisch geladen. **3** (living), lebend(ig); **transport of live animals**, Transport lebender Tiere

load *n* (on a vehicle), Ladung *nf*; **please collect the load from . . .**, bitte holen Sie die Ladung von . . . ab

load *vb* (transp, comp), laden

loan *vb*, leihen

lobby *n*, Lobby *nf*

local *adj*, lokal, Lokal-, Orts-; **local paper**, Lokalblatt *nn*; **local call**, Ortsgespräch *nn*; **local area network** (comp), lokales Rechnernetz *nn*, LAN

locally *adv*, vor Ort

locate *vb* (find), ausfindig machen

located *adj*, **1** (gen), liegen; **the hotel is centrally located**, das Hotel liegt zentral. **2** (company site), seinen Standort haben; **located in Wales**, mit Standort in Wales

location *n* (of company), Standort *nm*

lock out *vb* (pers), aussperren

lodge *vb* **a complaint against** (law), Beschwerde einlegen gegen (+ acc)

logo *n*, Firmenzeichen *nn*

long *adj*, lang; **long form** (bill of lading) (imp/exp), detaillierter Frachtbrief *nm*

long *adv* (long time), lange; **you won't need to wait long**, Sie brauchen nicht lange zu warten

long-distance *adj*, Fern-; **long-distance call** (telec), Ferngespräch *nn*; **long-distance flight**, Fernstreckenflug *nm*

long-range *adj*, langfristig; **long-range economic forecast**, langfristige Konjunkturprognose *nf*

long-standing customer *n*, Stammkunde *nm*, Stammkundin *nf*

long-term *adj*, langfristig; **long-term loan** (fin), langfristiges Darlehen *nn*; **long-term planning**, langfristige Planung *nf*

loose *adj* (not fixed, not packed), lose

lorry *n* (transp), Last(kraft)wagen *nm*, Lkw *nm*; **lorry driver**, Last(kraft)wagenfahrer *nm*, Lkw-Fahrer *nm*; **lorry load**, Lkw-Ladung *nf*

lose *vb* (gen, comm), verlieren; **we have lost a lot of time**, wir haben viel Zeit verloren

loss *n* (gen, comm), Verlust *nm*; **make a loss**, einen Verlust machen; **loss adjuster** (ins), Schadenssachverständiger *nm*; **loss leader** (mktg, sales), Lockartikel *nm*

lost *adj*, verloren

lot *n*, **a lot of**, viel(e); **a lot of problems**, viele Probleme

low *adj*, niedrig; **low figures**, niedrige Zahlen *nfpl*; **low price**, niedriger Preis *nm*; **low interest loan** (fin), Darlehen *nn* zu niedrigen Zinsen; **lower than**, niedriger als

lower *vb*, senken; **lower prices**, die Preise senken

loyalty *n*, **brand loyalty**, Markentreue *nf*; **customer loyalty**, Kundentreue *nf*

LSD, **loading, storage and delivery** (imp/exp, transp), Beladen *nn*, Lagerung *nf* und Lieferung *nf*

Ltd, **private limited company**, ≈ Gesellschaft *nf* mit beschränkter Haftung

luggage *n*, Gepäck *nn*

lump sum *n*, Pauschalbetrag *nm*

lunch *n*, Mittagessen *nn*

luncheon voucher *n*, **LV**, Essensmarke *nf*

luxury *n*, Luxus *nm*; **luxury goods**, Luxuswaren *nfpl*

machine *n*, Maschine *nf*; **machine tools**, Maschinenwerkzeuge *nnpl*

machinery *n*, **1** (several machines), Maschinen *nfpl*. **2** (working parts), Mechanismus *nm*

made *adj*, **made in** (imp/exp), made in . . . ; **made of** (material), aus . . . ; **made of leather**, aus Leder; **made to measure**, maßgefertigt; **made up of**, bestehend aus (+ dat); **a group made up of four experts**, eine aus vier Experten bestehende Gruppe

magazine *n* (gen), Zeitschrift *nf*

magistrate *n* (law), Friedensrichter *nm*

mail *n*, Post *nf*

mail *vb*, (ab)senden

mailing *n* (mktg, sales), Sendung *nf*; **mailing list**, Adressenliste *nf*

mail order *n* (mktg, sales), Postversand *nm*; **mail order company**, Versandhaus *nn*

mailshot *n* (mktg, sales), Direktwerbung *nf*; **send out a mailshot**, Werbebriefe verschicken

main *adj*, Haupt-; **main activity**, Haupttätigkeit *nf*; **main station**, Hauptbahnhof *nm*

mainframe *n* (comp), Großrechner *nm*

mains *n* (electr), Hauptschalter *nm*; **runs on mains electricity**, mit Netzanschluß

maintain *vb*, **1** (keep), (aufrecht) erhalten; **maintain order**, die Ordnung aufrecht erhalten. **2** (e.g., a machine), warten

maintenance *n*, **1** (keeping things going), (Aufrecht-)Erhaltung *nf*. **2** (of machines), Wartung *nf*; **(building) site maintenance**, Baustellenwartung *nf*

major *adj*, bedeutend; **a major manufacturer**, ein bedeutender Hersteller

majority *n*, Mehrheit *nf*; **the majority of shareholders**, die Mehrheit der Aktionäre

make *n* (of goods), Marke *nf*

make *vb*, **1** (manufacture), herstellen. **2** (oblige), zwingen; **make an application**, **1** (ask for something in writing), einen Antrag einreichen. **2** (for a post), eine Bewerbung einreichen; **make an appointment**, einen Termin festmachen; **make an offer**, ein Angebot machen; **make redundant** (pers), entlassen

make up *vb*, **1** (a loss, a delay), wettmachen. **2** (an order), aufstellen

maker *n* (e.g. of cars), Hersteller *nm*

malpractice *n* (law), Berufsvergehen *nn*; **be guilty of malpractice**, sich eines Berufsvergehens schuldig machen; **be accused of malpractice**, eines Berufsvergehens beschuldigt werden

manage *vb*, **1** (pers), leiten. **2** (achieve), schaffen; **we managed to reduce our costs**, es ist uns gelungen, die Kosten zu senken

management *n*, Management *nn*; **management accounting**, Kosten- und Leistungsrechnung *nf*; **management accounts**, Geschäftsbilanz *nf*

manager(ess) *n* (pers), Manager(in) *nm/f*

managing director *n* (pers), geschäftsführender Direktor *nm*, geschäftsführende Direktorin *nf*

manifest *n* (transp), Ladeliste *nf*

man-made *adj*, Kunst-; **man-made fibres**, Kunstfasern *nfpl*

manpower *n*, Personal *nn*; **manpower planning**, Personalplanung *nf*

manual *n*, Handbuch *nn*; **operating manual**, Bedienungshandbuch *nn*; **user manual**, Benutzerhandbuch *nn*

manual *adj*, manuell; **manual control**, manuelle Steuerung *nf*; **manual worker**, Handarbeiter(in) *nm/f*

manufacture *vb* (gen), herstellen

manufacturer *n*, Hersteller *nm*

manufacturing industries *npl*, verarbeitende Industrien *nfpl*

margin *n*, **1** (paper), Rand *nm*. **2** (scope), Spielraum *nm*; **margin of error**, Fehlerspielraum *nm*. **3** (comm), Spanne *nf*; **profit margin**, Gewinnspanne *nf*. **4** (fin), Marge *nf*

marginal *adj*, geringfügig; **marginal profit**, geringfügiger Gewinn *nm*

marine insurance *n* (ins), See(transport)versicherung *nf*

mark *vb*, markieren

mark down *vb* (prices), heruntersetzen

mark up *vb* (prices), erhöhen

marker pen *n*, Textmarker *nm*

market *n*, Markt *nm*; **there is a big market for . . .**, es gibt einen großen Markt für . . .; **market analysis**, Marktanalyse *nf*; **market economy**, Marktwirtschaft *nf*; **market forces**, Marktkräfte *nfpl*; **market leader**, Marktführer *nm*; **market penetration**, Marktdurchdringung *nf*; **marketplace**, Markt(platz) *nm*; **market price**, Marktpreis *nm*; **market research**, Marktforschung *nf*; **market sector**, Marktbereich *nm*; **market share**, Marktanteil *nm*; **market trend**, Marktentwicklung *nf*; **market value**, Marktwert *nm*

market *vb* (a product), auf den Markt bringen

marketable *adj*, marktfähig

marketing *n*, Marketing *nn*; **marketing department**, Marketingabteilung *nf*; **marketing mix**, Marketing-Mix *nm*

mark-up *n*, **1** (increase in price), Erhöhung *nf*. **2** (percentage profit margin), Gewinnspanne *nf*; **we have a 20% mark-up**, wir haben eine 20%ige Gewinnspanne

married *adj* (CV), verheiratet

mass mailing *n*, Massensendung *nf*

mass memory *n* (comp), Massenspeicher *nm*

mass production *n*, Massenproduktion *nf*

match *vb*, **1** (e.g. colours), (zusammen)passen. **2** (price), einen vergleichbaren Preis bieten

material *n*, Stoff *nm*; **dress material**, Kleiderstoff *nm*; **raw material**, Rohstoff *nm*

mature *adj*, **1** (person), reif. **2** (economy), entwickelt

mature *vb* (fin), fällig werden

maturity date *n* (fin), Fälligkeitstermin *nm*

maximise *vb*, maximieren

maximum *adj*, maximal

maximum *n*, Maximum *nn*

md, months after date (fin), Monate nach Datum

mean *n* (maths), Mittelwert *nm*

means *npl*, Mittel *nn*

measure *n*, **1** (measuring), Maß *nn*. **2** (action), Maßnahme *nf*. **3** (tape), Maßband *nn*

measure *vb*, messen

measurement *n*, **pay by measurement** (transp), nach Volumen bezahlen; **measurements**, Maße *nnpl*

mechanical *adj*, mechanisch

mechanism *n*, Mechanismus *nm*

media, the media *npl*, die Medien *npl*

medical *adj*, medizinisch

medicine *n*, Medizin *nf*

meet *vb*, **1** (commitments/conditions), Verpflichtungen/Bedingungen erfüllen. **2** (demand), die Nachfrage befriedigen. **3** (have a meeting), eine Sitzung abhalten. **4** (at the station), abholen. **5** (in the street etc), treffen. **6** (a deadline), eine Frist einhalten. **7** (a target), ein Ziel erreichen

memo *n*, Memorandum *nn*; **an internal memo**, ein internes Memorandum; **write/send a memo to . . . about . . .**, ein Memorandum an . . . schreiben/senden über (+ acc)

memory *n* (comp), Speicher *nm*

mend *vb*, reparieren

menu *n* (comp), Menü *nn*

merchandising *n*, Merchandising *nn*

merchant bank *n* (fin), Handelsbank *nf*

merge with *vb* (comm), fusionieren mit (+ dat)

merger *n* (comm), Fusionierung *nf*

message *n* (offce), Mitteilung *nf*; **send a message**, eine Mitteilung machen; **receive a message**, eine Mitteilung empfangen

messenger *n*, Bote *nm*

Messrs (in name of firm), Firma *nf*; **Messrs Swan and Smith** (corr), Firma Swan and Smith

meter *n*, **1** (100 cm), Meter *nm*. **2** (for gas etc), Zähler *nm*

method *n*, Methode *nf*; **method of payment**, Zahlungsweise *nf*; **method of production**, Produktionsmethode *nf*

microphone *n*, Mikrofon *nn*

mile *n* (= 1.625 km), Meile *nf*

mileage *n*, gefahrene Meilen *nfpl*

minicomputer *n* (comp), Minicomputer *nm*

minimal *adj*, minimal; **maintenance costs are minimal**, die Wartungskosten sind minimal

minimise *vb*, auf ein Minimum beschränken

minimum *n*, Minimum *nn*

minimum *adj*, Mindest-; **minimum wage**, Mindestlohn *nm*

minor *adj*, unbedeutend; **a minor fault**, ein unbedeutender Fehler

minority *n*, Minderheit *nf*; **be in a minority**, in der Minderheit sein; **minority interest** (fin), Minderheitsbeteiligung *nf*; **minority shareholder** (fin), Minderheitsaktionär *nm*; **minority shareholding** (fin), Minderheitsbeteiligung *nf*

minutes *npl* (of meeting), Protokoll *nn*

miscellaneous *adj*, verschieden

mislead *vb*, irreführen

misleading *adj*, irreführend; **misleading advertising**, irreführende Werbung *nf*

miss *vb*, **1** (flight), verpassen. **2** (target), verfehlen

missing *adj*, fehlend; **missing articles** (from list), fehlende Posten; **be missing**, fehlen

mistake *n*, Fehler *nm*; **make a mistake**, einen Fehler machen

mobile phone *n*, drahtloses Telefon *nn*

model *n*, Modell *nn*; **the latest model**, das neuste Modell

mode of transport *n* (imp/exp, transp), Transportmittel *nn*

modern *adj*, modern

modification *n*, Modifizierung *nf*; **make a modification to . . .**, eine Modifizierung anbringen an (+ dat)

modify *vb*, modifizieren

modular *adj*, modular

module *n*, Modul *nn*

monetary *adj*, monetär, Währungs-; **monetary system**, Währungssystem *nn*; **European Monetary System, EMS**, Europäisches Währungssystem; **monetary unit**, Währungseinheit *nf*

money *n*, Geld *nn*; **earn money**, Geld verdienen; **easy money**, leicht verdientes Geld; **money order**, Postanweisung *nf*; **money supply**, Geldreserve *nf*

money-making *adj*, gewinnbringend

money-spinner *n*, Kassenschlager *nm*

monitor *n*, **1** (comp, TV), Monitor *nm*. **2** (process control), Überwachungssystem *nn*

monitor *vb* (control), überwachen

month *n*, Monat *nm*; **calendar month**, Kalendermonat *nm*

monthly *adj*, monatlich; **monthly deliveries**, monatliche Lieferungen *nfpl*; **monthly payment**, monatliche Zahlung *nf*; **monthly ticket**, Monatskarte *nf*

moor *vb* (shipping), anlegen

mooring *n* (shipping), Liegeplatz *nm*

more *adj*, mehr; **please send more copies of the brochure**, bitten senden Sie mehr Exemplare der Broschüre

more *adv*, **more attractive**, attraktiver; **more economical**, sparsamer; **more expensive**, teurer; **more than . . .**, mehr als . . .

mortgage *n*, Hypothek *nf*; **mortgage loan**, Hypothekenanleihe *nf*; **mortgage payments**, Hypothekentilgung *nf*

mortgage *vb*, hypothekarisch belasten

motivate *vb*, motivieren

motivation *n*, Motivation *nf*

motor *n*, **1** (engine), Motor *nm*. **2** (automobile), Kraftfahrzeug *nn*, Kfz; **motor insurance**, Kraftfahrzeugversicherung *nf*, Kfz-Versicherung

motorist *n* Autofahrer(in) *nm/f*

motorway *n* (transp), Autobahn *nf*; **motorway junction**, Autobahnkreuz *nn*

mouse *n* (comp), Maus *nf*

move *vb* (office, house), umziehen; **we have moved**, wir sind umgezogen

MP, Member of Parliament, Parlamentsabgeordnete(r) *nf/m*

mpg, miles per gallon, the car does 27 miles to the gallon, der Wagon verbraucht eine Gallone auf 27 Meilen

MR, **mr**, **mate's receipt** (imp/exp), Verladeschein *nm*

Ms, no equivalent in German; use 'Frau' for all female adults

m/s, months after sight (fin), Monate nach Sicht

multicoloured *adj*, mehrfarbig

multilateral *adj*, multilateral; **multilateral trade**, multilateraler Handel *nm*

multiple copies *npl*, in mehrfacher Ausfertigung

multiply by *vb* (maths), multiplizieren mit (+ dat)

NA, N/A, not applicable (form), entfällt

name *n*, Name *nm*; **brand name**, Markenname *nm*; **company name**, Firmenname *nm*

name *vb*, (be-)nennen; **person named in the policy** (ins), der in der Police benannte Versicherungsnehmer

national *adj*, **1** (politics, economy), national. **2** (distribution), landesweit; **have a national reputation**, landesweit bekannt sein; **national advertising campaign**, landesweite Werbekampagne *nf*; **national insurance contribution**, Sozialversicherungsbeitrag *nm*

nationalise *vb* (industries), verstaatlichen

nationalised *adj*, verstaatlicht

nationality *n* (CV), Staatsangehörigkeit *nf*

naval *adj*, See-; **naval warfare**, Seekrieg *nm*

NCV, no commercial value (imp/exp), unverkäufliche Warenprobe *nf*

near *adj*, nahe; **in the near future**, in naher Zukunft; **£100 or nearest offer**, £100 oder das nächstbeste Angebot

near *prep* (location), in der Nähe (+ genitive); **near the airport**, in der Nähe des Flughafens

nearly *adv*, fast

need *n*, **1** (felt), Bedürfnis *nn*. **2** (material), Bedarf *nm*; **there is a need for . . .**, es besteht ein Bedarf an (+ dat)

need *vb*, **1** brauchen; **we need your advice**, wir brauchen Ihren Rat; **the money is urgently needed**, das Geld wird dringend gebraucht. **2** müssen; **we need to know whether . . .**, wir müssen wissen, ob . . .

needs analysis *n*, Bedarfsanalyse *nf*; **carry out a needs analysis**, eine Bedarfsanalyse durchführen

neglect *vb*, **1** (not look after), vernachlässigen. **2** (forget to do), versäumen

negotiable *adj*, **1** (gen), verhandlungsfähig. **2** (bankable), bankfähig. **3** (endorsable), indossierfähig. **4** (saleable), verkäuflich. **5** (cheque), "**not negotiable**", „nicht übertragbar"; **negotiable cheque**, Inhaberscheck *nm*

negotiate *vb*, **1 negotiate with . . . about . . .**, verhandeln mit (+ dat) über (+ acc); **the management promised to negotiate with the Union**, die Betriebsleitung versprach, mit der Gewerkschaft zu verhandeln. **2 negotiate a contract**, einen Vertrag aushandeln. **3 negotiate a sale**, einen Verkauf tätigen

negotiation *n*, Verhandlung *nf*; **break off negotiations**, Verhandlungen abbrechen; **start negotiations**, Verhandlungen aufnehmen; **wage negotiations**, Lohnverhandlungen *nfpl*

net *vb* (make a net profit), netto einnehmen

net *adj* (fin), netto, Netto-; **terms strictly net**, Bezahlung strikt netto; **net cashflow**, Netto-Cashflow *nm*; **net contribution**, Nettobeitrag *nm*; **net income**, Nettoeinkommen *nn*; **net price**, Nettopreis *nm*; **net profit**, Nettogewinn *nm*; **net sales**, Nettoumsatz *nm*; **net weight**,

Nettogewicht *nn*

network *n* (gen, comp), Netz(werk) *nn*; **computer network**, Computernetz(werk) *nn*; **distribution network**, Vertriebsnetz *nn*; **television network**, Sendenetz *nn*

network *vb* (comp), vernetzen

networked system *n* (comp), Rechnerverbund *nm*

networking *n*, Vernetzung *nf*

new *adj*, neu; **a new model**, ein neues Modell; **as new**, wie neu; **under new management**, unter neuer Leitung

news *npl*, **1** (news item), Nachricht *nf*; **the news of the merger**, die Nachricht von der Fusion. **2** (collection of items) (TV, radio), Nachrichten *nfpl*

newsletter *n* (mktg, sales), Mitteilungsblatt *nn*

niche *n*, Nische *nf*; **market niche**, Marktnische *nf*

niche market *n*, Nischenmarkt *nm*

nil *n*, Null *nf*; **the response was nil**, die Reaktion war gleich Null

no claim(s) bonus *n* (ins), Schadenfreiheitsrabatt *nm*

non-payment *n* (fin), Nichtzahlung *nf*

non profit-making organisation *n*, gemeinnütziges Unternehmen *nn*

non-returnable *adj*, Einweg-; **non-returnable bottle**, Einwegflasche *nf*; **non-returnable packing**, Einweg(ver)packung *nf*

not applicable *adj* (filling in form), entfällt

not as ordered (mktg, sales), entspricht nicht unserer Bestellung

note *n*, **1** (to jog memory), Notiz *nf*; **take notes**, Notizen machen. **2** (a few non-personal lines to someone), (kurze) Mitteilung *nf*, Nachricht *nf*; **thank you for your note of 4 April**, ich danke Ihnen für Ihre Mitteilung/Nachricht vom 4. April. **3** (informal note), Zettel *nm*; **I left you a note on your desk**, ich habe dir auf deinem Schreibtisch einen Zettel hinterlassen. **4** (bank note), Banknote *nf*

note *vb*, **1** (make a note on paper), notieren. **2** (register mentally), zur Kenntnis nehmen; **we have noted your order**, wir haben Ihre Bestellung zur Kenntnis genommen

noted for *adj*, bekannt für (+ acc)

note-pad *n*, Notizblock *nm*; **electronic note-pad**, elektronischer Notizblock

notice *n*, **1** (official warning), Bescheid *nm*. **2** (on wall), Anschlag *nm*. **3** (written announcement that someone is losing job), Kündigung *nf*; **period of notice**, Kündigungsfrist *nf*; **give notice**, kündigen; **he gave in his notice**, er kündigte; **they were given notice**, ihnen wurde gekündigt

noticeboard *n*, Anschlagbrett *nn*

notification *n*, Mitteilung *nf*; **receive notification of . . .**, die Mitteilung bekommen, daß . . .

notify *vb*, mitteilen; **he was notified that . . .**, ihm wurde mitgeteilt, daß . . .

novel *adj*, neuartig; **a novel solution**, eine neuartige Lösung

novelty *n*, Neuheit *nf*

null and void *adj* (law), null und nichtig

number *n*, **1** (several things/people), Zahl *nf*; **a large number of mistakes**, eine große Zahl Fehler; **the number of people who . . .**, die Zahl der Leute, die . . . **2** (figures in directories, on houses, cars etc), Nummer *nf*; **box number**, Postfachnummer *nf*; **car registration number**, Autonummer *nf*; **fax number**, (Tele)Faxnummer *nf*; **house**

number, Hausnummer *nf*; **telephone number**, Telefonnummer *nf*; **number plate**, Nummernschild *nn*

number *vb*, numerieren

numerical order *n*, **in numerical order**, in zahlenmäßiger Folge

numeric data *npl*, numerische Daten *nnpl*

o/a, on account (fin), für Rechnung

object *n*, **1** (thing), Gegenstand *nm*; **a large object**, ein großer Gegenstand. **2** (aim), Zweck *nm*; **the object of the meeting**, der Zweck der Sitzung

object *vb*, einwenden gegen (+ acc), dagegen sein; **he objected that . . .**, er wandte ein, daß . . . ; **"I object"**, „ich bin dagegen"

objection *n*, Einwand *nm*; **make an objection**, einen Einwand machen

objective *n*, Ziel *nn*; **the sales team reached their objectives**, das Verkaufsteam hat seine Ziele erreicht

obligatory *adj*, obligatorisch

oblige *vb*, verpflichten

obsolete *adj*, obsolet

obstacle *n*, Hindernis *nn*; **an obstacle to . . .**, ein Hindernis für (+ acc)

obtain *vb*, erhalten; **obtain permission**, Erlaubnis erhalten; **qualifications obtained: . . .** (CV), Qualifikationen: . . .

occupation *n* (CV), Beruf *nm*

occupy *vb*, **1** (house), bewohnen. **2** (seat), belegen. **3** (require time, space, energy), beanspruchen. **4** (person, oneself), beschäftigen. **5** (post), innehaben

odd numbers *npl*, ungerade Zahlen *nfpl*

offence *n* (law), Straftat *nf*; **commit an offence**, eine Straftat begehen

offer *n*, Angebot *nn*; **make an offer**, ein Angebot machen; **receive an offer**, ein Angebot bekommen; **refuse an offer**, ein Angebot ablehnen

offer *vb*, anbieten; **he was offered £4,000**, ihm wurden £4.000 angeboten; **the producer offered to take back the goods**, der Hersteller bot an, die Waren zurückzunehmen

office *n*, **1** (place of work), Büro *nn*. **2** (authority), Amt *nn*; **office block**, Bürohaus *nn*; **office equipment** (furniture and machines), Büroausstattung *nf*; **office furniture**, Büromöbel *nnpl*; **office hours**, Bürostunden *nfpl*; **office manager(ess)**, Büroleiter(in) *nm/f*; **Office of Fair Trading**, Amt *nn* für Verbraucherschutz

official *adj*, offiziell; **official channels** (bureaucracy), Dienstweg *nm*

official *n*, Beamter *nm*, Beamtin *nf*

off label *adj* (price), unter dem angegebenen Preis

offset *vb*, **1** (gen), ausgleichen. **2** **offset costs**, Kosten anrechnen

OHP, overhead projector (mktg, sales), Overhead Projektor *nm*

oil *n*, Öl *nn*; **oil tanker**, Öltanker *nm*

old-fashioned *adj*, alt modisch

O Level, Ordinary Level *n* (educ), ≈ mittlere Reife *nf*

omission *n*, Auslassung *nf*

one-man business *n*, Einmannbetrieb *nm*

one-way street *n*, Einbahnstraße *nf*

on line, online *adv* (comp), online

on-the-job training *n*, betriebliche Ausbildung *nf*

o/o, (to the) order of (fin), an die Order von

open *adj*, offen; **open day**, Tag *nm* der offenen Tür; **open-ended questions** (mktg, sales), offene Fragen *nfpl*; **the open market**, der freie Markt; **open-plan office**, Großraumbüro *nn*; **open ticket** (transp), offenes Ticket *nn*

open *vb*, **1** (gen), öffnen. **2** (branch, computer file), eröffnen

opening *n*, **1** (sales point, event), Eröffnung *nf*. **2** (in the market), Marktöffnung *nf*

operate *vb* (machine), bedienen; **operated by**, **1** (controls), betätigt durch (+ acc). **2** (power source), betrieben mit (+ dat); **the system is operated by hydraulic pressure**, das System wird mit Wasserdruck betrieben

operating *adj*, Betriebs-; **operating budget** (fin, acct), Betriebswirtschaftsplan *nm*; **operating capital** (fin), Betriebskapital *nn*; **operating costs** (fin), Betriebskosten *npl*; **operating expenses** (gen, acct), Betriebsaufwendungen *nfpl*; **operating income** (fin), Betriebseinkommen *nn*; **operating instructions**, Betriebsanweisungen *nfpl*; **operating ratio** (fin), Wirtschaftlichkeitskoeffizient *nm*; **operating system** (comp), Betriebssystem *nn*

operations *npl* (of a company), Aktivitäten *nfpl*

operator *n*, **1** (of telephone switchboard), Telefonzentrale *nf*. **2** (of machines), Maschinist(in) *nm/f*. **3** (tour operator), Reiseveranstalter *nm*

opinion *n*, Meinung *nf*; **public opinion**, öffentliche Meinung; **opinion poll** Meinungsumfrage *nf*

opportunity *n*, Chance *nf*; **investment opportunity**, Investitionschance *nf*; **market opportunity**, Absatzchance *nf*

optimal *adj*, optimal

optimise *vb*, optimieren

optimum *adj*, optimal

option *n*, Option *nf*

optional *adj* (comm), auf Wunsch erhältlich; **cancellation insurance is optional**, Rücktrittsversicherung ist auf Wunsch erhältlich; **optional extras** (comm), Extras *nnpl*

order *n*, **1** (sales), Auftrag *nm*; **export order**, Exportauftrag *nm*; **telephone/fax order**, telefonischer Auftrag/Auftrag per Fax; **banker's order/standing order**, Dauerauftrag *nm*; **order book**, Auftragsbuch *nn*; **order form**, Auftragsformular *nn*. **2** (instruction to pay money), Anweisung *nf*; **postal order**, Postanweisung *nf*. **3** (sorting), Reihenfolge *nf*; **in alphabetical order**, in alphabetischer Reihenfolge

order, be in order *vb*, **1** (in proper sequence), in der richtigen Reihenfolge sein. **2** (OK), in Ordnung sein

order, be out of order *vb*, **1** (in wrong sequence), in der falschen Reihenfolge sein. **2** (not working), kaputt sein

order *vb* (sales), bestellen

ordinary *adj*, gewöhnlich; **ordinary shareholder**, Stammaktionär *nm*

ore *n*, Erz *nn*; **ore carrier** (ship), Erzfrachter *nm*

organic *adj*, **1** (science), organisch. **2** (farming), Bio-; **organic products**, Bioprodukte *nnpl*

organisation *n*, Organisation *nf*; **organisation chart**, Organogramm *nn*

organise *vb*, organisieren

origin *n*, Ursprung *nm*; **country of origin**, Ursprungsland *nn*

original *adj*, **1** (first), Original-; **original equipment**, Originalausstattung *nf*; **original packaging**, Originalverpackung *nf*. **2** (unusual), originell

other information *n* (forms, CV), weitere Informationen

outbid *vb*, überbieten; **they outbid XYZ Plc**, sie haben XYZ Plc überboten

outcome *n*, Ergebnis *nn*

outlay *n*, Auslagen *nfpl*; **capital outlay**, Investitionsauslagen *nfpl*; **at a modest outlay**, mit geringen Auslagen

outlet *n* (sales), Verkaufsstelle *nf*

outline *vb* (plan), skizzieren

outlook *n* (future), Aussichten *nfpl*; **the outlook is good**, die Aussichten sind gut

out of stock *adj*, nicht vorrätig

outperform *vb*, übertreffen

outplacement *n*, Weitervermittlung *nf* von Führungskräften

output *n*, **1** (of factory), Produktion *nf*. **2** (of electricity), Leistung *nf*. **3** (comp), Output *nm*

outsell *vb*, im Absatz übertreffen

outsider *n*, Outsider *nm*

outside use *n*, **for outside use only**, nur im Freien benutzen!

outsourcing *n*, Produktionsverlagerung *nf* ins Ausland

outstanding *adj*, **1** (quality), hervorragend; **of outstanding quality**, von hervorragender Qualität. **2** (not delivered, paid for), ausstehend; **outstanding items**, ausstehende Waren *nfpl*

out-tray *n* (offce), Ausgänge *nmpl*; **the letter is still in the out-tray**, der Brief liegt noch bei den Ausgängen

over *prep*, **1** (above, during), über (+ acc or dat); **over 10%**, über 10%; **over the year**, über das Jahr. **2 over the telephone** am Telefon

overbook *vb* (hotel/flight), überbelegen

overcapacity *n*, Überkapazität *nf*

overcharge *vb*, zuviel berechnen; **he was overcharged**, ihm wurde zuviel berechnet

overdraft *n*, Überziehung *nf*

overdrawn *adj*, **OD, O/D** (fin), überzogen; **I am overdrawn**, ich habe mein Konto überzogen; **my account is overdrawn**, mein Konto ist überzogen

overdue *adj*, überfällig; **payments are overdue**, die Zahlungen sind überfällig

overheads *npl*, Festkosten *npl*

overload *vb*, überladen

overlook *vb*, **1** (survey), überschauen. **2** (forget, not notice), übersehen; **this item was overlooked**, dieser Posten wurde übersehen

overnight delivery service *n*, Zustellung *nf* über Nacht

overpayment *n* (fin), Überbezahlung *nf*

overprice *vb* (mktg, sales), einen Preis zu hoch ansetzen; **this product is overpriced**, der Preis für dieses Produkt ist zu hoch

overtime *n*, Überstunden *nfpl*; **work overtime**, Überstunden machen

owe *vb*, schulden; **they owe us . . .**, sie schulden uns . . .

own *vb*, besitzen

own brand *n* (mktg, sales), Eigenmarke *nf*

owner *n*, Besitzer(in) *nm/f*; **owner's equity to debt** (acct), Eigners Anspruch *nm* auf Forderung; (ins), **goods sent at owner's risk**, Warensendung *nf* mit Gefahr beim Absender

P

pa, per annum, im/pro Jahr

pack *n* (mktg, sales), Packung *nf*; **a 5 kg pack**, eine 5-kg-Packung

pack *vb*, **1** (imp/exp), verpacken. **2** (comp), verdichten

package *n*, **1** Paket *nn*. **2** (set of services or facilities), Pauschal-; **package deal**, Pauschalarrangement *nn*; **package tour**, Pauschalreise *nf*

packaging *n* (mktg, sales), **1** (action) Verpacken *nn*. **2** (material), Verpackung *nf*

packed *adj* (imp/exp), verpackt; **packed in Belgium**, in Belgien verpackt; **packed in 5 kg plastic containers**, in Kunststoffbehältern von je 5 kg verpackt

packet *n* (mktg, sales), Päckchen *nn*; **a packet of cigarettes**, ein Päckchen Zigaretten

packing note/list *n* (imp/exp), Packzettel *nm*

P+D, pick-up and delivery service (imp/exp, transp), Abhol- und Zustelldienst *nm*

pad *n* (offce), (writing), Block *nm*; **writing pad**, Schreibblock *nm*; **note pad**, Notizblock *nm*

padded *adj* (imp/exp), mit Einlage

padding *n* (imp/exp), Polstermaterial *nn*

page *n* (print), Seite *nf*

page *vb* (communications), ausrufen lassen; "**paging Mr Jones**", „Herr Jones bitte!"

pager *n* (communications), Funkrufempfänger *nm*

paid *adj* (on bills), „bezahlt"; **money paid in advance** (fin, as part of later payment), Vorschuß *nm*; **paid on delivery, POD** (mktg, sales, transp), Zahlung *nf* bei Lieferung

paid-up capital *n* (fin), voll einbezahltes Kapital *nn*

pallet *n* (transp), Palette *nf*

palletise *vb* (transp), palettieren

paper *n*, **1** (for writing), Papier *nn*; **on paper** (in theory), auf dem Papier. **2** (newspaper), Zeitung *nf*

paperclip *n* (offce), Büroklammer *nf*

paperwork *n*, **1** (admin, pejorative), Papierkram *nn*. **2** (documents, forms), Dokumentation *nf*; **we will complete the paperwork**, wir vervollständigen die Dokumentation

par *n* (stock market), Nennwert *nm*; **above par**, über dem Nennwert; **at par**, zum Nennwert; **below par**, unter dem Nennwert

parcel *n* (offce, transp), Paket *nn*

parent company *n*, Muttergesellschaft *nf*

park *n*, **1** Park *nm*. **2 industrial park**, Industriegebiet *nn*. **3 theme park**, Themenpark *nm*. **4 car park**, Parkplatz *nm*

park *vb*, parken; **where can I park my car?**, wo kann ich parken?

parking meter *n*, Parkuhr *nf*

part *n*, **1** (spare part), Ersatzteil *nn*. **2** (component), Teil *nm*

part *adj* (incomplete), Teil-; **part delivery**, Teillieferung *nf*; **part load**, Teilladung *nf*; **part payment**, Teilzahlung *nf*

participate in *vb* teilnehmen an (+ dat)

participation in *n*, Teilnahme *nf* an (+ dat)

particular average *n* (ins), besondere Havarie *nf*

particulars *npl*, nähere Angaben *nfpl*; **would you like to give me your particulars?**, darf ich Sie um nähere Angaben zu Ihrer Person bitten?; **please let us have particulars of the load**, wir bitten Sie um nähere Angaben bezüglich der Ladung

partner *n*, Partner(in) *nm/f*

partnership *n*, **1** (gen), Partnerschaft *nf*. **2** (comm, law), Personengesellschaft *nf*

part-time work *n*, Teilzeitbeschäftigung *nf*

pass *vb*, **1** (approve), annehmen. **2** (exam), bestehen. **3** (overtake), überholen. **4** (exceed), übertreffen; **interim results show that sales have passed last year's total**, die Zwischenergebnisse zeigen, daß der Absatz den des Vorjahres übertrifft

passenger *n*, Passagier *nm*

password *n* (comp), Paßwort *nn*

past *adj* (former), ehemalig; **past president of . . .**, ehemaliger Präsident von . . .

paste *vb*, **1** (gen, offce), kleben. **2 cut and paste** (comp), den Text löschen und einfügen

patent *vb*, patentieren

patented *adj*, patentiert

pattern *n*, Muster *nn*; **pattern book** (comm), Musterbuch *nn*

pay *n*, **1** (gen), Bezahlung *nf*. **2** (wages), Lohn *nm*; **pay packet** Lohntüte *nf*

pay *vb*, **1** bezahlen, zahlen; **pay in advance**, im voraus bezahlen; **pay back**, zurückzahlen; **pay cash**, bar (be)zahlen; **pay for itself**, amortisieren; **pay in money**, Geld einzahlen; **pay into an account**, auf ein Konto einzahlen; **pay on delivery, POD** (mktg, sales, transp), Zahlung *nf* bei Lieferung. **2 pay a visit**, einen Besuch abstatten

payable *adj* (fin), fällig; **payable at the end of June**, fällig Ende Juni

payee *n*, Zahlungsempfänger *nm*

payload *n* (transp), Nutzlast *nf*

payment *n* (fin), Zahlung *nf*; **payment against documents** (fin), Zahlung bei Erhalt der Papiere; **payment in instalments** (fin), Ratenzahlung *nf*

payphone *n*, Münzfernsprecher *nm*

payroll *n* (fin), **1** (wages), Lohnliste *nf*. **2** (salaries), Gehaltsliste *nf*

payround *n*, Tarifrunde *nf*

PC, personal computer *n*, PC, Personalcomputer *nm*; **PC operator**, PC-Operator *nm*

peak *n* (of results), Höchststand *nm*; **exports reached peak in March**, die Exporte erreichten im März ihren Höchststand

peak *vb* (results), seinen Höchststand erreichen; **we believe that demand has peaked**, wir glauben, die Nachfrage hat ihren Höchststand erreicht

peg *vb* **prices** (mktg, sales), Preise stabilisieren

penalise *vb*, bestrafen

penalty *n*, Strafe *nf*; **penalty for late delivery**, Vertragsstrafe *nf* bei verspäteter Lieferung; **penalty clause**, Strafklausel *nf*

pencil *n*, Bleistift *nm*; **pencil sharpener** (offce), Bleistiftspitzer *nm*

pending *prep* **a decision**, bis zu einer Entscheidung

pending tray *n* (offce), Wiedervorlage *nf*

pension *n*, Rente *nf*; **pay a pension**, (eine) Rente (be)zahlen; **receive a pension**, (eine) Rente beziehen; **pension scheme**, Rentenversicherung *nf*

per *prep*, pro; **per year**, pro Jahr; **per quarter**, pro Quartal

percentage *n*, Prozentsatz *nm*; **a high/small percentage of all customers**, ein großer/kleiner Prozentsatz aller Kunden

perform *vb* (company), abschneiden; **the company performed badly**, das Unternehmen hat schlecht abgeschnitten

performance *n* (of company), Leistung *nf*; **performance bonus** (pers), Leistungsprämie *nf*; **performance-related pay** (pers), Lohnzahlung *nf* nach Arbeitsleistung

period *n*, Zeit *nf*; **period of probation** (pers), Probezeit *nf*

periodical *n* (magazine), Zeitschrift *nf*

peripherals *npl* (comp), periphäre Geräte *nnpl*

perishable *adj*, (leicht) verderblich; **perishable goods**, (leicht) verderbliche Waren *nfpl*

perk *n* (pers), Vergünstigung *nf*; **receive perks**, Vergünstigungen bekommen

permanent *adj* (pers), fest; **permanent employment**, feste Anstellung *nf*

permission *n*, **1** (gen), Erlaubnis *nf*. **2** (official), Genehmigung *nf*; **obtain permission**, die Genehmigung bekommen

permit *n*, Genehmigung *nf*

permit *vb*, **1** (gen), erlauben. **2** (official), genehmigen

personal *adj*, persönlich; **personal assistant, PA**, persönlicher Assistent *nm*/persönliche Assistentin, *nf*; **personal computer, PC**, Personalcomputer *nm*, PC; **personal details** (forms, CV), Angaben *nfpl* zur Person; **personal organiser** (paper-based), Terminplaner *nm*; **personal property** (customs), persönliches Eigentum *nn*; **personal secretary**, Privatsekretär(in) *nm/f*

personalised *adj* (mktg, sales), mit persönlicher Note

personnel *n*, **1** (staff), Personal *nn*. **2** (department), Personalabteilung *nf*; **personnel manager** (pers), Personalleiter(in) *nm/f*

petrol *n*, Benzin *nn*

petroleum products *npl*, Rohölprodukte *nnpl*

pharmaceutical industry *n*, pharmazeutische Industrie *nf*

pharmaceutical products *npl*, pharmazeutische Produkte *nnpl*

phase *n*, Phase *nf*; **the first phase of the project**, die erste Projektphase

phase in *vb*, schrittweise einführen

phasing *n*, Synchronisierung *nf*

PhD, ~ Doktor, Dr.

phone *n*, Telefon *nn*; **internal phone**, Haustelefon *nn*; **phone book**, Telefonbuch *nn*; **phone call**, Telefonanruf *nm*; **make a phone call**, einen Telefonanruf machen; **phone card**, Telefonkarte *nf*; **phone number**, Telefonnummer *nf*

phone *vb*, anrufen; **please phone me at 4 p.m.**, bitte rufen Sie mich um 16 Uhr an; **someone phoned**, jemand hat angerufen

phone back *vb*, zurückrufen; **can I phone you back later?**, kann ich Sie später zurückrufen?

photocopier *n*, Fotokopierapparat *nm*

photocopy *n*, Fotokopie *nf*

photocopy *vb*, fotokopieren

pick *vb*, **1** (choose), (aus)wählen. **2** (fruit, flowers), pflücken

pick up *vb*, **1** (a load) (transp), abholen; **please pick up the goods from the station**, bitte holen Sie die Waren am Bahnhof ab. **2** (improve, e.g. sales, profits), sich erholen; **sales picked up in the second quarter**, der Absatz hat sich im 2. Quartal erholt

pie chart *n* (fin), Kreisdiagramm *nn*

piggyback *adv* (transp), huckepack

pile up *vb* (transp) (put things on top of each other), stapeln

pilfering *n* (imp/exp), geringfügiger Diebstahl *nm*

place *vb*, **1 place a contract**, einen Auftrag vergeben. **2 place an order**, eine Bestellung aufgeben. **3 place staff**, Personal unterbringen

plan *n*, Plan *nm*; **contingency plan**, Krisenplan *nm*; **a strategic plan**, ein strategischer Plan; **street plan**, Stadtplan *nm*

plan *vb*, planen; **everything was carefully planned**, alles war sorgfältig geplant

planner *n* (offce), Kalender *nm* (zur Arbeitsplanung)

planning *n*, Planung *nf*

plant *n*, **1** (factory), Werk *nn*; **the company has a new plant in Dortmund**, das Unternehmen hat ein neues Werk in Dortmund. **2** (production unit), Anlage *nf*; **the packing plant**, die Verpackungsanlage *nf*. **3** (number of large machines, e.g. earthmoving machines), Baumaschinen *nfpl*

plastic *n* (gen), Plastik *nn*

plastic *adj*, Plastik-; **plastic bag**, Plastiktüte *nf*

platform *n*, **1** (at railway), Bahnsteig *nm*. **2** (comp), Platform *nf*

Plc, plc, public limited company ~ Aktiengesellschaft *nf*, AG *nf*

plug in *vb* (electr, comp), einstecken

plummet *vb* (gen, fin), stark fallen, absacken; **the pound has plummeted to DM 2.30**, das Pfund ist auf DM 2,30 abgesackt

plunge *vb* (figures, rates), stark fallen

p.m., post meridiem 1 (until about 6 p.m.), nachmittags. **2** (from about 6 p.m.), abends

PM, Prime Minister *n*, Premierminister(in) *nm/f*

poach *vb*, **1** (gen), wildern. **2** (pers), abwerben

POD, pay on delivery (mktg, sales, transp), Zahlung *nf* bei Lieferung

POE, 1 port of embarkation, Verladehafen *nm*. **2 port of entry**, Landehafen *nm*

point *n*, **1** Punkt *nm*; **a major point**, ein Hauptpunkt *nm*; **a point on the agenda**, ein Punkt auf der Tagesordnung; **this is an interesting point**, das ist ein interessanter Punkt. **2 make a point**, ein Argument *nn* anbringen. **3** Stelle *nf*; **decimal point**, Dezimalstelle *nf*. **4** (arithmetic), Komma *nn*; **twenty-three point zero three (23.03)**, dreiundzwanzig Komma null drei. **5** (purpose), Zweck *nm*; **there is no point**, es hat keinen Zweck. **6 point of sale, POS**, Verkaufsstelle *nf*; **point of sale advertising** Verkaufsstellenwerbung *nf*

pointer *n*, **1** (sign), Hinweis *nm*. **2** (presentations), Zeigestock *nm*. **3** (comp), Zeiger *nm*

police *n*, Polizei *nf*

policy *n*, **1** (gen), Politik *nf*; **company policy**, Unternehmenspolitik *nf*. **2** (ins), Police *nf*; **insurance policy** Versicherungspolice *nf*

poll *vb* (opinion), eine Meinungsumfrage durchführen

pollute *vb*, verschmutzen

pollution *n*, Verschmutzung *nf*

pool *n*, **1** (swimming), Schwimmbecken *nn*. **2** (shared resource), **typing pool**, zentraler Schreibdienst *nm*

pool *vb*, zusammenlegen; **pool all resources**, alle Mittel zusammenlegen

poor *adj*, **1** (no money), arm. **2** (not very good), schlecht; **poor quality** (imp/exp), schlechte Qualität *nf*; **poor results**, schlechte Ergebnisse *nnpl*

popular *adj*, (goods), beliebt

population *n*, Bevölkerung *nf*

port *n*, Hafen *nm*; **port of call**, Anlaufhafen *nm*; **port of embarkation, POE**, Verladehafen *nm*; **port of entry, POE**, Landehafen *nm*; **port charges**, Hafengebühren *nfpl*; **port risks, PR** (ins), Hafenrisiken *nnpl*

portable *adj*, tragbar; **portable computer**, Portable *nn*

portfolio *n*, Portfolio *nn*

position *n*, Lage *nf*; **be in a position to . . . ,** in der Lage sein, zu . . .; **the site is in an ideal position**, das Grundstück hat eine ideale Lage

possess *vb*, besitzen

post *n*, **1** (job), Stelle *nf*. **2** (letters delivered), Post *nf*; **by return of post**, postwendend; **post code**, Postleitzahl *nf*; **post office**, Postamt *nn*

post *vb*, **1** (letter), abschicken. **2** (entry in accounts), buchen

postage *n* (rate), Porto *nn*; **postage and packing**, Porto und Verpackung *nf*; **what is the postage to England?**, wie hoch ist das Porto nach England?; **postage paid**, portofrei

postal service *n*, Postdienst *nm*

poster *n* (mktg, sales), Plakat *nn*; **poster campaign**, Plakatkampagne *nf*

postman *n*, Postbote *nm*

postmark *n*, Poststempel *nm*

post-paid *adj* (corr, transp), Gebühr bezahlt

postpone *vb*, verschieben

potential *n*, Potential *nn*; **sales potential**, Absatzpotential *nn*

potential *adj*, potentiell; **there is a potential market of 3 million units**, es gibt einen potentiellen Markt von 3 Millionen Einheiten

power *n*, **1** (political, economic), Macht *nf*. **2 bargaining power**, Verhandlungsstärke *nf*. **3 borrowing power**, Kreditfähigkeit *nf*. **4 purchasing power**, Kaufkraft *nf*. **5** (electr), Strom *nm*; **power cut**, Stromausfall *nm*; **power point**, Steckdose *nf*

powerful *adj*, **1** (political, economic), mächtig. **2** (effect), stark. **3** (speech), mitreißend

p.p, p.p a letter *vb* (corr), im Auftrag unterschreiben

PR, public relations, PR, PR-Arbeit *nf*, Public Relations *npl*

practise *vb*, **1** (skill), üben. **2** (profession), ausüben

precedent *n* (law), Präzedenzfall *nm*

precision *n*, Präzision *nf*; **high precision**, hohe Präzision; **precision instrument**, Präzisionsinstrument *nn*

prefer *vb*, **1** (to do something), lieber tun. **2** (one thing to another), vorziehen; **our customers prefer the old model to the new one**, unsere Kunden ziehen das alte Modell dem neuen vor

preference *n*, **1** Vorliebe *nf*; **there is a general preference for . . .**, es herrscht eine allgemeine Vorliebe für (+ acc). **2** (give preference), Vorzug *nm*; **preference shares** (fin), Vorzugsaktien *nfpl*

premises *npl*, **1** (land), Gelände *nn*. **2** (business), Geschäftsräume *nmpl*. **3** (office), Büroräume *nmpl*. **4 on the premises**, in diesem Gebäude

premium *n*, **1** (ins), Prämie *nf*. **2** (prices), Zuschlag *nm*; **be at a premium**, schwer zu finden sein

prepacked *adj* (comm), abgepackt

prepaid *adj* (fin), vorausbezahlt

prescription *n* (med), Rezept *nf*

present *n*, Geschenk *nn*

present *vb*, **1** (hand over), überreichen; **may I present you with . . .**, darf ich Ihnen . . . überreichen. **2** (fin), vorlegen; **present a bill for acceptance**, eine Rechnung zur Zahlung vorlegen

presentation *n* (about a product etc), Präsentation *nf*; **make a presentation**, eine Präsentation machen; **presentation pack** (mktg, sales), Informationsmaterial *nn*

press *n*, Presse *nf*; **press coverage**, Pressebericht *nm*; **press release**, Pressemitteilung *nf*; **press report**, Pressebericht *nm*

pressure *n*, Druck *nm*; **high/low pressure**, Hochdruck *nm*/Tiefdruck *nm*; **be under pressure**, unter Druck sein; **working pressure**, Arbeitsdruck *nm*

price *n*, Preis *nm*; **the price is very high/low**, der Preis ist sehr hoch/niedrig; **price cut**, Preissenkung *nf*; **price/earnings ratio** (fin), Kurs-Gewinn-Verhältnis *nn*; **price freeze**, Preisstopp *nm*; **price increase**, Preiserhöhung *nf*; **price list**, Preisliste *nf*; **price rigging**, Preisabsprache *nf*; **price tag**, Preisschild *nn*

price *vb* **(at)**, einen Preis auf (+ acc) festsetzen

pricing policy *n*, Preispolitik *nf*

prime *adj*, Haupt-; **prime site** (property), erstklassiges Grundstück *nn*; **prime time** (TV, mktg, sales), Hauptsendezeit *nf*

principle *n*, Prinzip *nn*; **in principle**, im Prinzip

print *vb*, **1** (e.g. a brochure), drucken. **2** (type of writing), in Druckschrift schreiben; **please print**, bitte Druckschrift verwenden

print off/out *vb* (comp), ausdrucken; **this still needs printing out**, das muß noch ausgedruckt werden

printed matter *n* (corr), Drucksache *nf*

printer *n* (comp, occupation), Drucker *nm*

printing *n* (gen), Drucken *nn*

printout *n* (comp), Ausdruck *nm*; **make a printout**, ausdrucken

priority *n*, Priorität *nf*; **give priority to**, vorrangig behandeln; **we would be grateful if you could give priority to this matter**, wir wären Ihnen dankbar, wenn Sie diese Sache vorrangig behandeln könnten; **priority order**, vorrangiger Auftrag *nm*

private *adj*, privat; "**private and confidential**" (corr), „streng vertraulich"; **private enterprise**, Privatunternehmen *nn*; **private limited company**, Gesellschaft *nf* mit beschränkter Haftung, GmbH

privatise *vb*, privatisieren

privatised *adj*, privatisiert

prize *n*, Preis *nm*; **prize draw**, Preisverlosung *nf*

procedure *n*, **1** Verfahren *nn*. **2 correct procedure**, Vorschrift *nf*

proceedings *npl* (law), Prozeß *nm*

proceeds *npl* (acct), Erlös *nm*; **the proceeds from . . .**, der Erlös aus . . . (+ dat)

process *n* (gen, industrial), Prozeß *nm*; **production process**, Produktionsprozeß *nm*

process *vb*, **1** (deal with something, ins), bearbeiten; **process an order**, einen Auftrag bearbeiten. **2** (figures), aufbereiten. **3** (data, materials, comp), verarbeiten

processing *n* (data, materials), Verarbeitung *nf*; **data processing**, Datenverarbeitung *nf*; **waste processing**, Abfallverarbeitung *nf*

procurement *n* (purchasing), Beschaffung *nf*; **procurement manager**, Beschaffungsmanager *nm*

produce *n* (agriculture), Agrarerzeugnisse *nnpl*

produce *vb* (industry), herstellen, produzieren

producer *n* (industry), Hersteller *nm*, Produzent *nm*

product *n*, Produkt *nn*; **product benefits**, Produktnutzen *nm*; **product design**, Produktgestaltung *nf*; **product liability** (law), Produkthaftung *nf*; **product line**, Sortiment *nn*; **product life**, Haltbarkeit *nf*; **product manager**, Produktmanager *nm*; **product range**, Sortiment *nn*

production *n*, **1** Fertigung *nf*, Produktion *nf*. **2** (department), Fertigungsabteilung *nf*; **production cost**, Produktionskosten *npl*; **production line**, Fertigungsstraße *nf*, Fließband *nn*

productivity bonus *n*, Produktivitätsprämie *nf*

profession *n*, Beruf *nm*

professional *adj*, professionell, Berufs-; **professional experience**, Berufserfahrung *nf*; **professional translator**, Berufsübersetzer(in) *nm/f*

profile *n* (gen, pers), Profil *nn*; **have a high/low profile**, sehr/wenig bekannt sein; **keep a low profile**, sich zurückhalten

profit *n*, Gewinn *nm*; **a profit of 10%**, 10% Gewinn; **gross/net profit**, Brutto-/Nettogewinn *nm*; **record profits**, Rekordgewinne *nmpl*; **level of profits**, Gewinniveau *nn*; **profit/earnings per share** (fin), Mehrgewinne *nmpl*; **profit margin**, Gewinnspanne *nf*; **profit sharing** (pers), Gewinnbeteiligung *nf*

profitability *n*, Rentabilität *nf*

profitable *adj*, rentabel

pro forma invoice *n*, Pro-forma-Rechnung *nf*

programme *n* (gen, comp), Programm *nn*

programme *vb* (comp), programmieren

programmer *n* (comp), Programmierer(in) *nm/f*

progress *n*, Fortschritt *nm*; **make progress**, Fortschritte machen

prohibit *vb*, verbieten; **this should be prohibited**, das sollte verboten werden

prohibitive *adj* (cost), unerschwinglich

project *n*, Projekt *nn*; **project manager**, Projektleiter(in) *nm/f*

project *vb* (e.g. result, fin), vorhersagen

promise *n*, Versprechen *nn*

promise *vb*, versprechen; **he promised me a wage increase**, er hat mir eine Lohnerhöhung versprochen

promote *vb*, **1** befördern; **she has been promoted to the post of manager**, sie ist zur Managerin befördert worden. **2** (product), werben für (+ acc)

promoter *n*, **1** (of company), Mitbegründer *nm*. **2 sales promoter**, Verkaufsleiter(in) *nm(f)*

promotion *n*, **1** Beförderung *nf*. **2** (mktg, sales), Werbung *nf*

proof *n*, Beweis *nm*

property *n*, Eigentum *nn*; **private property**, Privateigentum *nn*; **property developer**, Immobilienmakler *nm*

proposal *n*, **1** (gen), Vorschlag *nm*; **make a proposal**, einen Vorschlag machen; **we have studied your proposal**, wir haben Ihren Vorschlag durchgesehen. **2** (formal, for decision), Antrag *nm*; **make a (formal) proposal**, einen Antrag stellen; **the (formal) proposal was rejected**, der Antrag wurde abgelehnt

propose *vb*, **1** (gen), vorschlagen; **I propose that . . .**, ich schlage vor, daß . . .; **I would like to propose a solution**, ich möchte eine Lösung vorschlagen. **2** (formal), beantragen

proposition *n*, Angebot *nn*

prospect *vb* (mktg, sales), akquirieren

prove *vb*, beweisen

provision *n* (fin), Rücklage *nf*

provisional *adj*, provisorisch

proviso *n* (law), Vorbehalt *nm*; **with the proviso that . . .**, unter dem Vorbehalt, daß . . .

public *adj*, öffentlich; **public company**, staatliches Unternehmen *nn*; **public limited company, plc**, Aktiengesellschaft *nf*, AG *nf*; **public prosecutor** (law), Staatsanwalt *nm*, Staatsanwältin *nf*; **public transport**, öffentlicher Verkehr *nm*; **public works**, staatliches Bauvorhaben *nn*

publicly owned company *n*, Unternehmen *nn* im öffentlichen Besitz

publisher *n*, Verleger *nm*

publishing industry *n*, Verlagswirtschaft *nf*

punter *n* (fin), Börsenspekulant *nm*

purchase *vb*, kaufen

purchase price *n* (fin), Kaufpreis *nm*

purchaser *n*, Käufer *nm*

purpose *n*, Zweck *nm*; **the purpose of the visit will be to . . .**, der Zweck der Reise ist, . . . zu . . .

put *vb*, **1** (position upright), stellen; **please put the filing cabinet in the corner**, bitte stellen Sie den

Aktenschrank in die Ecke. **2** (place, gen), setzen; **put one's signature under a document**, seine Unterschrift unter ein Dokument setzen; **put something on the agenda**, etwas auf die Tagesordnung setzen. **3** (lay down flat), legen; **I shall put the letter on your desk**, ich lege den Brief auf Ihren Schreibtisch. **4** (push in), stecken; **just put the plug in the socket**, stecken Sie einfach den Stecker in die Dose

put off *vb* (e.g. a meeting), verschieben; **the meeting has been put off until 5 September**, die Sitzung ist auf den 5. September verschoben worden

put up *vb*, **1** (a stand), einen Stand errichten. **2** (money), Geld zur Verfügung stellen. **3** (for sale), zum Verkauf anbieten. **4** (prices), die Preise erhöhen

qualifications *npl* (CV), Qualifikationen *nfpl*

qualified acceptance *n*, bedingte Annahme *nf*

qualify *vb*, **1** (pass exam), sich qualifizieren. **2** (statement), einschränken. **3 qualify for** . . . Anspruch *nn* haben auf (+ acc)

quality *n*, Qualität *nf*; **best quality**, beste Qualität; **poor quality**, schlechte Qualität; **quality circle** (pers), Qualitätszirkel *nm*; **quality control** (gen), Qualitätskontrolle *nf*

quantity *n*, Quantität *nf*, Menge *nf*; **a small/large quantity**, eine kleine/große Menge

quarter *n*, **1** (gen), Viertel *nn*. **2** (of year), Quartal *nn*. **3** (of town), Stadtviertel *nn*; **business quarter**, Geschäftsviertel *nn*

quay *n* (transp), Kai *nm*; **price ex quay**, Preis ab Kai

query *n*, **1** (gen), Frage *nf*. **2** (question concerning something assumed to be clear), Rückfrage *nf*. **3** (question regarding correctness, quality etc), Beanstandung *nf*

query *vb* (an order, a figure), beanstanden

questionnaire *n* (mktg, sales), Fragebogen *nm*; **fill in a questionnaire**, einen Fragebogen ausfüllen

quick *adj*, **1** (high speed), schnell. **2** (prompt), prompt; **a quick reply**, eine prompte Antwort

quickly *adv*, schnell

quota *n* (imp/exp), Quote *nf*; **impose a quota**, ein Quotensystem einführen

quota system *n*, Quotensystem *nn*

quotation *n*/**quote** *n* (a quoted price for a contract), Preisangabe *nf*

quote *vb* (e.g. a figure, name, price), angeben; **quoted on the stock exchange**, an der Börse zugelassen

R

R & D, Research and Development, Forschung *nf* und Entwicklung *nf*

radio *n*, Radio *nn*; **on the radio**, im Radio; **radio pager**, Funkrufempfänger *nm*

radio *vb*, **1** (send a message), per Funk durchgeben. **2** (contact), sich per Funk verständigen

rail, *n*, Bahn *nf*; **by rail**, per Bahn; **rail freight** Bahnfracht *nf*; **rail transport**, Bahntransport *nm*

railway *n* Bahn *nf*; **railway station**, Bahnhof *nm*

raise *vb*, **1** (loan), ein Darlehen aufnehmen. **2** (point), einen Punkt vorbringen. **3** (prices), die Preise erhöhen

RAM, random access memory (comp), RAM, Direktzugriffspeicher *nm*

range *n*, **1** (of goods), Auswahl *nf*. **2** (of prices), Preislage *nf*. **3** (of vehicle), Fahrbereich *nm*. **4** (of machine), Aktionsradius *nm*

rapid delivery *n* (transp), prompte Lieferung *nf*

rate *n*, Satz *nm*; **daily rate**, Tagessatz *nm*; **rate of interest** (fin), Zinssatz *nm*; **rate of exchange** (fin), Wechselkurs *nm*; **rate of return** (fin), Rendite *nf*

ratings *npl* (TV, radio), Einschaltquote *nf*

ratio *n* (maths), Verhältnis *nn*

ration *vb*, rationieren

rationalisation *n*, Rationalisierung *nf*

rationalise *vb*, rationalisieren

raw materials *npl*, Rohstoffe *nmpl*

reach *vb* (e.g. a level), erreichen; **reach an agreement**, eine Vereinbarung erzielen; **reach break-even** (fin), kostendeckend arbeiten

reader *n*, Leser(in) *nm/f*

readership *n*, Leserschaft *nf*, Leser *nmpl*

ready *adj*, fertig, bereit; **the order is now ready**, die Bestellung ist jetzt bereit; **ready for use**, gebrauchsfertig

real *adj*, **1** (materials, genuine), echt; **real leather**, echtes Leder *nn*. **2** (actual), Real-; **real wages**, Reallohn *nm*; **real estate**, Grundbesitz *nm*

reason *n*, Grund *nm*

reasonable offer *n*, reelles Angebot *nn*

reassess *vb*, neubewerten

reassessment *n*, Neubewertung *nf*; **make a reassessment of . . .**, eine Neubewertung von (+ dat) vornehmen

rebate *n* (mktg, sales), **1** (money back), Rückvergütung *nf*. **2** (discount), Rabatt *nm*; **give a rebate**, Rabatt gewähren

receipt *n*, **1** (document issued after purchase), Quittung *nf*; **make out a receipt**, eine Quittung ausstellen. **2** (delivery of goods), Empfang *nm*; **payment on receipt**, Zahlung *nf* bei Empfang

receipted invoice *n*, quittierte Rechnung *nf*

receive *vb*, **1** (gen), bekommen. **2** (more formal), empfangen, erhalten; "**received with thanks**", „dankend erhalten"

receiver *n*, **1** (gen), Empfänger *nm*. **2** (fin), Konkursverwalter *nm*

reception *n*, **1** (hotel), Rezeption *nf*, Empfang *nm*. **2** (for drinks), Empfang *nm*; **hold a reception**, einen Empfang geben

receptionist *n*, Empfangsdame *nf*, Herr *nm* am Empfang

reciprocal *adj* (gen), wechselseitig, gegenseitig; **reciprocal agreement**, gegenseitige Vereinbarung *nf*

recognise *vb*, **1** (acknowledge), anerkennen. **2** (identify), erkennen

recommend *vb*, empfehlen

recommended price *n* (comm), unverbindlicher Richtpreis *nm*

record *n* (offce), **1** (gen), Aufzeichnung *nf*; **we have no record of your letter**, Ihr Brief ist bei uns nicht registriert worden. **2** (of meeting) Protokoll *nn*

record *adj* (best), Rekord-; **record results**, Rekordergebnisse *nnpl*; **record exports**, Rekordexporte *nmpl*; **record sales**, Rekordabsatz *nm*; **a record number of sales inquiries**, eine Rekordzahl *nf* von Verkaufsanfragen

record *vb*, **1** (electronically), aufnehmen; **record a message** (on answerphone), eine Nachricht aufnehmen; **a recorded message**, eine Tonbandnachricht. **2** (write down, make a note of), notieren, aufzeichnen

records *npl* (offce), Unterlagen *nfpl*, Akten *nfpl*

recover *vb*, **1** (get back, e.g. money), zurückbekommen. **2** (improve, e.g. market), sich erholen

recruit *vb* (pers), einstellen

recruitment *n* (pers), Personalbeschaffung *nf*; **recruitment agency**, Personalagentur *nf*

recycle *vb* (gen), wiederaufbereiten

recycling *n*, Recycling *nn*, Wiederaufbereitung *nf*; **a recycling plant**, eine Wiederaufbereitungsanlage *nf*

red, be in the red *vb* (fin), in den roten Zahlen sein

reduce *vb*, **1** (gen), reduzieren; **we have reduced our prices by 10%**, wir haben unsere Preise um 10% reduziert; **we have reduced costs by using . . .**, wir haben unsere Kosten durch die Verwendung von (+ dat) reduziert; **the interest rate has been reduced to 4%**, der Zinssatz ist auf 4% reduziert worden. **2** (special concession), ermäßigen

reduction *n*, **1** (gen), Reduzierung *nf*; **price reduction**, Preisreduzierung *nf*. **2** (special concession), Ermäßigung *nf*

redundancy *n* (pers), **1** (making redundant), Entlassung *nf*. **2** (losing one's job), Arbeitsplatzverlust *nm*

redundant *adj*, arbeitslos; **make redundant**, entlassen

refer to *vb*, **1** (make reference to), sich beziehen auf (+ acc); **we refer to your letter of May 10th**, wir beziehen uns auf Ihren Brief vom 10. Mai. **2** (pass on, e.g. a query), weiterleiten; **we have referred your query to our Sales Department**, wir haben Ihre Anfrage an unsere Verkaufsabteilung weitergeleitet

reference *n*, **1** (for job application), Referenz *nf*, Empfehlungsschreiben *nn*. **2** (mentioning, referring to), Bezug *nm*; **with reference to your letter of . . .**, mit Bezug auf Ihren Brief vom . . . **3** (to identify document), Zeichen *nn*; **reference number**, Aktenzeichen *nn*

refine *vb*, verfeinern

refrigerated storage *n* (transp), Kühllagerung *nn*

refuel *vb* (ship, plane), auftanken

refund *n*, Rückerstattung *nf*; **full refund**, Rückerstattung in voller Höhe

refund *vb*, rückerstatten; **all costs will be refunded**, alle Kosten werden rückerstattet

refuse *vb*, **1** (something), ablehnen; **I have to refuse your offer**, ich muß Ihr Angebot ablehnen. **2** (to do something), sich weigern; **they refuse to cooperate**, sie weigern sich zu kooperieren

regional manager *n*, Bereichsleiter(in) *nm/f*

register *n*, Register *nn*, Verzeichnis *nn*

register *vb*, **1** (note in a list), registrieren, eintragen; **register a company**, eine Firma registrieren/eintragen. **2** (sign up for course, exhibition), sich anmelden

registered *adj*, **1** (noted in list), registriert, eingetragen; **registered office** (of company), eingetragener Sitz *nm*; **registered trademark**, eingetragenes Warenzeichen *nn*. **2 by registered post**, per Einschreibe

registration *n*, **1** (noting in list), Registrierung *nf*, Eintragung *nf*. **2** (signing up for course, exhibition), Anmeldung *nf*; **registration fee** (for course, exhibition), Anmeldegebühr *nf*; **registration form** (for course, exhibition), Anmeldeformular *nn*; **registration number** (of car), Kraftfahrzeugkennzeichen *nn*, Kfz-Kennzeichen *nn*

regret *vb*, bedauern

regulation *n*, Vorschrift *nf*

reimburse *vb*, (zurück)erstatten; **your expenses will be reimbursed**, Ihre Auslagen werden Ihnen (zurück)erstattet

reinforced *adj* **with** (imp/exp), verstärkt mit (+ dat); **reinforced concrete** Stahlbeton *nm*

reject *n* (comm), Ausschußware *nf*, zweite Wahl *nf*

reject *vb*, **1** (offer), ablehnen. **2** (criticism), zurückweisen

release *vb* (goods) (imp/exp), freigeben

relevant *adj*, **1** (details, facts), relevant. **2** (person, department), zuständig

reliability *n* (of product, person), Zuverlässigkeit *nf*

reliable *adj* (product, person), zuverlässig

relocate *vb* (move premises), seinen Standort verlegen; **the company is relocating to . . .**, das Unternehmen verlegt seinen Standort nach . . .

rely on *vb*, sich verlassen auf (+ acc); **we are relying on your information**, wir verlassen uns auf Ihre Informationen

remind *vb*, erinnern; **I must remind you that . . .**, ich muß Sie (daran) erinnern, daß . . .

reminder (letter) *n* (offce), Mahnung *nf*

remit *vb* (fin), überweisen

remittance *n* (fin), Überweisung *nf*

remote control *n*, Fernsteuerung *nf*

renew *vb*, erneuern

rent *n*, Miete *nf*

rent *vb*, **1** (hire), mieten; **rent a stand** (mktg, sales), einen Stand mieten; **rent offices in . . .**, Büroräume in . . . mieten. **2** (rent out), vermieten

rental *n*, Mietgebühr *nf*

reorganisation *n*, Reorganisation *nf*

reorganise *vb*, reorganisieren

repair *n*, Reparatur *nf*; **all repairs were carried out**, alle Reparaturen wurden ausgeführt

repair *vb*, reparieren

replace *vb* (gen, ins), ersetzen; **any defective items will be replaced**, alle schadhaften Artikel werden ersetzt

reply *n*, Antwort *nf*; **receive a reply**, eine Antwort bekommen; **reply coupon**, Antwortcoupon *nm*; **reply-paid envelope**, Freiumschlag *nm*

reply to *vb* (gen), beantworten; **he has not replied to our letter**, er hat unseren Brief nicht beantwortet; **reply to a job advertisement**, sich auf eine Stellenannonce hin bewerben

report *n*, Bericht *nm*; **write a report on/about**, einen Bericht über (+ acc) schreiben

report on *vb* (gen), berichten über (+ acc)

report to *vb*, **1** (inform someone), melden; **I will report the accident to our insurers**, ich werde den Unfall unserer Versicherung melden. **2** (to a superior), unterstehen; **he reports directly to the head of department**, er untersteht direkt dem Abteilungsleiter

reputable *adj*, angesehen

reputation *n*, Ansehen *nn*, Ruf *nm*; **have a good reputation**, einen guten Ruf haben

reschedule *vb*, einen Plan umstellen

research *n*, Forschung *nf*; **carry out research into . . .**, Forschung über (+ acc) betreiben; **market research**, Marktforschung *nf*; **research and development**, Forschung und Entwicklung

research *vb*, forschen

reservation *n*, Reservierung *nf*; **cancel a reservation**, eine Reservierung rückgängig machen; **have a reservation**, eine Reservierung haben; **make a reservation**, eine Reservierung machen

residence permit *n*, Aufenthaltsgenehmigung *nf*

resources *npl*, Mittel *nnpl*, Ressourcen *nfpl*; **financial resources**, finanzielle Mittel *nnpl*

responsible *adj*, verantwortlich; **be responsible for . . .** (pers), verantwortlich sein für (+ acc)

restitution *n* (of property), Rückgabe *nf*

restock *vb*, das Lager auffüllen

restricted market *n*, beschränkter Markt *nm*

restrictions on imports *npl*, Importbeschränkungen *nfpl*

restructure *vb* (a company), umstrukturieren

result *n* (gen), Ergebnis *nn*, Resultat *nn*; **results** (fin), Jahresergebnisse *nnpl*

retail *n*, Einzelhandel *nm*; **retail bank** (fin), Einzelhandelsbank *nf*; **retail outlet**, Einzelhandelsgeschäft *nn*; **retail price**, Einzelhandelspreis *nm*; **retail trade**, Einzelhandel *nm*

retail *vb*, im Einzelhandel verkaufen; **the product retails at a recommended price of . . .**, das Produkt wird im Einzelhandel zum Richtpreis von . . . verkauft

retailer *n*, Einzelhändler *nm*

retire *vb* (pers), in Pension/Rente gehen

retirement *n*, Pension *nf*, Rente *nf*; **early retirement**, Frühpensionierung *nf*, Frührente *nf*

retrain *vb*, umschulen

retraining *n*, Umschulung *nf*

return *vb*, **1** (goods to supplier), zurückgeben. **2** (come back to), zurückkehren; **he will return to Pavia shortly**, er wird in Kürze nach Pavia zurückkehren

return *n*, **1** (gen), Rückkehr *nm*. **return ticket**, Rückfahrkarte *nf*. **2** (fin), Rendite *nf*, Gewinn *nm*; **return on investment** (fin), Investitionsrendite *nf*

revenue *n* (fin), Einkünfte *npl*

reverse *vb*, **1** (trend), umkehren. **2** (car), rückwärts fahren

reverse-charges call *n* (telec), R-Gespräch *nn*

revise *vb*, revidieren; **revise the terms of payment**, die Zahlungsbedingungen revidieren

revision *n*, Revision *nf*

revival *n* (fin, economic), Aufschwung *nm*, Belebung *nf*; **a revival in sales**, eine Absatzbelebung *nf*

revolving credit *n* (fin), Revolving-Kredit *nm*; **arrange revolving credit**, Revolving-Kredit besorgen; **obtain a revolving credit of . . .**, einen Revolving-Kredit von . . . bekommen

revolving letter of credit *n* (imp/exp), revolvierender Kreditbrief *nm*

rider *n* (law), Zusatzklausel *nf*

right *n*, Recht *nn*; **have the right to . . .**, das Recht haben zu . . .; **sole rights to . . .**, alleinige Rechte an . . .

right *adj*, **1** (correct), richtig; **be right**, recht haben; **you are quite right**, Sie haben ganz recht. **2** (not left), recht; **the right side**, die rechte Seite

right *adv*, **on the right**, rechts

right-hand drive *n*, Rechtssteuerung *nf*

rights issue *n* (fin), Bezugsrechtsausgabe *nf*

ring *vb*, **1** (phone someone), anrufen; **ring back**, zurückrufen. **2 the phone is ringing**, das Telefon klingelt. **3** (make a ring around), einkreisen

ring binder *n* (offce), Ringbuch *nn*

rise *n*, Anstieg *nm*; **a steep rise**, ein steiler Anstieg; **a rise in prices**, ein Preisanstieg *nm*

rise *vb*, steigen; **rise sharply/slightly/steadily**, steil/leicht/stetig steigen

risk *n*, Risiko *nn*, Gefahr *nf*; **all risks** (ins), alle Risken; **take out an all risks policy**, eine Vollkaskoversicherung abschließen

risk *vb*, riskieren

rival *n*, Rivale *nm*, Rivalin *nf*; **the main rival is . . .**, der Hauptrivale ist . . .

road *n*, Straße *nf*; **be on the road**, unterwegs sein; **road haulage** (transp), Güterkraftverkehr *nm*

rob *vb* (law), (be)rauben

robot *n*, Roboter *nm*; **robot assembly** (assembly by robots), Roboter-Montage *nf*

roll *vb*, rollen

rolled steel *n*, Walzstahl *nm*

ROM *n* (comp), ROM *nn*

roro, roll on roll off (imp/exp, transp), Ro-Ro-

rough *adj* (approximate), grob; **rough estimate**, grobe Schätzung; *nf* **rough copy**, Konzept *nn*

roughly *adv*, etwa, ungefähr

round *adj* (shape), rund

round down *vb* (figures), abrunden

round up *vb* (figures), aufrunden

route *n*, Route *nf*; **en route**, unterwegs

row *n*, **a row of . . .** eine Reihe *nf* von (+ dat); **in a row**, nacheinander

rubber *n* (material), Gummi *nm*

rubber-stamp *vb*, **1** stempeln. **2** (approve automatically), automatisch genehmigen

rule *n*, Regel *nf*; **as a rule**, in der Regel; **work to rule**, Dienst nach Vorschrift tun

run *vb*, **1** (department, company), leiten. **2** (computer programme), benutzen. **3 run into debt**, in Schulden geraten

running costs *npl*, **running expenses** *npl*, Betriebskosten *npl*, Festkosten *npl*

rush hour *n*, Rush-hour *nf*

rush order *n* (mktg, sales), Eilauftrag *nm*

rust *n*, Rost *nm*; **there were patches of rust on the surface of the product**, die Produktoberfläche hatte Roststellen

rust *vb*, rosten

rustproof *adj*, rostfrei

S

sack *n* (container) (imp/exp), Sack *nm*

sack *vb* (staff), entlassen

SAE, stamped addressed envelope, frankierter Rückumschlag *nm*

safe *adj*, sicher; **a safe investment**, eine sichere Investition *nf*

safe *n* (offce, banks), Safe *nm*

safeguard *vb*, schützen

safety *n*, Sicherheit *nf*; **safety standards**, Sicherheitsnormen *nfpl*

sail *vb* (leave port), auslaufen

salaried *adj* (pers), fest angestellt

salary *n*, Gehalt *nn*

sale *n*, Verkauf *nm*; **summer sale**, Sommerschlußverkauf *nm*; **end of season sale**, Saisonschlußverkauf *nm*; **on sale**, zum Verkauf; **sale by tender**, Verkauf durch Ausschreibung; **for sale**, zu verkaufen; **sale or return**, Kauf *nm* mit Rückgaberecht

sales *npl*, Verkauf *nm*, Absatz *nm*; **sales chart**, Verkaufsstatistik *nf*; **sales department**, Verkaufsabteilung *nf*; **sales figures**, Verkaufszahlen *nfpl*; **sales force**, Verkaufsstab *nm*; **sales forecast**, Absatzprognose *nf*; **sales girl**, Verkaufsdame *nf*; **sales incentive**, Kaufanreiz *nm*; **sales lead**, Absatzvorsprung *nm*; **salesman**, Vertreter *nm*; **sales manager**, Verkaufsleiter *nm*; **sales outlet, sales point**, Verkaufsstelle *nf*; **sales promotion**, Verkaufsförderung *nf*

sample *n* (mktg, sales), (Waren)Muster *nn*, (Waren)Probe *nf*; **not up to sample**, entspricht nicht dem Muster; **free sample**, Gratisprobe *nf*; **sample opinion**, Stichprobenbefragung *nf*

sample *vb* (mktg, sales), **1** (opinion), eine Stichprobe machen. **2** (food), probieren

sampling *n* (mktg, sales), Stichprobenverfahren *nn*

satellite TV *n* (mktg, sales), Satellitenfernsehen *nn*

satisfied *adj*, zufrieden; **according to our research customers are very satisfied with the new service**, nach unserer Umfrage sind unsere Kunden mit dem neuen Service sehr zufrieden

satisfy *vb*, **1** (customers), zufriedenstellen. **2** (conditions), erfüllen; **not all conditions have been satisfied**, nicht alle Bedingungen sind erfüllt

saturation point *n*, Sättigungspunkt *nm*

save *vb*, **1** (comp, data), speichern. **2** (reduce expenditure, use less), sparen; **save electricity**, Elektrizität sparen; **save money**, Geld sparen

scale *n* (of set charges, rates), Skala *nf*, Tabelle *nf*; **on a sliding scale**, gestaffelt; **scale of charges**, Gebührenordnung *nf*

scanner *n* (comp), Scanner *nm*

scarce *adj*, knapp; **scarce resources**, knappe Mittel *nnpl*

schedule *n* (gen), Plan *nm*

schedule *vb* (plan, fix), ansetzen; **the next meeting is scheduled for . . .**, die nächste Sitzung ist für . . . angesetzt

scheduled flight *n*, Linienflug *nm*

scheme *n* (plan), Plan *nm*, Programm *nn*

scissors *npl*, Schere *nf*

scrap *n* (waste material), Abfall *nm*; **scrap iron**, Schrott *nm*

scrap *vb*, **1** (plan), einen Plan fallenlassen. **2** (product), ausrangieren. **3** (car, ship), verschrotten

screen *n*, **1** (partition), Trennwand *nf*. **2** (for film) Leinwand *nf*. **3** (TV, comp), Bildschirm *nm*

screw *vb* (gen), schrauben

sea *n*, See *nf*; **by sea**, auf dem Seewege

seal *n*, Siegel *nn*; **company seal**, Firmensiegel *nn*; **customs seal**, Plombe *nf*, Zollverschluß *nm*

seal *vb*, versiegeln

sealed *adj*, versiegelt

season *n*, Saison *nf*; **the quiet season**, die Nebensaison *nf*; **the busy season**, die Hauptsaison *nf*

seasonal *adj*, saisonbedingt; **seasonal demand**, saisonbedingte Nachfrage *nf*; **seasonal employment**, saisonbedingte Beschäftigung *nf*

second *n* (comm), zweite Wahl *nf*; **this is a second**, das ist zweite Wahl

second *adj*, zweite(r, s); **the second point is . . .**, der zweite Punkt ist . . .

second *vb* (proposal), unterstützen

second-hand *adj*, gebraucht; **second-hand car**, Gebrauchtwagen *nm*

secondly *adv*, zweitens

second-rate *adj*, zweitklassig

secret *n*, Geheimnis *nn*

secret *adj*, geheim

secretary *n*, Sekretär(in) *nm/f*

sector *n*, Sektor *nm*

secure *vb* **an order**, einen Auftrag gewinnen

securities *npl* (fin, stock exchange), Effekten *npl*, Wertpapiere *nnpl*; **securities market** (fin, stock exchange), Wertpapiermarkt *nm*

security *n* (gen, fin, for a loan), Sicherheit *nf*; **lend money on security**, Geld gegen Sicherheit leihen

see from *vb*, ersehen aus (+ dat); **we see from your report that . . .**, aus Ihrem Bericht ersehen wir, daß . . .

see to *vb*, sich kümmern um (+ acc)

segment *n*, **market segment** (mktg, sales), Marktsegment *nn*

segmentation *n* (mkgt, sales), Segmentierung *nf*

seize *vb*, ergreifen; **seize an opportunity**, eine Chance ergreifen

select *vb*, auswählen

selection *n*, Auswahl *nf*; **make a selection**, eine Auswahl treffen; **selection procedure** (pers, recruitment), Auswahlverfahren *nn*

self-confidence *n* Selbstvertrauen *nn*

self-financing *adj*, selbstfinanzierend

self-service *n*, Selbstbedienung *nf*

sell *vb*, verkaufen

sell off *vb* (e.g., surplus stock), abstoßen

seller *n*, Verkäufer *nm*

send *vb* **1** (gen), senden. **2** (post), **send back**, zurücksenden; **send off**, absenden

sender *n* (corr), Absender *nm*

senior executive *n*, leitende(r) Angestellte(r) *nf/m*

senior partner *n*, Seniorpartner(in) *nm/f*

sensitive *adj* (gen), empfindlich; **be sensitive to . . .**, empfindlich reagieren auf (+ acc); **price-sensitive**, preisempfindlich

sentence *n* (law), Urteil *nn*

separate *vb* (gen), trennen

separate *adj*, getrennt; **send under separate cover**, mit getrennter Post senden

serial connector *n* (comp), serieller Anschluß *nm*

serial number *n*, Seriennummer *nf*

series *n*, Serie *nf*

service *n*, Bedienung *nf*, Dienst *nm*; **after sales service**, Kundendienst *nm*; **fast service**, prompte Bedienung; **maintenance service**, Wartungsdienst *nm*; **24-hour service**, Tag- und Nachtdienst *nm*; **secretarial service**, Schreibdienst *nm*; **translation service**, Übersetzungsdienst *nm*; **service contract** (mktg, sales), Wartungsvertrag *nm*; **service industries**, Dienstleistungsbranche *nf*

service *vb* (machine), warten

servicing *n*, Wartung *nf*; **regular servicing is essential for XYZ**, XYZ bedarf unbedingt regelmäßiger Wartung

set *n*, Satz *nm*; **a complete set of documents**, ein kompletter Dokumentationssatz *nm*

setback *n*, Rückschlag *nm*; **receive a setback**, einen Rückschlag erleiden

settle *vb* **a bill** (fin), eine Rechnung *nf* begleichen

settle *vb* **a disagreement/a dispute**, eine Streitigkeit *nf* beilegen

settlement *n* (fin), Abrechnung *nf*

several *adj*, mehrere (*pl*); **several problems**, mehrere Probleme

share *n*, **1** (gen), Anteil *nm*; **market share**, Marktanteil *nm*. **2** (shareholding), Anteil *nm*, Aktie *nf*; **share certificate** (fin), Aktienzertifikat *nn*; **share ownership**, Aktienbesitz *nm*; **share warrant**, Aktiengarantie *nf*

share *vb*, teilen; **share the cost of repair**, die Reparaturkosten teilen

shareholder *n* (fin), Anteilseigner *nm*, Aktionär *nm*

shed a load *vb* (transp), ausladen

shelf-life *n* (of goods), Haltbarkeit *nf*

shelf-space *n*, Regalfläche *nf*

shelve a project *vb*, ein Projekt aufschieben

shelving *n*, Regale *nnpl*

shift *n*, Schicht *nf*; **night shift**, Nachtschicht *nf*; **shift manager**, Schichtleiter *nm*

shift *vb*, rutschen; **the load/cargo has shifted**, die Ladung ist gerutscht

ship *n* (transp), Schiff *nn*

ship *vb*, **1** (send off goods), verschiffen. **2** (load goods), an Bord nehmen

shipbuilding *n*, Schiffbau *nm*

shipment *n*, Sendung *nf*, Ladung *nf*

shipped bill of lading *n* (imp/exp), Verschiffungskonnossement *nn*

shipper *n*, **1** (loader), Spediteur *nm*. **2** (sender), Absender *nm*

shipping agent *n* (arranging transport), Spediteur *nm*

shipping documents *npl* (imp/exp, transp), Versanddokumente *nnpl*

shipping instructions *npl* (transp), Versandanweisungen *nfpl*

shipping note *n* (imp/exp, transp), Frachtbrief *nm*

ship's papers *npl* (imp/exp, transp), Schiffspapiere *nnpl*

shock-absorbent *adj*, stoßdämpfend

shock-proof *adj*, stoßfest, stoßsicher

shop *n*, Laden *nm*, Geschäft *nn*

shopping *n*, Einkaufen *nn*; **shopping around**, preisbewußtes Einkaufen;

shopping centre, Einkaufszentrum *nn*

shop-soiled *adj*, **1** (not clean), angeschmutzt. **2** (damaged), leicht beschädigt

short *adj*, **1** kurz; **a short letter**, ein kurzes Schreiben. **2** (incomplete), unvollständig; **short shipment**, unvollständige Ladung *nf*. **3** (not enough), zu wenig; **they were short of staff**, sie hatten zu wenig Personal. **4** (credit), kurzfristig

shortage *n*, Mangel *nm*; **a shortage of raw materials**, ein Mangel an Rohstoffen

shorthand *n*, Stenografie *nf*; **shorthand and typing** (pers), Stenografie und Schreibmaschine; **shorthand notes**, stenografierte Notizen *nfpl*; **shorthand typist**, Stenotypist(in) *nm/f*

short-term *adj*, kurzfristig; **short-term contract**, Zeitvertrag *nm*; **short-term debts**, kurzfristige Schulden *nfpl*; **short-term loan**, kurzfristiger Kredit *nm*

show *n*, Ausstellung *nf*, Schau *nf*; **fashion show**, Modeschau *nf*

show *vb*, zeigen; **the figures show that . . .**, die Zahlen zeigen, daß . . .; **our agent will be happy to show you the new model**, unser Vertreter wird Ihnen gern das neue Modell zeigen

showcase *n*, Schaukasten *nm*

shown *adj*, gezeigt

showroom *n*, Ausstellungsraum *nm*

shrink *vb*, schrumpfen

shrinking *adj*, schrumpfend; **a shrinking market**, ein schrumpfender Markt *nm*

shrink wrapping *n*, Schrumpfpackung *nf*

shrunk *adj*, geschrumpft

shut *adj*, geschlossen

shut *vb* (gen), schließen

shut down *vb* (company), schließen, stillegen

shuttle service *n*, Pendelverkehr *nm*

sick *adj*, krank; **be on sick leave**, krank geschrieben sein

side effect *n*, Nebenwirkung *nf*

sight *n*, Sicht *nf*; **after sight** (fin), nach Sicht

sight draft *n* (fin), Sichtwechsel *nm*

sign *n* (for road, shop etc), Schild *nn*; **neon sign**, Neonschild *nn*; **road sign**, Straßenschild *nn*

sign *vb* (a document), unterschreiben

sign for *vb* (goods), bestätigen

signatory *n*, **authorised signatory**, Zeichnungsberechtigte(r) *nf/m*

signature *n*, Unterschrift *nf*

signed copy *n* (documents), unterschriebene Kopie *nf*; **please return the signed copies**, die unterschriebenen Kopien bitte zurücksenden

significant *adj*, **1** (change), signifikant. **2** (facts, events), wichtig; **a significant fact**, eine wichtige Tatsache

single fare *n*, **1** (price), einfacher Fahrpreis *nm*. **2** (ticket), einfache Fahrkarte *nf*

single room *n*, Einzelzimmer *nn*

site *n*, **1** (gen), Stelle *nf*, Platz *nm*. **2** (construction), Baustelle *nf*

site, be sited *vb*, liegen; **the supermarket will be sited near the M5**, der Supermarkt wird in der Nähe der M5 liegen

site engineer *n*, Bauleiter *nm*

situation *n* (gen, fin), Lage *nf*; **the economic situation**, die wirtschaftliche Lage

size *n*, Größe *nf*; **what is the size of the load?**, wie groß ist die Ladung?

skilled worker *n*, Facharbeiter(in) *nm/f*

skills *npl*, Fertigkeiten *nfpl*

slack *adj* (economy), flau; **the market is very slack at present**, der Markt ist gegenwärtig sehr flau

slacken *vb* (rates, trends), nachlassen

slash *vb* (prices), stark reduzieren

sleeper *n* (train), Schlafwagen *nm*

sleeping compartment *n* (trains), Schlafwagenabteil *nn*

sleeping partner *n* (fin), stiller Teilhaber *nm*

slide *n* (presentations), Dia(positiv) *nn*

slide *vb*, **1** (gen, slip down), abrutschen. **2** (fall behind target, slip back), zurückfallen

slide projector *n* (mktg, sales), Diaprojektor *nm*

sliding *adj* (rates), gleitend; **a sliding scale**, eine gleitende Skala

slight *adj* (insignificant), leicht; **a slight fall in profits**, ein leichter Gewinnrückgang *nm*

slightly *adv*, etwas; **slightly higher/lower than . . .**, etwas höher/niedriger als . . .

slip *n* (of paper), Zettel *nm*

slip *vb*, **1** (skid), rutschen. **2** (trend), fallen

slippage *n*, Rückstand *nm*

slip-up *n*, Fehler *nm*

slogan *n* (mktg, sales), Slogan *nm*, Werbespruch *nm*

slot *n*, **1** (mktg, sales, TV), Sendezeit *nf*; **advertising slot**, Werbezeit *nf*. **2** (in machines), Schlitz *nm*. **3 slot machine**, Automat *nm*

slow *adj*, langsam

slow down *vb*, verlangsamen

slowdown *n*, Verlangsamung *nf*

sluggish *adj* (e.g. sales), flau

slump *n* (fin), Baisse *nf*

slump *vb* (mktg, sales, rates), plötzlich fallen; **profits have slumped to . . .**, die Gewinne sind plötzlich auf . . . gefallen

small *adj*, klein; **a small quantity of . . .**, eine kleine Menge *nf* . . .; **small ad** (mktg, sales), Kleinanzeige *nf*

SME, **small or medium-sized enterprise**, kleines oder mittleres Unternehmen *nn*

S/N, **SN**, **shipping note** (imp/exp), Frachtbrief *nm*

snowball *vb*, eskalieren

soar *vb* (sales, rates), sprunghaft ansteigen

soaring *adj* (fin), sprunghaft ansteigend; **soaring costs**, sprunghaft ansteigende Kosten

society *n*, Gesellschaft *nf*

soft *adj*, **1** (gen), weich; **soft currency**, weiche Währung *nf*. **2 soft furnishings** (mktg, sales), Heimtextilien *npl*

software *n* (comp), Software *nf*

soiled *adj* (goods), **1** (not clean), angeschmutzt. **2** (damaged), leicht beschädigt

sole agent *n* (mktg, sales), Alleinvertreter *nm*

sole distributor *n* (mktg, sales), Alleinvertrieb *nm*

solicitor *n* (law), Rechtsanwalt *nm*, Rechtsanwältin *nf*

solve *vb* **a problem**, ein Problem lösen

sort *vb* (comp), sortieren

soundproof *adj*, schalldicht

source *n*, Quelle *nf*; **deduction at source** (fin), Quellenbesteuerung *nf*

sourcing *n* (obtaining supplies), Beschaffung *nf*

space *n*, Raum *nm*; **advertising space**, Anzeigenraum *nm*

space out *vb* (e.g. payments), verteilen

spare part *n* (gen), Ersatzteil *nn*

speak *vb*, sprechen; **speak about . . .**, sprechen über (+ acc)

speak to *vb*, **1** (meeting), eine Rede halten vor (+ dat). **2** (an individual), mit jemandem sprechen

special *adj*, Sonder-; **special courier** (transp), Expreßbote *nm*; **special offer** (mktg, sales), Sonderangebot *nn*; **special price**, Sonderpreis *nm*; **special qualifications** (CV), besondere Qualifikationen *nfpl*; **special terms**, Sonderbedingungen *nfpl*

specialise in *vb*, sich spezialisieren auf (+ acc)

speciality *n*, Spezialität *nf*

specifications *npl*, **1** (technical features required), technische Voraussetzungen *nfpl*. **2** (description of technical features), Spezifikationen *nfpl*

specify *vb*, spezifizieren

speculate *vb*, spekulieren

speed *n*, Tempo *nn*, Geschwindigkeit *nf*

speed up *vb*, beschleunigen

spell *vb*, **1** buchstabieren; **could you spell your name please?**, würden Sie bitte Ihren Namen buchstabieren? **2** schreiben; **how do you spell your name?**, wie schreibt man Ihren Namen?

spend *vb*, **1** (money), ausgeben. **2** (time), verbringen

spill *vb* (liquid, load), verschütten

spin-off *n*, **1** (negative, unwanted side-effect), Nebenwirkung *nf*. **2** (positive), Nebenprodukt *nn*

split into *vb*, (auf)teilen in (+ acc)

spoil *vb* (affect quality), verderben

spokesman *n*, Sprecher(in) *nm/f*

sponsor *n* (mktg, sales), Sponsor(in) *nm/f*

sponsor *vb*, **1** (mktg, sales), sponsern. **2** (government support), fördern

sports equipment *n*, Sportausrüstung *nf*

spot *n* (purchase), Lokoware *nf*

spot cash *n*, sofortige Bezahlung *nf*

spray *vb* (crops, paint etc), spritzen

spread *vb*, **1** (spread over), verteilen. **2** (gain support, strikes), sich verbreiten

spreadsheet *n* (comp), Spreadsheet *nn*

square *n*, Quadrat *nn*

square *adj*, quadratisch; **square metre**, Quadratmeter *nm*, qm; **the rate is £15 per square metre**, die Miete beträgt £15 pro Quadratmeter (qm); **the stand covers 15 square metres**, der Stand nimmt 15 Quadratmeter (qm) ein

squeeze *vb*, **1** (make smaller), verkleinern. **2** (press), drücken

stabilise *vb*, stabilisieren

stable *adj*, stabil; **stable currency**, stabile Währung *nf*

stack *n* (transp), Stapel *nm*

stack *vb* (transp), stapeln

stacked *adj* (transp), gestapelt

staff *n* (pers), Personal *nn*

stage *n* (of a project), Phase *nf*; **stage payments** (fin), Zahlung *nf* in Etappen; **stage report** Zwischenbericht *nm*

stagnate *vb*, stagnieren

stake *n*, **1 a lot is at stake**, es steht viel auf dem Spiel; **that is precisely the issue at stake**, genau darum geht es. **2 have a financial stake in the company**, einen Anteil an dem Unternehmen haben

stamp *n*, **1** (for making marks on documents), Stempel *nm*.

2 (postage), Briefmarke *nf*

stamp *vb*, **1** (making mark), stempeln; **2** (a letter), frankieren

stamped addressed envelope *n*, frankierter Rückumschlag *nm*

stand *n* (mktg, sales), Stand *nm*; **stand manager** (mktg, sales), Standmanager *nm*

stand *vb*, **1** (gen), stehen. **2** (withstand, resist), aushalten; **the case can stand temperatures of up to 100 degrees C**, die Kiste hält Temperaturen bis zu 100 Grad Celsius aus

staple *vb* (offce), zusammenheften

stapler *n*, Hefter *nm*

start *vb*, **1** (gen), anfangen. **2** (a company), gründen

start-up costs *npl* (fin), Startkosten *npl*

state *n*, **the State**, der Staat

state *adj*, staatlich; **state aid**, staatliche Unterstützung *nf*; **state-controlled**, unter staatlicher Aufsicht

state *vb*, behaupten; **the report states that . . .**, in dem Bericht wird behauptet, daß . . .

statement *n*, **1** (gen, court), Aussage *nf*. **2 bank statement**, Kontoauszug *nm*. **3 financial statement**, Finanzbericht *nm*. **4 statement of account** (fin), Abrechnung *nf*

station *n* (for trains, coaches) Bahnhof *nm*

stationary *n*, **1** (notepaper), Briefpapier *nn*. **2** (writing materials), Schreibwaren *nfpl*; (office stationery), Büromaterial *nn*

statistics *npl*, Statistik *nf*

status *n*, **1** (gen), Status *nm*. **2** (fin), Finanzlage *nf*. **3 status line** (comp), Statuszeile *nf*

statutory *adj*, gesetzlich; **statutory holiday**, gesetzlicher Feiertag *nm*

stay *n* (period of residence), Aufenthalt *nm*

stay in *vb* (spend time in a place), sich aufhalten in; **how long did you stay in X?**, wie lange haben Sie sich in X aufgehalten?

STD code *n*, Vorwahl(nummer) *nf*

steady *adj*, **1** (worker), zuverlässig. **2** (demand), stabil, beständig

steel *n*, Stahl *nm*; **stainless steel**, rostfreier Stahl; **steel industry**, Stahlindustrie *nf*

steep *adj*, steil; **a steep rise in prices**, ein steiler Preisanstieg *nm*

step up *vb*, **1** (speed up), beschleunigen. **2** (e.g., a campaign), intensivieren

sterling *n* (currency), Sterling *nm*

stick *vb*, kleben

stick on *vb*, aufkleben

sticky label *n* (offce), Aufkleber *nm*, Etikett *nn*

stipulate *vb*, (vertraglich) vereinbaren

stock *n*, **1** (goods), Lagerbestand *nm*; **be out of stock**, ausverkauft sein; **have in stock**, auf Lager haben; **stock list**, Lagerbestandsverzeichnis *nn*; **stock turnover**, Lagerumschlag *nm*. **2** (on stock market), Aktie *nf*; **stock market** (fin), Börse *nf*; **stock option** (fin), Aktienoption *nf*; **stock option plan** (fin), Aktienoptionsplan *nm*

stock *vb*, führen; **we no longer stock . . .**, wir führen . . . nicht mehr

stockist *n* (mktg, sales), Fachhändler *nm*

stockpile *vb*, horten

stock-take *vb*, Inventur machen

stock-taking *n*, Inventur *nf*; **stock-taking sale**, Jahresschlußverkauf *nm*

stolen *adj*, gestohlen

stop *vb*, **1** aufhören. **2** (account, leave, cheque, electricity, wages), sperren; **stop wages**, den Lohn sperren. **3 stop work**, (strike) die Arbeit niederlegen. **4** (prevent), hindern

stop at *vb* (travel), haltmachen in (+ dat)

stopover *n* (aviation), Zwischenlandung *nf*

stoppage *n*, **1** (of work) (pers), Streik *nm*. **2** (of pay), Sperrung *nf*

storage *n* (transp), Lagerung *nf*; **storage space**, Lagerraum *nm*

store *n*, **1** (shop), Geschäft *nn*, Laden *nm*. **2** (for storage), Lager *nn*. **3** (comp), Speicher *nm*

store *vb*, **1** (gen, keep), aufbewahren. **2** (keep in warehouse), lagern. **3** (comp), speichern

stow *vb* (transp), verladen, verstauen

strategy *n*, Strategie *nf*; **our marketing strategy**, unsere Marketingstrategie *nf*

streamline *vb* (production, a company), rationalisieren

strength *n* (of materials), Festigkeit *nf*

strengthen *vb*, **1** (materials), (ver)stärken, festigen. **2** (market), festigen

strengthened *adj* **(with)**, verstärkt (mit) (+ dat)

stress *vb* (insist, point out), hervorheben

strike *n* (pers), Streik *nm*; **go on strike**, in den Streik treten

strike *vb* (pers), streiken

strong *adj*, stark

strong room *n*, Tresorraum *nm*

structural *adj*, strukturell

structure *n*, Struktur *nf*

study *vb*, **1** (examine), untersuchen. **2** (in higher education), studieren. **3** (a text), lesen

style *n*, Stil *nm*

subcontract *vb*, einen Unterauftrag vergeben

subcontracting *n*, Untervergabe *nf* von Aufträgen

subcontractor *n*, Subunternehmer *nm*

subject *n*, **1** (citizen), Staatsbürger(in) *nm/f*. **2** (topic), Thema *nn*

subject to *adj*, **1** (condition), **subject to government approval**, vorausgesetzt, die Regierung genehmigt es; **offer subject to availability**, solange der Vorrat reicht. **2** (possible risk), **subject to overheating**, anfällig für Überhitzung; **subject to change**, Änderungen vorbehalten. **3** (law), **subject to XYZ law**, unterliegt dem XYZ-Recht

subscribe to *vb*, **1** (a journal), abonnieren. **2** (an appeal), spenden

subscriber *n*. **1** (to magazine), Abonnent(in) *nm/f*. **2** (to new share issue), Zeichner *nm* von neuen Aktien. **3** (telec), Teilnehmer *nm*

subscription *n*, **1** (of magazine), Abonnement *nn*. **2** (of new share issue), Zeichnungsangebot *nn*

subsidiary *n* (company), Tochtergesellschaft *nf*

subsidise *vb* (fin), subventionieren

subsidy *n* (fin), Subvention *nf*

substandard *adj*, minderwertig

substitute *n* (materials), Ersatz *nm*

substitute for *vb* (goods), ersetzen durch (+ acc); **please substitute plastic for aluminium**, bitte ersetzen Sie Aluminium durch Plastik

suburb *n*, Vorstadt *nf*

succeed *vb*, **1** (manage to), gelingen (+ dat); **he succeeded in delivering the goods on time**, es gelang ihm, die Waren rechtzeitig zu liefern; **will you succeed in persuading him?**, wird es Ihnen gelingen, ihn zu überreden? **2** (do well), Erfolg haben; **the company succeeded best in Poland**, das Unternehmen hatte in Polen den größten Erfolg

success *n*, Erfolg *nm*

successful *adj*, erfolgreich

sue *vb* (law), gerichtlich belangen

suffer *vb* **from**, leiden unter (+ dat); **the company suffered from poor management**, das Unternehmen litt unter schlechtem Management

suitable *adj*, passend; **a suitable location**, ein passender Standort

sum *n* (of money), Summe *nf*

summarise *vb*, zusammenfassen; **please summarise the article in 150 words**, bitte fassen Sie den Artikel in 150 Wörtern zusammen

summary *n*, Zusammenfassung *nf*; **make a summary of a report**, einen Bericht zusammenfassen

summons *n* (law), Vorladung *nf*; **issue a summons**, vorladen

supermarket *n*, Supermarkt *nm*

superstore *n* (mktg, sales), Einkaufsmarkt *nm*

supervisor *n* (pers), **1** (factory, production) Polier *nm*. **2** (gen, offce), Aufseher *nm*

supplementary *adj*, zusätzlich, Zusatz-; **supplementary charge**, Zusatzgebühr *nf*

supplier *n* (gen), Lieferant *nm*

supplies *npl*, **1 electrical supplies**, Elektrowaren *nfpl*. **2 office supplies**, Bürobedarf *nm*

supply *n*, **1** (supplying), Versorgung *nf*; **electricity supply**, Elektrizitätsversorgung *nf*. **2** (what is supplied), Lieferung *nf*; **supply problems**, Lieferungsprobleme *nnpl*. **3** (stock), Vorrat *nm*; **a large supply of salt**, ein großer Salzvorrat *nm*. **4 supply and demand**, Angebot *nn* und Nachfrage *nf*

supply *vb*, **1** (provide), versorgen. **2** (deliver), liefern

support *vb*, unterstützen; **support a proposal**, einen Vorschlag unterstützen

surcharge *n*, **1** (gen), Zuschlag *nm*. **2** (customs), Abgabe *nf*. **3** (postal), Strafporto *nn*

surface mail *n*, gewöhnliche Post *nf*; **by surface mail**, mit gewöhnlicher Post

surge *n*, plötzlicher Anstieg *nm*; **a surge in imports**, ein plötzlicher Anstieg der Importe; **surge protector** (comp), Überspannungsableiter *nm*

surrender *vb* (documents), übergeben

surrender value *n* (fin), Rückkaufwert *nm*

survey *n*, **1** (gen, of surroundings etc), Überblick *nm*. **2** (opinion poll), Umfrage *nf*; **market survey**, Marktumfrage *nf*. **3** (report), Gutachten *nn*

survey *vb*, **1** (gen), überblicken. **2** (study), begutachten; **survey the market**, den Markt begutachten; **survey the damage** (ins), den Schaden begutachten

suspend *vb* (stop), suspendieren; **suspend payments** (fin), Zahlungen *nfpl* suspendieren

switch *n*, Schalter *nm*

switch off *vb*, abschalten

switch on *vb*, einschalten

switchboard *n* (offce), Telefonzentrale *nf*; **switchboard operator** (offce), Telefonist(in) *nm/f*

synthetic *adj*, synthetisch

system *n*, System *nn*

T

table *n*, (figures), Tabelle *nf*; **the table shows the sales figures for this month**, die Tabelle zeigt die Verkaufszahlen für diesen Monat

table *vb* (put on agenda), auf die Tagesordnung setzen

tacit *adj*, stillschweigend; **we have the tacit agreement of the manufacturer**, wir haben die stillschweigende Zustimmung des Herstellers

tackle *vb*, in Angriff nehmen; **I would like you to tackle the problem of . . .**, ich möchte Sie bitten, das Problem . . . in Angriff zu nehmen

tactic *n*, Taktik *nf*; **their usual tactic is to ignore the problem as far as possible**, ihre gewöhnliche Taktik ist, das Problem so weit wie möglich zu ignorieren; **a negotiating tactic**, eine Verhandlungstaktik *nf*

tag *n* (price tag), Schild *nn*, Preisschild *nn*

tailor *vb*, **we can tailor our service to your exact needs**, wir können uns ganz auf Ihre Bedürfnisse einstellen

tailor-made for *adj*, **1** (clothes), maßgeschneidert für (+ acc). **2** (fig, meeting certain needs), zugeschnitten auf (+ acc)

take *vb*, **1** (gen, buy), nehmen. **2** (accommodate), fassen; **the tank can take 3000 litres**, der Tank faßt 3000 Liter; **take into account**, in Betracht ziehen; **take back**, **1** (goods), zurücknehmen; **we are willing to take back the unsatisfactory goods**, wir sind bereit, die mangelhaften Waren zurückzunehmen. **2** (pers), wieder einstellen; **take to court** (law), gerichtlich belangen; **take down a stand** (at exhibitions), abbauen; **stands must be taken down within 24 hours of the end of the exhibition**, die Stände müssen innerhalb von 24 Stunden nach Ende der Ausstellung abgebaut werden; **take an exam in**, ein Examen in . . . machen; **take legal action**, gerichtlich vorgehen; **take a load to Bonn** (transp), eine Ladung nach Bonn fahren; **take notes/minutes**, Protokoll führen; **take off**, anlaufen; **sales have begun to take off**, der Absatz ist gut angelaufen; **take on** (pers), einstellen; **take out an insurance**, eine Versicherung abschließen; **take over** (company), übernehmen; **Schilke GmbH have been taken over by . . .**, Schilke GmbH sind von . . . übernommen worden; **take over from** (pers), ablösen; **Mr Jones has taken over from Mrs Smith in your sector**, Mr Jones hat in Ihrem Bereich Mrs Smith abgelöst; **take place**, stattfinden; **the conference will take place on . . . at . . .**, die Konferenz wird am . . . in . . . stattfinden; **take steps**, Schritte ergreifen; **take up an option**, sein Optionsrecht ausüben

takeover *n* (of a company), Übernahme *nf*; **takeover bid** (fin), Übernahmeangebot *nn*; **make a takeover bid**, ein Übernahmeangebot machen; **receive a takeover bid**, ein Übernahmeangebot bekommen

talk *vb*, sprechen

talk *n*, **give a talk on**, einen Vortrag halten über (+ acc)

talks *npl*, Gespräche *nnpl*; **have talks with . . .**, mit (+ dat) Gespräche führen

tamper *vb* (with goods), sich an . . .

zu schaffen machen; **the boxes have been tampered with**, jemand hat sich an den Kisten zu schaffen gemacht

tangible *adj* (acct), materiell

tank *n* (imp/exp), Tank *nm*

tanker *n* (transp), **1** (sea), Tanker *nm*. **2** (road, rail), Tankwagen *nm*

tape *n*, **1** (gen), Band *nn*. **2** (sound), Tonband *nn*; **tape recorder**, Tonbandgerät *nn*. **3** (video), Videoband *nn*

tape *vb*, auf Band aufnehmen

tapering rates *npl*, Staffeltarif *nm*

target *n*, **1** Ziel *nn*; **target market**, Zielmarkt *nm*; **target price**, Richtpreis *nm*. **2 on target**, nach Plan *nm*. **3 sales target**, Absatzsoll *nn*

target *vb* (mktg, sales), abzielen auf (+ acc); **the new product targets the under 21's**, das neue Produkt zielt auf die Unter-21-Jährigen ab

tarpaulin *n* (transp), Plane *nf*

task *n*, Aufgabe *nf*

taste *n*, Geschmack *nm*; **a new taste**, ein neuer Geschmack; **poor taste**, schlechter Geschmack

taste *vb*, **1** (good/bad), schmecken. **2** (sample), probieren; **we will want to taste the wine before buying**, wir möchten den Wein vor dem Kauf probieren

tax *n*, **1** (imp/exp), Gebühr *nf*. **2** (fin), Steuer *nf*; **tax accountant**, Steuerberater(in) *nm/f*; **tax consultant**, Steuerberater(in) *nm/f*; **tax disc** (vehicles), Kraftfahrzeugsteueraufkleber *nm*; **tax-free**, steuerfrei; **tax relief**, Steuererlaß *nm*; **tax year**, Steuerjahr *nn*

taxable *adj*, steuerpflichtig

team *n*, Team *nn*

tear *vb* (materials), zerreißen

technical *adj*, technisch

technician *n*, Techniker(in) *nm/f*

technique *n*, Technik *nn*

technology *n*, Technik *nf*; **incorporates the latest technology**, entspricht den neusten technischen Anforderungen

telegraphic address *n*, Telegrammadresse *nf*

telegraphic transfer *n* (fin), telegrafische Uberweisung *nf*

telemarketing *n*, Telemarketing *nn*

telephone *n*, Telefon *nn*; **telephone answering machine**, Telefonbeantworter *nm*; **telephone call**, (Telefon)Anruf *nm*; **following your recent telephone call . . .**, in Beantwortung Ihres kürzlichen Anrufs . . . ; **receive a telephone call from . . .**, einen Anruf von . . . bekommen; **telephone sales** (mktg, sales), Telefonverkauf *nm*

telephone *vb*, **1** (make a call), telefonieren, anrufen. **2** (ring someone), anrufen; **please ring me at 5 p.m.**, bitte rufen Sie mich um 5 Uhr nachmittags an

teleprinter *n*, Fernschreiber *nm*

telesales *n* (mktg, sales), Telefonverkauf *nm*

television *n*, Fernsehen *nn*; **on television**, im Fernsehen; **television programme**, Fernsehprogramm *nn*; **television set**, Fernseher *nm*

telewriter *n* (comp), Fernschreiber *nm*

telex *n*, **1** (machine), Fernschreiber *nm*. **2** (message), Telex *nn*, Fernschreiben *nn*; **by telex**, per Telex/per Fernschreiber; **telex number** Telexnummer *nf*

telex *vb*, ein Telex schicken; **telex a company**, einem Unternehmen ein Telex schicken; **telex an order to a company**, eine Bestellung per

Telex an ein Unternehmen schicken; **please telex details on the load**, bitte senden Sie Ladungsdaten per Telex

temporary *adj*, vorübergehend; **temporary address**, vorübergehende Adresse *nf*; **temporary employment** (pers), vorübergehende Beschäftigung *nf*

tendency *n*, **have a tendency to . . .**, die Neigung haben, zu . . .

tender *n* (offer), Angebot *nn*; **invite tenders**, Angebote einholen

tender *vb* (offer a price), ein Preisangebot machen; **tender for a contract**, sich um einen Auftrag bewerben

tentative *adj* (agreement), unverbindlich

terminate *vb* **a contract**, einen Vertrag beenden

terms *npl*, Bedingungen *nfpl*; **attractive terms** (mktg, sales), attraktive Bedingungen; **terms of payment**, Zahlungsbedingungen *nfpl*

territory *n* (mktg, sales), Bezirk *nm*, Verkaufsbezirk *nm*

test *n*, Test *nm*; **the interview included a test**, das Vorstellungsgespräch schloß einen Test ein; **the product was subjected to several tests**, das Produkt wurde mehreren Tests unterworfen

test *vb*, testen

test-drive *vb* **a car**, ein Auto probefahren

think *vb*, **1** denken; **we think it would be useful to meet next month**, wir denken, es wäre nützlich, wenn wir uns nächsten Monat träfen. **2** (reflect on), nachdenken über (+ acc); **I will think about the question of distribution and try to suggest a suitable agent**, ich werde über die Frage des Vertriebs nachdenken und versuchen, einen passenden Vertreter vorzuschlagen

third *n* (fraction), Drittel *nn*

third party fire and theft *n*, (ins), Haftpflichtversicherung *nf* (Feuer und Diebstahl)

thorough *adj* (research, report), gründlich

threshold *n*, Schwelle *nf*; **reach the 5% threshold**, die 5%-Schwelle erreichen

thriving *adj*, blühend

through bill of lading *n* (transp), Durchkonnossement *nn*

through flight *n*, Direktflug *nm*

through freight *n*, Durchgangsfracht *nf*

through train *n*, durchgehender Zug *nm*

tick *n* (form), Kreuz *nn*

tick *vb* (documents), ankreuzen; **please tick the appropriate box**, Zutreffendes bitte ankreuzen

ticket *n*, **1** (gen), Fahrkarte *nf*. **2** (air), (Flug)Ticket *nn*. **3** (on goods), Etikett *nn*, Schild *nn*

tide *n*, Gezeiten *nfpl*; **high tide**, Flut *nf*; **low tide**, Ebbe *nf*

tidy (up) *vb*, aufräumen

tie up *vb* (capital, resources), festlegen

tight *adj*, **1** (strict), streng. **2** (scarce), knapp

tighten up *vb* (regulation), verschärfen

timber *n* (gen), Holz *nn*

time *n*, Zeit *nf*; **an interesting time**, eine interessante Zeit; **lead time**, Lieferzeit *nf*; **local time**, Ortszeit *nf*; **a suitable time for a meeting**, eine passende Zeit für eine Sitzung

timetable *n*, **1** (transp), Fahrplan *nm*. **2** (appointments), Terminkalender *nm*. **3** (conference), Konferenzprogramm *nn*

tin *n* (container), Dose *nf*

tip *n*, **1** (information, help), Tip *nm*. **2** (peak), Spitze *nf*. **3** (waste), Halde *nf*. **4** (gratuity), Trinkgeld *nn*

tip *vb* (e.g. a load), kippen

title *n*, **1** (of book etc or person), Titel *nm*. **2** (right to property), Anrecht *nn*, Rechtstitel *nm*; **title deed**, Grundeigentumsurkunde *nf*

token ring network *n* (comp), Tokenring-Netzwerk *nn*

tolerance *n* (measurement), Toleranz *nf*

tolerate *vb* (materials), tolerieren

toll *n* (on road), Benutzungsgebühr *nf*

ton *n*, Tonne *nf*; **long ton**, britische Tonne (= 1016 kg); **short ton**, amerikanische Tonne (= 907 kg)

tonnage *n*, Tonnage *nf*

tool *n*, Werkzeug *nn*

top *adj* (best), Spitzen-

top *n*, **1** (highest point), Spitze *nf*. **2** (highest part of a machine/building), Oberteil *nn*. **3** (lid), Deckel *nm*. **4 come top of . . .**, der/die/das Beste sein

top *vb* (beat), übertreffen; **this year's profits will top £5m**, die Gewinne dieses Jahres werden £5 Mill. übersteigen

total *n* (money), Gesamtsumme *nf*; **a total of £23 664**, eine Gesamtsumme von £23 664

total *vb*, **1** (add up to), sich belaufen auf (+ acc); **costs total £3m**, die Kosten belaufen sich auf £3 Mill. **2** (add up figures), zusammenzählen

touch *n*, **please get in touch with our office in . . .**, bitte setzen Sie sich mit unserem Büro in . . . in Verbindung

tourism *n*, Tourismus *nm*

tourist *n*, Tourist(in) *nm/f*

tour operator *n*, Reiseveranstalter *nm*

tow *vb*, abschleppen; **your car needs to be towed**, Ihr Wagen muß abgeschleppt werden

town *n*, Stadt *nf*

TPND, **theft, pilferage, non-delivery** (imp/exp, ins), Diebstahl, Beraubung, Nichtlieferung

TQM (pers), **total quality management**, TQM *nn*, Total-Quality-Management *nn*

trackball *n* (comp), Steuerungsball *nm*

track record *n*, Erfolgs- und Leistungsnachweis *nm*; **the company has a good track record in . . .**, das Unternehmen hat in . . . gute Erfolge zu verzeichnen; **unfortunately, the applicant has no track record in this area**, leider kann der Bewerber in diesem Bereich keine Leistungen nachweisen

trade *n*, **1** (business of buying and selling), Handel *nm*; **export trade**, Exporthandel *nm*; **foreign trade**, Auslandshandel *nm*; **import trade**, Importhandel *nm*; **international trade**, internationaler Handel. **2** (individual trade, occupation), Gewerbe *nn*;

trade balance *n*, Handelsbilanz *nf*

trade fair *n*, Handelsmesse *nf*

trade in *vb*, handeln mit (+ dat); **the company trades in plastics**, die Firma handelt mit Kunststoff

trade magazine *n*, Fachzeitschrift *nf*

trademark *n*, Handelsmarke *nf*, Warenzeichen *nf*

trade press *n*, Fachpresse *nf*

trade supplier *n*, Zulieferer *nm*

trade(s) union *n*, Gewerkschaft *nf*

trading account *n* (fin), Erfolgskonto *nn*; **the trading account shows a small deficit for the month of**

. . ., das Erfolgskonto weist ein geringes Defizit für den Monat . . . auf

trading estate *n*, Gewerbegebiet *nn*

trading profit *n* (fin), Geschäftsgewinn *nm*

trading year *n*, Geschäftsjahr *nn*

traffic *n*, Verkehr *nm*; **road traffic**, Straßenverkehr *nm*

trailer *n* (transp), Anhänger *nm*

train *n* (transp), Zug *nm*; **freight/goods train**, Güterzug *nm*; **express train**, Schnellzug *nm*; **passenger train**, Personenzug *nm*

train *vb* (pers), ausbilden

trainee *n*, Auszubildende(r) *nf/m*

training *n* (pers), Ausbildung *nf*; **training centre** (pers), Ausbildungszentrum *nn*

transaction *n* Transaktion *nf*

transfer *n* (fin), Transfer *nm*, Überweisung *nf*; **bank transfer**, Banküberweisung *nf*; **credit transfer**, Kredittransfer *nm*

transfer *vb* (fin, law), **1** (stocks), transferieren, übertragen. **2** (money, funds, from one account to another), überweisen. **3** (property), überschreiben

transferable *adj* (money, securities), transferierbar

transhipment *n* (transp), Umladung *nf*

transit *n* (transp, ins), Transport *nm*; **goods damaged or lost in transit . . .**, beim Transport beschädigte oder verlorengegangene Güter; **transit freight**, Transitfracht *nf*

translate *vb*, übersetzen; **the letter has been translated into English**, der Brief ist ins Englische übersetzt worden

translation *n*, Übersetzung *nf*

transmit *vb*, übermitteln nach/von (+ dat); **the message was transmitted this morning**, die Botschaft wurde heute morgen übermittelt

transparency *n*, Folie *nf*

transport *n*, Transport *nm*

transport *vb*, transportieren

transporter *n* (company), Transportunternehmen *nn*

travel *vb*, reisen

travel *n*, Reise *f*; **travel agency**, Reisebüro *nn*; **travel allowance**, Reisekostenzuschuß *nm*; **travel expenses**, Reiseaufwendungen *npl*; **travel insurance**, Reiseversicherung *nf*

traveller *n*, Reisende(r) *nf/m*; **business traveller**, Geschäftsreisende(r) *nf/m*; **traveller's cheque**, Reisescheck *nm*

trial *n*, **1** (law), Prozeß *nm*. **2** (test), Test *nm*, Probe *nf*; **free trial**, kostenlos zur Probe; **trial period**, Probezeit *nf*; **trial sample**, Probestück *nn*

trip *n*, Reise *nf*; **he is away on a trip to Venice**, er ist gerade auf einer Reise nach Venedig; **business trip**, Geschäftsreise *nf*

triple *vb*, sich verdreifachen; **profits have tripled**, die Gewinne haben sich verdreifacht

true *adj*, **1** (not false), wahr. **2** (accurate, faithful), (wahrheits)getreu; **a true and fair view** (law), eine wahrheitsgetreue Darstellung; **a true copy**, eine getreue Kopie

trust *n* (gen), Vertrauen *nn*; **we have complete trust in our agent**, wir haben volles Vertrauen in unseren Vertreter

trust *vb*, **1** (a person), vertrauen; **you may trust Ms Smith completely**, Sie können Ms Smith völlig vertrauen; **I don't trust him**, ich traue ihm nicht. **2** (trust that), hoffen; **we trust (that) our**

proposal meets with your approval, wir hoffen, daß unser Vorschlag Ihre Zustimmung findet; **I trust not**, ich hoffe nicht

try *vb*, **1** (attempt), versuchen; **we will try to have the order ready by the end of the month**, wir werden versuchen, den Auftrag bis Ende des Monats zu erledigen. **2** (sample, try out), (aus)probieren; **you may try the machine for one week at no expense**, Sie dürfen die Maschine für eine Woche kostenlos ausprobieren

TUC, Trades Union Congress, Gewerkschaftsdachverband *nm*, ≈ Deutscher Gewerkschaftsbund *nm*, DGB

turn down *vb* **a proposal/an offer**, einen Vorschlag/ein Angebot ablehnen

turn on *vb*, **1** (machine), anstellen. **2** (comp), einschalten

turnover *n*, **1** (acct), Umsatz *nm*. **2** (of stock), Lagerumschlag *nm*

twice *adv* zweimal; **twice as high as . . .**, zweimal so hoch wie . . .

type *n*, **1** (sort, kind), Typ *nm*; **a new type of machine**, ein neuer Maschinentyp. **2** (print), Type *nf*, Schrift *nf*

type *vb* (print), tippen

typewriter *n*, Schreibmaschine *nf*

typist *n*, Schreibkraft *nf*, Stenotypist(in) *nm/f*

tyre *n*, Reifen *nm*

U

UK, United Kingdom, Vereinigtes Königreich *nn*

ultimatum *n*, Ultimatum *nn*

unanimously *adv*, einstimmig

unanswered *adj*, unbeantwortet; **our letter of complaint has remained unanswered**, unser Beschwerdebrief ist unbeantwortet geblieben

unapproved *adj*, nicht bewilligt

unauthorised *adj*, nicht genehmigt

unavailable, be unavailable *vb*, **1** (goods, out of stock), nicht vorrätig/verfügbar sein. **2** (person away), nicht im Hause sein. **3** (person busy), nicht zu sprechen sein; **I am afraid Mrs Smith is unavailable at the moment**, Frau Smith ist leider im Augenblick nicht zu sprechen

unbranded *adj*, markenlos

unchanged *adj*, unverändert

unconditional *adj*, vorbehaltlos

unconfirmed *adj*, unbestätigt

uncorrected *adj*, unkorrigiert

undamaged *adj*, unbeschädigt

undelivered *adj*, nicht zustellbar

under *prep*, **1** unter (+ dat or acc); **under 15%**, unter 15%. **2** (law, according to), gemäß (+ dat), laut (+ dat); **under the terms of . . .**, gemäß/laut den Bedingungen von . . .

undercut *vb*, unterbieten; **undercut competitors/the competition**, Konkurrenten/die Konkurrenz unterbieten

underdeveloped countries *npl*, unterentwickelte Länder *nnpl*

underestimate *vb*, unterschätzen

undersigned *n*, Unterzeichnete(r) *nf/m*; **we, the undersigned . . . declare . . .**, wir, die Unterzeichneten, erklären . . .

understand *vb*, **1** (comprehend, sympathise), verstehen. **2** (believe, hear), **we understand that you are currently seeing an agent in . . .**, wie wir hören, besuchen Sie gerade einen Vertreter in . . .

understanding *n*, **1** (sympathy, forgiveness), Verständnis *nn*; **I am grateful for your understanding**, ich bin Ihnen für Ihr Verständnis dankbar. **2** (condition), Voraussetzung *nf*; **we accept on the understanding that . . .**, wir akzeptieren unter der Voraussetzung, daß . . . **3** (agreement), Übereinkunft *nf*; **we have reached an understanding about . . .**, wir haben eine Übereinkunft über (+ acc) erzielt

undertake *vb*, sich verpflichten

undervalue *vb*, unterbewerten

underwrite *vb*, **1** (gen, agree to), billigen. **2** (finance a project, a loss), tragen. **3** (ins, share risks), garantieren, bürgen für (+ acc)

uneconomical *adj*, unwirtschaftlich

unemployed *adj*, arbeitslos

unemployment *n*, Arbeitslosigkeit *nf*

uneven *adj*, ungleich

unexpected *adj*, unerwartet

unfair *adj*, unfair; **unfair competition**, unfairer Wettbewerb *nm*

unfavourable *adj*, **1** (results, prospects etc), ungünstig. **2** (expressing approval), negativ. **3** (trade balance), passiv

unforeseen *adj*, unvorhergesehen

uniform *adj*, einheitlich

union *n* (trade(s) union), Gewerkschaft *nf*; **union representative** (pers), Gewerkschaftsvertreter(in) *nm/f*

unit *n* (of goods), Einheit *nf*, Stück *nn*; **unit cost**, Einheits-, Stückkosten *npl*; **unit price**, Einheits-, Stückpreis *nm*; **unit trust** (fin), Unit Trust *nm*, Investmentgesellschaft *nf*

unlawful *adj*, **1** (action), gesetzwidrig. **2** (assembly), ungesetzlich

unlikely *adj*, unwahrscheinlich; **it is unlikely that economic conditions will improve in the short term**, es ist unwahrscheinlich, daß sich die wirtschaftlichen Bedingungen in der nahen Zukunft verbessern

unload *vb* (transp), ausladen

unofficial *adj*, inoffiziell; **unofficial strike** (pers), wilder Streik *nm*

unpack *vb*, auspacken

unpacking *n*, Auspacken *nn*

unpaid *adj*, **1** (bills), nicht beglichen; **there is an unpaid bill for £ 200**, eine Rechnung über £ 200 ist noch nicht beglichen; **our invoice No. 38382 is still unpaid**, unsere Rechnung Nr. 38382 ist noch nicht beglichen. **2** (work), unbezahlt, ehrenamtlich

unsaleable *adj*, **be unsaleable**, sich nicht verkaufen lassen; **we fear that the damage has made the goods unsaleable**, wir befürchten, daß sich die Waren wegen des Schadens nicht verkaufen lassen

unserviceable *adj*, unbrauchbar; **the equipment is now unserviceable**, die Ausrüstung ist jetzt unbrauchbar

unsold *adj*, unverkauft, nicht verkauft; **according to the agreement, unsold items may be returned**, vereinbarungsgemäß konnen nicht verkaufte Waren zurückgegeben werden

unsuitable *adj*, unpassend

untrue *adj*, unwahr

unused *adj*, unbenutzt

up, be *vb*, **up 2%**, um 2% gestiegen sein; **be DM 5,000 up**, um 5.000 DM gestiegen sein

upgrade *vb* (pers), **1** (promote), befördern. **2** (post), anheben

upswing *n*, Aufschwung *nm*

upturn *n*, Aufschwung *nm*

upward trend *n*, Aufwärtstrend *nm*

urban *adj*, städtisch

USA, United States of America, USA *npl*, Vereinigte Staaten *nmpl* von Amerika

use *n*, Gebrauch *nm*

use *vb*, gebrauchen

used *adj* (second-hand), gebraucht

user *n*, **1** (gen), Benutzer(in) *nm/f*. **2** (comp), Benutzer *nm*, Anwender *nm*; **user-friendly,** benutzerfreundlich, anwenderfreundlich

USP, Unique Selling Proposition (mktg, sales), einzigartiges Verkaufsargument *nn*

usual *adj*, gewöhnlich

utility programme *n*, Hilfsprogramm *nn*

vacancy *n*, freie/offene Stelle *nf*

vacuum-sealed *adj*, vakuumverpackt

valid *adj*, gültig; **valid from . . .**, gültig vom . . .

validity *n*, Gültigkeit *nf*; **period of validity**, Gültigkeitsdauer *nf*

valuable *adj*, wertvoll

valuables *npl*, Wertgegenstände *nmpl*

value *n*, Wert *nm*; **face value** (fin), Nennwert *nm*; **good value for money**, preiswert

value *vb*, **1** (appreciate), schätzen; **I value your support**, ich schätze Ihre Unterstützung. **2** (estimate value), den Wert von . . . schätzen; **we value this car at . . .**, wir schätzen den Wert dieses Wagens auf (+ acc) . . .

van *n* (transp), Lieferwagen *nm*

variable, be variable *vb*, variieren; **demand is very variable**, die Nachfrage variiert sehr

variation *n*, Abweichung *nf*; **seasonal variations,** saisonbedingte Abweichungen

vary *vb*, **1** abändern, ändern; **we can vary the contents according to the customer's needs**, wir können den Inhalt den Kundenbedürfnissen entsprechend (ab)ändern. **2** (be subject to change), sich verändern, sich ändern. **3** (oscillate), schwanken; **the price varies according to season**, der Preis schwankt je nach Saison

VAT, value-added tax, Mehrwertsteuer *nf*

VCR, video cassette recorder, Videorekorder *nm*

vehicle *n*, Fahrzeug *nn*

vending machine *n* (for drinks etc), Automat *nm*

vendor *n*, Verkäufer *nm*; **street vendor**, Straßenhändler *nm*

Venn diagram *n* (comp), Venn-Diagramm *nn*

venture capital *n*, Risikokapital *nn*

venue *n*, **1** (for meeting), Sitzungsort *nm*. **2** (for conference), Tagungssort *nm*

verbal *adj*, mündlich; **a verbal agreement**, eine mündliche Vereinbarung

verify *vb*, verifizieren

vessel *n* (transp), Schiff *nn*; **merchant vessel**, Handelsschiff *nn*

veto *vb*, sein Veto einlegen gegen (+ acc); **they vetoed the trade embargo**, sie legten ihr Veto gegen das Handelsembargo ein

via *prep*, über (+ acc); **she is coming via Munich**, sie kommt über München

vice-chairman *n*, stellvertretender Vorsitzender *nm*

vice-president *n*, Vizepräsident(in) *nm/f*

video *n* (film), Videofilm *nm*; **corporate video**, Werbefilm *nm* für ein Unternehmen; **promotional video**, Werbevideofilm *nm*

video *vb*, auf Video(band) aufnehmen

view *vb*, **1** (a property), besichtigen. **2** (a film), ansehen

view *n*, **in view of . . .**, angesichts (+ genitive); **in view of the cost of raw materials we have . . .**, angesichts der Rohmaterialkosten haben wir . . .

virus *n* (comp), Virus *nm*; **virus protection**, Virusschutz *nm*

visit *n*, Besuch *nm*; **pay someone a visit**, jemandem einen Besuch abstatten

visit *vb*, besuchen

visitor *n*, Besucher(in) *nm/f*

voluntary *adj*, freiwillig

vote *n*, **1** (at meeting etc), Abstimmung *nf*. **2** (election), Wahl *nf*. **3** (vote cast), Stimme *nf*

vote for/against *vb*, für/gegen (+ acc) stimmen

vote on, *vb* abstimmen über (+ acc)

voucher *n* (exchanged for goods or service), Gutschein *nm*; **gift voucher**, Geschenkgutschein *nm*

wage(s) *n(pl)*, Lohn *nm*; **wage claim**, Lohnforderung *nf*; **wage earner**, Lohnempfänger *nm*; **wage freeze**, Lohnstopp *nm*; **wage increase**, Lohnerhöhung *nf*; **wage levels**, Lohnniveau *nm*; **wage packet**, Lohntüte *nf*

wagon *n* (transp), Waggon *nm*

wait *n*, Wartezeit *nf*

wait *vb*, warten; **we are still waiting for the goods**, wir warten immer noch auf die Waren

waiting-room *n*, Warteraum *nm*

waive *vb* (law, ins), verzichten auf (+ acc)

waiver *n* (ins), **1** (act of foregoing something), Verzicht *nm* auf (+ acc). **2** (document), Verzichterklärung *nf*. **3** (law, contract), Außerkraftsetzung *nf*

walk-out *n*, Arbeitsniederlegung *nf*

walkway *n* (between exhibition stands), Gang *nm*

wall chart *n* (offce), Plantafel *nf*

want *vb*, wollen

warehouse *n*, Lagerhaus *nn*; **warehouse warrant**, Lagerhausgarantie *nf*

warehouseman *n* (transp), Lagerarbeiter *nm*

warehousing *n* (transp), Lagerung *nf*; **warehousing charges**, Lagerungsgebühren *nfpl*

warn *vb*, warnen; **please warn your driver that there is a strike at the port**, bitte warnen Sie Ihren Fahrer, daß am Hafen gestreikt wird

warning *n*, **1** (gen, of danger), Warnung *nf*. **2** (early notice), Vorankündigung *nf*; **warning letter** Warnbrief *nm*

warrant *vb*, **1** (guarantee), garantieren. **2** (justify), rechtfertigen

warranty *n*, **1** (guarantee), Garantie *nf*. **2** (promise in a contract, ins), Gewähr *nf*

waste *vb*, verschwenden

wasteful *adj*, verschwenderisch

waterproof *adj*, wasserdicht

waybill *n* (imp/exp), Frachtbrief *nm*

weak *adj*, schwach

weaken *vb*, schwächen

weakness *n*, Schwäche *nf*

week *n*, Woche *nf*

weekly *adj*, wöchentlich; **weekly deliveries**, wöchentliche Lieferungen *nfpl*; **weekly magazine**, Wochenzeitschrift *nf*

weigh *vb*, wiegen

weight *n*, Gewicht *nn*; **net weight**, Nettogewicht *nn*

weighted *adj* (calculations), Bewertungs-; **weighted average**, Bewertungsdurchschnitt *nm*

weld *vb*, löten

well-paid *adj*, gut bezahlt

wet *adj*, naß

wharf *n*, Kai *nm*

wheel *n*, Rad *nn*

white *adj*, weiß; **white goods** (mktg, sales), elektrische Haushaltsgeräte *nnpl*

wholesale *n* (mktg, sales), Großhandel *nm*; **wholesale price**, Großhandelspreis *nm*

wholesaler *n* (mktg, sales), Großhändler *nm*

wholly-owned subsidiary *n*,

100%ige Tochtergesellschaft *nf*

wide *adj*, breit; **the box is 16 cm wide and 12 cm long**, die Schachtel ist 16 cm breit und 12 cm lang; **a wide selection of . . .**, eine große Auswahl an (+ dat) . . .

widen *vb*, erweitern

width *n*, Breite *nf*

win *vb*, gewinnen

wind up *vb* (a company), auflösen

with *prep*, mit (+ dat); **with much regret**, mit großem Bedauern; **with particular average** (ins), mit besonderer Havarie *nf*

withdraw *vb*, **1** (money), abheben. **2** (offer), zurücknehmen. **3** (from a post), zurücktreten

without *prep*, ohne (+ acc); **without many difficulties**, ohne viele Schwierigkeiten

witness *n* (law), Zeuge *nm*, Zeugin *nf*; **act as a witness**, als Zeuge/Zeugin auftreten

witness *vb* (law), **1** (see), **he witnessed the accident**, er war bei dem Unfall Zeuge. **2** (testify), bezeugen. **3** (attest by signature), bestätigen; **witness a document**, ein Dokument bestätigen

wood *n*, Holz *nn*

wooden *adj*, hölzern, aus Holz

wool *n*, Wolle *nf*

woollen *adj*, wollen, aus Wolle

word *n*, Wort *nn*

word *vb* (an agreement), formulieren

wording *n*, Wortlaut *nm*; **according to the wording of the agreement**, nach dem Wortlaut der Vereinbarung

word processing *n*, Textverarbeitung *nf*; **word processing software**, Textverarbeitungs-Software *nf*

work *n*, Arbeit *nf*; **work experience** (pers), **1** (gen, CV), Berufserfahrung *nf*. **2** (education), Praktikum *nn*; **work in hand/work in progress** (acct), unfertige Erzeugnisse *nnpl*; **work permit**, Arbeitserlaubnis *nf*; **work placement** (education), Praktikum *nn*; **work station**, Arbeitsplatz *nm*

work *vb*, **1** (machines, method of operation), funktionieren; **the demonstration will show how the machine works**, die Demonstration wird zeigen, wie die Maschine funktioniert. **2** (gen, employee), arbeiten; **work for . . .** (pers), arbeiten für (+ acc); **work to rule** (pers), nach Vorschrift arbeiten

work out *vb* (calculate), errechnen

workforce *n* (pers), Belegschaft *nf*; **the company has a workforce of 1,200**, die Firma hat eine Belegschaft von 1.200

working capital *n* (fin), Betriebskapital *nn*; **working capital turnover** (fin), Betriebskapitalumsatz *nm*

working conditions *npl* (pers), Arbeitsbedingungen *nfpl*

working day *n*, Arbeitstag *nm*

working week *n*, Arbeitswoche *nf*

works manager *n* (pers), Betriebsleiter *nm*

worldwide *adj, adv*, weltweit; **worldwide sales**, weltweiter Absatz *nm*; **we operate worldwide**, wir operieren weltweit

worth *n*, Wert *nm*

worth, be worth *vb*, wert sein

worthwhile, be worthwhile *vb*, sich lohnen

WP *n* (comp), **1 word processor**, Textverarbeiter *nm*. **2 word processing**, Textverarbeitung *nf*

wrap *vb*, einpacken

wrapped *adj* (imp/exp), verpackt;

wrapped in wood wool, in Holzwolle verpackt

wrapper *n*, **wrapping** *n*, Verpackung *nf*

writ *n* (law), Verfügung *nf*

write *vb*, schreiben; **write a report**, einen Bericht schreiben; **we wrote to you last week**, wir haben Ihnen letzte Woche geschrieben

write off *vb*, abschreiben

write off *n* (ins), Totalschaden *nm*; **in our opinion the vehicle is a write off**, unserer Ansicht nach muß das Fahrzeug als Totalschaden abgeschrieben werden

writing pad *n*, Notizblock *nm*

written off, **be written off** *vb* (acct), vollständig abgeschrieben werden

wrong *adj*, falsch; **the wrong items**, die falschen Waren *nfpl*; **the wrong price**, der falsche Preis

wrong, **be wrong** *vb* (opinion, judgement), sich irren

X-ml, **X-mll**, **ex-mill** (imp/exp), ab Werk

X-ship, **ex-ship** (imp/exp), ab Schiff

x-stre, **ex-store** (imp/exp), ab Lager

x-whf, **ex-wharf** (imp/exp), ab Werft

x-whse, **ex-warehouse** (imp/exp), ab Lagerhaus

x-wks, **ex-works** (imp/exp), ab Werk

Y

year *n*, Jahr *nn*; **calendar year**, Kalenderjahr *nn*; **financial year**, Finanzjahr *nn*; **fiscal year**, Steuerjahr *nn*

yearly *adj*, jährlich; **a yearly payment**, eine jährliche Zahlung *nf*

Yellow Pages *npl*, Gelbe Seiten *nfpl*

yield *n* (fin), Ertrag *nm*, Rendite *nf*

yield *vb* (fin), bringen

Yours faithfully, Yours sincerely (corr), Mit freundlichem Gruß

Z

zero *n*, Null *nf*; **zero growth**, Nullwachstum *nn*; **zero inflation**, Nullinflation *nf*

zipcode *n*, Postleitzahl *nf*

TEACH YOURSELF BUSINESS FRENCH

Barbara Coultas

Now that the European market place is truly with us, thousands of business people are finding that they need to be able to say more than just 'Bonjour, Monsieur' if they are to survive. If you are one of them, and you've never learnt French before, or if your French needs brushing up, this is the ideal course.

Barbara Coultas has created a practical course that is both fun and easy to work through. She explains the language clearly along the way and gives you plenty of opportunities to practise what you've learnt. The course structure means that you can work at your own pace, arranging your learning to suit your needs.

The course contains:

- A range of units of dialogues, culture notes, grammar and exercises
- Further units of cultural briefings – in French to give you more practice
- Verb tables
- A quick reference list of key phrases
- An extensive French–English vocabulary

By the end of the course you'll be able to participate fully and confidently in meetings, on the shop floor, on the telephone or in the bar after work.

This title is also available in a book/cassette pack.